Contents

KT-164-175

OPPOSITE SWIMMERS AT GELLÉRT BATHS **PREVIOUS PAGE** CHAIN BRIDGE AT DUSK

Introduction to

Budapest

With a wonderful natural setting straddling the River Danube, beautiful architecture and flavoursome Magyar cuisine, Budapest is one of the most rewarding cities in Europe to visit. Its magnificent bridges and boulevards and its grand riverside views invite comparisons with Paris, Prague and Vienna – as do many features of its cultural life, from coffee houses and a love of music to its restaurants and its wine-producing tradition, while it has recently acquired a new modern edge all its own, with cool boutique hotels and its hip bars springing up in artfully decaying buildings. The city is also distinctively Hungarian, its inhabitants displaying fierce pride in their Magyar ancestry. Their language, too, whose nearest European relative is Finnish, underlines the difference – that can represent a challenge to visitors but is no barrier to enjoyment of this most cosmopolitan of European cities.

Fundamental to the city's layout and history, the **River Danube** (Duna) – which is seldom blue – separates **Buda** on the hilly west bank from **Pest** on the eastern plain. Until 1873 these were separate cities, and they still retain a different feel. Buda is older and more dignified: dominated by the Vár (Castle Hill), a mile-long plateau overlooking the Danube, it was the capital of medieval monarchs and the seat of power for successive occupying powers. Built during the city's golden age in the late nineteenth century, with boulevards of Haussmann-like apartment blocks sweeping out from the old medieval centre, **Pest** holds most of the capital's magnificent Art Nouveau edifices and has a noisy, bustling feel. Following construction of the first permanent bridge between the two cities in 1849, power gradually moved across the river, culminating in the building of the grandiose Parliament on the Pest side. The two halves of the city still retain their differences, but as a whole Budapest is a vibrant place today, never in danger of being overwhelmed by tourism but nonetheless offering plenty for visitors to enjoy.

ABOVE MILLENNIUM MONUMENT, HŐSÖK TERE

THE ROUGH GUIDE TO

Budapest

This sixth edition updated by

Charles Hebbert and Norm Longley

Rough
GUIDES

roughguides.com

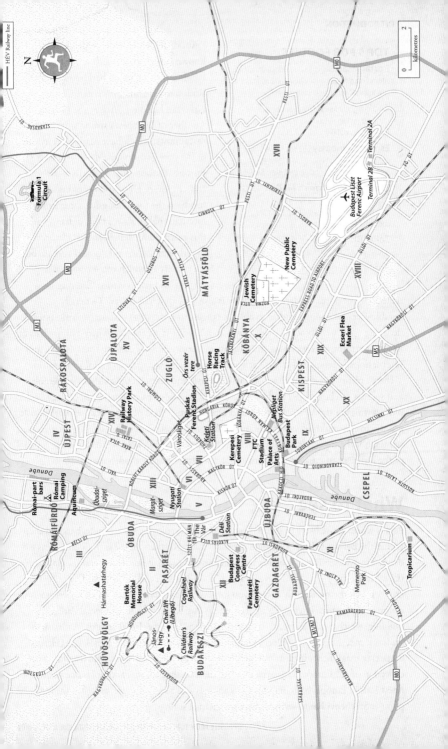

TOP 5 FOR FOODIES

Bortársaság Sample the best Tokaj, Bull's Blood and lesser-known wines at this traditional vintners. **See p.190**

Cooking classes Why eat restaurant goulash when you can learn to make your own? **See p.164**

Espresso Embassy One of Budapest's hip, new-style cafés, whose interior is as interesting as the coffee on offer. **See p.168**

Szimplakert Farmer's Market Head to Szimpla on a Sunday morning, and you'll find all manner of delectable foodstuffs. **See p.185**

Zeller Bistro Inventive Hungarian food in a fabulously chic basement restaurant. **See p.164**

Above all, Budapest is probably best known for its **spas**, which range from fabulous Ottoman-era bathhouses like the Rudas, to fine nineteenth-century Art Nouveau buildings such as the Gellert. Another of Budapest's strong suits is its **restaurants**, which have made the city one of the new gastronomic destinations of Europe. Fantastically-innovative, contemporary Hungarian cooking is now firmly to the fore, alongside some brilliant international cuisine. Hand in hand with this gastronomic renaissance is Hungary's superb **wine**, often overlooked abroad, but the quality of which often comes as a surprise to many visitors. Catering for a wide range of tastes, Budapest's **nightlife** is also very much of a draw. Generally trouble-free, welcoming and accessible, it ranges from the city's distinctive "ruin pubs" in decaying apartment blocks or courtyards to *táncház* (dance houses) where Hungarians of all ages perform wild stamping movements to the rhythms of darkest Transylvania, and internationally renowned artists such as Márta Sebestyén appear in an informal setting.

There's plenty to offer in terms of **classical music and opera**, too: world-class ensembles and soloists can be enjoyed in the Palace of Arts' state-of-the-art concert hall or the grander, older settings of the Music Academy and Opera House. Fans of **pop**, **rock** and **world music** can discover a wealth of local talent, especially on the folk scene, alongside big international names, but the biggest event of the year is the **Sziget Festival**, held on an island just north of the centre in August, which is one of Europe's largest musical celebrations.

What to see

Pest is where you're likely to spend most of your time, enjoying the streetlife, bars and shops within the **Belváros** (Inner City) and the surrounding districts. These surrounding areas are defined by two semicircular boulevards – the **Kiskörút** (Small Boulevard) and the **Nagykörút** (Great Boulevard) – and radial avenues such as Andrássy út and Rákóczi út. Exploring the area between them can easily occupy you for several days. In the financial and government centre of **Lipótváros**, interest lies in St Stephen's Basilica and the monumental Parliament building, which rivals the grand structures across the Danube. In **Terézváros**, Andrássy út leads out past the grandiose Opera House and the House of Terror to Hősök tere (Heroes' Square), a magnificent imperial set piece where the Fine Arts Museum displays a first-rate collection of old European masters. Beyond, the **Városliget** (City Park) holds one of the finest zoos in Europe, both in terms of its animals and its architecture, as well as the hugely popular Széchenyi Baths, served by its own thermal springs.

OFFBEAT BUDAPEST

Chess on the water Watch old timers ponder their moves while taking a soak at Széchenyi Baths. **See p.74**

Communist trainers Check out retro brand Tisza for some cult 1970s Hungarian footwear. **See p.189**

Escape rooms Fancy being locked up in a ruined Soviet-era apartment block? Thought so… **See p.193**

Odd medicine Dried bats and mummified skulls are just some of the exhibits in the Semmelwies medical collection. **See p.109**

Sleep in a work of art Full of antiques, bric-a-brac and witty drawings – the Lavender Circus is a fantastically eccentric place to stay. **See p.152**

Of Pest's remaining inner-city districts, **Erzsébetváros** and **Józsefváros** hold the most appeal. The former is Budapest's old Jewish quarter, with a rich and tragic history that's still palpable in the bullet-scarred backstreets behind the great synagogue on Dohány utca. But its old apartment blocks have also spawned a new genre of bars, the "ruin pubs", which have become a popular destination for younger Budapestis. From here, it's not far to the National Museum, a well-presented introduction to Hungarian history, and the Great Market Hall, further round in **Ferencváros**, whose hinterland harbours the Applied Arts Museum, Holocaust Memorial Centre and the Palace of Arts, one of Budapest's foremost cultural venues.

The Vár (Castle) on the **Buda** side was once the seat of Hungary's monarchs, and its palace, museums, churches and Baroque streets offer some absorbing sightseeing; the historic Turkish baths along the banks of the Danube are also well worth experiencing, as is the remarkable Cave Church in **Gellért-hegy**. There's more history to the north in **Óbuda**, with its extensive Roman remains and a clutch of worthwhile museums clustered around the old centre. In fine weather, people flock to

Margit-sziget, the large, leafy island mid-river between Buda and Pest, to swim and sunbathe at the enormous lido and party through the night. Encircling the city to the west, the **Buda Hills** have a different kind of allure, with fun rides on the Cogwheel and Children's railways and chairlift, and intriguing caves to be visited. **Further out**, the steam trains of the Hungarian Railway History Park and the redundant Communist monuments within the Memento Park rate as major attractions.

There is plenty to see on **excursions** from Budapest. Top of the list is Szentendre, a picturesque artists' colony with a superb open-air ethnographic museum. Further upriver, the Danube Bend offers gorgeous scenery, a Renaissance palace and citadel and an amazing treetop zip-ride at Visegrád, while Esztergom boasts its basilica and a remarkable Turkish relic, while on the east bank of the Danube sits Vác, with its well-preserved Baroque centre. Classical-music lovers, meanwhile, will also enjoy concerts in the former Habsburg palace of Gödöllő, to the east of Budapest.

When to go

The best times to visit Budapest are **spring** (late March to the end of May) and **autumn** (Sept–Oct), when the weather is mild and there are fewer tourists (though things tend to get busy during the **Budapest Spring Festival** in late March/early April). The majority of visitors come in the summer, when many residents decamp to Lake Balaton and those who remain flock to the city's pools and parks to escape the heat and dust. Though some concert halls are closed over summer, there are all kinds of outdoor events to compensate – and also major international events such as the Sziget Festival and Formula One Grand Prix, in July/August. Winter is cold and may be snowy, but you can still enjoy all the city's sights and cultural attractions (as well as trying roasted chestnuts from street vendors), while the thermal baths take on an extra allure. It's wise to book accommodation in advance for Christmas, New Year, the Spring Festival and Grand Prix.

A TRIBAL NATION

As a small, landlocked country whose language sets it apart from its neighbours, Hungary is a tribal nation, whose citizens still identify with their ancestors, pagan Magyar tribes who conquered the Carpathian Basin in 896 AD. Since the epochal Christmas Day when the Magyar ruler Vajk was baptized and crowned as King Stephen by a papal envoy, Hungary has identified itself with Europe while simultaneously remaining aware of its "otherness" – a sentiment reinforced by successive foreign occupations and the loss of much of its territory to neighbouring states.

The symbol of statehood is **St Stephen's Crown**, whose bent cross – caused by it being squashed in the eighteenth century – is a cherished sign of the vicissitudes that Hungary has endured, and features on the national **coat of arms** that you'll see everywhere in Budapest. The shield beneath the crown bears a Catholic cross of Lorraine, and the red and white "Árpád stripes" of the early Magyar tribal kings; today, the latter signify far-right loyalties, having formerly been employed as the flag of the Fascist Arrow Cross. With the fall of Communism, St Stephen's Crown returned to the coat of arms, but not to the national **flag** – which is a simple red, white and green tricolour.

17

things not to miss

It's not possible to see everything that Budapest has to offer in one trip – and we don't suggest you try. What follows is a selective taste of the city's highlights: magnificent Art Nouveau treasures, unique thermal baths, and gastronomic treats. All highlights have a page reference to take you straight into the Guide, where you can find out more. Coloured numbers refer to chapters in the Guide section.

1 THERMAL BATHS
Page 194
Bathe in splendour at the city's magnificent Ottoman-era and Art Nouveau spas, which are fed by hot springs.

2 WINE
Page 177
Hungary's vineyards turn out excellent wines – taste them at the Budapest Wine Festival in September, or all year round in the city's top-class restaurants.

3 BUDA HILLS
Page 118
Both children and adults will enjoy this delightful ride up into the verdant Buda Hills.

4 LIVE MUSIC
Page 181
Catch the irrepressible sounds of Gypsy fiddlers, folk singers or one of Budapest's world-class ensembles in the city's lively music scene.

5 #2 TRAM RIDE
Page 25
This route past Parliament and along the Pest embankment affords some of the best views of the city.

6

7

8

9

10

6 FISHERMEN'S BASTION
Page 90

Take a stroll along the Fishermen's Bastion for superlative views of the Danube and Pest beyond.

7 HUNGARIAN NATIONAL GALLERY
Page 96

Showcased in the imposing Royal Palace, this is Hungary's premier collection of home-grown art, from Gothic altarpieces to Art Nouveau and Abstract Expressionism.

8 DESIGN HOTELS
Page 148

Awash with colour, creativity and flair, Budapest possesses an impressive ensemble of superbly conceived design hotels.

9 SZIGET FESTIVAL
Page 179

Hungary's Glastonbury, this enormous mid-August bash draws some of the biggest bands on the planet.

10 COFFEE HOUSES
Page 167

Ponder the world over a coffee and cake – after all, it's an old Central European tradition.

11 MEMENTO PARK
Page 124

Lenin and his comrades in Communist statuary are now laid out in a park on the outskirts of Budapest.

11

14

A MI
POLITIKAI NYOMOZÓINK
ÁLLAMVÉDELMI HATÓS
DOLGOZÓI,

NÉP LEGJOBBJAIBÓL K

15

16

17

Itineraries

Budapest is essentially two cities in one: Buda and Pest, but on both sides of the Danube, you'll find glorious architecture alongside remnants of the city's Communist past, not to mention all manner of superb music – and there are some fun ways to get around, too.

ARCHITECTURAL BUDAPEST

Museum of Applied Arts Lechner's flamboyantly–designed Secessionist building is as much an exhibit as the voluminous displays inside. **See p.82**

Gellért Baths Soothe any aching limbs with a wallow in the hot pool and steam rooms of these magnificent Art Nouveau baths. **See p.196**

Centrál Kávéház If you only take coffee – alright then, cake too – in one place, then make it *Centrál*, which has retained its pre-World War II grandeur, when it was the meeting place of the Budapest literati. **See p.168**

Great Synagogue The crowning glory of the Jewish District is the Byzantine-inspired Great Synagogue, the largest in Europe; admire, too, Imre Varga's Holocaust Memorial, beautifully cast in the shape of a willow tree. **See p.63**

Budapest Zoo As famous for its architecture as its animals, the city's fabulous zoo will entertain kids and parents alike – don't miss the elephant house. Afterwards, take a stroll through Városliget Park. **See p.73**

Mátyás Church and Fishermen's Bastion At the heart of cobbled Castle Hill stands the glorious, colourfully-patterned Mátyás Church, and just across the way, the Fishermen's Bastion with its sweeping views of Pest. **See p.89 & p.90**

ON THE RAILS AND ON THE WATER

Sikló Hop on the nineteenth-century funicular perched atop Castle Hill, and enjoy a great view of the city as you ride down to the riverside. **See p.101**

Millennium Line Completed in 1896 for the millennium celebrations – making it the second oldest metro in the world after London – a ride on yellow line #1 from Vörösmarty tér to Hősök tere is sure to conjure up images of a bygone era. **See p.39**

Tram Ride Tram #2 along the Pest embankment offers the best views of Buda, so jump aboard at the southern terminus near the Palace of Arts, and take in the sights all the way up to the Parliament building and beyond. **See p.25**

River Cruise What better way to appreciate the not always so blue Danube than on a lazy afternoon cruise. **See p.24**

Cogwheel and Children's Railway Kids and adults alike will love this 3km climb up into the Buda Hills; and once you've reached the upper terminus, you can board the narrow-gauge railway, which runs for a further 11km through deep woods. **See p.119**

Castle Bus It might not be the most comfortable ride in the world, but as it rattles through the cobbled streets of the Vár, you'll get to see the pick of the sights hereabouts. **See p.88**

ABOVE THE DANUBE **OPPOSITE** APPLIED ARTS MUSEUM

RED BUDAPEST

House of Terror Housed in the former headquarters of the Secret Police, this gripping, and often sobering, museum commemorates the victims of the Communist regime. **See p.60**

Memento Park Head to the city outskirts and wander amongst Red Army soldiers and Communist dictators, then have your picture taken in the Trabant. **See p.124**

Soviet Army Memorial This typically stern Cold War-era memorial honours the soldiers killed during the liberation of the city from the Nazis. **See p.51**

Budapest Poster Gallery Pick up a piece of Communist chic at this fabulous poster shop, specializing in Soviet-era art. **See p.186**

Hospital in the Rock The Cold War comes to life in this fascinating former military hospital-cum-nuclear bunker located deep below Castle Hill. **See p.94**

MUSICAL BUDAPEST

Akvárium A semi-subterranean hub for live bands and DJs, plus an "underwater" restaurant – what's not to like? **See p.181**

Liszt Academy of Music Get your classical kicks by attending a concert in the Grand Hall of the prestigious, and recently renovated, academy building, named after Hungary's most revered musician. **See p.180**

Music History Museum Learn more about Hungary's rich musical heritage at this engaging collection, from the irrepressible sounds of the Roma to the classical genius of Liszt and Bartók. **See p.92**

Cocoa concerts Children-themed concerts run by the Budapest Festival Orchestra – a fun way to introduce a bit of culture to the under-12s. **See p.200**

Opera House Take a backstage tour through one of central Europe's great opera houses, or, better still, take in a performance. **See p.180**

Jazz A strong jazz tradition prevails in Budapest, but for the very best, seek out the Budapest Jazz Club or the Opus Jazz Club, both of which feature a regular roster of high-class acts. **See p.181**

Folk Music One of the most prominent aspects of Magyar culture is folk music, and one of the best places to appreciate these traditional sounds is a *Táncház* (dance house); the Fonó Music Hall is a good place to start. **See p.182**

GETTING AROUND ON TWO WHEELS

Basics

Getting there

Budapest is easy to reach by air from the UK, with a number of airlines flying from several airports. There are no direct flights from North America, Australasia or South Africa so you will need to change planes at a European hub. Travelling overland from the UK is another option, though this inevitably takes much longer and usually works out far more expensive.

To get the very cheapest fares, you'll need to book weeks, if not months, in advance, with the highest fares from June to September, Christmas and New Year. You'll get the best prices during the low season, November to February.

Most airlines prefer you to book online these days, and you can find some great deals, but always check the small print as most budget airlines are non-changeable and non-refundable. Another option is to contact a general flight or **travel agent** – these have similar deals on flights and services, and some are particularly geared towards youth, student and independent travel. Other specialist **tour operators** can book you onto a variety of city breaks or themed tours in Budapest.

Flights from the UK and Ireland

Flying time to Budapest from the UK or Ireland is between two and a half and three hours, depending on your departure airport.

There are currently several budget airlines flying from the UK to Budapest: easyjet (Ⓦeasyjet.com), which flies from London Gatwick and Luton; Norwegian Air (Ⓦnorwegian.com), which flies from London Gatwick; Wizz Air (Ⓦwizzair.com), which flies from Luton; Ryanair (Ⓦryanair.com), which flies from Bristol, Manchester and Stansted; and Jet2 (Ⓦjet2.com), which flies from East Midlands, Leeds Bradford, Manchester and Edinburgh. Tickets with these airlines can be obtained from as little as £80 return, including tax.

The demise of Malév, the Hungarian national airline, in 2012 left British Airways (Ⓦba.com) as the only national carrier flying direct from the UK (daily from Heathrow). Return fares start around £180 high season and £120 low season, though the earlier you book, the cheaper the price.

From **Ireland**, both Aer Lingus (Ⓦaerlingus.com) and Ryanair (Ⓦryanair.com) fly between Dublin and Budapest – flights take three hours. Fares start at around €150 in low season.

Flights from the US and Canada

With no direct flights from North America to Budapest, your best bet is to fly with one of the major European-based airlines like Air France (Ⓦairfrance.com), British Airways or Lufthansa (Ⓦlufthansa.com), where you'll probably be routed via their respective European hubs.

Fares from New York to Budapest are around US$900 high season and US$550 low season, and from the west coast around US$1200 high season and US$850 low season. From **Canada**, fares rise from Can$1000 to at least Can$1600 in high season.

Flights from Australia, New Zealand and South Africa

There are no direct flights to Budapest from Australia, New Zealand or South Africa, so the best option is to fly to a western European gateway and get a connecting flight from there. A standard return **fare** to Budapest with Qantas from eastern **Australia** via Frankfurt is around Aus$2600 in low season, rising to Aus$3500 in high season. From **New Zealand**, a standard return ticket via London with Air New Zealand costs around NZ$3500 in low season, NZ$4000 in high season. Flying from **South Africa**, you can get return flights for ZAR8900 in low season and ZAR9600 in high season.

City breaks and tours

Budapest is an extremely popular city-break destination and this is reflected in the number of operators offering the city as a destination in itself

---

A BETTER KIND OF TRAVEL

At Rough Guides we are passionately committed to travel. We believe it helps us understand the world we live in and the people we share it with – and of course tourism is vital to many developing economies. But the scale of modern tourism has also damaged some places irreparably, and climate change is accelerated by most forms of transport, especially flying. All Rough Guides' flights are carbon-offset, and every year we donate money to a variety of environmental charities.

or as part of a two- or three-centre trip, usually combined with Prague and Vienna.

AGENTS AND OPERATORS

Cox & Kings UK ☏ 020 7873 5000, Ⓦ coxandkings.co.uk. Upmarket cultural trips to Budapest staying in five-star hotels such as the *Four Seasons* and the *Corinthia Royal*: three-night breaks starts at around £470 including flights and transfers. There are also luxury and private group tours aboard the Danube Express, which stops off in Budapest.

Kirker Holidays UK ☏ 020 7593 1899, Ⓦ kirkerholidays.co.uk. Three-night cultural breaks in four- and five-star hotels from around £500 per person, including flights and transfers. They can reserve opera tickets and arrange walking tours of the city.

Martin Randall Travel UK ☏ 020 8742 3355, Ⓦ martinrandall .com. Well-respected art, architecture and music tours led by a lecturer, with prices for a six-day trip starting at around £2500, which includes flights from the UK, hotels, transfers, excursions, concert tickets and some meals.

North South Travel UK ☏ 01245 608 291, Ⓦ northsouthtravel .co.uk. Friendly, competitive travel agency, offering discounted fares worldwide. Profits are used to support projects in the developing world, especially the promotion of sustainable tourism.

Osprey City Holidays UK ☏ 0131 243 8098, Ⓦ ospreyholidays .com. Two-night breaks in one of several three-, four- and five-star hotels, from around £330 per person, including flights and transfers.

Page & Moy UK ☏ 01858 415407, Ⓦ pageandmoy.com. Twelve-day river cruises taking in Budapest as part of a four- or five-centre trip, typically with Austria, Slovakia, Serbia and Romania; £2500.

Regent Holidays UK ☏ 020 7666 1244, Ⓦ regent-holidays.co.uk. Central and Eastern European specialist offering three-night city breaks in three-, four- and five-star accommodation from £345 (including flights from the UK), as well as tailor-made itineraries.

Stag Republic UK ☏ 0845 686 0619, Ⓦ stagrepublic.co.uk. A Budapest-based operation that arranges stag packages that can include Trabant treks, quad biking, visits to the baths and stag dinners. Prices start at around £55 per person for a two-night hostel stay, on top of which you add the various activities.

STA Travel UK ☏ 0871 2300 040, US ☏ 1 800 781 4040, Australia ☏ 134 782, New Zealand ☏ 0800 474 400, South Africa ☏ 0861 781 781; Ⓦ statravel.co.uk. Worldwide specialists in independent travel; also student IDs, travel insurance, car rental, rail pass and more. Good discounts for students and under-26s.

Thermalia Spas UK ☏ 01843 864 688, Ⓦ thermaliaspas.co.uk. Spa holiday specialists offering stays centred around health and fitness at four-star thermal resorts in Budapest. Prices from around £400 for three nights and £720 for seven nights, including flights from the UK and Ireland.

Trailfinders UK ☏ 0845 054 6060, Ireland ☏ 021 464 8800, Australia ☏ 1300 780 212; Ⓦ trailfinders.com. One of the best-informed and most efficient agents for independent travellers.

Trains

Getting to Budapest by **train** is likely to be considerably more expensive than flying, though it's a great deal more fun. First stop should be Ⓦ seat61 .com, an excellent website that provides route, ticket, timetable and contact information for all European train services.

The quickest and most straightforward option from the UK is to take the **Eurostar** from London's St Pancras International to Paris, and then continue from Gare de l'Est to Munich before catching the night train to Budapest; the entire journey takes around twenty hours in total. A standard second-class **return ticket** on this route costs around £320. An alternative is to go via Brussels, Cologne and Vienna: it involves more changing of trains and takes up to twenty-four hours but the views along the Rhine Valley are delightful. There are discounts for students, and those under 26 or over 60.

A **train pass from** InterRail (Ⓦ interrail.eu) or Eurail (Ⓦ eurail.com) – both cover Hungary – makes it convenient to take in the country as part of a wider rail trip around Europe.

RAIL CONTACTS

European Rail UK ☏ 020 7619 1083, Ⓦ europeanrail.com.
Eurostar UK ☏ 0843 218 6186, Ⓦ eurostar.com.
Rail Europe UK ☏ 0844 848 5848; Ⓦ raileurope.com.

By bus

Eurolines (Ⓦ eurolines.co.uk) operates two **buses** a week directly from London to Budapest, which take around 28 hours. Otherwise, you can change in Vienna. A standard return fare costs around £140, though advance deals and special offers can bring this down considerably. Although by no means a particularly comfortable journey, buses are air-conditioned and have on-board toilets. The usual route is to take the ferry across the Channel to Calais and then on via Brussels and Vienna.

Driving to Budapest

Driving to Hungary from the UK can be a pleasant proposition, particularly if you want to make stops in other places along the way. It's about 1600km from London to Budapest, which, with stops, takes two days to drive. To plan your route, try **motoring organizations** such as the AA (Ⓦ theaa.com), the RAC (Ⓦ rac.co.uk) and Via Michelin (Ⓦ viamichelin.com).

The most common cross-Channel options are the **ferry** links between Dover and Calais or Ostend. However, the quickest way of crossing the Channel is to go via the **Eurotunnel** service (Ⓦ eurotunnel .com), which operates drive-on drive-off shuttle trains between Folkestone and Calais/Coquelles. The 24-hour service runs every twenty minutes throughout the day.

Once across the Channel, the most direct route to Budapest is via Brussels, Aachen, Cologne, Frankfurt, Nürnberg, Linz and Vienna. To avoid the long queues at Hegyeshalom, consider entering Hungary from Deutsch-Kreutz, just south of Einstadt, instead. The main cause for any queues is the need to buy an electronic motorway **vignette** (e-Vignette) – compulsory if you are driving on Hungarian motorways. The shortest vignette you can get is the ten-day one which costs 2975Ft (around €11); see Ⓦmotorway.hu for details. You can buy the vignette online ahead of travelling, or at one of the petrol stations in Austria before you cross the border, which should reduce any waiting. A system of mobile patrols and electronic number-plate readers enforces the scheme, and there are steep fines for travelling on a motorway without one. See p.25 for information on driving in Budapest.

FERRY CONTACTS

P&O Ferries UK ☎ 08716 642 121, International ☎ 01304 863 000, Ⓦ poferries.com.
Stena Line UK ☎ 0844 770 7070, Ⓦ stenaline.co.uk.

Arrival

Other than the airport, all points of arrival are fairly central and most within walking distance or just a few stops by metro from downtown Pest. Budapest's excellent public transport system ensures that few parts of the city are more than thirty minutes' journey from the centre; many places can be reached in half that time. Three of the city's four metro lines and three main roads meet at the major junction of Deák tér in Pest, making this the main transport hub of the city; there's a transport map at the back of this book.

By air

Liszt Ferenc International Airport (☎1 296 7000, Ⓦbud.hu), 20km southeast of the centre in Ferihegy (which it is still sometimes known as), has two passenger terminals. Terminal 2A serves countries covered by the Schengen Agreement, while 2B serves all non-Schengen destinations (UK, the US etc). Before leaving, it is worth checking which terminal you're flying from, as the Schengen divide might be subject to revision. There are **ATMs**, exchange facilities, tourist information desks and car-rental offices in all the terminal buildings.

The easiest – but most expensive – way to get into the centre is an **airport taxi**. Run by Fótaxi (☎1 222 2222), these charge a fixed fee to different zones (you'll pay around 6500Ft or €22 to the centre). The next fastest option is the **Airport Shuttle** minibus (☎1 296 8555, Ⓦairportshuttle .hu), which will take you directly to any address in the city. Tickets (3200Ft/€11 for one person, 4790Ft/€16 for two) can be bought at the Airport Shuttle minibus desk in arrivals, or you can make a reservation online. Travelling from the city centre to the airport, you can either reserve online or by phone.

Far cheaper is **public transport**; bus #200E departs every fifteen minutes from the stop between terminals 2A and 2B to Kőbánya-Kispest metro station; from here, you switch to the blue metro line to get to the centre. Buses run between 4am and 11pm and the journey time to Kőbánya-Kispest is about 40 minutes. Both bus and metro tickets cost 350Ft each, but assuming you need to travel into the centre from Kőbánya-Kispest, you'll save money by buying a transfer ticket (530Ft); just remember to validate the second portion of the ticket before you board the metro. Your best bet is to buy your tickets (and collect a public transport map) from the **BKK (Budapest Transport Centre)** desk inside arrivals, next to the Budapest Informa-tion desk. Otherwise, you can buy tickets from the vending machine next to the bus stop (350Ft), or from the driver on board, though this will cost you 450Ft. With a Budapest Card (see p.30), available from the Budapest Information desk, it's free to travel on the bus from the airport.

By train

The Hungarian word *pályaudvar* (abbreviated "*pu*." in writing) is used to designate a **train station**. Of the six in Budapest, only three are important for tourists, but note that their names, which are sometimes translated into English, refer to the direction of services handled rather than their location.

Most international trains terminate at Pest's **Keleti Station**, on Baross tér in the VIII district. It's still something of a hangout for hawks and hustlers – particularly people offering currency exchange – but just simply ignore them all. The best source of tourist information here is the Mellow Mood agency (June–Aug daily 7am–10pm; Sept–May

Mon–Sat 8am–4pm; ☎1 343 0748, ⓦmellowmood
.hu), whose offices are to the right of the big glass
doorways at the station entrance. It can also book
accommodation and organize transport to its
hostels. You can get all tickets and passes from the
excellent BKK public transport customer centre
(daily 5.30am–10pm) located in the underpass.
There are also 24-hour left-luggage lockers here
(400Ft/600Ft for 24hr).

Nyugati Station, north of central Pest in the VI
district, is the second most useful terminus. It has
left-luggage lockers next to the international ticket
office. To reach Deák tér, take the blue metro line
two stops in the direction of Kőbánya-Kispest.

Some trains from Vienna arrive at **Déli Station**,
near the Vár in Buda, and just four stops from Deák
tér on the red metro line. There are left-luggage
lockers here but no tourist office.

Avoid all offers of a **taxi** at any of these stations –
you'll almost certainly be ripped off. Instead, look
out for taxis from the companies listed on p.25,
such as Fótaxi. Better still, call one.

By bus or hydrofoil

International buses and services from the Great
Plain and Transdanubia terminate at **Népliget bus
station**, 5km southeast of the centre at Üllői út 131
in the IX district. The international ticket counters
are on the main concourse, where there's a travel
centre, with domestic ticket counters located
downstairs, which is where you'll also find the left-
luggage office (daily 6am–9pm; 300Ft). An
underpass links the bus station to metro line #3
(blue), from where it's just six stops to Deák tér in
the centre.

Of the other bus stations, the **Újpest Városkapú**
in the XIII district (on the blue metro line) is the
jumping-off point for buses to and from Szentendre
and the Danube Bend; the **Stadion bus station** in
the XIV district (on the red metro line) serves the
Northern Uplands and the **Etele tér bus station** in
the XI district (take bus #7 or #7E to the centre)
serves the Buda hinterland. None of the city's bus
stations has any tourist facilities.

Hydrofoils (operated by Mahart; ☎1 484 4013,
ⓦmahartpassnave.hu) from Vienna (June–Sept)
dock at the **international landing stage**, on the
Belgrád rakpart (embankment), near downtown Pest.

By car

Most drivers enter Budapest along the M1
motorway from Vienna via Hegyeshalom, which is a

busy road, heavily policed to fine speeding
foreigners. It approaches Budapest from the
southwest, and goes straight through to Erzsébet
híd in the centre, with turn-offs signed to Petőfi híd
in the south of the centre, and Széll Kálmán tér and
Margít híd to the north.

Getting around

**Budapest's well-integrated transport
system comprises the metro, buses,
trams and trains, all of which reach most
areas of interest to tourists, while the
outer suburbs are well served by the
overground HÉV rail network. Services
operate generally between 5am and
11pm, and there are also night-time
buses covering much of the city.**

There is a whole array of **tickets** available for use
on public transport, but since validating your ticket
can be complex and is easy to forget, it's best to get
a **travel pass** if you're staying for more than half a
day. The local transport authority, the **Budapest
Transport Centre** (BKK; ⓦbkk.hu) operates an
increasing number of customer service points
(Budapesti Közlekedési Központ), and also has a
useful website with full timetable and ticket
information.

Tickets and passes

Standard single **tickets** (*Vonaljegy*) valid for the
metro, buses, trams, trolleybuses, the Cogwheel
Railway (see p.119) and suburban HÉV lines (up to
the edge of the city) cost 350Ft per journey and
are sold at train and metro stations, newspaper
kiosks and tobacconists. There are also an
increasing number of coin-operated vending
machines at bus and tram stops. Metro tickets
also come in a variety of other types, depending
on whether you are changing trains and how
many stops you want to go: a short section metro
ticket (*Metrószakasz*; 300Ft) takes you three stops
on the same line; a metro transfer ticket
(*Átszállójegy*; 530Ft) is valid for as many stops as
you like with one line change. Tickets bought on
board buses, trams and trolleybuses cost 450Ft.
Books of ten standard single tickets (*tíz-darabos
gyüjtőjegy* – 3000Ft) are also available – these are
still valid if torn out of the book but cannot be
used on night services.

Tickets must be **validated** when you use them.
On the metro and HÉV you punch them in the

BUDAPEST ADDRESSES

Finding your way around Budapest is easier than the welter of names might suggest. Districts and streets are well signposted, and those in Pest conform to an overall plan based on radial avenues and semicircular boulevards.

Budapest is divided into 23 districts, numbered using Roman numerals. Except when addressing letters, a Budapest **address** always begins with the district number, a system used throughout this book. On letters, a four-digit **postal code** is used instead, the middle two digits indicating the district (so that 1054 refers to a place in the V district). For ease of reference, we list below the district numbers you're most likely to encounter, along with the areas within those districts that you'll probably spend most time in.

I	The Vár and Víziváros	X	Kőbánya
II	Rószadomb and Hűvösvölgy	XI	The area south and east of
III	Óbuda and Aquincum		Gellért-hegy
IV	Újpest	XII	The area from the Vár west into
V	Belváros and Lipótváros		the Buda Hills
VI	Terézváros	XIII	Újlipótváros and Angyalföld
VII	Erzsébetváros	XIV	Városliget and Zugló
VIII	Józsefváros	XXII	Budafok and Nagytétény
IX	Ferencváros		

As a rule of thumb, **street numbers** ascend away from the north–south axis of the River Danube and the east–west axis of Rákóczi út/Kossuth utca/Hegyalja út. Even numbers are generally on the left-hand side as you head outwards from these axes, odd numbers on the right. One number may refer to several premises or an entire apartment building, while an additional combination of numerals denotes the floor and number of individual **apartments** (eg Kossuth utca 14.III.24). Confusingly, some old buildings in Pest are designated as having a half-floor (*félemelet*) or upper ground floor (*magas földszint*) between the ground (*földszint*) and first floor (*elsőemelet*) proper – so that what the British would call the second floor, and Americans the third, Hungarians might describe as the first. This stems from a nineteenth-century taxation fiddle, whereby landlords avoided the higher tax on buildings with more than three floors.

machines at station entrances (remember to validate a new ticket if you change lines, unless you have a metro transfer ticket); on trams, buses and trolleybuses, you punch the tickets on board in the small red or orange machines.

Day **passes** (*napijegy*) cost 1650Ft and are valid for unlimited travel from midnight to midnight on the metro, buses, trams, trolleybuses, the Cogwheel Railway and suburban HÉV lines; three-day passes cost 4150Ft and weekly passes 4950Ft. **Season tickets** cost 6300Ft for two weeks and 9500Ft for a month, and are available from metro stations, but you'll need a passport photo for the accompanying photocard; there are photo booths inside the entrance of Deák tér and Széll Kálmán tér stations.

Children up to the age of 6 and EU citizens over the age of 65 travel free on all public transport, though in both cases some form of official documentation must be shown if challenged by inspectors.

As in any big city, **beware of pickpockets** on all forms of public transport. Gangs distract their victims by pushing them or blocking their way, and empty their pockets or bags at the same time.

The metro

The second oldest underground system in the world after London, the Budapest **metro** has four lines, usually referred to by their colour and shown on the colour map at the end of this book. Line #4 was completed in 2014 and runs from Keleti station to Kelenföld station; the three other lines intersect at Deák tér in downtown Pest. Line #1 – also known as the Millennium Underground railway – was the first to be constructed, and in 2002 it was listed as a UNESCO World Heritage Site. Trains run at two- to twelve-minute intervals. There's little risk of going astray once you've learned to recognize the signs *bejárat* (entrance), *kijárat* (exit), *vonal* (line) and *felé* (towards). The train's direction is indicated by the name of the station at the end of the line. The trains on the superb new metro line #4 have announcements in

JUST THE TICKET

The myriad rules on Budapest's public transport system make it easy to catch foreigners out, and **inspectors** (who wear blue or purple armbands saying *jegyellenőr*) tend to be strict in levying 16,000Ft fines (8000Ft if you pay on the spot) for travelling without a valid ticket. Inspectors are plain-clothed, and only whip out their armbands once aboard. The easiest way to get fined is to fail to validate your ticket or when changing lines. If you feel you've been fined unfairly you can try taking your complaint to the office at Akácfa utca 22 (Mon–Fri 7am–8pm, Sat 8am–2pm; ☎ 1 258 4636).

English telling you the next stop (and some line #2 trains too), but on lines #1 and 3, these are in Hungarian only (and barely audible), so you're better off looking out for the signs at each station.

Buses, trams and trolleybuses

There is a good **bus** (*autóbusz*) network across the city, especially in Buda, where Széll Kálmán tér (on the red metro line) and Móricz Zsigmond körtér (southwest of Gellért-hegy) are the main terminals. Bus stops are marked by a picture of a bus on a white background in a blue frame, and have timetables underneath; most buses run every ten to twenty minutes (*utolsó kocsi indul* … means "the last one leaves …"). On busier lines express buses – with an E at the end of the number – run along the same route making fewer stops: for example, the bus #7E that runs along most of the route of the #7. There is a comprehensive network of **night buses**, all of which have a three-digit number beginning with a 9, and which run every hour or half-hour from around midnight or whenever the service they replace finishes.

The network of yellow (or the newer orange) **trams** (*villamos*) is smaller, but they provide a crucial service round the Nagykörút and along the Pest embankment. **Trolleybuses** (*trolibusz*) mostly operate northeast of the centre near the Városliget. Interestingly, their route numbers start at 70 because the first trolleybus line was inaugurated on Stalin's 70th birthday in 1949. Trolleybus #83 was started in 1961, when Stalin would have been 83.

HÉV trains

The green overground **HÉV trains** provide easy access to Budapest's suburbs, running roughly three to five times an hour between 4.30am and 11.30pm. As far as tourists are concerned, the most useful line is the one from **Batthyány tér** (on the red metro line) out to **Szentendre**, which passes through Óbuda, Aquincum and Rómaifürdő. The other lines originate in Pest, with one running

northeast from **Örs vezér tere** (also on the red metro line) to **Gödöllő** via the Formula One racing track at Mogyoród; another southwards from Boráros tér at the Pest end of Petőfi híd to Csepel; and the third from **Közvágóhíd** (bus #23 or #54 from Boráros tér) to **Ráckeve**.

Boats and other transport

There are several **passenger boat services on the Danube**, which makes for an enjoyable way to see the Buda and Pest embankments. On weekdays, service D11 plies the route between Újpest and Haller utca (just beyond Petőfi híd towards the Palace of the Arts); while service D12 starts at Rómaifürdő and also travels down to Haller utca. At weekends and on holidays, service D13 runs between Rómaifürdő and Haller utca. All services stop at Árpád Híd, Margit-sziget, Batthyány tér, Petőfi tér and Szent Gellért tér, running roughly hourly between 7am and 7pm. Tickets (750Ft) can be obtained from kiosks (where timetables are posted) or machines at the docks.

In the Buda Hills, there's also the **Cogwheel Railway** (Fogaskerekűvasút, now officially designated as tram #60), the **Children's Railway** (Gyermekvasút), and the **chairlift** (*libegő*) between Zugliget and János-hegy; see Chapter 9 for details. Note that BKK tickets and passes are also valid for the Cogwheel Railway and BKK passes can be used on boats on weekdays – for the others, you'll need to buy tickets at the point of departure or on board.

Taxis

Though not nearly as bad it used to be, Budapest's **taxis** still have a reputation for ripping off foreigners. Make sure your taxi has a meter that is visible and **switched on** when you get in, and that the rates are clearly displayed. **Fares** are fixed though, with a starting fee of 450Ft, and a price per kilometre of 280Ft.

Taxis can be flagged down on the street, and there are **ranks** throughout the city. For a slightly

USEFUL BUS, TRAM AND TROLLEYBUS ROUTES (LISTED WITH KEY STOPS)

BUSES

#7 Bosnyák tér–Keleti Station–Móricz Zsigmond körtér (via Ferenciek tere, Rudas Baths, *Gellért Hotel*).

#16A Dísz tér (Castle District)–Széll Kálmán tér.

#16 Deák tér–Dísz tér (Castle District)–Bécsi kapu tér–Széll Kálmán tér.

#26 Margit-sziget–Árpád híd metro station.

#65 Kolosy tér–Pálvölgyi Caves–*Fenyőgyöngye* restaurant at the bottom of Hármashatár-hegy.

#86 Southern Buda–Gellért tér–Batthyány tér–Margit Bridge–Flórián tér (Óbuda).

#105 Apor Vilmos tér–Lanchíd–Deák tér–Oktogon–Gyöngyösi utca.

#116 Fény utca market–Széll Kálmán tér– Dísz tér (Castle District).

NIGHT BUSES

#906 Széll Kálmán tér–Margit-sziget–Nyugati Station–Nagykörut (Great Boulevard)–Móricz Zsigmond körtér.

#907 Örs vezér tere–Bosnyák tér–Keleti Station–Erzsébet híd–*Gellért Hotel*–Etele tér (Kelenföld).

#914 and **#950** Kispest (Határ út metro station)–Deák tér–Lehel tér–Újpest, along the route of the blue metro and on to the north and south.

TRAMS

#2 Margit Bridge (Jászai Mari tér)–Belgrád rakpart (along embankment)–Petőfi híd–Vágóhíd ter.

#4 Széll Kálmán tér–Margit-sziget–Nyugati Station–Nagykörut (Great Boulevard)–Petőfi Bridge–Október 23 utca.

#6 Széll Kálmán tér–Margit-sziget–Nyugati Station– Nagykörut (Great Boulevard)–Petőfi Bridge–Móricz Zsigmond körtér.

#19 Batthyány tér–the Víziváros–Kelenföld Station.

#47 Deák tér–Szabadság híd–*Gellért Hotel*–Móricz Zsigmond körtér–Budafok.

#61 Móricz Zsigmond körtér–Villányi út–Déli Station–Széll Kálmán tér–Huvősvölgy.

TROLLEYBUSES

#72 Arany János utca metro station–Nyugati Station–Zoo–Széchenyi Baths–Hermina út.

#74 Dohány utca (outside the Main Synagogue)–Városliget.

---

cheaper rate, order a cab by phone. Avoid unmarked private cars, and drivers hanging around the stations and airport.

TAXI COMPANIES

Citytaxi ☎ 1 211 1111
Főtaxi ☎ 1 222 2222
Volantaxi ☎ 1 433 3322

Driving

If you're coming just to Budapest, it's unlikely you'll need, or want, to drive around the city, especially given the excellent public transport system. In any case, **driving** in Budapest can't be recommended; road manners are nonexistent, parking spaces are scarce and traffic jams are frequent – careering trams, bumpy cobbles, swerving lane markings and unexpected one-way systems make things worse.

In addition, access to the Castle District and parts of the Belváros are strictly limited.

If you are driving, however, the most important **rules** to bear in mind are: you must give way to cars on your right if there are no road markings to indicate otherwise; at night, many traffic lights go into flashing orange mode, which means that priority is given to the right; drinking and driving is totally prohibited, as is the use of a hand-held mobile phone. The speed limit in built-up areas is 50kph (30mph), and 90kph (60mph) outside built-up areas. On main roads, it's 110kph (68mph), and on motorways 130kph (80mph).

In terms of **parking**, you might be better off leaving your car outside the centre and using public transport to travel in – there are park and ride facilities at most metro termini. If you must park in the centre, the best options are the underground car parks in Szent István tér by the Basilica and underneath Szabadsag tér, both in Lipótváros. Parking on the street in the central districts typically costs 120–440Ft per hour – you get a ticket from the nearest machine; alternatively, there are an increasing number of car parks that have been set up in areas where blocks of buildings have been knocked down.

Renting a car is easy, with prices inevitably cheaper the further in advance you book – expect to pay around €45 for a day's rental (unlimited mileage) and upwards of €250 per week. When checking prices, make sure the price quoted includes the twenty-percent ÁFA (VAT). Before signing, check on mileage limits and any other restrictions or extras, as well as what you're liable for in the event of an accident.

CAR RENTAL COMPANIES

All these companies have offices at the airport, except for Regina.

Avis V, Szabadság tér 7 ☏ 1 318 4240, ⓦ avis.hu.

Budget Hotel Mercure Buda, I, Krisztina körút 41–43 ☏ 1 214 0420, ⓦ budget.hu.

Europcar V, Erzsébet tér 7–8 ☏ 1 505 4400, ⓦ europcar.hu.

Hertz V, Váci utca 135–139 ☏ 1 237 0407, ⓦ hertz.hu.

Regina X, Regina köz 1 ☏ 1 367 3663, ⓦ reginaauto.hu.

Cycling

Cycling is finally catching on in Budapest, with rising numbers of cyclists and the emergence of dedicated cycle lanes (red with yellow lines on either side). That said, it isn't easy riding: drivers are generally oblivious and you also have to contend with sunken tramlines, bumpy cobbles and bad air pollution. **Cycle routes** are still patchy and don't link up to form a coherent network yet, so you're best off sticking to the city's green areas like Margaret Island and the City Park. There are also good routes out of town, such as along the Buda bank of the Danube to Szentendre and on up towards Slovakia. Bicycles can be carried on HÉV trains and the Cogwheel Railway for the price of a one-way ticket, but not on buses or trams. For trail-biking in the Buda Hills, see p.119.

There are several excellent bike-rental outfits in the city, as well as a number of bike shops that do repairs, including Nella Bikes, off Bajcsy-Zsilinszky út at V, Kálmán Imre utca 23 (☏ 1 331 3184, ⓦ nella.hu). For an in-depth look at cycling from a local's point of view visit ⓦ cyclingsolution.blogspot.hu.

BIKE RENTAL

Expect to pay around 2000Ft for half a day's rental and 3000Ft for a full day's rental, including a lock and helmet.

Bikebase VI, Podmaniczky utca 19 ☏ 1 269 5983, ⓦ bikebase.hu. Excellent operation near Nyugati Station, with friendly staff who dole out maps and advise on cycling routes. Repair service available too. March to mid-Nov daily 9am–7pm.

BuBi Bike ⓦ molbubi.bkk.hu. Bike-sharing scheme with docking stations all over Budapest; pre-registration is required however; 30mins free then 500Ft for one hour, 1500Ft for two hours.

Budapest Bike VII, Wesselényi utca 13 ☏ 30 944 5533, ⓦ budapestbike.hu. Bike rental and bike tours. Mid-March to mid-Oct daily 9am–6pm.

Yellow Zebra VI, Lázár utca 16 ☏ 1 269 3843, ⓦ yellowzebra budapest.com. See below.

City tours

There is now a wide range of city tours available in Budapest; indeed you can't move these days without being accosted by someone offering a tour of some description. But if you're hard-pressed for time, you might appreciate one of the city's bus tours, which generally take you past the Parliament, along Andrássy út, across to the Várhegy and up to Gellért-hegy for panoramic photo opportunities.

That said, Budapest's backstreets and historic quarters are eminently suited to walking, and this is much the best way to appreciate their character. Moreover, traffic is restricted in downtown Pest and around the Vár in Buda, and fairly light in the residential backstreets off the main boulevards, which are the nicest areas to wander around. The Budapest Card (see p.30) entitles you to two free guided walks, one of Buda, one of Pest.

BIKE TOURS

Yellow Zebra VI, Lázár utca 16 ☏ 1 269 3843, ⓦ yellowzebra budapest.com. Excellent outfit offering both scheduled and private cycling tours of the city. Between April and October, there's a standard four-hour bike tour (€20) which departs at 11am daily (March & Nov Fri–Sat only). They also offer two-hour Segway tours (€60) – all year-round – on the strange-looking, two-wheel Segway bikes.

BUS TOURS

Budapest Sightseeing ☏ 1 317 7767, ⓦ programcentrum.hu. Two-and-a-half-hour hop-on hop-off city tour taking in all the major sights; buses depart from Erzsébet tér every thirty minutes. Tickets (5000Ft), though, are valid for 48 hours. April–Oct.

Giraffe Hop-On Hop-Off VI, Andrassy utca 2 ☏ 1 374 7070, ⓦ citytour.hu. Another hop-on hop-off bus tour taking in all the key sights, but on red double-decker buses. There are two lines, both of which depart every thirty minutes; red from József Nádor tér, and yellow from

Erzsébet tér. Tickets (5000Ft) are valid on both lines for 48 hours. They also do a hop-on hop-off cruise departing hourly from Vigadó tér (3000Ft). April–Oct.

WALKING TOURS

Absolute Walking Tours VI, Lázár utca 16 ☎ 1 269 3843, Ⓦ absolutetours.com. Run by the same team as Yellow Zebra (in the Discover Budapest office). Aside from the standard three-hour city walk (€26), Absolutes offer a terrific range of themed tours, such as Food & Wine (€68) and Hammer & Sickle (€45), as well as an evening pub crawl (€28).

Free Budapest Tours ☎ 20 534 5819, Ⓦ freebudapesttours.hu. Aimed at backpackers, tours depart from Déak tér daily at 10.30am (Pest to Buda City Tour; 2hr 30min) and 2.30pm (Faith, Terror, Communism Tour; 1hr 30min). Both tours are free, though tips are welcome.

Jewish Heritage ☎ 1 317 2754, Ⓦ ticket.info.hu. Three tours of the Jewish quarter, ranging from one and half hours (4900Ft) to four hours (9900Ft), though all include a guided visit of the Dohany synagogue. Daily except Sat, either at 10am or 2pm (and 11am on Sun). Advance booking required.

RIVER TOURS

RiverRide ☎ 1 332 2555, Ⓦ riverride.com. Jump aboard the floating bus for a slightly more unorthodox sightseeing tour; starting in Széchenyi tér, the bus takes in all the main sights in Pest before splashing into the Danube and continuing down to the Chain Bridge and winding up in Buda. Departures daily April–October at 10am, noon, 3pm and 5pm; Nov–March at 11am, 1pm and 3pm. (€30).

The media

Hungary has a long tradition of lively print media, and there are several broadsheets available, in addition to a handful of local English-language papers. Television differs little from that in other European countries, with foreign cable and satellite television dominating the airwaves.

Newspapers and magazines

There are several Budapest-based English publications, including the weekly magazine *Budapest Times* (Ⓦ budapesttimes.hu), which offers a useful commentary on current affairs, and the *Budapest Business Journal* (Ⓦ bbj.hu), which covers mainly business and politics. You can often find them for free in the lobbies of larger hotels.

The best place to find foreign newspapers and magazines are the newsagents (such as Relay) at stations and shopping malls, though all the major bookshops should have a decent stock of foreign-language material; the best of these is Bestsellers (see p.188).

There are several sources of English-language **listings information**: the fortnightly *Budapest Funzine* (Ⓦ funzine.hu), distributed free in cafés and bars, is aimed at the expat market and has nightlife listings, as well as information on other happenings in Budapest. The free monthly magazine *Where Budapest* has information on current events. The Hungarian-language listings bible *Pesti Est* (free in bars and cinemas) has extensive details of film and music events, and sometimes has an English section in the summer.

Television

Hungarian **television** is not particularly exciting, with state TV (MTV) screening a dreary diet of gameshows and low-budget soaps from morning to night. In addition, there are numerous commercial channels such as ATV, TV2, the RTL Klub and Duna TV, a state-supported channel geared to Hungarian minorities abroad, though these are little better. For this reason many Hungarians subscribe to satellite channels, with whole apartment blocks sharing the cost of installation. The majority of hotels have satellite TV, though the programming is dominated by German channels or those from neighbouring countries. Most, though, will also feature the likes of BBC World, Sky or CNN.

Websites

You can find English-language news and entertainment **listings** online at Ⓦ xpatloop .com and Ⓦ caboodle.hu. For up-to-the-minute restaurant, club and bar reviews check out Ⓦ welovebudapest.com. As for **blogs** Ⓦ pestiside .hu provides an irreverent expat take on life and events in Hungary, Ⓦ horinca.blogspot.hu are the entertaining musings of an long-term Budapest resident and klezmer player while Ⓦ lostandfoundin budapest.wordpress.com focuses on the city from a student's point of view. Slightly quirkier are Ⓦ disappearingbudapest.blogspot.com which looks at undiscovered or disappearing features of the city and architectural blog Ⓦ budapest100.hu.

Festivals

Whatever time of the year you visit Budapest, there's almost certain to be something happening. The two biggest events by far are the Spring Festival in

March and the Café Budapest Contemporary Arts Festival in October, both of which feature world-class music, film and drama. Indeed, music is a constant theme throughout the festival year, with none bigger than the mega Sziget Festival in August.

Many theatres, concert halls and dance houses close down during the long, hot months of July and August, when open-air performances are staged instead. The city's population returns from the countryside for the fireworks on August 20, and life returns to normal as school starts the following week. The new arts season kicks off in the last week of September with a rash of music festivals and political anniversaries. Great fun, too are the growing number of food and drink festivals during which stalls are often set up in Vörösmarty tér and in Varosháza park, on Károly körút.

JANUARY AND FEBRUARY

Farsang Jan 6 to Ash Wednesday. Held in the run-up to Lent, this Hungarian carnival sees revellers taking to the streets in fancy dress, parading across the Lánchíd and down to Vörösmarty tér. Unfortunately the inclement weather at this time of year often dampens the event's spirit.

Mangalica Festival First weekend in Feb; **W** mangalicafesztival .hu. A pig-out in every sense of the word, as the nation's favourite curly-haired swine is celebrated in Szabadság tér; hog roasts aside, there are cooking competitions and a stack of other foodie treats.

MARCH AND APRIL

Declaration of Independence of 1848 March 15. A public holiday in honour of the 1848 Revolution, which began with Petőfi's declaration of the National Song from the steps of the National Museum. Budapest decks itself out with Hungarian tricolours (red, white and green), and there are speeches and gatherings outside the museum and by Petőfi's statue on Marcius 15 tér. The more patriotic citizens wear little cockades in the national colours pinned to their lapels.

Budapest Spring Festival (Budapest Tavaszi Fesztivál) Mid- to late March; **W** btf.hu. The city's most prestigious arts festival is an intensive, two-week jamboree of classical music, with orchestral, chamber and operatic performances taking place in venues across the city. There's also theatre, cinema, exhibitions (including the World Press Photos show) and dance, including a big folk dance gathering and market (*Országos Táncháztalálkozó és Kirakodóvásár*; **W** tanchaz.hu).

Easter (Húsvét) Late March/early April. Easter has strong folk traditions in Hungary. In the city this is limited to some processions in churches Easter Saturday, while on Easter Monday *locsolkodás* (splashing) takes place, when men and boys visit female friends to spray them with cologne in a tamer version of an older village tradition involving a bucket of water. Kids get a painted egg or money in return for splashing, while the men receive *pálinka* (schnapps).

There is an arts and craft fair in the Royal Palace (**W** budavarihusvet .hu), with traditional skills such as egg painting on display, accompanied by music and dancing. There are lots of Easter stalls in Vörösmarty tér in central Pest, and folk skills are on display in situ at the Hungarian Open-Air Museum in Szentendre (p.132). You can also catch performances of the Bach Passions in the big, yellow Lutheran church on Deák tér.

Titanic International Film Festival Mid-April; **W** titanicfilmfest .hu. Superb ten-day programme of independent films from all over the world, with separately themed categories. The venues include the Uránia and Toldi cinemas. Most films have English subtitles. See p.182.

MAY, JUNE AND JULY

Labour Day May 1. These days, Budapest's citizens are no longer obliged to parade past the Lenin statue that once stood behind the Műcsarnok; instead, the major trade unions put on a big do in the park, with shows, games, talks and food and drink in large quantities.

Pálinka Festival May; **W** budapestipalinkafesztival.hu. This colourful four-day event in Varosháza Park features some two dozen distilleries offering several hundred variations on the quintessential Hungarian tipple, alongside sausages, cheese and the like.

Book Week (Könyvhét) Early June. Established in 1929, and as popular as ever, Book Week sees Hungarian writers from all over the world gather around stalls on Vörösmarty tér. There are signings – politicians have now joined the book circus – as well as dancing on the temporary stages in the two squares.

Craft Beer and Street Food Festival (Főzdefeszt) early June; **W** fozdefeszt.hu. The celebration of the growing popularity of Hungarian microbreweries joins forces with the Street Food Festival on the riverfront by the Technical University, below the *Gellért Hotel* for a true fest of food and drink. A week later the official beer festival opens in the Vár.

Night of Museums (Múzeumok Ejszakája) around June 21; **W** muzej.hu. Most of the city's big museums take part, opening their doors to visitors till late into the night with exhibitions, concerts and shows. The 1500Ft ticket gets you into all the sights and covers bus travel, as well – special bus services run till 2am.

Gay Pride Mid-late June; **W** budapestpride.com. The largest event in the gay calendar, this is a week-long celebration of gay and lesbian culture. The week culminates in a march along Andrássy út , either to or from the Városliget. See p.202.

AUGUST

Sziget Festival Mid-Aug; **W** sziget.hu. A stamina-sapping eight days long, Sziget is now firmly established as one of Europe's biggest rock and pop festivals. Staged on Óbudai sziget, an island north of the centre, it features a stellar line-up of rock, pop and world music acts, alongside dance, theatre, films and children's events. See p.179.

Festival of Crafts (Mesterségek Ünnepe) In the days leading up to Aug 20, the Vár is taken over by a huge festival of traditional crafts, accompanied by folk music and dancing.

St Stephen's Day Aug 20. A public holiday in honour of Hungary's national saint and founder, with day-long rites at his Basilica, and a spectacular fireworks display fired off between the Erzsébet and Margit bridges at 9pm, watched by over a million people who line the Danube; the traffic jam that follows is equally mind-blowing. Restaurants are packed that night, so book well ahead if you want to eat out.

Jewish Summer Festival End Aug; ⓦ jewishfestival.hu. Vibrant, week-long jamboree, attracting an international range of classical, jazz and klezmer music performances, films and exhibitions.

SEPTEMBER AND OCTOBER

Budapest Wine Festival (Budapest Bor Fesztivál) Early Sept; ⓦ winefestival.hu. The country's top producers set out their wares on the terrace of the Royal Palace in the Castle District: for the price of a day ticket you get unrestricted access, a glass and a glass holder. Individual tasting tickets are available once inside.

Café Budapest Contemporary Arts Festival (Kortárs Művészeti Fesztivál) Mid-Oct; ⓦ cafebudapestfest.hu. The old Budapest Autumn Festival has been rebranded, but it is still strong on contemporary music and also features an excellent programme of film, dance and photography.

Anniversary of the Arad Martyrs Oct 6. Commemoration of the shooting of the thirteen Hungarian generals in 1849 in Arad (Nagyvárad) in present-day Romania, when the 1848 revolution was crushed by the Austrians with Russian help. Wreaths are laid at the Eternal Flame.

Commemoration of the 1956 Uprising Oct 23. A national holiday to mark the 1956 Uprising and the declaration of the Republic in 1990. Ceremonies take place in Kossuth tér, by the nearby Nagy Imre statue, and at Nagy's grave in the New Public Cemetery. Bear in mind that 1956 has left a divided inheritance and tempers can flare.

LGBTQ Film Festival Oct–Nov; ⓦ budapestpride.com. Budapest's major gay film festival. There is also the Lesbian Identities Festival (LIFT – Leszbikus Identitások Fesztiválja; ⓦ labrisz.hu/english) in early Nov.

NOVEMBER AND DECEMBER

All Saints' Day (Mindenszentek napja) Nov 1. Cemeteries stay open late and candles are lit in memory of departed souls, making for an incredible sight as darkness falls.

St Nicholas's Day (Mikulás) Dec 5 & 6. On Dec 5, children clean their shoes and put them in the window for "Mikulás", the Santa Claus figure, to fill with sweets; naughty children are warned that if they behave badly, all they will get is *virgács*, a gold-painted bunch of twigs from Mikulás's little helpers.

Christmas (Karácsony) Dec 24 & 25. The main celebration is on Dec 24, when the city becomes eerily silent by late afternoon. Children are taken out while their parents decorate the Christmas tree (until then the trees are stored outside, and on housing estates you can often see them dangling from windows). When the kids return home, they wait outside until the bell rings, which tells them that "little Jesus" (Jézuska) has come. Inside, they sing carols by the tree, open presents, and start the big Christmas meal, which traditionally includes spicy fish soup. In the preceding weeks there are Christmas fairs in several locations around town, the best being in the Museum of Ethnography, where traditional crafts are demonstrated.

New Year's Eve (Szilveszter) Dec 31. Revellers gather on the Nagykörút during the evening, engaging in paper trumpet battles at the junction with Rákóczi út.

Culture and etiquette

Forty years of Communism swept away Hungary's archaic semi-feudal society but you can still find remnants of the old ways, for instance in the language. As a foreigner, you are not obliged to know these details, but Hungarians will love it if you can get them right.

Hungarians preserve certain formalities in meeting and greeting. Young people will usually go straight into the informal form of address with each other (the Hungarian equivalent of the French "*tu*" is to use the second person), but with their elders or in the more formal settings of work or school they would use the formal mode, talking to people in the third person, until invited to use the **informal** mode. So "*Hogy vagy?*" is the informal "how are you?", "*Hogy van?*" is the **formal** – and then to be awfully polite, talking to someone's granny for instance, you can say "*Hogy tetszik lenni?*" (literally, "How does it please you to be?").

When introduced to someone you shake hands and say your name. You would usually **shake hands** when meeting people, though between friends, kissing on both cheeks is the norm – between men, too. Some older men still bow to kiss a woman's hand – but it looks rather affected when anyone else does it, so it is best not to try. You will hear an echo of this social convention in the greeting "*Csókolom*", which means "I kiss [your hand]". Adults will say it to elderly ladies and children will say this to adults – responding in kind is an easy error to make and will provoke much laughter.

The formal salutation – to say hello or goodbye – is "*Jó napot*" (or "*Jó reggelt*" before 9am) while with friends "*Szia*", "*Szervusz*" or even "*Helló*" is normal. For more on language see p.222.

A sense of social formality is preserved in other ways too. When visiting someone at home, taking flowers is always acceptable: there are many complex rules and codes in flower-giving that you need not worry about – but do take an odd number of flowers (not 13, though).

Two other useful points when visiting: it is common to take off your shoes when you go into people's houses; and if eating at someone's house it is customary to compliment the host(ess) on the food early on after the first couple of mouthfuls.

Smoking is pretty universal in Budapest – though in someone's home, of course, it is polite to ask if it is permitted. The smoking ban in restaurants and bars is strictly enforced, but this does not apply to attached terraces and in gardens, where everyone lights up at will. Smoking is also banned on all public transport.

Religion

The majority of the Hungarian population is officially **Roman Catholic**, with the remainder comprising Calvinists, smaller numbers of Lutherans and Jews and even smaller groups such as Serb and Greek Orthodox. The 2012 constitution declared Hungary to be a "Christian" country, though official recognition initially left out Methodists, among others.

Churches may prohibit sightseeing during services and charge for entry. Visitors are expected to wear "decorous" dress – that is, no shorts or sleeveless tops. Several churches offer services in English: Anglican: 10.30am on the first Sunday of the month XII, Eötvös út 35 in Buda, and the other Sundays at VII, Almássy utca 6 in Pest ❶06 20 269-5161, ⓦanglican budapest.com; Baptist: Sunday 10.30am, International Baptist Church, II, Törökvész út 48–54 (Móricz Zsigmond Gimnázium) ❶1 319 8525, ⓦibcbudapest .org; Roman Catholic: Saturday 5pm, Pesti Jézus Szíve Templom, VIII, Mária utca 25 ❶1 318 3479.

Hungary has a rich **Jewish heritage** and Budapest boasts a sizeable and increasingly active Jewish community. The city is also the focus of huge donations aiming to restore buildings that were devastated in the Holocaust.

Travel essentials

Admission charges

The majority of the city's museums charge between 600Ft (€2) and 800Ft (€2.50), though the showpiece ones, such as the Museum of Fine Arts and the House of Terror cost around 1800–2200Ft (€6–7).

THE BUDAPEST CARD

If you're doing a lot of sightseeing, the **Budapest Card** (ⓦbudapest-card.com) represents great value. It's available for 24hr (4500Ft), 48hr (7500Ft) or 72hr (8900Ft), and grants free public transport in the city, free entrance to eight museums (Museum of Fine Arts, the Hungarian National Museum, the National Gallery and the Budapest History Museum), free entry to the Lukács Baths, and two free guided walking tours. In addition, there are discounts of between ten and fifty percent on lots of other attractions, including some of the baths, plus shops and restaurants. The card is available online, from tourist offices, hotels, central metro stations and at the airport, and comes with a booklet explaining where it can be used.

There's usually a reduction or free entrance if you show a student, youth or senior citizen card. If you're planning on visiting multiple museums, consider buying the Budapest Card (see above), which offers good savings. For details of admission charges to Budapest's baths, see p.195. Churches may charge a small fee to see their crypts and treasures.

Climate

Budapest has quite distinct **seasons**; summers can be extremely hot with prolonged periods of sunshine and temperatures regularly reaching the mid-30s (°C). Winters, by contrast, can be bitterly cold, with snow common in the months either side of Christmas – though this can make for a wonderful sight around the festive season, particularly with the markets in full flow. The most reliable seasons are spring and autumn, which are generally pretty mild; spring is invariably beautiful, and it's not

BUDAPEST CLIMATE											
	Jan	**Feb**	**Mar**	**Apr**	**May**	**Jun**	**Jul**	**Aug**	**Sep**	**Oct**	**Nov**	**Dec**
AVERAGE DAILY TEMPERATURE												
Avg Minimum C° (F°)	-4 (25)	-2 (28)	2 (36)	7 (45)	1 (52)	15 (59)	16 (61)	16 (61)	12 (54)	7 (45)	3 (37)	-1 (30)
Avg Maximum C° (F°)	1 (34)	4 (39)	10 (50)	17 (63)	22 (72)	26 (79)	27 (82)	27 (82)	23 (73)	16 (61)	8 (46)	4 (39)
AVERAGE RAINFALL												
mm	37	44	38	45	72	69	56	47	33	57	70	46

uncommon for the city to experience long days of sunshine throughout March and April, though May can get showery. The sun, meanwhile, often lingers well into September, and even October. This makes the city a perfect time to visit for the prestigious Spring and Autumn Festivals respectively.

Costs

Although Budapest is not the bargain destination it once was, it's still very good value, especially when compared to cities in Britain, France or Italy, for example.

If you're not staying in a hostel, the main drain on your resources will be hotel accommodation; while rates fluctuate wildly according to season and demand, expect to pay around €60 a night for a double room in a three-star hotel, and somewhere In excess of €100 for a four-star. A two-course lunch or dinner with a glass of wine in one of the better restaurants should set you back around 5500Ft (€18). Public transport is cheap, with a one-day pass covering all modes of transport costing 1650Ft (€5.50).

Foreigners are easy targets for overcharging, so it is always worth checking the price of what you are buying ("*Mennyibe kerül?*" means "how much is it?"). One hidden extra is the ÁFA or sales tax (the equivalent of VAT in Britain) of up to 25 percent, which can hike up the cost of rental cars and hotels, for example: look out for the phrase "*az árak nem tartalmaznak Áfát*", meaning "prices do not include tax". There is also a three percent tourist tax on hotel prices, and it is worth checking that both taxes are included in any prices quoted. The simplest way to ask is "*Ez az ár bruttó vagy nettó?*" – "Is this price with or without tax?".

Crime and personal safety

Hungary is one of the safest European countries, and there's little reason to worry about your personal security while visiting. Violent crime is extremely rare, though petty theft is common, with downtown Budapest a prime area for pickpocketing and scams directed at tourists, such as luring them into rip-off restaurants. It is also advisable not to take valuables to the baths, as lockers are sometimes targeted by thieves.

The Hungarian **police** (*rendőrség*) have a milder reputation than their counterparts in other Eastern European states, and are generally keen to present a favourable image. During the summer, **tourist police** patrol the streets and metro stations mainly to act as a deterrent against thieves, and to assist in any problems tourists may encounter. Most Hungarian police have at least a smattering of German, but rarely speak any other foreign language. To contact the police, call ☎107, or ☎112, which is also the number for the ambulance and fire services. Alternatively, Tourinform has a 24-hour English-speaking service on ☎1 483 8080.

Electricity

The Hungarian system runs on 220 volts. Round two-pin plugs are used. A standard continental adapter allows the use of 13-amp square-pin plugs.

Entry requirements

Hungary is part of the Schengen Agreement, so citizens of the other Schengen states can enter Hungary with just an ID card and stay for up to ninety days. Citizens of the UK, Ireland, US, Canada, Australia and New Zealand, and most other European countries, can enter Hungary with just a passport and stay for the same period. South African citizens will need to apply to their local Hungarian consulate for a visa, though note that visas valid for another Schengen country are also valid for Hungary.

FOREIGN CONSULATES IN BUDAPEST

Canada II, Ganz utca 12–14 ☎1 392 3360, ⓦkanada.hu.
Ireland V, Szabadság tér 7, Bank Center, seventh floor ☎1 301 4960, ⓦembassyofireland.hu.
South Africa II Gárdonyi Géza út 17 ☎1 392 0999.
UK V, Harmincad utca 6 ☎1 266 2888, ⓦbritishembassy.hu.
US V, Szabadság tér 12 ☎1 475 4400, ⓦhungary.usembassy.gov.

Health

No inoculations are required for Hungary and standards of public health are good, although hospital services vary considerably and are probably best avoided, unless it's an emergency. The **European Health Insurance Card** gives EU citizens access to Hungary's national health service (OTBF) under reciprocal agreements. While this will provide free or reduced-cost medical care in the event of minor injuries or emergencies, it won't cover every eventuality – so **travel insurance** is essential (see p.32).

Budapest has plentiful **pharmacies** (*gyógyszertár* or *patika*), which normally open Monday to Friday from 8am to 7 or 8pm, and on Saturday from 8am until noon or 1pm; signs in the window give the location or telephone number of the nearest all-night (*éjjeli* or *ügyeleti szolgálat*) pharmacy. There is one in Buda at XII, Alkotas utca 1/b, near Déli pu, and in Pest at VI, Teréz körút 41.

In **emergencies**, dial ❶104 for the Mentok ambulance service (or ❶112, the central number for emergencies), or get a taxi to the nearest **hospital** (*kórház*). For non-urgent treatment, tourist offices can direct you to a local **medical centre** or doctors' surgery (*orvosi rendelő*), and your embassy in Budapest will have the addresses of foreign-language-speaking **doctors** and **dentists**, who will probably be in private (*magán*) practice.

Sunburn (*napszúrás*) and insect bites (*rovarcsípés*) are the most common **minor complaints** for travellers, so take plenty of sunscreen and repellent. Mosquitoes can be annoying, but the bug to beware of in forests around Budapest is the *kullancs*, a tick which bites and then burrows into human skin, causing inflammation of the brain. The risk of one biting you is fairly small, but if you get a bite that seems particularly painful, or are suffering from a high temperature and stiff neck following a bite, have it checked out as quickly as possible.

Insurance

You should take out a comprehensive insurance policy before travelling to Budapest, to cover against loss, theft, illness or injury. A typical policy will provide cover for loss of baggage, tickets and – up to a certain limit – cash or travellers' cheques, as well as cancellation or curtailment of your journey.

If you need to make a **claim**, you should keep receipts for medicines and medical treatment, and in the event you have anything stolen, you must obtain an official statement from the police.

Internet

Budapest has excellent wi-fi coverage, with most hotels and youth hostels, and many cafés and bars offering free access, though in the latter you will be obliged to buy a drink for using this facility.

Kids

Budapest is a child-friendly city, with plenty to entertain young ones – see p.198 for details. Hungarians tend to be welcoming to kids without making them the centre of attention as you might find in, say, Italy.

Facilities are a bit patchy, though; while the network of playgrounds is marvellous, nappy-changing facilities (*pelenkázó*) are hard to find – they're mostly concentrated in big shopping malls. Buildings don't tend to be very accessible if you're pushing a buggy, but help is usually quickly forthcoming when you're trying to negotiate stairs. On public transport people will readily give up seats to pregnant women and to parents with babies. They will also happily chat to children – the flipside is that old ladies may also loudly berate parents for not looking after their babies "properly", such as for not putting a hat on a baby even in the mildest of weather.

The malls are also the best bet for nappies, baby toiletries and clothes, while many also have indoor play areas. Restaurants usually have high chairs, and although there isn't a culture of whole families dining out in the evening, waiting staff (even in smart places) are usually accommodating. In many places you can ask for a small child's portion –*kisadag*.

Laundry

There are very few self-service launderettes (*mosoda*) in Budapest, but you could try the following: Laundromat Mosómata at VI, Ó utca 24–26 (Mon–Fri 9am–7pm, Sat & Sun 10am–4pm) near the Basilica; and Liliom Szalon, IX, Liliom utca 7–9 (Mon–Fri 8am–8pm, Sat 8am–noon; ⓦliliom szalon.hu). Expect to pay around 1800Ft for a wash

---

ROUGH GUIDES TRAVEL INSURANCE

Rough Guides has teamed up with WorldNomads.com to offer great travel insurance deals. Policies are available to residents of over 150 countries, with cover for a wide range of adventure sports, 24hr emergency assistance, high levels of medical and evacuation cover and a stream of travel safety information. Roughguides.com users can take advantage of their policies online 24/7, from anywhere in the world – even if you're already travelling. And since plans often change when you're on the road, you can extend your policy and even claim online. Roughguides.com users who buy travel insurance with WorldNomads.com can also leave a positive footprint and donate to a community development project. For more information go to ⓦroughguides.com/shop.

and dry. Otherwise, most youth hostels have laundry facilities, with a small fee payable; hotels will charge considerably more.

Living in Budapest

Teaching English has traditionally been the main opportunity for **work** in Hungary, and it remains a big business, with many native speakers working in Budapest and a number of schools in and around the capital. The most reputable **language school** is International House, whose Budapest branch is at I, Vérmező út 4 (❶1 212 4010, ⓦih.hu); its minimum requirement is a CELTA or TESOL qualification, and preferably one year's experience. It offers a range of teacher training qualifications in Budapest. There are also teaching opportunities at the British Council, VI, 1075 Madách Imre út 13–14 (❶1 483 2020, ⓦbritishcouncil.org).

Study programmes

Several schools in Budapest cater for foreigners wishing to **learn Hungarian**, the best of which is the Hungarian Language School at VIII, Bródy Sándor utca 4 (❶1 266 2617, ⓦmagyar-iskola.hu). The school runs a comprehensive range of short- and long-term courses, from beginners to advanced, as well as organizing cultural programmes and workshops. The Debrecen Summer School also runs year-round courses in Budapest (V, Báthory utca 4.II.1 ❶1 320 5751, ⓦsummerschool.hu/bp).

Lost property

For items left on public transport go to the BKV office at VII, Akácfa utca 18 (Mon 8am–8pm, Tues–Thurs 8am–5pm, Fri 8am–3pm; ❶1 258 4636). Lost or stolen passports should be reported to the police station in the district where they were lost.

Mail

Post offices (posta) are usually open Monday to Friday 8 or 9am to 5pm, though these following main offices keep longer hours: by Keleti Station at VIII, Baross tér 11c (Mon–Fri 7am–9pm, Sat 8am–2pm); by Nyugati Station at VI, Teréz körút 51 (Mon–Fri 7am–8pm, Sat 8am–6pm); at the Mammut Mall by Széll Kálmán tér (Mon–Fri 8am–8pm, Sat 9am–2pm); while the branch in the Tesco at XIV, Pillangó utca 15 near the Pillangó utca stop on the red metro is open 24 hours a day. **Stamps** (bélyeg) can be bought at tobacconists or post offices, though the latter are usually pretty crowded and very few staff speak English. Stamps for sending postcards and letters abroad cost the same. You'll do better choosing the slightly more expensive elsőbbségi ("priority" – airmail) rate, 295Ft up to 20g within Europe, 340Ft for further afield, rather than the nem-els őbbségi rate. If you are sending anything of value, it is worth forking out the 1500Ft or so for recorded delivery. The Magyar Posta website ⓦposta.hu has further details of post offices and mailing costs.

Maps

The maps in this guide, together with the small freebies supplied by tourist offices and hotels, should be sufficient to help you find your way around. Larger folding maps are sold all over the place, but their size makes them cumbersome. For total coverage you can't beat the wire-bound **Budapest Atlasz**, available in bookshops in a range of sizes (from 2500Ft), which shows every street, bus and tram route, and the location of restaurants, museums and such like. It also contains enlarged maps of the Vár, central Pest, Margit-sziget and the Városliget, plus a comprehensive index.

Money

Hungary's unit of currency is the **forint** (Ft or HUF), with notes issued in denominations of 200, 500, 1000, 2000, 5000, 10,000 and 20,000 forints, and coins in denominations of 5, 10, 20, 50 and 100 forints. At the time of writing, the **exchange rate** was around 370Ft to the pound sterling, 310Ft to the euro and around 220Ft to the US dollar. You

---

HUNGARIAN NAMES

Surnames precede forenames in Hungary, to the confusion of foreigners. In this book, the names of historical personages are rendered in the Western fashion, for instance, Lajos Kossuth rather than Kossuth Lajos (Hungarian-style), except when referring to the names of buildings, streets, etc. The Hungarian order has a clear logic: in Hungarian the stress in any word always comes on the first syllable; since Hungarian, like most other languages, puts the main stress on the family name when saying a person's name, that means putting the family name first.

might be able to buy forints at some banks or exchange offices, or in the UK at post offices, but you will probably have to order them in advance.

By far the easiest way to get money is to use your bank **debit card** (or credit card) to withdraw cash from an ATM, found all over the city. All major credit cards are accepted in hotels, restaurants and shops, though not necessarily in some of the smaller ones.

As a rule, you're best off changing money in **banks**, which are normally open Monday to Thursday from 8am to 4 or 5pm, and on Friday from 8am to 3pm, although the ubiquitous private exchange offices offer similar rates. Banks charge no commission, but you will need to show your passport; exchange offices do levy a commission, but no passport is required. Large hotels will change most hard currencies.

If taking cash, and you are not able to obtain forints in advance, a modest amount of low-denomination euros is advisable, although pound sterling and dollars are widely accepted. Avoid anyone who approaches you on the street or at stations offering to exchange money – you will almost certainly be fleeced.

Opening hours and public holidays

Shops are generally open Monday to Friday from 10am to 6pm, and on Saturdays from 10am to 2pm; grocery stores and supermarkets open slightly longer hours at both ends of the day. The shopping malls are open Monday to Saturday 10am to 8pm or 9pm, and Sunday 10am to 6pm. There are also a growing number of 24-hour shops (signed "non-stop", "0–24" or "*éjjel-nappali*").

PUBLIC HOLIDAYS

January 1 New Year's Day
March 15 Independence Day
Easter Monday
May 1 Labour Day
Whitsun Monday
August 20 St Stephen's Day
October 23 National holiday
November 1 All Saints' Day
December 25 Christmas. (Since celebrations start on Christmas Eve, many shops will be closed the whole day, and by the afternoon everything closes down.)
December 26

Museums are generally open Tuesday to Sunday 10am to 6pm, and in winter 9 or 10am to 4 or 5pm. Budapest's **thermal baths** are usually open daily from 6 or 7am to 8pm. Office hours are usually Monday to Friday from 8am to 4pm.

Most things in Hungary shut down on the **public holidays** listed below. When these fall on a Tuesday or Thursday, the Monday before or the Friday after may also become a holiday, and the previous or next Saturday a working day to make up the lost day.

Phones

Telephone numbers in Budapest have seven digits, and the area code for all landline phone numbers is 1. To make a call to another part of Hungary, dial ☎06, followed by the area code and the subscriber's number. Hungarian mobile numbers have nine digits, and begin with ☎06 20, 06 30 or 06 70, depending upon the network.

If you want to use your home mobile phone in Budapest, check with your phone provider whether it will work in Hungary, and what the call charges will be; US cell phones need to be tri-band to work. If you plan on staying in Budapest for a while, you might want to consider buying a Hungarian pay-as-you-go **SIM card**; T-Mobile or Vodafone are the most ubiquitous outlets. Both have pay-as-you-go offers.

To call Hungary from abroad, dial your international access code, then 36 for Hungary, then the area code (omitting the initial zero where present) and the number. If the Hungarian number begins with 06, omit these two digits. **Within Hungary**, directory enquiries is on ☎198, international directory enquiries on ☎199.

Time

Hungary is one hour ahead of GMT, six hours ahead of Eastern Standard Time and nine ahead of Pacific Standard Time. A word of caution: Hungarians express time in a way that might confuse the Anglophone traveller. As in German, 10.30am is expressed as "half eleven" (written 1/2 11 or f11), 10.45am is "three-quarter-eleven" (3/4 11 or h11), and 10.15am is "a quarter of eleven" (1/4 11 or n11).

Tipping

Tipping is standard practice in most restaurants; ten percent or thereabouts is fine, unless the service was not worth it. Note that ten, twelve or even fifteen percent may have quietly been added to the bill, though restaurant menus really should state whether a service charge is included. Otherwise, include the tip when you are paying the bill – say the amount you want to pay and they will give you the change – or give the tip to the staff rather than leaving it on the table. Taxi drivers usually get five to ten percent, more if they have helped you with bags or been similarly useful. It's also customary to tip bath attendants who unlock your cubicle (100–200Ft is usual). In all cases, when tipping be warned that if you expect change back, don't say *köszönöm* (thank you) when handing over payment, as it will be assumed that you want the change to be kept.

Tourist information

The official tourist office, Budapestinfo (**Ⓦ** budapestinfo.hu), has several branches in town, as well as desks at both airport terminals. There are also a couple of independent tourist offices providing similar information, but with more enthusiasm.

INFORMATION OFFICES

Budapestinfo V, Sütő utca 2, by the Deák tér metro (daily 8am–8pm; **Ⓣ** 1 438 8080, **Ⓦ** budapestinfo.hu); VI, Liszt Ferenc tér 11, on the corner of Andrássy út (daily: 10am–6pm **Ⓣ** 1 486 3311); and XIV, Hősök tere, in the City Park Ice Rink building (daily 10am–6pm). Good for getting maps, brochures and the Budapest Card, but otherwise they have limited information.

Discover Budapest VI, Lázár utca 16 (Mon–Sat 9am–4pm, June–Aug open Sun too **Ⓣ** 1 269 3842, **Ⓦ** discoverbudapest.com). Handy office just behind the Opera House, with information on the city and on walking, cycle and Segway tours.

Kazimir VII, Kazinczy utca 34 (Mon–Fri 10am–6pm **Ⓣ** 1 798 5748, **Ⓦ** info.kazimir.hu). One of the city's friendliest tourist information points in the middle of the Seventh district that can guide you on tours of the old Jewish quarter – but also has information on the rest of the city. The staff speak English – the website will follow shortly.

HUNGARIAN TOURIST OFFICES ABROAD

UK Hungarian National Tourist Office, 46 Eaton Place, London SW1 8AL, **Ⓦ** uk.gotohungary.com. There is also a free tourist hotline with information on the city (**Ⓣ** 0800 360 0000). The website of the Hungarian Cultural Centre in London (**Ⓦ** hungary.org.uk) is a useful place to keep up Hungarian links after your visit.
US Hungarian National Tourist Office, 447 Broadway, Fifth Floor, New York, NY 10013 **Ⓣ** 212/695 1221, **Ⓦ** gotohungary.com.

Travellers with disabilities

Hungary has been painfully slow to acknowledge the needs of the disabled traveller, and while progress is being made, don't expect much in the way of special facilities. However, the rapid growth of new hotels in Budapest has meant much better access for those with disabilities, with particular emphasis on specially designed rooms. Moreover, an increasing number of museums are providing ramps for wheelchairs.

The website of the **Hungarian Disabled Association** or Meosz, III, San Marco utca 76, 1032 Budapest (**Ⓣ** 1 250 9013 or 388 2387, **Ⓦ** meosz.hu), has useful – though not always up-to-date – information about access to the main museums, cultural and historical sites. On public transport, there are a growing number of low-floor buses and trams in the city – for example most of the #4 and #6 trams on the Nagykörút. Access to the metro system is more limited: only the new fourth metro line has lifts at all stations. Note also that station escalators tend to move suprisingly fast. On bus and tram timetables, accessible services are underlined. If you want help finding a wheelchair-friendly route, go to the route planner **Ⓦ** bkv.hu/en, which has an accessibility setting.

Meosz operates three accessible buses in Budapest that you can book. You can also contact Angyálkerék (Angel Wheel **Ⓣ** 20 356 3921 **Ⓦ** angyalkerek.hu), which operates a 24-hour bus service; and the Danish-Hungarian travel company Skagerrak Tours (**Ⓣ** 1 780 8123 **Ⓦ** skagerrak.hu), which has its own bus and can organise trips and accommodation, too.

ART NOUVEAU MOSAIC, SZERVITA TÉR

The Belváros

Abuzz with pavement cafés, street artists, vendors, boutiques and nightclubs, the Belváros or Inner City is the hub of Pest and, for tourists at least, the centre of what's happening. Commerce and pleasure have been its lifeblood as long as Pest has existed, first as a medieval market town and later as the kernel of a city whose *belle époque* rivalled that of Vienna. Unquestionably the focal point of the Belváros is pedestrianised Váci utca, running parallel to the Danube; the magnet for most first-time visitors to the city, this popular promenade is actually little more than a glorified shopping street, but you can still get a sense of the old atmosphere in the quieter backstreets south of Kossuth utca, where café life fans out in the shadow of some dramatic architecture.

1

The **Kiskörút** (Small Boulevard; comprising Károly körút, Múzeum körút and Vámház körút) that surrounds the Belváros follows the course of the medieval walls of Pest, showing how compact it was before the phenomenal expansion of the nineteenth century. However, little remains from further back than the eighteenth century, as the "liberation" of Pest by the Habsburgs in 1686 left the town in ruins. Some Baroque churches and the former Greek and Serbian quarters attest to its revival by settlers from other parts of the Habsburg empire, but most of the **architecture** dates from the era when Budapest asserted its right to be an imperial capital, between 1860 and 1918. Today, first-time visitors are struck by the statues, domes and mosaics on the Neoclassical and Art Nouveau piles, which are reflected in the mirrored banks and luxury hotels that symbolize the post-Communist era. While restaurant prices in the Belváros are above average for Budapest, and there are few bargains to be had in the shops, one of the most enjoyable activities is people-watching from one of the many café terraces.

ARRIVAL AND GETTING AROUND

By public transport With three metro lines (#1, 2 and 3) converging at Deák tér (line #1 continues to Vörösmarty tér), the Belváros is easily reached. Moreover, several trams and buses run the length of the Kiskörút, which skirts the Belváros, while tram #2 runs the entire length of the embankment, a worthwhile ride in itself.

On foot Once in the Belváros, the best way to appreciate it is simply by wandering around, perhaps taking a stroll from Vörösmarty tér down through Váci utca, occasionally breaking off to admire the views of the Vár from the embankment.

Vörösmarty tér

Vörösmarty tér, the leafy centre of the Belváros, is a good starting point for exploring the area. Crowds eddy around the food kiosks and craft stalls that fill the square, which is also the setting for the wonderful Christmas market and the Budapest Book Week in June. While children play on the Lion fountain, teenagers lounge around the **statue of Mihály Vörösmarty** (1800–55), a poet and translator whose hymn to Magyar identity, *Szózat* ("Appeal"), is publicly declaimed at moments of national crisis. Its opening line "Be faithful to your land forever, Oh Hungarians" is carved on the statue's pedestal. Made of Carrara marble, the statue has to be wrapped in plastic sheeting each winter to prevent it from cracking. The black spot below the inscription is reputedly a "lucky" coin donated by a beggar towards the cost of the monument.

Gerbeaud patisserie

Gerbeaud cukrászda • V, Vörösmarty tér 7 • Daily 9am–9pm • ☎ 1 429 9000, ⊕ gerbeaud.hu

On the north side of Vörösmarty tér is the **Gerbeaud patisserie**, Budapest's most famous confectioners. Founded in 1858 by Henrik Kugler, it was bought in 1884 by the Swiss confectioner Emile Gerbeaud, who invented the *konyakos meggy* (cognac-cherry bonbon) – still a popular sweet with Hungarians. He sold top-class cakes at reasonable prices, making the *Gerbeaud* a popular rendezvous for the middle classes. While the prices are now astronomical by Hungarian standards, and the service can be surly, it still has an undeniable appeal. Emile's portrait hangs in one of the rooms, whose gilded ceilings and china recall the *belle époque*.

HIDDEN GEMS: THE BELVÁROS

Párisi Udvar See p.40
Tram #2 along Pest Embankment
See p.43
Károlyi-kert playground See p.40
River Danube statue in Erzsébet tér
See p.45

Jacques Liszt bakery and café
See p.158
Coffee and cake at Centrál Kávéház
See p.168
Rózsavölgyi record shop See p.190
Underground Railway Museum See p.45

1

RESTAURANTS, CAFÉS & BARS		Ibolya	14	SHOPS			
Action	23	Jacques Liszt	4	BÁV	4	Nanushka	3
Al-Amir	8	Központ	5	Bio ABC	15	Retrock	2
Belvárosi		Madrid	12	Emilia Anda	6	Rododendron	10
Disznótoros	17	My Little Melbourne	6	Hecserli	17	Rózsavölgyi Music	5
Café Alibi	21	Sonka Arcok	19	Holló Folk Art Gallery	9	Rózsavölgyi	
Café Astoria	13	Sonkapult	9	Intuita	14	Chocolates	18
Castro Bistro	7	Szamos Gourmet Ház	2	Insitu	11	Valéria Fazekas	12
Centrál Kávéház	16	Tako Café	11	Kodály Zoltán		Vass	8
Csendes	18	Tip Top Bar	22	Zeneműbolt	16		
Fekete	15	Trattoria Toscana	20	Központi Antikvárium	13		
Gerbeaud	1	Vapiano	3	Magma	7		
Gerlóczy	10	Why Not?	24	Malatinszky	1		

Underground Railway

From the terrace outside the *Gerbeaud* patisserie you can observe the entrance to the **Underground Railway** (Földalatti Vasút, the yellow #1 metro line), whose vaguely Art Nouveau cast-iron fixtures and elegant tilework stamp it as decades older than the other metro lines. For its centenary in 1996, the line's stations were restored to their original decor. If you're curious to know more about its history, visit the Underground Railway Museum at Deák tér (see p.45). The Underground Railway's route along Andrássy út is covered in Chapter 3, with Hősök tere described in Chapter 4.

Bershka store and former Bank Palace

Directly behind Vörösmarty's statue stands the **Bershka store**, its 1911 facade adorned with bronze panels with plant motifs. In the Communist era the Luxus Áruház, as it was then known, was *the* place to get your Western-style clothes. Now it sells the real thing, Western clothes as produced by the Spanish fashion company and aimed at the younger market.

Another early twentieth-century building, the former **Bank Palace**, stands at the southern end of the square on the corner of Váci utca. When the Budapest **Stock Exchange** reopened its doors in 1990, this was its new home. Built in the heyday of Hungarian self-confidence by Ignác Alpár, who also designed the prewar Stock Exchange on Szabadság tér (see p.50), it has now been turned into a major retail centre.

Váci utca and around

Váci utca has been famous for its shops and **korzó** (promenade) since the eighteenth century. During the 1980s, its vivid street life became a symbol of the "consumer socialism" that distinguished Hungary from other Eastern Bloc states. It's now prime tourist territory, hence the endless souvenir shops, not to mention the myriad hawks and hustlers endeavouring to entice visitors into their restaurants and bars.

Today the northern half of the street, down to Ferenciek tere, has at least gained a touch of style from a number of outlets for big Western fashion names. Moreover, there are a few landmarks along the way that might catch your eye: the scantily clad **Fisher-girl fountain** on **Kristóf tér**; the **Pest Theatre** (no. 9) on the site of the *Inn of the Seven Electors*, where the 12-year-old Liszt performed in 1823 – note also the gorgeous Art Nouveau florist's and the former **Auction House** (no. 11a), with its Gothic Revival facade of majolica tiles and toothy wrought-ironwork.

An underpass further south brings you out on Március 15 tér, where a weird stone **monument** resembling a giant cactus flower commemorates the 125th anniversary of the unification of Buda and Pest. Beyond here, the pedestrianized continuation of Váci is infested with tourist-trap restaurants and shops, but retains some imposing architecture: worth a look are the prewar **Officers' Casino** (no. 38) guarded by statues of halberdiers (now a bank's headquarters), and the sculptural **plaque** on the wall of no. 47, commemorating the fact that the Swedish king Charles XII stayed here during his lightning fourteen-day horseride from Turkey to Sweden, in 1714. Further along at nos. 62–64 looms the red-brick, griffon- and majolica-encrusted **Budapest City Hall**, where the city council still meets.

1

Serbian Orthodox Church

Szerb Ortodox templom • V, Szerb utca 2–4 • Daily 10am–5pm if staff are available to open it • 300Ft • High Mass on Sun 10am

A left turn off Váci utca into Szerb utca brings you to the **Serbian Orthodox Church**, built by the Serbian artisans and merchants who settled here after the Turks were driven out. Secluded in a high-walled garden, it's best visited during High Mass on Sunday, when the singing of the liturgy, the clouds of incense and flickering candles create an unearthly atmosphere.

A block or so south of the church, part of the **medieval wall** of Pest can be seen behind a children's playground on the corner of Bástya utca and Vernes Pálné utca. There is more of the wall near the eastern end of Bástya utca, tucked away inside the bank at Kecskeméti utca 19, on the corner of Kalvin tér.

Petőfi Literary Museum

Petőfi Irodalmi Múzeum • V, Károlyi utca 16 • Tues–Sun 10am–6pm • 600Ft • ☎ 1 317 3611, ⓦ pim.hu

A short walk up Szerb utca, and just beyond the University Law Faculty, stands the Károlyi Palota, the birthplace of Count Mihály Károlyi, the liberal politician who briefly led the government after World War I. Today the palace houses the **Petőfi Literary Museum**, which has a permanent exhibition on the life of Sándor Petőfi, the nineteenth-century revolutionary poet (see box, p.44). The wealth of personal effects on display includes his first manuscript of poetry, and the engagement ring belonging to his wife of just two years, Júlia Szendrey – there are also several gifts exchanged between Petőfi and his lifelong friend, Arany János, the other pre-eminent poet of that time. As one of the key figures in the 1848 Revolution, prominent coverage is given to Petőfi's role both here and as a soldier in the Hungarian Revolutionary Army, where he fought under the Polish general, József Bem; the warrant issued for his arrest by the Germans is the most poignant item on display in this section. During the summer you may be able to see round the rest of the palace rooms (separate entry fee).

The mansion's garden, the **Károlyi-kert**, is a delightful green haven in the centre of the city, and has a children's playground. It was here that Lajos Batthyány, head of the independent Hungarian government following the 1848 revolution, was arrested in 1849, and General Haynau, the "Butcher of Vienna", signed the death warrants of Batthyány and other rebel leaders after finishing his morning exercises.

Ferenciek tere

Heading north from the Petőfi Literary Museum, you'll pass the **Centrál Kávéház** (see p.168), one of Pest's grand old coffee houses where, in the early twentieth century, writers and intellectuals lingered day and night, while to the right rises the coloured dome of the university library. Beyond here is **Ferenciek tere** (Franciscans' Square) – though it's more L-shaped than square, and is dominated by the network of roads approaching the Erzsébet bridge. Yet even the six-lane highway that runs across the top of the square cannot detract from the magnificence of the buildings.

Párisi Udvar

The most notable building on Ferenciek tere is the **Párisi Udvar**, a flamboyantly eclectic shopping arcade constructed in 1915. Upon completion, its fifty naked statues above the third floor were deemed incompatible with its intended role as the headquarters of the city savings bank, symbolized by images of bees throughout the building. Long neglected and still awaiting its fate, the gloomy interior is as ornate as an Andalusian mosque, with its hexagonal stained-glass dome designed by Miksa Róth, carved wooden statues, and majolica tiles from the Zsolnay factory. The side gate is normally open so you should be able to have a wander around inside.

FROM TOP LITTLE PRINCESS STATUE, VIGADÓ TÉR (P.44); CAFÉ GERBEAUD (P.37) >

1

The Klotild Palaces

The traffic roars into the western end of Ferenciek tere between a pair of imposing *fin-de-siècle* office buildings – designed by Flóris Krob and Kálmán Giergl, the same team behind the Bershka department store building (see p.39) and the Music Academy (se p.60). Named the **Klotild Palaces** after the Habsburg princess who commissioned them, the northern one is home to the luxury *Buddha Bar* hotel, while the southern one once housed a restaurant owned by Egon Ronay's father – after it was nationalized in 1946, the young Ronay moved to London where he was appalled by cooking standards.

Kossuth Lajos utca

Heading out the eastern end of Ferenciek tere, the road seamlessly becomes **Kossuth Lajos utca**, where the noise and the fumes deter the visitor from lingering. Immediately on the right is the **Franciscan Church** that gave the square its name. The relief on the church's wall recalls the great flood of 1838, in which over four hundred citizens were killed; it depicts the heroic efforts of Baron Miklós Wesselényi, who personally rescued scores of people in his boat.

Some 200m further along, the junction of Kossuth Lajos utca with the Kiskörút is named after the **Astoria Hotel** on the corner, a prewar haunt of spies and journalists that was commandeered as an HQ by the Nazis in 1944 and the Soviets after the 1956 Uprising. Today, its Neoclassical coffee lounge is redolent of Stalinist chic.

Szervita tér

North from Ferenciek tere, Petőfi Sándor utca leads up to **Szervita tér**, a square containing the best and the worst of twentieth-century architecture. Three remarkable buildings from the golden age of Hungarian architecture line its western side. No. 3, the former Turkish Bank House dating from 1906, has a gable aglow with a superb **Art Nouveau mosaic** of *Patrona Hungariae* (Our Lady) flanked by key figures from Hungarian history, one of the finest works of Miksa Róth (see p.66). No. 2 (1908) is one of the earliest Modernist buildings in Budapest, with its geometric motifs and its decorative screws, while at no. 5 the **Rózsavölgyi Building** (1911–12) was built by the "father" of Hungarian Modernism, **Béla Lajta**, whose earlier association with the National Romantic school is evident from the majolica bands on its upper storeys, typical of the style. The Rózsavölgyi music shop on the ground floor is one of the oldest, and best, in the city – sadly Lajta's interior fittings were lost in a fire in 1955.

Servite Church

Szervita Templom • V, Szervita tér 6 • Daily 10am–1pm & 2–6pm • Free; concerts Wed noon, donations accepted

Szervita tér is named after the eighteenth-century **Servite Church** (otherwise known as St Anne's Church), built following liberation from Turkish rule, indeed on the site of a former mosque. Its badly crumbling facade bears a relief of an angel cradling a dying horseman, in memory of the Seventh Kaiser Wilhelm Hussars killed in World War I. The interior, meanwhile, is standard Baroque exuberance, the pick of the paintings being those of the seven founders of the Servite order, located on the right-hand side of the nave. The attached monastery was damaged in World War II and in 1964 was replaced with the brutalist communications centre that now hems in the church.

Along the embankment

The riverbank bore the brunt of the fighting in 1944–45, when the Nazis and the Red Army exchanged salvoes across the Danube. As with the Vár in Buda, postwar clearances exposed historic sites and provided an opportunity to integrate them into the environment – but the magnificent **view** of the Royal Palace and Gellért-hegy is

1

hardly matched by the row of modern hotels on the Pest side. While such historic architecture as remains can be seen in a fifteen-minute stroll between the Erzsébet híd and the Lánchíd, tram #2 enables you to see a longer stretch of the waterfront between Szabadság híd and Kossuth tér in the north, interrupted by a tunnel at the Lánchíd.

Erzsébet híd

The bold white pylons and cables of the **Erzsébet híd** (Elizabeth Bridge) are as dominant a feature of the panorama as the stone Lánchíd to the north or the wrought-iron Szabadság híd to the south. Of all the Danube bridges blown up by the Germans as they retreated to Buda in January 1945, the Erzsébet híd was the only one not rebuilt in its original form. In fact it was not replaced until 1964 – and even then had to be closed down immediately due to faulty engineering.

Március 15 tér

A largely nondescript square today, **Március 15 tér** nevertheless betrays strong military associations – in one corner you can peer down through the glass covers at the remains of **Contra-Aquincum**, a Roman fort that was an outpost of the settlement at Óbuda at the end of the third century. More pertinently to Hungarian history, the name of the square refers to March 15, 1848, when the anti-Habsburg Revolution began.

Belváros Parish Church

Belvárosi Főplébánia Templom • V, Március 15 tér 2 • Mon–Sat 7am–7pm, Sun 8am–7pm • Free

Dominating Március 15 tér is the **Belváros Parish Church**, the oldest church in Pest. Founded in 1046 as the burial place of St Gellért (see p.106), it was rebuilt as a Gothic hall church in the fifteenth century (his remains had long been shipped off to Venice), turned into a mosque by the Turks and then reconstructed as a church in the eighteenth century. This history is reflected in the interior, and after Latin Mass at 10am on Sunday you can see the Gothic sedilia and Turkish *mihrab* (prayer niche) behind the high altar, which are otherwise out of bounds. The austere Gothic interior is largely devoid of ornamentation save for a few splashes of colour on the rib-vaulted nave.

Petőfi tér and Duna-korzó

Petőfi tér to the north is named after Sándor Petőfi, whose poem *National Song* – the anthem of 1848 – and romantic death in battle the following year made him a patriotic icon (see box, p.44). Erected in 1882, the square's **Petőfi statue** has long been a focus for demonstrations as well as patriotic displays – especially on March 15, when the statue is bedecked with flags and flowers.

The concrete esplanade running north from the square is a sterile attempt at recreating the prewar **Duna-korzó**, the most informal of Budapest's promenades, where it was socially acceptable for strangers to approach celebrities and stroll beside them. The outdoor cafés here, which boast wonderful views, charge premium rates.

Cathedral of the Dormition

Nagyboldogasszony magyar ortodox székesegyház • V, Petőfi tér 2 • Wed, Fri & Sat 3–5pm, Sun noon–5pm; services Mon–Fri 5pm, Sat 6pm, Sun 8, 9 & 10am • Free

On the eastern side of Petőfi tér looms the Greek Orthodox **Cathedral of the Dormition**, built by the Greek community in the 1790s and, more recently, the object of a tug-of-war between the Patriarchate of Moscow that gained control of it after 1945 and the Orthodox Church in Greece that previously owned it. One of the church's towers was lost in the siege of Budapest in 1944, and in its place there now sits an awkward-looking temporary replacement. The cathedral has services in Hungarian, Church Slavonic and Greek, according to the make-up of the congregation, accompanied by singing in the Orthodox fashion. The big feast here is on August 28, the Dormition of Mary (the Assumption) in the Orthodox calendar.

1

SÁNDOR PETŐFI

Born on New Year's Eve, 1822, of a Slovak mother and a southern Slav butcher-innkeeper father, **Sándor Petőfi** was to become obsessed by acting and by poetry, which he started to write at the age of 15. As a strolling player, soldier and labourer, he absorbed the language of working people and composed his lyrical poetry in the vernacular, to the outrage of critics. Moving to Budapest in 1844, he fell in with the young radical intellectuals who met at the *Pilvax Café* on nearby Pilvax koz (the café is no more), and embarked on his career as a revolutionary hero. He declaimed his *National Song* from the steps of the National Museum on the first day of the 1848 Revolution, and fought in the War of Independence with General Bem in Transylvania, where he disappeared during the Battle of Segesvár in 1849. Though he was most likely trampled beyond recognition by the Cossacks' horses (as predicted in one of his poems), Petőfi was long rumoured to have survived as a prisoner. In 1990, a Hungarian entrepreneur sponsored an expedition to Siberia to uncover the putative grave, but it turned out to be that of a woman.

Vigadó tér

Vigadó tér is an elegant square named after the **Vigadó** concert hall, whose name translates as "having a ball" or "making merry". Inaugurated in 1865, this Romantic pile by Frigyes Feszl is encrusted with statues of the Muses and plaques recalling performances by Liszt, Mahler and Wagner and other renowned artists. Badly damaged in World War II, it didn't reopen until 1980, such was the care taken to recreate its sumptuous decor. Following another lengthy closure between 2004 and 2014, during which time the facade was cleaned up and the interior renovated, the magnificent main hall is once again staging classical concerts.

On the other side of Vigadó tér, it's easy to miss the statue of the impish **Little Princess**, which has been sitting on the railings by the tram line since 1990. After dusk, you'll hardly notice that she isn't a person, if you notice her at all. By day, she looks like a cross-dressing boy in a Tinkerbell hat. Prince Charles was so taken by her that he invited her creator, László Marton, to hold an exhibition of his work in Britain.

Deák tér

Three metro lines and several important roads meet at **Deák tér**, to form a jumping-off point for the Belváros and Lipótváros. However, finding local addresses can be confusing since Deák Ferenc tér merges seamlessly into the far larger **Erzsébet tér** to the north.

Anker Palace

The vast, mustard-coloured **Anker Palace** (Anker palota), to the east of the square, is one of several imposing edifices in the centre of Budapest built for a foreign insurance company, in this case the Viennese Insurance Company. Its design by Ignác Alpár, the man behind the former Stock Exchange and the National Bank on Szabadság tér, was widely admired for its clever use of an awkward plot. Not everyone was impressed: when it opened in 1910, Alpár's wife said, "Oh Ignác, aren't you ashamed of yourself? What have you done here?"

Lutheran Church and Museum

Deák téri Evangélikus Templom & Evangélikus Múzeum • V, Deák tér 4 • Tues–Sun 10am–6pm • 500Ft • ⓦ evangelikusmuzeum.hu

The large, spireless **Lutheran Church**, which looms over the metro pavilion on the edge of the Belváros, was built in 1808 according to designs by Mihály Pollack. Both the exterior and interior exhibit typical early Neoclassical styles, exemplified by minimal ornamentation. More interestingly, the church hosts some excellent concerts that include regular free Sunday evening organ recitals and Bach's *St John Passion* over the

1

fortnight before Easter. Next door, the **Lutheran Museum** displays a facsimile of Martin Luther's last will and testament, and a copy of the first book printed in Hungarian, a New Testament from 1541.

Underground Railway Museum

Földalattivasút Múzeum • V, Deák tér underpass by the entrance to the metro station • Tues–Sun 10am–5pm • 350Ft

Accessible via the upper sub-level of Deák tér metro, the enjoyable little **Underground Railway Museum** extols the history of Budapest's original metro. The exhibition is set up in an original stretch of tunnel, which was abandoned in 1955 when the line was altered, while the constant rumble of the trains close by adds another layer of authenticity. Sitting on the track are three old wooden carriages (one used up until 1973), while exhibits include construction diaries, models, and period fixtures and posters, which enhance the museum's nostalgic appeal.

The metro's genesis was a treatise by Mór Balázs, proposing a steam-driven tram network starting with a route along Andrássy út, an underground line being suggested as a fallback in case the overground option was rejected. Completed in under two years, it was inaugurated in 1896 – in time for the Millennial Exhibition – by Emperor Franz Josef, who agreed to allow it to bear his name, which it kept until 1918. The metro was the first on the European continent and the second in the world (after London's Metropolitan line), and originally ran from Vörösmarty tér as far as the Millennial Exhibition grounds at Hősök tere. The exhibition also recalls the role of women on the underground, more precisely their recruitment as conductors during World War I owing to male staff shortages.

Erzsébet tér

Once the site of a cemetery beyond the medieval city walls, **Erzsébet tér** has gone through many names since then, notably Sztálin tér from 1946 until 1953, when it became Engels tér, before getting its older name back. The statue in the middle of the park is of **Old Father Danube** with his three tributaries, the Dráva, Száva and Tisza, and was designed in 1880 by Miklós Ybl.

On the east side of the square a small **skateboard park** attracts youngsters keen to perfect their skills. The long, low functionalist building next door is the former bus station, protected by a conservation order and so unable to be demolished, much to the ire of locals. However, it does now function as a cool alfresco bar in warmer months, while just a few paces from here, a glass-bottomed pool sits above a series of stepped terraces leading down to a cafe/club – the whole area has become one of the most popular places to gather on summer evenings, as the crowds spill out across the square.

Lipótváros and Újlipótváros

Lipótváros (Leopold Town), lying to the north of the Belváros, started to develop in the late eighteenth century, first as a financial centre and later as the seat of government. Several institutions of national significance are found here, including Parliament, St Stephen's Basilica and the National Bank and the Television headquarters. Though part of the V District, as is the Belváros, Lipótváros has quite a different ambience, with sombre streets of Neoclassical buildings interrupted by squares flanked by monumental Art Nouveau piles. That said, the area has developed into quite a social hub, with bars sprawled across Szent István tér and Zrinyi utca, and some of the city's best restaurants sited along Sas utca. Across the Nagykörút, Újlipótváros (New Leopold Town; the XIII district) is worth visiting for the lively Lehel tér market.

ARRIVAL AND GETTING AROUND

Lipótváros It makes sense to start a Lipótváros visit either with Széchenyi István tér, by the Lánchíd, or St Stephen's Basilica, two minutes' walk from Deák tér. Most of the streets between them lead towards the set-piece expanse of Szabadság tér, whence you can head on towards

Parliament – though the Kossuth tér metro station or tram #2 along the river will provide quicker access.

Újlipótváros The way to get here is either by tram #4 or #6 along the Nagykörút or on the blue #2 metro line to the Lehel tér stop.

Széchenyi Istvan tér

2

At the Pest end of the Lánchíd, **Széchenyi István tér** is named after "the greatest Hungarian", the man responsible for building the bridge (see p.101). Blitzed by traffic crowding on and off the bridge, it's also dominated by huge trees – including one propped-up acacia said to be the oldest tree in the city – that make it hard to get a feel for this historic square. It was here that the Austrian emperor Franz Josef was crowned King of Hungary in 1867 – paradoxically symbolizing Hungary's increasing independence within the Habsburg empire. Soil from every corner of the nation was piled into a Coronation Hill, on the site of the present square. The emperor flourished the sword of St Stephen and promised to defend Hungary against all its enemies – a pledge that proved almost as ephemeral as the hill itself. In 1947 the square was renamed **Roosevelt tér** in honour of the late US president – a rare example of Cold War courtesy that survived until 2011 when the new mayor set about sweeping away the old Communist names.

Gresham Palace

Unquestionably the finest building on **Széchenyi István tér,** and one of Budapest's landmark hotels, is the magnificent Art Nouveau **Gresham Palace** on its eastern side. Commissioned by a British insurance company in 1904, it's named after the financier Sir Thomas Gresham, the author of Gresham's law that bad money drives out good, whereby the circulation of coins of equal face value but different metals leads to those made of more valuable metal being hoarded and disappearing from use.

The building was in an awful state when it was acquired by the Four Seasons hotel chain in 2001, but fears of a crass refurbishment were dispelled by a loving restoration: authentic materials and even the original workshops were sought out to do the job. Today you can once again see Gresham's bust high up on the facade, and members of the public may walk in to admire the subtle hues of the tiled lobby and glass-roofed arcade, with wrought-iron peacock gates and stained-glass windows by Miksa Róth.

Hungarian Academy of Sciences

Magyar Tudományos Akadémia • V, Széchenyi István tér 9 • Mon & Fri 11am–4pm • Free • ☎ 1 411 6489

Statues of Count Széchenyi (see box, p.101) and Ferenc Deák, another major nineteenth-century politician who helped to forge Hungary's agreement with the Austrians in 1867, stand at opposite ends of Széchenyi István tér. The statue of the former isn't far from the **Hungarian Academy of Sciences,** founded after Széchenyi pledged a year's income from his estates towards its establishment in 1825 – as depicted on a relief on the wall facing Akadémia utca. The only part of the Academy that is open is its small collection of paintings, mainly portraits but including the odd Munkácsy landscape.

HIDDEN GEMS: LIPÓTVÁROS AND ÚJLIPÓTVÁROS

Bestsellers Bookshop See p.188
**Drink in the glass-roofed arcade of
the Gresham Palace** See p.47
Art Nouveau Bedő House See p.51

Post Office Savings Bank See p.50
Dinner at Borkonyha See p.159
St Stephen's Basilica Treasury See p.49
Coffee in Espresso Embassy See p.168

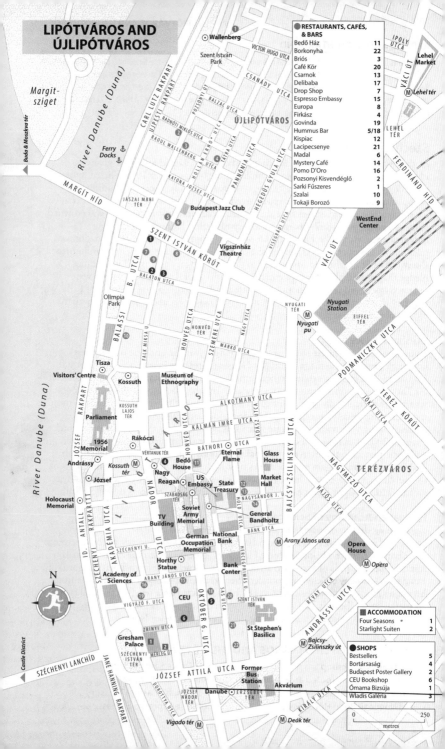

LIPÓTVÁROS AND ÚJLIPÓTVÁROS

RESTAURANTS, CAFÉS, & BARS

Bedő Ház	11
Borkonyha	22
Briós	3
Café Kör	20
Csarnok	13
Delibaba	17
Drop Shop	7
Espresso Embassy	15
Europa	8
Firkász	4
Govinda	19
Hummus Bar	5/18
Kispiac	12
Lacipecsenye	21
Madal	6
Mystery Café	14
Pomo D'Oro	16
Pozsonyi Kisvendéglő	2
Sarki Fűszeres	1
Szalai	10
Tokaji Borozó	9

ACCOMMODATION

Four Seasons	1
Starlight Suiten	2

SHOPS

Bestsellers	5
Bortársaság	4
Budapest Poster Gallery	2
CEU Bookshop	6
Ómama Bizsúja	1
Wladis Galéria	3

0 — 250 metres

St Stephen's Basilica

Szent István-Bazilika • **Basilica** Mon–Sat 9am–7pm, Sun 1–6pm • Free but a 200Ft donation is encouraged • Mass on weekdays 7am, 8am & 6pm, Sun 8.30am, 10am, noon & 6pm. **Chapel** Mon–Sat 10am–4pm, Sun 1–4.30pm • Free • **Panorama Tower** Daily: Oct–June 10am–4.30pm; July–Sept 10am–6.30pm, closing earlier in bad weather • 500Ft • **Treasury** Same hours as tower • 400Ft • ☏ 1 311 0839, Ⓦ bazilika.biz

St Stephen's Basilica took so long to build that Budapestis once joked, when borrowing money, "I'll pay you back when the basilica is finished." Work began in 1851 under the supervision of József Hild, continued after his death under Miklós Ybl, and was finally completed by Joseph Krauser in 1905. At the inaugural ceremony Emperor Franz Josef was seen to glance anxiously at the dome, whose collapse during a storm in 1868 had set progress back. At 96m, it is exactly the same height as the dome of the Parliament building – both allude to the putative date of the Magyars' arrival in Hungary (896 AD). After recent restoration work that seemed to take as long as the original construction, the basilica looks very grand today. Its beauty lies in the combined effect of the frescoes, marble and gilded stucco rather than in any particular works of art, though the mosaics by Károly Lotz in the cupola are worth admiring. The **organ**, too, is quite splendid, and put to good use every Thursday evening with a concert at 8pm. In the second chapel to the right is a painting of King Stephen offering the Crown of Hungary to the Virgin (see box, p.92), while a statue of him haloed as a saint (but with a sword at his side) forms the centrepiece of the altar.

For most visitors, though, the chief attraction lies inside the **Holy Right Chapel**, where the gnarled **mummified hand of St Stephen**, Hungary's holiest relic, resides. Over the centuries, the relic was variously kept in Bihar (Transylvania), Ragusa (now Dubrovnik) and Vienna, before being returned to Buda in 1771. Each year, on August 20, the Szent Jobb (literally, "holy right") is paraded with great pomp through the surrounding streets, the anniversary of his death.

If you've time, make a beeline for the **treasury** (*kincstár*), reachable via a lift next to the entrance. As well as the usual chalices, monstrances and suchlike, there's a fascinating display on the life of Cardinal Mindszenty, the head of the church who is much honoured for his challenge to the Communist regime (see box, p.141). Photos, robes and mitres, as well as various items garnered whilst in exile, including a suitcase (presumably the one he took with him), attest to his life's work.

Finally, you shouldn't miss the grand view over the city from the Panorama **tower** (Körkilátó) reached by lift to the base of the cupola, or by climbing 302 stairs.

Bajcsy-Zsilinszky út

While Stephen is revered as the founder and patron saint of Hungary, the pantheon of national heroes includes a niche for **Endre Bajcsy-Zsilinszky** (1866–1944), after whom the avenue that runs past the Basilica is named. Originally a right-winger, he ended up an outspoken critic of Fascism, was arrested in Parliament and shot as the Russians approached. **Bajcsy-Zsilinszky út** is the demarcation line between the Lipótváros and Terézváros districts, running northwards to **Nyugati Station**, an elegant, iron-beamed terminal built in 1874–77 by the Eiffel Company of Paris.

Szabadság tér and around

For more than a century, Lipótváros was dominated by a gigantic barracks where scores of Hungarians were imprisoned or executed, until this symbol of Habsburg tyranny was demolished in 1897 and the site redeveloped as **Szabadság tér** (Liberty Square). Invested with significance from the outset, it has become a kind of record of the vicissitudes of modern Hungarian history, where each regime added or removed **monuments**, according to their political complexion. For an excellent vantage point from which to admire the square's buildings, head to the café pavilion in the centre of the square.

The Stock Exchange

In the early twentieth century, Hungary's burgeoning prosperity was expressed by two monumental temples to capitalism on opposite sides of Szabadság tér. To the west stands the former **Stock Exchange**, one of the grandest buildings in Budapest. Designed by Ignác Alpár, it has blended motifs from Greek and Assyrian architecture and is crowned with twin towers resembling Khmer temples. After the Communists closed down the Exchange in 1948, it became the **headquarters of Hungarian Television**. During the riots of 2006, protesters broke into the building, but generally it is closed to the public.

2

National Bank

Magyar Nemzeti Bank • V, Szabadság tér 8 • Visitor Centre Mon–Fri 9am–4pm, open till 6pm Thurs • Free • Ⓦ mnb.hu

Ignác Alpár, the man behind the former Stock Exchange, also designed the **National Bank** on the eastern side of Szabadság tér, which still functions as such and is notable for the bas-reliefs on its exterior, representing such diverse aspects of wealth creation as Magyars ploughing and herding, ancient Egyptians harvesting wheat, and Vikings loading longships with loot. The stones for its columns were hauled all the way from Transylvania by oxen. The main entrance on the south facade of the building leads to a stylish **Visitor Centre** featuring curiosities like the "Kossuth" banknotes that were issued in America during the politician's exile after the failed War of Independence, and notes denominated in trillions of forints from the period of hyper-inflation in 1946. The bank also has some fine stained-glass windows on the stairs, but you can only see these during European Heritage Days in September.

The US embassy

The northern neighbour of the National Bank on the eastern side of Szabadság tér is the imposing **US Embassy**; for fifteen years, the latter sheltered Cardinal Mindszenty, the Primate of Hungary's Catholic Church, in the aftermath of the 1956 Uprising. Later, however, the US became embarrassed by his presence, as did the Vatican, which finally persuaded him to leave for Austria in 1971 (see box, p.141).

In front of the US embassy, the stocky figure of **General Harry Bandholtz** commemorates the US general who intervened with a dogwhip to stop Romanian troops from looting the Hungarian National Museum in 1919. The statue was erected in the 1930s, removed after World War II, and reinstated by the Communists prior to President George Bush's visit in 1989.

Hungarian State Treasury

Right behind the US embassy lies a fine example of Hungarian Art Nouveau. The tiled facade of the **Hungarian State Treasury** is patterned like a quilt, with swarms of bees symbolizing thrift – this was originally the **Post Office Savings Bank** (Postatakarékpénztár). The polychromatic roof with its beehives and dragon tails is the wildest part of the building. Its architect, Ödön Lechner, once asked why birds shouldn't enjoy his buildings too, and amazing roofs are a feature of his other masterpieces in Budapest, the Geological Institute (p.74) and the Applied Arts Museum (p.82). The interior is only open to the public on European Heritage Days, but a small display of photographs of the interior gives you a taste of the design in the foyer, accessible during banking hours.

Belvárosi market hall

Vásárcsarnok • V, Hold utca 13 • Mon–Thurs 6.30am–5pm, Fri 6.30am–6pm

Diagonally across the street from the State Treasury is a wrought-iron **market hall**, one of five opened on a single day in 1896 and which still serve the centre of Pest; it's much less touristy than the Great Market Hall on Vámház körút (see p.81) and also has a few simple eateries catering for workers hereabouts. Its rear entrance will bring you out on Vadász utca, not far from one of Budapest's least-known memorials to the Holocaust.

Glass House Memorial Room

Üvegház Emlékszoba • V, Vadász utca 29 • Daily 1–4pm • Free, donations accepted • ☎ 1 242 6964, ⓦ uveghaz.org

The **Glass House Memorial Room** was named both for the extensive use of glass in its Modernist design and for its erstwhile role as a glass showroom. From 1944 to 1945, it was one of many properties in Budapest that was designated as neutral territory by the Swiss consul Carl Lutz (1895–1975) serving as a refuge for three thousand Jews and the underground Zionist Youth organization. An **exhibition** (to the right in the courtyard) explains how Lutz and other "Righteous Gentiles" managed to save thousands of Jews from the SS and Arrow Cross death squads by issuing Schutzpasses to Jews, attesting that they were Swiss or Swedish citizens – a ruse subsequently used by Wallenberg. After the war Lutz was criticized for abusing Swiss law and, feeling slighted, proposed himself for the Nobel Peace Prize. While their co-religionists from the provinces were transported en masse to Auschwitz, the Jews of Budapest faced random executions in the heart of the capital, within full view of Parliament (see p.53) and their Gentile compatriots, who seemed more offended by the bloodshed than outraged by their murder. Inside, exhibits include a letter to Lutz from Admiral Horthy, as well as the shattered marble tablet to Artur Weisz, the owner of the Glass House who was shot in 1944: it stood on the wall outside until it was smashed by neo-Nazis a few years ago.

German occupation monument

At the southern end of Szabadság tér stands its latest memorial, this time marking the **Nazi takeover** on 19 March 1944. Depicting archangel Gabriel – representing Hungary – being menaced by a Germanic eagle, the monument has caused much debate. The government insists that it stands for all victims of the occupation, while Jewish groups see it as part of an official attempt to absolve Hungary of responsibility in the Holocaust. Nearby, in front of the Church of Homecoming (*Hazatéres Temploma*), stands a bust of **Admiral Horthy** – put up by a right-wing priest who belongs to the Jobbik party.

Soviet Army Memorial

The top end of Szabadság tér has also been the scene of controversy. From 1921 to 1945 it was dominated by the Monument to Hungarian Grief in protest at the 1920 Treaty of Trianon, which awarded two-thirds of Hungary's territory and a third of its Magyar population to the "Successor States" of Romania, Czechoslovakia and Yugoslavia. After World War II, this was replaced by a **Soviet Army Memorial** commemorating the liberation of Budapest from the Nazis, with bas-reliefs of Red Army troops and tanks advancing on Ferenciek tere and Parliament. Today, the Soviet obelisk is fenced off to protect it from vandalism by right-wing nationalists.

Statue of Ronald Reagan

The statue of **Ronald Reagan** was set up to mark the 100th anniversary of the former US president's birthday in 2011. The 2m-high statue, which presents him striding from Parliament into the square (he never visited the city), was erected in recognition of his role in ending the Cold War.

The Bedő House

Bedő Ház, or Magyar Szecesszió Háza • V, Honvéd utca 3 • Mon–Sat 10am–5pm • 2000Ft • ☎ 1 269 4622, ⓦ magyarszecessziohaza.hu

Behind the Soviet Army Memorial, look out for the pistachio facade of the **Bedő House**, a superb example of Hungarian Art Nouveau architecture, built by Emil Vidor in 1903. Restored to its original state after decades of neglect, it now holds the **Museum of Hungarian Art Nouveau**, an extensive but rather haphazard collection of furniture, ceramics, interior design and other knick-knacks; check out the toilets in the basement too. If you find the entrance price off-putting, settle instead for a browse around the shop, with its reproduction and original pieces, or enjoy a coffee in the very pleasant café.

The Batthyány and Nagy monuments

Two monuments off the northern corners of Szabadság tér recall very different historical figures. To the northeast at the far end of Aulich utca, in the centre of a small roundabout, a badly weathered lantern flickers with an **Eternal Flame** commemorating **Count Lajos Batthyány**. The Prime Minister of the short-lived republic declared after the 1848 War of Independence, Batthyány was executed by the Habsburgs on this spot on October 6, 1849. As a staunch patriot – but not a revolutionary – he is a hero for conservative nationalists, and his monument is the destination of marches on October 6.

To the northwest of Szabadság tér at the far end of Vécsey utca a figure stands on a footbridge in Vértanuk tere (Martyrs' Square), gazing towards Parliament. This is **Imre Nagy**, the reform Communist who became Prime Minister during the 1956 Uprising and was shot in secret two years afterwards. With his raincoat, trilby and umbrella hooked over his arm, Nagy cuts an all-too-human, flawed figure – and is scorned by those who pay homage to Batthyány.

Kossuth tér

The apotheosis of the government district and Hungary's romantic self-image comes at **Kossuth tér**, with its colossal Parliament building and its memorials to national heroes. The square is named after **Lajos Kossuth**, the leader of the 1848 Revolution (see box below), who is represented by a sculptural tableau showing him and his ministers downcast by their defeat in 1849. The Communists had replaced it with a more heroic version, but that has been removed as the square is returned to its pre-March 1944 state. Two restored statues stand to the north and south of Parliament: by the visitor centre is the grandiose monument to **István Tisza**, the prime minister of Hungary in 1914, while to the south is the equestrian statue of **Gyula Andrássy**, prime minister after the 1867 compromise. The equestrian statue on the grass in front of Parliament is of **Prince Ferenc Rákóczi II**, a hero of the struggle for Hungarian independence, whose plinth is inscribed: "The wounds of the noble Hungarian nation burst open!" This is a

---

LAJOS KOSSUTH

Lajos Kossuth was the incarnation of post-Napoleonic bourgeois nationalism. Born into landless gentry in 1802, he began his career as a lawyer, representing absentee magnates in Parliament. His Parliamentary reports, which advocated greater liberalism than the Habsburgs would tolerate, became widely influential during the Reform era, and he was jailed for sedition. While in prison, Kossuth taught himself English by reading Shakespeare. Released in 1840, he became editor of the radical *Pesti Hírlap*, was elected to Parliament and took the helm during the 1848 Revolution.

After Serbs, Croats and Romanians rebelled against Magyar rule and the Habsburgs invaded Hungary, the Hungarians proclaimed a republic with Kossuth as de facto dictator. After the Hungarians surrendered in August 1849, Kossuth escaped to Turkey and later toured Britain and America, espousing liberty and trying to win support for the Hungarian cause. So eloquent were his denunciations of Habsburg tyranny that London brewery workers attacked General Haynau, the "Butcher of Vienna", when he visited the city. One man who did his best to undermine Kossuth's efforts was Karl Marx, who loathed Kossuth as a bourgeois radical and wrote hostile articles in the New York *Herald Tribune* and the London *Times*.

As a friend of the Italian patriot Mazzini, Kossuth spent his last years in Turin, where he died in 1894. His remains now lie in the Kerepesi Cemetery (see p.80).

reference to the anti-Habsburg war of 1703–11, but also perfectly describes the evening of October 23, 1956, when crowds filled the square, chanting anti-Stalinist slogans at Parliament – the prelude to the Uprising that night. Down the steps between the two equestrian statues is the new 1956 memorial to those who died on Kossuth tér on October 25, when ÁVO snipers opened fire on a peaceful crowd that was fraternizing with Soviet tank-crews.

Statue of Attila József

Immediately south of the Andrássy statue, close to the river, sits the brooding figure of **Attila József**, one of Hungary's finest poets, who was expelled from the Communist Party for trying to reconcile Marx and Freud, and committed suicide in 1937 after being rejected by his lover. His powerful, turbulent verse has never lost its popularity, and he earns his place here for his poem *By the Danube*.

2

Holocaust Memorial

Right on the riverbank 200m south of Parliament is a poignant **Holocaust Memorial**: dozens of shoes cast in iron, marking the spot where hundreds of Jewish adults and children were machine-gunned by the Arrow Cross and their bodies thrown into the Danube. Before being massacred, they were made to remove their coats and footwear, which were earmarked for use by German civilians. (Access from Parliament is dangerous as it means crossing the busy embankment road; the nearest crossing is down by the tram stop before the Lánchíd.)

Parliament

Országház • V, Kossuth Lajos tér • Tours in English daily at 10am, noon, 1pm, 2pm & 3pm (no tours on national holidays); tours in other major languages at different times • The ticket office opens at 8am (tickets sell fast) and entry is through the Visitor Centre (Látogatóközpont), down the steps at the northern end of the Parliament by the Tisza monument • EU citizens with passport 2000Ft, otherwise 4000Ft • ℗ parlament.hu

The Hungarian **Parliament** building makes the Houses of Parliament in London look humble, its architect Imre Steindl having larded Pugin's Gothic Revival style with Renaissance and Baroque flourishes. Sprawling for 268m along the embankment, its symmetrical wings bristle with finials and 88 statues of Hungarian rulers, surmounted by a dome 96m high (alluding to the date of the Magyar conquest; see p.67). Though most people are impressed by the building, the poet Gyula Illyés once famously dismissed it as "no more than a Turkish bath crossed with a Gothic chapel" – albeit one that cost 38,000,000 gold forints. One weakness in the design was the white limestone of the exterior, which has been degraded by the elements and pollution; since 1925 it has required almost constant cleaning and replacement.

For centuries, Hungarian assemblies convened wherever they could, and it wasn't until 1843 that it was resolved to build a permanent "House of the Motherland" in Pest-Buda (as the city was then called). By the time work began in 1885, the concept of Parliament had changed insofar as the middle classes were now represented as well, though over ninety percent of the population still lacked the right to vote. Gains were made in 1918, but they were soon curtailed under the Horthy regime, just as the attainment of universal adult suffrage in 1945 was rendered meaningless after 1948 by a Communist dictatorship. The introduction of multiparty democracy in 1990 was symbolized by the removal of the red star from Parliament's dome and the replacement of Communist emblems by the traditional coat of arms featuring the crown of King Stephen – whose Coronation Regalia is now on show in the building's Cupola Hall.

The interior – and the Coronation Regalia

Having passed through a security check, the extent to which the interior is accessible depends on Parliament's activities, but you can be sure of seeing the main staircase, the Cupola Hall and the Lords Chamber, if nothing else.

2

ST STEPHEN'S CROWN

The much revered **St Stephen's Crown**, the jewel of the Coronation Regalia on display in the Parliament building, consists in fact of two crowns joined together: the cruciform crown that was sent as a gift by Pope Sylvester II to Stephen for his coronation in 1000, and a circlet given by the Byzantine monarch to King Géza I. The distinctive bent cross was caused by the crown being squashed as it was smuggled out of a palace in a baby's cradle. At other times it has been hidden in a hay-cart or buried in Transylvania, abducted to Germany by Hungarian Fascists and thence taken to the US, where it reposed in Fort Knox until its return home in 1978, together with Stephen's crystal-headed sceptre, a fourteenth-century gold-plated orb and a sixteenth-century sword made in Vienna, used by his successors. Under the Dual Monarchy, Habsburg emperors ruled Hungary in the name of St Stephen, and travelled to Budapest for a special coronation ceremony, traditionally held in the Mátyás Church in the Vár.

Despite its archaic style, the building was high-tech for its time, being air-conditioned via blocks of ice in the basement that kept it at the constant temperature of 25°C which the architect reckoned was most conducive to thought – since modern air conditioning was installed, MPs have complained of back pains. Statues, carvings, gilding and mosaics are ten a penny, lit by lamps worthy of the Winter Palace – but there are also cosy touches such as the individually numbered brass ashtrays where peers left their cigars smouldering in the lounge while they popped back into the chamber to hear someone speak; a good speaker was said to be "worth a Havana".

Guards holding drawn sabres flank the **Coronation Regalia**, whose centrepiece, **St Stephen's Crown** (see box above), has symbolized Hungarian statehood for over a thousand years. Don't be surprised to see loyal citizens prostrating themselves in its sacred presence. On a humbler note, you'll be shown a **scale model** of Parliament made of 100,000 matchsticks, built by a patriotic family over three years.

Museum of Ethnography

Néprajzi Múzeum • V, Kossuth Lajos tér 12 • Tues–Sun 10am–6pm • 1000Ft • ☎ 1 473 2400, ⑩ neprajz.hu

Across the road from Kossuth's statue stands a neo-Renaissance building housing the **Museum of Ethnography**. Little visited by tourists, it's actually one of the finest museums in Budapest, originally built as the Palace of the Supreme Court; petitioners would have been overawed by its lofty, gilded main hall, whose ceiling bears a fresco of the goddess Justitia surrounded by allegories of Justice, Peace, Revenge and Sin.

The museum's permanent exhibition on Hungarian folk culture occupies thirteen rooms on the first floor (off the left-hand staircase) and is fully captioned in English, with an excellent catalogue available. Exhibits from all over the Carpathian Basin, including a reconstructed church interior, bear traps, painted furniture and plentiful photos, are well presented under headings such as "Institutions" and "Peasant Work", but there's only occasional reference to the range of ethnic groups who lived in Habsburg-ruled Hungary. Though few of the beautiful costumes and objects on display are part of everyday life in Hungary, you can still see them in parts of Romania, such as Maramureş and the Kalotaszeg, which belonged to Hungary before 1920.

Temporary exhibitions (on the ground and second floors) cover anything from Hindu rituals to musical instruments from around the world, while over Easter and Christmas there are **concerts** of Hungarian folk music and dancing, and **craft fairs**.

Újlipótváros

Szent István körút, the section of the Nagykörút running from Nyugati Station to the Danube, marks the end of Lipótváros – but there are a few sights further out in **Újlipótváros** (the XIII District) that are worth a mention.

Holocaust memorials

Running up from the *körút* parallel to the river is Pozsonyi út, a bustling tree-lined street leading to **Szent István Park**, the prewar social hub of a wealthy Jewish neighbourhood. The park is an apt site for a **monument to Raoul Wallenberg**, who gave up a playboy life in neutral Sweden to help the Jews of Budapest in 1944 (see p.64). The monument was constructed in the 1950s but "exiled" to Debrecen in eastern Hungary before being stashed away for decades, only taking its rightful place in Budapest in 1999.

There is another less well-known Holocaust memorial some 100m north in the riverside Vizafogó park at the end of Vesŏ utca. The **Martyrs' Memorial**, by the Greek sculptor Agamemnon Makrisz, is a copy of the composition he made earlier for the Mauthausen concentration camp, and has nine figures standing with their arms upraised. Erected in 1986, this was the first major public memorial to the wartime murder of the Jews – and typically it was hidden away up here.

Lehel tér market hall

Lehel Csarnok • XIII, Lehel tér • Mon 6am–5pm, Tues–Fri 6am–6pm, Sat 6am–2pm

Heading 500m eastwards along Csanádi utca will take you to **Lehel tér**, notable for its picturesque 1930s reconstruction of the ruined **Romanesque church** at Zsámbék, west of Budapest. Beyond lies the **Lehel tér market hall**, which may look like a stylistic mishmash but it's a true locals' market and has a great set of stalls selling vegetables, fruit, meat and dairy products, and loads of freshly baked goodies.

DOHÁNY UTCA SYNAGOGUE

Terézváros and Erzsébetváros

Terézváros (Theresa Town, the VI District) is home to the State Opera House, the Academy of Music and several bar-filled squares, making it one of the most vibrant parts of the city. Its main thoroughfare, Andrássy út, is Budapest's longest, grandest avenue, running in a perfect straight line for two and a half kilometres up from Erzsébet tér to Hősök tere and the Városliget. With its coffee houses, high-end fashion shops and grey stone edifices laden with dryads, not to mention the Opera House, the avenue retains something of the style that made it so fashionable in the 1890s, when "Bertie" the Prince of Wales drove its length in a landau, offering flowers to women as he passed.

To the south of Király utca, the mainly residential **Erzsébetváros** (Elizabeth Town, the VII District) is composed of nineteenth-century buildings whose bullet-scarred facades, adorned with fancy wrought-ironwork, conceal a warren of dwellings and leafy courtyards. There is certainly no better part of Pest to wander around, soaking up the atmosphere. The old buildings have made the district popular for a distinctive form of nightlife in the "ruin gardens": bars set up in derelict plots or old houses that were previously awaiting development or demolition.

This is also the old **Jewish quarter** of the city, which was transformed into a ghetto during the Nazi occupation and almost wiped out in 1944–45, but has miraculously retained its cultural identity. Its current resurgence owes much to increased contacts with international Jewry, and a revival of interest in their religion and roots among the eighty-thousand-strong Jewish community of Budapest, which had previously tended towards assimilation, reluctant to proclaim itself in a country where anti-Semitic prejudices linger.

ARRIVAL AND GETTING AROUND

Terézváros The stretch of Andrássy út up to the Oktogon – where it meets the Nagykörút (Great Boulevard) – is within walking distance of Deák tér, and the whole length of the boulevard is served by metro line #1. Trams circle the Nagykörút night and day, and several trolleybus lines run through the two districts out to the Városliget.

Erzsébetváros The obvious starting point for exploring the area is the Dohány utca Synagogue, a short walk down the Kiskörút from the metro interchange at Deák tér.

Terézváros

Laid out in the late nineteenth century, **Terézváros** was heavily influenced by Haussmann's redevelopment of Paris, and at that time it was one of the smartest districts in the city. Under Communism, the area became pretty run-down, but the appeal of the old apartment blocks lining its streets is now bringing in the middle classes; luxury brands such as Gucci and Louis Vuitton have moved in, the villas near the park have recovered their value and café society flourishes around Liszt Ferenc tér.

Andrássy út was inaugurated in 1884 as the Sugár (Radial) út, but was soon renamed after the statesman Count Gyula Andrássy, and it was this name which stayed in popular use throughout the years when this was officially Stalin Avenue (1949–56) or the Avenue of the People's Republic (1957–89).

The State Opera House

Állami Operaház • VI, Andrássy út 22 • English-language tours of the interior daily 3pm & 4pm • 2900Ft • ☎ 1 332 8197 , ⓦ opera.hu (for programmes), ⓦ operavisit.hu (for tours)

The **State Opera House** was founded by Ferenc Erkel, the composer of Hungary's national anthem, and occupies a magnificent neo-Renaissance pile built in 1875–84 by Miklós Ybl. It can boast of being directed by Mahler (who was driven out by the anti-Semitism he experienced in the city), hosting performances conducted by Otto Klemperer and Antal Doráti, and sheltering two hundred local residents (including Kodály) in its cellars during the siege of Budapest. The 1260-seat auditorium was the first in Europe to feature an iron fire curtain (installed after a blaze at the Vienna Opera House), underfloor heating and air conditioning. Its chandelier weighs three tonnes, and 2.7 kilos of gold were used to gild the fixtures. To the left of the stage is the box used by Emperor Franz Josef's wife Sisi (see p.146), who loved Hungarian opera as much as he detested it. The upstairs reception rooms and downstairs foyer are equally lavish, festooned with portraits and busts of Hungarian divas and composers. Tickets for tours are available from the shop to the left in the foyer; see p.180 regarding tickets for performances.

Nagymező utca

Continuing from the Opera House along Andrássy út, you'll pass one of Budapest's venerable coffee houses on the right-hand side, the *Művész* (no. 29), where the

● ACCOMMODATION

Astoria City	17	K&K Opera	12
Benczúr	3	Mamaison Hotel	
Casati	13	Andrássy	2
Caterina	8	Marco Polo	16
City Comfort		Medosz	9
Apartments	4	Mirage Fashion	1
Continental Hotel Zara	15	Radisson Blu Béke	5
Corinthia Grand Royal	11	Soho	14
easy Hotel	6	Star Inn	7
Home-Made Hostel	10		

● SHOPS

ACB	3	Judaica	20
Alexandra	9	Knoll	6
Bamo	19	Kultúr Barlang	11
Brush Shop	22	Ludovika	16
Deák Erika Galéria	2	Mai Manó	7
Gardrob	13	Manier	5
Hass & Czjzek	10	Massolit Books	15
Herend	12	Sóos	21
In Vino Veritas	18	Térképkirály	8
Irók Boltja	4	Tisza Shoes	23
Játékszerek anno	1	Wave	14
Játék Udvar	17		

● RESTAURANTS, CAFÉS & BARS

2Spaghi	46	Félix Hélix	32	Krizia	9
Amigo Bar	39	Frici Papa	23	Kuplung	25
À Table	51	Fröhlich	36	Lokál	45
Bobek Café	28	Funky Pho	13	M	24
Bock Bisztró	21	Ganga	17	Mai Manó	15
Bors	54	Garzon	43	Menza	14
Butcher's Kitchen	44	Il Terzo Cerchio	53	Mika Tivadar	29
Café Bouchon	8	Instant Bar	11	Montengrói Gurman	47
Chocodeli	7	La Pizza di		Most Bar	16
Cirkusz	41	Mamma Sofia	34	Művész	22
Coffee Cat	6	Kádár Etkézde	31	New York	38
CoXx	52	Kadarka	27	Podma Café	3
Csak a Jó Sör	26	Kazimír	42	PRLMNT	2
Dang Muoi	5	Két Szerecsen	19	Rácskert	33
Doblo	40	Kiadó	12	Spinoza	49
Eco Café	4	Kis Parázs	55	Szimplakert	50
Falafel	20	Kisüzem	30	Szóda	48
Fausto	57	Klassz	18	Zeller	10
Fekete Kutya	37	Kőleves	35	Zokni	56

Zoo

Városliget

Museum of Fine Arts

Millennary Monument

WestEnd Center

Hősök tere

Vajdahunyad Castle

The Southeast Asian Gold Museum

Műcsarnok

Városliget

RADNÓTI MIKLÓS UTCA

VÁCI ÚT

FERDINÁND HÍD

KATONA JÓZSEF UTCA

Nyugati pu

Nyugati Station

EIFFEL TÉR

Ferenc Hopp Museum

Bajza utca

Post Office Museum

Kodály Körönd

Kodály Memorial Museum

György Ráth Museum

Koestler

N

Margit-sziget & Buda

TERÉZVÁROS

Vörösmarty utca

House of Terror

Liszt Memorial Museum

VI

Oktogon

Market Hall

Music Academy

Operetta Theatre

Mai Manó House

Opera House

Opera

Robert Capa Photographic Center

Madách Theater

Miksa Róth Museum

Keleti Station

ERZSÉBETVÁROS

Keleti pu

New Theatre

Orthodox Synagogue

Post Office Museum

VII

BKV Office

Rumbach utca Synagogue

Deák tér

New York Palace

Erkel Theatre

Lutz

Blaha Lujza tér

Museum of Electro-technology

II János Pál Pápa tér

Dohány utca Synagogue

BELVÁROS

V

Stadiums

Kerepesi Cemetery

Párisi Udvar

Astoria

Buda

KOSSUTH LAJOS U.

0		500

metres

TERÉZVÁROS AND ERZSÉBETVÁROS

magnificent interior is more enticing than the cakes or service. The next major junction is **Nagymező utca** – somewhat optimistically nicknamed "**Broadway**" because of its theatres and nightclubs. Outside the Operetta Theatre at no. 17, take a look at the **statue** of the composer **Imre Kálmán**, lounging on a bench. Better known to the world as Emmerich Kalman, he penned such operetta favourites as *The Gypsy Princess* and *Countess Maritsa* – it's a genre that wins Hungarian hearts with its combination of music and melodrama. Strangely, the statue has a bronze computer beside it: the idea was that you could look at the theatre's website on it, but that did not account for vandals. Two blocks down from Nagymező utca, on Paulay Ede utca, take a peek at the **New Theatre**, whose blue and gold early Art Deco facade and foyer (by Béla Lajta in 1909) look superb.

Mai Manó House (Hungarian House of Photography)

Mai Manó Ház (Magyar Fotográfusok Háza) • VI, Nagymező utca 20 • Mon–Fri 2–7pm, Sat, Sun & holidays 11am–7pm •1500Ft • ☎ 1 473 2666, Ⓦ maimano.hu

During the interwar years, the best-known club on Nagymező utca was the Arizona at no. 20: "the most glamorous nightclub I have ever visited," said Patrick Leigh Fermor, who went there on his way across Europe. It was run by Sándor Rozsnyai and his wife, Miss Arizona. However, he was sent to a concentration camp and she was murdered by the Arrow Cross in 1944 (which inspired Pál Sándor's 1988 film, *Miss Arizona*, starring Hanna Schygulla and Marcello Mastroianni). The bottle-green-tiled building was the former home of the Habsburg court photographer **Mai Manó**, which made it a fitting choice for the photography museum that occupies it today. It hosts temporary exhibitions in three separate galleries, and an excellent photographic bookshop on the first floor – the colourful café on the ground floor is a well-frequented haunt.

Robert Capa Contemporary Photographic Centre

Robert Capa Kortárs Fotográfiai Központ • VI, Nagymező utca 8 • Tues–Sun 11am–7pm • 1500Ft • ☎ 1 413 1310, Ⓦ capacenter.hu

On the opposite side of Andrássy út is the **Robert Capa Contemporary Photographic Centre,** named after the renowned war photographer (and founder of Magnum Photos) who was born in Budapest in 1913. A fabulous exhibition space, it is the venue for the city's most important photographic exhibitions, including the annual Hungarian Press Photo Competition, which usually takes place in April. In any case, it's worth a peek inside to see the Art Nouveau features by József Rippl-Rónai and Ödön Lechner; take a look at the Art Deco lobby of the Tivoli Theatre next door, too.

Miklós Radnóti statue

Across the road, outside the theatre at no. 11 that takes his name, lounges a statue of one of Hungary's finest poets, **Miklós Radnóti**, whose most powerful poems were written while serving in a Jewish labour brigade in the war. When his body was exhumed eighteen months after he was shot in 1944, a notebook of his last poems was discovered in his pocket.

Paris Department Store

Back on Andrássy út, you can't miss the striking Art Nouveau frontage of Budapest's first department store, with a glass facade that soars up five floors. When the **Paris Department Store** opened in 1911 it boasted a roof terrace and even an ice rink. It's now a large bookstore, with an excellent selection of English-language books, but in any case it's worth having a look inside to see how the restoration has preserved the sweeping lines of the interior. There is a surprising contrast on the first floor at the back of the shop: the **Lotz terem**, which was a ballroom dating from 1885 in a neighbouring casino, is magnificently decorated in frescoes by Károly Lotz, and today holds a posh café, complete with resident pianist.

Jókai Mór tér and Liszt Ferenc tér

Close to the Oktogon, two elongated squares stretch out on either side of Andrássy út, lined with pavement **cafés**. On the left is **Jókai Mór tér**, with a large statue of the novelist Mór Jókai, while on the right is **Liszt Ferenc tér**, crammed with the terraces of bars and restaurants. In the middle of the square, the composer +Liszt hammers an imaginary keyboard with his vast hands, blind to the drinkers and diners surrounding him.

Presiding over the far end of the square is the **Music Academy** that bears his name. Founded by the eponymous composer in 1875 – though it didn't move here until 1907 having originally been based in Liszt's apartment on Andrássy út – the entire building has been beautifully renovated after a lengthy closure, re-establishing the Academy's status as Budapest's most prestigious concert venue. The florid exterior is dominated by Stróbl's statue of a seated Liszt, while the magnificent Art Nouveau entrance hall, designed by Aladár Körösfői Kriesch, is flush with green Zsolnay tiles and golden mosaics. The two gilded auditoriums, meanwhile, manifest glorious decor that matches the quality of the music played here.

The Oktogon

Andrássy út meets the Nagykörút at the **Oktogon**, an eight-sided square flanked by eclectic buildings. With 24-hour fast-food chains, and trams and taxis running along the Nagykörút through to the small hours, the Oktogon never sleeps. During the Horthy era it rejoiced in the name of Mussolini tér, while under the Communists it was called November 7 tér after the date of the Bolshevik revolution.

The House of Terror

Terror Háza • VI, Andrássy út 60 • Tues–Sun 10am–6pm • 2000Ft • ☎ 1 374 2600 ⓦ terrorhaza.hu

Just beyond the Oktogon, the stern, dark grey walls, blacked-out windows and ominous black frame that surmounts the building at no. 60 marks this place out as the **House of Terror**, once the dreaded headquarters of the secret police. Dubbed the "House of Loyalty" by the Fascist Arrow Cross during World War II, it was subsequently used for the same purpose by the Communist **ÁVO**. After the reimposition of Soviet rule, the building was thoroughly sanitized before being handed over to the Communist Youth organization.

Before beginning, you might consider an audio-guide (1300Ft), which will save you the trouble of reading the English-language sheets in each room, but the latter pack far more information, and you can also take them away. Upon entering the atrium, you are confronted with a Soviet tank sitting in a pool of water, alongside hundreds of images of ÁVO victims, before you proceed to the second floor (you take the lift, then work downwards).

To the sound of thumping, industrial-style music, the exhibition begins with "Double Occupation", which documents the respective Nazi and Soviet occupations, courtesy of some powerful video footage. The next couple of rooms deal with the reign of the feared Arrow Cross, before you get to the main subject of the museum: the Soviet "liberation" and the emergence of Communism with its associated themes of religious persecution, resistance, interrogation and intimidation. The focus here is

THE ÁVO

The **Communist secret police** began as the Party's private security section during the Horthy era, when its chief, **Gábor Péter**, betrayed Trotskyites to the police to take the heat off their Stalinist comrades. After World War II it became the 9000-strong Államvédelmi Osztály or **ÁVO** (State Security Department), its growing power implicit in a change of name in 1948 – to the State Security Authority or **ÁVH** (though the old acronym stuck). Ex-Nazi torturers were easily persuaded to apply their skills on its behalf, and its network of 41,000 informers permeated society. So hated was the ÁVO that any members caught during the Uprising were summarily killed, and their mouths stuffed with banknotes (secret policemen earned more than anyone else).

inevitably on the activities of the Soviet-style **PRO (Political Security Department)**, which subsequently became the ÁVO and then the ÁVH, though all three organisations were headed up by Gábor Péter, whose desk and phone remain in situ. Throughout, there are moving testimonies from many of those arrested and detained on suspicion of anti-Bolshevik activities – tens of thousands of "class enemies" were interned in forced labour camps such as the notorious Recsk camp in northeastern Hungary.

No less compelling is the Communist propaganda film of Nagy and his cohorts in court attempting to defend themselves against charges of counter-revolutionary activities. The most sobering part is the **basement**, with its reconstructed torture chamber and cells, alongside pictures of some of those who were kept here, and further, even more harrowing testimonies.

The Liszt Memorial Museum

Liszt Ferenc Emlékmúzeum • Andrássy út 67 • Mon–Fri 10am–6pm, Sat 9am–5pm; closed on national holidays • 1300Ft • Concerts every Sat at 11am, 1300Ft, or 2000Ft for concert and museum • ☎ 1 413 0440, Ⓦ lisztmuseum.hu

Across the road from the House of Terror stands the old Liszt Music Academy, which was also where the composer – who was the Academy's first president – lived from 1881 until his death in 1886. The three rooms that once comprised the first floor apartment now harbour the **Liszt Memorial Museum**, the centrepiece of which is the drawing room and its extensive collection of pianos; the star exhibit is a Chickering Grand given to Liszt in 1880, atop which sits a silver music stand, complete with a bust of Beethoven, among others. Among the wealth of personal memorabilia on display in the study-bedroom are letters, books and scores, items of clothing, and a bronze cast of Liszt's right hand by Stróbl.

Kodály körönd

Kodály körönd, named after the composer Zoltán Kodály, is one of Budapest's most elegant squares, albeit flanked by four neo-Renaissance mansions in various states of disrepair. During World War II, the *körönd* (circus) was named Hitler tér, prompting the émigré Bartók to vow that he would not be buried in Hungary so long as anywhere in the country was named after Hitler or Mussolini. Curiously, there is no statue of Kodály here, but instead, there are statues of three military heroes who fought in the wars against the Ottomans, namely Miklós Zrinyi, János Botthány and György Szondy, in addition to a statue of the poet Bálint Balassa.

Kodály Memorial Museum

Kodály Emlékmúzeum • VI, Andrássy út 89 • Wed–Fri 10am–noon & 2–4.30pm by prior appointment only on ☎ 1 352 7106 • 900Ft • Ⓦ kodaly.hu

In the northeast corner of Kodály körönd, the ground-floor flat where Zoltán Kodály lived until his death in 1967 now houses the **Kodály Memorial Museum**, preserving his library, dining room and salon, the last of which keeps his grand piano as well as a rich assemblage of folk art, which Kodály was particularly fond of collecting during his various trips. A fourth room is used for temporary exhibitions, often pertaining to Kodály himself.

Ferenc Hopp Museum

Hopp Ferenc Múzeum • VI, Andrássy út 103 • Tues–Sun 10am–6pm • 1000Ft • ☎ 1 322 8476, ⓦ hoppmuzeum.hu

Lurking just beyond the Kodály körönd, the **Ferenc Hopp Museum** presents temporary displays of works from the vast collection of more than twenty thousand items amassed by optician and art collector Ferenc Hopp (1833–1919), with pieces from Japan, China, India, Korea, Indonesia and Vietnam. One item on permanent display is the imposing Chinese moon gate standing in the garden.

The Southeast Asian Gold Museum

Délkelet-Azsiai Aranymúzeum • VI, Andrássy út 110 • Tues–Thurs & Sun 11am–5pm, Fri & Sat 11am–7pm • 2500Ft • ☎ 1 482 3190, ⓦ thegoldmuseum.eu

Of all the many museums hereabouts, the most rewarding is the **Southeast Asian Gold Museum**, an extraordinary private collection of a former diplomat to the region. The nine rooms of dazzling artefacts (ninety percent of which are gold) have been acquired from various tribal cultures, notably the Javanese, Khmer and Champa kingdoms (central/ southern Vietnam today). The latter's proximity to an abundance of gold and silver quarries is manifest in a spectacular output of both religious and secular metalwork, from ritual statues and jewellery to everyday objects like cutlery and pourers. Look out too for artefacts from the Cult of Shiva, a Hindu god, and in particular the amusingly precise phallic symbols (linga) made from stone or rock crystal. Intricately ornamented crowns (diadems) take star billing in the religious art section, and in another room, floor-to-ceiling high with Buddha statues, you can view a rare ritual drum with frogs crawling around the rim, supposedly denoting rains and agricultural fertility.

The **oriental teahouse** and adjoining **tropical sculpture garden** are well worth visiting once you're done, while the shop sells original pieces, though at prices most won't be able to afford.

Post Office Museum

Posta Múzeum • VI, Benczúr utca 27 • Tues–Sun 10am–6pm • 500Ft • ☎ 1 269 6838, ⓦ postamuzeum.hu

Since being established in 1881, the wonderful **Post Office Museum** has had a somewhat nomadic existence, only moving to its current home here in the Benczúr House (with which the postal service has long had various associations) in 2012. The Hungarian Postal Service (Magyar Posta) itself was founded in 1867, following the country's separation from Austria, and its history since is surprisingly noteworthy. Indeed, it can boast a series of notable firsts: in 1869, it became the first country in the world (along with Austria) to introduce the postcard, while in 1881 it was one of the first to install a telephone exchange – thanks largely to the work of inventor and telephone pioneer Tivadar Puskás, a colleague of Thomas Edison. More impressive, though, were the technical innovations, from the manufacture and introduction of mechanically emptied mailboxes, to the use of petrol-driven vehicles for mail collection and delivery, at the end of the nineteenth century – as testified by the vintage delivery vehicles designed by engineer János Csonka.

György Ráth Museum

Ráth György Múzeum • VI, Városligeti fasor 12 • Open by appointment only: ask at the Ferenc Hopp Museum (see above) or ring ☎ 1 456 5110 • 600Ft

In an Art Nouveau villa on Városligeti fasor, which runs parallel to Andrássy and is lined with even finer mansions, the **György Ráth Museum** displays artefacts from the same collection as the Ferenc Hopp Museum. The statue in the garden of a Buddhist monk actually depicts Sándor Kőrösi-Csoma, a Hungarian who achieved fame by

THE JEWISH QUARTER

In the streets fanning out to the east of Károly körút lies Budapest's old **Jewish quarter**. After Josef II's reforms in 1783 allowed Jews back into Pest for the first time since the defeat of the Turks, they were invited to live in the grounds of Count Orczy's house between Király utca and Madách tér. Thereafter they flourished, and the Pest community grew from eight percent of the population in 1800 to twenty-three percent in 1920. In April 1944 this was chosen by the Nazis as the location of Budapest's Jewish **ghetto** – a sign on Wesselényi utca by the synagogue marks where the ghetto gate stood. All Jews living outside the ghetto were compelled to move in. As their menfolk had already been conscripted into labour battalions intended to kill them from overwork, the 70,000 inhabitants of the ghetto were largely women, children and old folk, crammed into 162 blocks of flats, with over 50,000 of them (in buildings meant for 15,000) around Klauzál tér alone.

JEWISH QUARTER WALKING TOURS

English-language guided walking tours of the area, run by Aviv (Sip utca 12 ☎ 1 462 0477, 🌐 aviv.hu), depart from the Dohány utca Synagogue (daily except Sat at 10.30am, 11.30am, 12.30pm, 1.30pm & 2.30pm; April–Oct also 3.30pm & 4.30pm). The cheapest tour (2850Ft) simply covers the synagogue and memorial garden; another (3200Ft) includes the Jewish Museum, while the most expensive (3800Ft) also features the Rumbach utca Synagogue. For a fascinating personalized walking tour of the entire quarter, contact Eszter Gömöri (🅴 bp. cityguide@gmail.com), who charges €20 an hour.

3

compiling the first English–Tibetan dictionary, though his real goal was a vain search for the ancestors of the Hungarian people. Highlights include an early fourteenth-century lacquer Water-Moon Guanyin Bodhisattva in the Chinese collection, a seventeenth- to eighteenth-century gilt bronze Buddha in the Mongolian collection, and a fifteenth-century Kalachakra mandala in the Tibetan Collection.

Erzsébetváros

One of the centres of the new cool Budapest is **Erzsébetváros**, separated from **Terézváros** by the narrow **Király utca** (the main road through the area before Andrássy út was built). The vibrant "ruin garden" (*romkocsma*) movement that has spread through the city started here among the decaying apartment blocks and empty plots of the old **Jewish quarter** (see box, p.173). The run-down stock of the district is also attracting big money in housing and retail developments such as the **Madách sétany**, cutting swathes through the old city, or doing up older parts such as the Gozsdu-udvar or Kazinczy utca.

The Dohány utca Synagogue

Dohány utcai Zsinagóga • VII, Dohány utca 2–8 • March–Oct Mon–Thurs & Sun 10am–5.30pm, Fri 10am–3.30pm; Nov–Feb Mon–Thurs & Sun 10am–3.30pm, Fri 10am–1.30pm • 2500Ft including the Jewish Museum • ☎ 70 533 5696, 🌐 greatsynagogue.hu

One of the landmarks of Pest, the splendid **Dohány utca Synagogue** (also known as the Great Synagogue, Nagy Zsinagóga) is Europe's largest synagogue and the second biggest in the world after the Temple Emmanuel in New York, with 3600 seats and a total capacity for over five thousand worshippers. It belongs to the **Neolog** community, a Hungarian denomination combining elements of Reform and Orthodox Judaism. Today, eighty percent of Hungarian Jewry are Neologs, but their numbers amounted to only twenty percent before the Holocaust, which virtually wiped out the Orthodox and Hasidic communities in the provinces. Neolog worship includes features that are anathema to other denominations, not least organ music during services.

Designed by a Viennese Gentile, Ludwig Förster, the building epitomizes the so-called Byzantine-Moorish style that was popular in the 1850s, and attests to the patriotism of Hungarian Jewry – the colours of its brickwork (yellow, red and blue) being those of Budapest's coat of arms. In the 1990s the synagogue was restored at a cost of over $40 million; the work was funded by the Hungarian government and the Hungarian-Jewish diaspora, notably the Emmanuel Foundation, fronted by the late Hollywood actor Tony Curtis who was born of 1920s emigrants.

The interior

The magnificent, cathedral-like **interior** was designed by Frigyes Feszl, the architect of the Vigadó concert hall. Arabesques and Stars of David decorate the ceiling, the balconies for female worshippers are surmounted by gilded arches, and the floor is inset with eight-pointed stars. The layout reflects the synagogue's Neolog identity, with the *bemah*, or Ark of the Torah, at one end, in the Reform fashion, but with men and women seated apart, according to Orthodox tradition. On Jewish festivals, the place is filled to the rafters with Jews from all over Hungary, whose chattering disturbs their more devout co-religionists. At other times, the hall is used for concerts of classical or klezmer music, as advertised outside.

The Jewish Museum

Heading up to the second-floor **Jewish Museum** (Zsidó Múzeum), to the left of the main synagogue entrance, note a relief of Tivadar (Theodor) Herzl, the founder of modern Zionism, who was born and taught on this site. In the foyer is a gravestone inscribed with a menorah (seven-branched candlestick) from the third century AD – proof that there were Jews living in Hungary six hundred years before the Magyars arrived. The first three rooms are devoted to Jewish festivals, with beautifully crafted objects such as Sabbath lamps and bowls for the Seder festival, some from medieval times. The final room focuses on the Holocaust in Hungary, with chilling photos and examples of anti-Semitic propaganda. Oddly, the museum says nothing about the huge contribution that Jews have made to Hungarian society, in every field from medicine to poetry.

The cemetery and Heroes' Temple

The **cemetery** beside the synagogue only exists at this spot because the Nazis forbade Jews from being buried elsewhere – one of many calculated humiliations inflicted on the Jewish quarter (by then a walled ghetto) by the local SS commander, Eichmann. Some 2281 Jews are interred beneath simple headstones, erected immediately after the Red Army's liberation of the ghetto on January 18, 1945. Beyond the cemetery looms the cuboid, domed **Heroes' Temple**, inaugurated in 1931 in honour of the ten thousand Jewish soldiers who died fighting for Hungary during World War I. It now serves as a synagogue for everyday use and so may not be open to tourists.

Raoul Wallenberg Memorial Park

Just beyond the cemetery, you enter the **Raoul Wallenberg Memorial Park**, named after the Swedish consul who saved twenty thousand Jews during World War II. Armed with diplomatic status and money for bribing officials, Wallenberg and his assistants plucked thousands from the cattle trucks and lodged them in "safe houses", manoeuvring to buy time until the Russians arrived. He was last seen alive the day before the Red Army liberated the ghetto; arrested by the Soviets on suspicion of espionage, he died in the Gulag. The park's centrepiece is a **Holocaust Memorial** by Imre Varga, shaped like a weeping willow, each leaf engraved with the names of a family killed by the Nazis. On the plinth are testimonials from their relatives living in Israel, America and Russia. Behind it, glass panels by the artist Klára Szilárd commemorate the sixtieth anniversary of the neighbouring Goldmark Hall.

Goldmark Hall

Goldmark terem, • VII, Wesselényi utca 7 • Mon–Thurs & Sun 10am–6pm, Fri 10am–4pm • 800Ft but it's cheaper to buy a combined ticket with the synagogue (2500Ft) which takes you through the memorial park

Named after Károly Goldmark, the composer of the opera *The Queen of Sheba*, the

Goldmark Hall houses the fascinating small Jewish Quarter exhibition. This display of objects from the **Jewish Archives** includes the screenplay for a performance of *The Magic Flute* performed here in 1942; opened in 1931, the hall was the only place where Jews were able to perform in the city at that time. There's also a coffee grinder that was one family's sole possession to survive the Holocaust, and a pair of weighty scales from the *Fröhlich* patisserie on Dob utca (see p.169), which opened in 1953 and is still going strong today.

Monument to Carl Lutz

Heading north up Rumbach Sebestyén utca from the Great Synagogue you'll cross Dob utca, where you'll see a **monument to Carl Lutz**, the Swiss consul who saved many Jewish lives during the war (see p.51). His monument – a gilded angel swooping down to help a prostrate victim – is locally known as "the figure jumping out of a window".

Rumbach utca Synagogue

Rumbach utca zsinagóga • VII, Rumbach Sebestyén utca 11–13 • Mon–Thurs 10am–3.30pm, Fri 10am–2.30pm, Sun 10am–5.30pm • 500Ft

In happier times, each Jewish community within the quarter had its own place of worship, with a *yeshiva* (religious school) and other facilities within an enclosed courtyard invisible from the surrounding streets – as epitomized by the **Rumbach utca Synagogue**. Built by Otto Wagner in 1872, for the so-called "Status Quo" or middling-conservative Jews, it now belongs to the Neolog community and stands restored but empty. Decorated in violet, crimson and gold, its octagonal Moorish interior hosts occasional exhibitions and concerts. As a plaque outside notes, the building served as a detention barracks in August 1941, from where up to 1800 Slovak and Polish refugees were deported to the Nazi death camps.

Király utca

The official boundary between Terézváros and **Erzsébetváros** runs down the middle of **Király utca**, once the main street here before Andrássy út was built. In the 1870s it contained fourteen of the 58 licensed brothels in Budapest, and as late as 1934 Patrick Leigh Fermor was told that "any man could be a cavalier for five pengöes" here. After decades of shabby respectability under Communism the street is undergoing a revival, with numerous cafés, bars and restaurants popping up here, plus interior design and furniture boutiques.

Gozsdu-udvar

At Király utca 13, a grey stone portal leads into the **Gozsdu-udvar**, a 200m-long passageway built in 1904 and running through to Dob utca 16. Connecting seven courtyards, it was a hive of life and activity before the Holocaust; after many years of dereliction, it has now been sensitively redeveloped and new restaurants, café and bars once again populate this atmospheric space, as well as a terrific Sunday flea market. As you walk down the Gozsdu-udvar, you cross the **Madách Walk** (Madách sétány), a controversial plan to modernize the district through the creation of new apartments, shops and restaurants. The Walk runs parallel to Király utca, stretching from Madách tér on the Kiskörút through to the Nagykörút, though it has only reached Kazinczy utca so far.

Dob and Kazinczy utcas

These two streets form the axis of the 3000-strong Orthodox community. At Dob utca 22 the *Fröhlich* patisserie is a popular haunt for locals and visitors, while further along there's a kosher butcher at no. 35. Down to the right on Kazinczy utca are a kosher baker and pizzeria, opposite the kosher *Carmel* restaurant. The recent pedestrianizing of this section of the street makes it all the more enjoyable to wander around.

Orthodox Synagogue

VII, Kazinczy utca 29 • Sun–Thurs 10am–3.30pm, Fri 10am–12.30pm • 1000Ft

Looming over the middle of Kazinczy utca is the **Orthodox Synagogue**, built by Béla and Sándor Löffler in 1913 in the Art Nouveau style, with a facade melding into the curve of the street, and an interior with painted rather than moulded motifs. A smaller wood-panelled synagogue for winter use, a *yeshiva* and the *Hanna* Orthodox kosher restaurant are all contained within an L-shaped courtyard that can also be entered via an arcade on Dob utca.

The Museum of Electrotechnology

Magyar Elektrotechnikai Múzeum • Kazinczy utca 21 • Tues–Fri 10am–5pm, Sat 10am–4pm • 800Ft • ☎ 1 342 5750, ⊛ elektromuzeum.hu

For something quite different from the rest of the sights in the Jewish quarter visit the **Museum of Electrotechnology**, set in a former electricity substation. Its devoted curators can demonstrate the world's first dynamo (invented in 1859 by Áynos Jedlik, a Benedictine monk), tie irons and a child-proof plug from 1902 in rooms devoted to such topics as the history of light bulbs and the Hungarian section of the **Iron Curtain**, along the border with Austria. Captions are in Hungarian only, but the beauty of early domestic electrical contraptions comes across anyway.

Dohány utca

Dohány utca takes its name – Tobacco Street – from the tobacco factory that once stood on the corner of Sip utca – close to the sadly neglected Art Deco **Metro Klub** that stands there now. This narrow thoroughfare sweeps through the lower part of Erzsébetváros from the Kiskörút and out across the Nagykörút towards the Garment District.

The Hungária Baths

Halfway between the two *körúts* you pass the magnificent Art Nouveau front of the ill-fated **Hungária Baths** at no. 44 Dohány utca. When the complex opened in 1908, its main selling point – its large number of private bathtubs – was its downfall, as the building of better-equipped apartments reduced demand. The baths closed in 1929, and were used after the war as a cinema and then as a theatre until 1965. By the 1980s the inside was crumbling fast and the baths were close to complete ruin – the little that could be saved can be seen on the facade and in the lobby of the *Zara* hotel that now stands in its place.

The New York Palace

At the junction of Dohány utca and the Nagykörút is a piece of old Budapest that for many years lay derelict. Like the *Gresham Palace* on Széchenyi tér (see p.47), the **New York Palace** on the corner of the Nagykörút is a Budapest landmark also associated with an insurance company, in this case the New York, which commissioned the building in 1895 and included in the plans a magnificent coffee house, which became one of the great literary cafés of interwar Budapest. Under Communism the edifice housed a publishers, and its Beaux-Arts facade – with a small Statue of Liberty high up on the corner – survived being rammed by a tank in 1956. Now a luxury hotel, its gilded and frescoed restaurant-cum-coffee house is worth a look, even if you don't want to fork out to eat there.

Miksa Róth Museum

Róth Miksa Múzeum • VII, Nefelejcs utca 26 • Tues–Sun 2–6pm • 800Ft • ☎ 1 341 6789, ⊛ rothmuzeum.hu

Beyond the *New York Palace*, among the backstreets near Keleti Station, the **Miksa Róth Museum** showcases the work of a leading figure in the Hungarian Art Nouveau movement. Located in Róth's former home, the museum reveals the diversity of his work – both in stained glass and in mosaics – which can also be seen in the Parliament, the *Gresham Palace*, the Music Academy and the Jewish Museum.

SZÉCHENYI BATHS

The Városliget and the stadium district

Both Hősök tere (Heroes' Square) and the Városliget (City Park), at the end of Andrássy út, were created in the late nineteenth century for the nationwide celebrations of the millennium of the Magyar conquest of Hungary, but as neither was ready on time, the anniversary was rescheduled for the following year, 1896, ever since. Aside from the park itself, the chief attractions are the Museum of Fine Arts and the romantic Vajdahunyad Castle, followed by a wallow in the Széchenyi Baths. It's also the setting for Budapest's wonderful zoo, the circus, and a handful of other museums, the best of which is the Transport Museum. Further out lie the city's most important stadia, and one of Budapest's Art Nouveau masterpieces, the Geological Institute.

ARRIVAL

Városliget The best ways to reach the Városliget from the centre are on the yellow #1 metro line or bus #105, but trolleybus #74 from the Dohány utca Synagogue, #75 from the Margít híd and #72 from Arany János utca metro station are also useful.

The stadium district To reach the stadium district, catch trolleybus #75 or the red #2 metro line from the centre of town to the Puskás Ferenc Stadion stop.

Hősök tere

The enormous ceremonial plaza of **Hősök tere** is flanked by two galleries resembling Greek temples. At its centre is the **Millennary Monument** – Budapest's version of Nelson's Column in London – consisting of a 36m-high column topped by the figure of the Archangel Gabriel who, according to legend, appeared to Stephen in a dream and offered him the crown of Hungary. Around the base are figures of Prince Árpád and his chieftains, who led the seven Magyar tribes into the Carpathian Basin. They look like a wild bunch; one of the chieftains, Huba, even has stag's antlers strapped to his horse's head. As a backdrop to this, a semicircular colonnade displays statues of Hungary's most illustrious leaders, from King Stephen to Kossuth.

During the brief Republic of Councils in 1919, when the country was governed by revolutionary Soviets, the square was decked out in red banners and the column enclosed in a red obelisk bearing a relief of Marx. In 1989, it was the setting for the ceremonial reburial of Imre Nagy and other murdered leaders of the 1956 Uprising (plus an empty coffin representing the "unknown insurgent") – an event which symbolized the dawning of a new era in Hungary. Today it's more likely to be filled with rollerbladers and skateboarders – for whom the smooth surface is ideal – and tourists, or for hosting **events** such as Army Day in May or the National Gallop in September.

Műcsarnok

XIV, Hősök tere • Tues, Wed & Fri–Sun 10am–6pm, Thurs noon–8pm • 1800Ft • ☎ 1 460 7000, ⓦ mucsarnok.hu

On the southeast side of the Hősök tere is the **Műcsarnok** (Exhibition Hall), also called the Palace of Art (not to be confused with the Palace of Arts, covered on p.85). A Grecian pile with gilded columns and a mosaic of St Stephen as patron of the arts, it was inaugurated in 1896 just in time for the Millenary celebrations. Its magnificent facade and foyer are in contrast to the four austere rooms used for **temporary exhibitions** (two or three at a time), often of modern art, though these are usually of a high quality – with anything from graphic art to multi-media and installation art.

Museum of Fine Arts

Szépművészeti Múzeum • XIV, Hősök tere • Tues–Sun 10am–6pm with late opening on alternate Thurs till 10pm • 1800Ft • Free guided tours in English Tues–Thurs 11am, 1pm & 2pm, Fri 11am & 2pm, Sat 11am • Audio-guide 500Ft • Temporary exhibitions 2600Ft which includes entry to permanent collection • ☎ 1 469 7100, ⓦ szepmuveszeti.hu

On the northwest side of the Hősök tere, the **Museum of Fine Arts** is the pan-European equivalent of the Hungarian National Gallery, housed in an imposing Neoclassical building completed in 1906, though without the gilt of the Műcsarnok. Most exhibits are labelled in English and a free floor-plan is available, but if you want more information you should go on an English-language **tour** or rent an **audio-guide**. Note that the continued rearrangement of the museum's collection, the loaning of pictures and **temporary exhibitions** can alter the layout of pictures described here. Special **events** – music and guided tours – are held on late-opening Thursdays, as advertised on the website. Art historians may be drawn to the **library** which is a treasure-trove of information in various languages, housed nearby at VI, Szondi utca 77 (ask at the museum information desk for more details).

Lower ground floor

In the museum's bowels, a hippopotamus-tusk wand carved with spells to protect a child presages the small but choice **Egyptian Collection**, chiefly from the Late Period and Greco-Roman eras of Egyptian civilization. The highlights of the first room are four huge painted coffins and a child-sized one from Gamhud in Middle Egypt; *shabti* figures, intended to perform menial tasks in the afterlife; and mummified crocodiles and other creatures from the Late Period, when animal cults reached their apogee. In the second room, look out for the sculpted heads of a priestess of Hathor and a bewigged youth from the New Kingdom, the painted coffin of a priestess of Amun, and a tautly poised bronze of the cat goddess Bastet.

Across the basement lobby, the section entitled **Art around 1900** starts with **Symbolist** and **Decadent** works such as Franz von Stuck's *The Kiss of the Sphinx*, Arnold Böcklin's *Spring Evening*, and Hans Makart's *Nessus Carries off Deianeira*. The remainder musters a few works by the Hungarian **Art Nouveau** masters József Rippl-Rónai and Károly Ferenczy, an Utrillo street scene, some Bonnards and two famous images by **Oscar Kokoschka**: *Veronica's Veil* and the poster *Der Sturm*.

Ground floor

The rooms to the right of the entrance lobby are devoted to **ancient Mediterranean cultures** from Etruria to Athens, mainly represented by jugs and vases. Highlights include a pair of bronze shin-guards decorated with rams' heads, terracotta tiles portraying bestial deities, a man's torso and head from the pediment of a Campanian temple, lifelike busts of Roman worthies, and an early fifth-century BC Etruscan grave marker with reliefs of funerary games.

Across the ground-floor lobby is an excellent **bookshop**, leading to a wing used for **temporary exhibitions** (requiring a separate ticket). Before heading upstairs, visit the grand **Renaissance Hall**, used for hanging large allegorical or religious works on loan from other museums; the **Baroque Hall** (often used for televised events), and the **Prints and Drawings Room** at the far end on the right, mounting temporary displays (free) drawn from the museum's holdings of works by Raphael, Leonardo, Rembrandt, Rubens, Dürer, Picasso and Chagall.

The first floor: the Spanish Collection

The museum's forte is its hoard of **Old Masters**, based on the collection of Count Miklós Esterházy, which he sold to the state in 1871. The room numbering can make navigation here confusing: the main rooms have Roman numerals and smaller ones down the sides have Arabic digits.

The **Spanish Collection** of seventy works is arguably the best in the world outside Spain. Located off to the right at the top of the stairs, it kicks off with vivid altarpieces by unknown Catalans, such as the *Bishop-Saint Enthroned* (whose bewilderment belies his magnificent attire) in room II. Room V, beyond, has seven **El Grecos** – including *The Disrobing of Christ, The Agony in the Garden, The Apostle St Andrew* and *The Penitent Magdalene* – and a superb *Adoration of the Magi* by Eugenio Cajes.

Murillo's *Flight into Egypt* and *Holy Family with the Infant St John the Baptist* hang beside a tender *Holy Family* by **Zurbarán** in room IV; across the room are two depictions of St Andrew, one by Zurbarán and the gory *Martyrdom of St Andrew* by **Ribera**, together with **Velázquez**'s *Tavern Scene*. Room III next door has five **Goyas** ranging from war scenes (*2nd of May*) to portraits of the rich (*Señora Ceán Bermudez*) and humble (*The Knife-Grinder*). Murillo's *Madonna and Child with Angels Playing Music* is a highlight of room VI, and there's an annexe of Habsburg court portraits by Juan Martínez (room 1).

The Flemish Collection

Entering the adjacent **Flemish Collection** in room VII, Snyders' gigantic *Hawk in the Barnyard* and Van Valckenborch's nocturnal *Pilgrims Before a Forest* are overshadowed by room VIII, where the serenity of **Van Dyck**'s *St John the Evangelist* contrasts with the melodrama of **Rubens**' *Mucius Scaevola before Porsenna* and **Jordaens**' *The Satyr and the Peasant.*

Room IX segues into the **Dutch Collection** with an array of **Brueghels**, from Pieter the Elder's *Sermon of St John the Baptist* to Pieter the Younger's *Blind Hurdy-Gurdy Player* and Jan's *Paradise Landscape* and *Garden of Eden with the Fall of Man.* A copy of **Bosch**'s *The Bacchus Singers* (featuring a man making himself vomit) hangs in room VII. The rest of the Dutch collection is on the floor above, reached by stairs (or a lift) off room IX. There you'll find the *Parable of the Hidden Treasure* by **Rembrandt** and his pupil Gerard Dou and other works from his studio in room XVIII to the right, with portraits by **Hals** and wildlife scenes by **Melchior de Hondecoeter Houdeleoter** in rooms XXVII and XXVI, off to the left.

The German Collection

Back on the first floor, in room X, the **German Collection** opens with **Angelika Kauffmann**'s *The Wife of Count Esterházy as Venus* – a strumpet with her jewellery box – and darkly Gothic works by **Cranach the Elder**, such as *Christ and the Adulteress* and *The Lamentation, and the Holy Virgin in Prayer* by **Dürer**. In *Salome with the Head of St John the Baptist,* Salome displays his head on a platter with the nonchalance of a hostess bringing out the roast. Every emotion from awe to jealousy appears on the faces in **Holbein**'s *Dormition of the Virgin*, at the far end of the room. Don't overlook **Dürer**'s *Young Man* with an enigmatic smile, sharing room XIV with pictures by **Altdorfer**.

From Romanticism to Postimpressionism

For a change of mood, cross the lobby and enter **From Romanticism to Postimpressionism**, where Room XII displays **Courbet**'s wild landscapes and life-sized *Wrestlers*, **Corot**'s *Remembrance of Coubrou* and **Rodin**'s sculpture *The Brazen Age*. In the small rooms alongside you'll find orchards and river-views by **Renoir** and **Monet** (room XIX), *Lady with a Fan* by **Manet**, a **Pissarro** Paris scene and **Toulouse-Lautrec**'s *These Ladies* (room XX), as well as a little-known **Gauguin**, *Black Pigs*, from his Tahitian period and more Monets (room XXII). Teutonic Romanticism rules in room XIII, with Von Lenbach's *The Triumphal Arch of Titus in Rome* and Böcklin's *Centaur at a Forge*.

English and French art

The single room (XIV) devoted to **English art** musters a dullish portrait apiece by Hogarth, Reynolds and Gainsborough, and a melodramatic theatre scene by Zoffany, while the highlight of **French art until 1800** in room XVI is *The Rest on the Flight into Egypt* by **Poussin**. However, both are totally outshone by the display of masters that follows.

Italian Collection

The superb **Italian Collection** occupies nine rooms and can be viewed in a very rough chronological order by entering from the lobby opposite the Spanish section, or in reverse from the English or French rooms; some backtracking is inevitable. A tradition of gilded altarpieces such as *The Mystic Marriage of St Catherine* (room XXIV) gave rise to **Boccacio**'s masterpiece *The Adoration of the Infant Christ*, usually displayed near **Titian**'s *Madonna and Child with St Paul* in the later rooms. **Bellini**'s pig-eyed *Queen of Cyprus* and a possible **Fra Angelico** landscape are the highlights of room XXIII.

Room XIX boasts **Raphael**'s exquisite *Esterházy Madonna* – a Virgin and Child with the infant St John – and two **Giorgione** paintings, one a self-portrait, leading to a powerful **Bronzino** portrait in room XX. The highlights of the neighbouring Room XVII are a couple of portrayals of Venetian Doges, a friendly one by **Titian** and another, more watchful character by **Tintoretto**, who is also represented by *Hercules Expelling the Faun from Omphale's Bed*; and a couple of **Veronese** paintings, including one of a disagreeable grandee in an ermine-trimmed robe.

Room XVIII hosts the biblical epic *Jael and Sara*, by **Artemisia Gentileschi**. Finally, up by the English collection, room XV has two superb **Canalettos**: one of Vienna and the other of the Pantheon, though the latter is poorly displayed high above a door. Also on show are a handful of landscapes by **Guardi** and some paintings by **Tiepolo**.

4

Ötvenhatosok tere

Ötvenhatosok tere, 56ers' Square, the wide avenue running off alongside the Városliget, was called Parade Square in Communist times, as it was here that Party leaders reviewed marching soldiers. Up to 1956 they did so beneath a 25m-high statue of Stalin that was torn down during the Uprising and hammered into bits for souvenirs. Later, a statue of Lenin was erected in its place, which in turn was removed to the Memento Park (see p.124) in 1989. Today it serves as the setting for occasional **fairs** and **concerts** but work is starting to transform it into Budapest's new **Museum Quarter**, moving the National Gallery and Ethnographical Museum here.

The three monuments

Today, three monuments mark the distance that Hungary has travelled since 1989. The **Timewheel** is the world's largest hourglass, a metal canister 8m in diameter that rotates 180° on the last day of each year, symbolizing Hungary's accession to the European Union in 2004. Where the Stalin statue once stood, you now see the **Monument to the Uprising**, a forest of oxidized columns merging into a stainless steel wedge, beside a Hungarian flag with a circle cut out, recalling the excision of the hated Soviet symbol in 1956. Beyond this, a crucifix rises over the foundations of the **Virgin Mary Church** that the Communists demolished in 1951.

The Városliget

The **Városliget** (City Park) starts just behind Hősök tere, where the fairy-tale towers of **Vajdahunyad Castle** rear above an island girdled by an artificial lake that's used for **boating** in the summer and transformed into a splendid outdoor **ice rink** in winter. Between May and September, pedaloes can be rented out (1800Ft/1hr) from the lakeside building just down from the tourist office. Otherwise, the park is a great spot to take the kids, with numerous play areas and acres of space to run around.

Vajdahunyad Castle

Like the park, **Vajdahunyad Castle** was created for the Millenary Anniversary celebrations of 1896, proving so popular that the temporary structures were replaced by permanent ones. Vajdahunyad is a catalogue in stone of architectural styles from the kingdom of Hungary, incorporating parts of two Transylvanian castles and a replica of the Romanesque **chapel at Ják** (May–Oct daily 10am–4pm; 100Ft), with a splendidly carved portal and a Renaissance courtyard that makes a romantic setting for evening **concerts** from July to mid-August.

Next to the church sits the hooded **statue of Anonymous**. Completed in 1903, this nameless chronicler to King Béla is the prime source of information about early medieval Hungary, though the existence of several monarchs of that name during the twelfth and thirteenth centuries makes it hard to date him (or his chronicles) with any accuracy.

Agriculture Museum

Mezőgazdasági Múzeum • XIV, Vajdahunyad Castle • Tues–Sun 10am–5pm • 1500Ft • ☎ 1 363 1117, ⓦ mezogazdasagimuzeum.hu

Filling the bulk of the castle these days are the extensive displays of the **Agriculture Museum**. It's generally a mixed bag, but what is certainly worth the entrance fee is the first section, which includes a superb hoard of archeological finds, including exquisitely produced items of pottery such as milk jugs and butter churns. The breeding of livestock became more extensive in the fourteenth and fifteenth centuries, particularly on the Great Plain, where **Hungarian breeds** such as the long-horned grey cattle and woolly Mangalica pigs were favoured. By the nineteenth century the **Great Plains** were one of Europe's most valuable grain-producing regions and by the time the Hungarian Ministry of Agriculture was established in 1889, only the USA produced more maize.

The remainder of the exhibition, comprising displays on forestry, hunting and fishing, is eminently missable, though the craftsmanship in antique crossbows and rifles exquisitely inlaid with leaping hares and other prey is undeniably impressive, as is a 270-year-old dugout boat carved from a single piece of oak, which was found at Lake Balaton, southwest of the capital.

Petőfi Csarnok and Aviation and Space Flight Exhibition

Petőfi Csarnok XIV, Zichy Mihály utca 14 • ☎ 1 848 0206, ⓦ petofirendezvenykozpont.hu • **Aviation and Space Flight Exhibition** Repüléstörténeti és Űrhajózási kiállítás • May–Sept Fri 10am–4pm, Sat & Sun 10am–5pm • 500Ft • Trolleybuses #70, #72 and #74 from the centre of town all go near the hall

Leaving Vajdahunyad island by the causeway at the rear, you're ten minutes' walk from the **Petőfi Csarnok** or "Pecsa" as it is often called, a 1970s "Metropolitan Youth Centre" that regularly hosts concerts (outdoors in summer), exhibitions, fairs, films and parties, as well as a fine **flea market** at weekends. At the back of the building is a stairway leading to the extensive **Aviation and Space Flight Exhibition** which, among other items, contains the spacesuit used by Hungary's first astronaut Bertalan Farkas on the Soyuz-35 mission of 1980; an L-2 monoplane sporting an Italian Fascist symbol, which broke world speed records in the Budapest–Rome races of 1927 and 1930; and cockpits of a Tu-154 and MiG 25. One familiar name is that of **Ernő Rubik**: the father of the inventor of the cube was a big name in plane design. Strangely, though, there's nothing about Count **László Almássy**, Hungary's foremost aviator of that time, better known abroad as the hero of the book and film *The English Patient*.

Transport Museum

Közlekedési Múzeum • XIV, Városligeti körút 11 • Tues–Fri 10am–5pm, Sat & Sun 10am–6pm; Nov–March closes 1hr earlier • 1600Ft • ☎ 1 273 3840

On the edge of the City Park is the **Transport Museum**, of which the aviation exhibition is an outgrowth. Captions in English explain that the Hungarian transport network of the 1890s was among the most sophisticated in Europe; despite the country starting from a low technological base, railways, canals, trams and a metro had all been created within fifty years. Displays include vintage locomotives and carriages that you can climb into, scale models of steamboats and a wonderful collection of Hungarian Railways posters from 1900 to 1980. A model train set on the floor above the foyer attracts a crowd when it's switched on – for fifteen minutes every hour, on the hour; there's also a small one on the ground floor that runs on the half-hour. Collectors, meanwhile, can buy Hungarian model trains in the museum shop. Outside the building are remnants of two of the Danube bridges that were wrecked in 1945: the cast-iron Erzsébet híd (replaced by a new bridge) and a few links of the original chains from the Lánchíd, which is now supported by cables.

While you're here, check out the **Hungarian Federation of the Blind and Partially Sighted** nearby at Hermina út 47, an extraordinary pink concoction designed by Lechner.

The northern end of the Városliget

Three major attractions lie on Állatkerti körút, the road that runs round the top of the Városliget. The best access is by foot from Hősök tere, by #72 trolleybus, which passes the door of all four, or by the yellow #1 metro line to the Széchenyi Fürdő stop.

The Zoo

Állatkert • XIV, Állatkerti körút 6 • Daily: Jan, Feb, Nov & Dec 9am–4pm; March & Oct 9am–5pm; April & Sept 9am–5.30pm; May–Aug 9am–6.30pm; animal houses open 1hr later and close 30min before the zoo itself • 2500Ft, family 7300Ft • ☎ 1 273 4900, ⓦ zoobudapest.com

Tucked behind the Fine Arts Museum you'll find the delightful Elephant Gates of Budapest's **Zoo**, which opened its doors in 1866, thus establishing itself as one of the world's oldest. The wonderful Art Nouveau pavilions, designed by Kornél Neuschloss and Károly Kós and originally dating back to 1912, seem like the last word in zoological architecture: the exotic **Elephant House**, resembling a Central Asian mosque, the **India House** with its big cats, and the **America Tropicana** (formerly the **Palm House**) with its magnificent **aquarium** below.

In recent years, there have been some notable arrivals: in 2007, the zoo announced the world's first birth of a rhino conceived by artificial insemination; and in 2013, the zoo welcomed its first elephant calf, Asha, for more than fifty years. Look out for **children's events**, evening concerts and exhibitions under the Great Rock. Next door to the zoo is the **Once Upon a Time Park** (Hol Nem Volt Park, 500Ft, or free with zoo entry), in the grounds of the former Funfair. As well as some of the old Funfair rides such as the magnificent carousel, you'll also find the Children's Corner and petting zoo.

The Municipal Circus

Fővárosi Nagycirkusz • XIV, Állatkerti körút 12 • Wed & Thurs 5pm, Fri 3pm, Sat 11am, 3pm & 7pm, Sun 11am & 3pm • 1900–3900Ft ; children 1500–2700Ft • ☎ 1 343 8300, ⓦ fnc.hu

Next door to the Zoo, the **Municipal Circus** traces its origins back to 1783, when the Hetz Theatre played to spectators on what is now Deák tér. Today the building has a changing programme featuring anything from tiger-taming and horse shows to musical clowns, illusionists and Chinese and Cuban acrobats. It also hosts a big international circus festival every even-numbered year in late January or early February – check the website for details.

The Széchenyi Baths

Széchenyi Gyógyfürdő • XIV, Állatkerti körút 11 • Daily 6am–10pm • ☎ 1 363 3210, ⓦ szechenyibath.com • See p.197 for details

Across the road from the Municipal Circus, the **Széchenyi Baths** could be mistaken for a palace, so grand is its facade. Outside is a statue of the geologist Zsigmondy Vilmos, who discovered the thermal spring that feeds its outdoor pool and Turkish baths. This is perhaps the best venue for mixed-sex bathing, and in one of the large outdoor pools you can enjoy the surreal spectacle of people playing **chess** while immersed up to their chests in steaming water – so hot that you shouldn't stay in for more than twenty minutes. The best players sit at tables around the pool's edge (the late former world champion **Bobby Fischer** among them in the 1980s); bring your own set if you wish to participate.

The stadium district

The **stadium district**, 1km south of Vajdahunyad Castle, is chiefly notable for the **Ferenc Puskás Stadium** (Puskás Ferenc Stadion), where league championship and international **football** matches, and **concerts** by foreign rock stars are held. Originally known as Népstadion ("People's Stadium") and built in the early 1950s by fifty thousand Budapestis who "volunteered" their labour, on Soviet-style "free Saturdays", it was renamed in 2002 after the legendary footballer Ferenc Puskás (1927–2006), who captained the Mighty Magyars in their remarkable 6–3 victory over England at Wembley Stadium in 1953 (a team that went unbeaten for a world record of 32 consecutive games), before defecting to forge a second career at Real Madrid.

To the west of the stadium is the smaller **Kisstadion**, which is commonly used for ice sports, while to the east Stalinist statues of healthy proletarian youth line the court that leads to the indoor **Papp László Sportaréna** (or Aréna), a mushroom-shaped silver structure which hosts both concerts and sporting events – Papp was the first boxer to win three Olympic gold medals (1948, 1952 and 1956). The **Stadion bus station** completes this concrete ensemble.

Geological Institute

Földani Intézet • XIV, Stefánia út 14 • Thurs, Sat & Sun 10am–4pm • 500Ft • ☎ 1 251 0999, ⓦ mfgi.hu • Trolleybus #75 from Puskás Ferenc Stadion metro station or from City Park

On Stefánia út, beyond the stadiums, you can admire the **Geological Institute**, one of the major edifices in Budapest designed by Ödön Lechner. Much of the original design has been preserved simply because the institute has never had enough money to make major changes. The exterior is as striking as his Post Office Savings Bank (see p.50) and Applied Arts Museum (see p.82), with a gingerbread facade, scrolled gables and steeply pitched Transylvanian roofs patterned in bright blue tiles, crowned by four figures supporting a globe on their backs. Lechner put numerous geological references into the design and originally planned to put dwarves holding up the globe. The institute has a small **Geological Museum**, but the helpful staff will happily show visitors round the building itself, with its gingerbread stucco and faux lapis lazuli stairways. (Ernő Rubik, the man behind the famous cube, left his mark here: he designed the museum's cataloguing system.) The little concrete turret on top of the rear of the building is said to be a 1950s machine-gun turret, though it never saw any action.

Józsefváros and Ferencváros

Separated from Erzsébetváros by Rákóczi út, which runs out to Keleti Station, Józsefváros (the VIII District) is an amalgam of high and low life. While the Hungarian National Museum, Eötvös Loránd University and the Szabó Ervin Library on Múzeum körút make for a lively student quarter, its seedier hinterland beyond the Nagykörút district – nicknamed "Chicago" between the wars – still has an association with vice and crime, though this is largely redundant now as the area around the old apartment blocks near the Rákóczi tér market hall has become increasingly gentrified. You can wander safely anywhere in Józsefváros by day, and between the Kiskörút and Nagykörút in the small hours, but elsewhere stick to main roads and avoid pedestrian underpasses after midnight – particularly around Keleti Station, where Kerepesi Cemetery and the Police History Museum are worth a visit by day.

5

Üllői út – leading to the airport – marks the boundary of the adjacent **Ferencváros** (Franz Town, the IX District), once the most solidly working-class of the inner-city districts. Today, **Ráday utca** and the backstreets behind the wonderful **Great Market Hall** on Vámház körút are full of hip restaurants and bars; luxury condos rise where teenage insurgents once fought, and the district's historic far-right sympathies are challenged by a **Holocaust Memorial Centre**. Along the riverbank there is much ongoing development all the way down to the **Palace of Arts** complex, which is transforming the balance of the district. Football fans will want to see Fradi in action at the **FTC Stadium**, and children will enjoy the **Natural History Museum**.

ARRIVAL

Public transport links for the two districts are excellent, and include metro lines #2, #3 and #4, trams #4 and #6 along the Nagykörút and tram #2, which runs down the Pest bank of the Danube to the Palace of Arts.

Józsefváros

Named after the heir to the Habsburg throne in 1777, Józsefváros has many faces. The grand but neglected apartment blocks speak of an old middle-class suburb that fell into decline. Rákóczi tér became the centre of the city's sex industry and cheap housing in the streets behind it attracted a big Roma population. The prostitutes have long since gone, however, and gentrification is spreading rapidly throughout the district, helped by the sparkling new metro line #4. Some of the sights further out in the district, such as the Museum of Applied Arts, the Corvin köz and the Natural History Museum, are covered under the Üllői út section of Ferencváros (see p.82).

Múzeum körút

Part of the Kiskörút, **Múzeum körút** separates the Belváros and Józsefváros. Aside from being curved rather than straight, it resembles Andrássy út in miniature, lined with trees, shops and grandiose buildings. Immediately beyond the East–West Business Centre by the Astoria junction stands the old faculty of the **Eötvös Loránd Science University** (known by its Hungarian initials as ELTE). It's named after the physicist Loránd Eötvös, whose pupils included many of the scientists who later developed the US atomic bombs at Los Alamos, including Edward Teller, "Father of the Hydrogen Bomb".

Across the street it is worth putting your head into the courtyard of no. 7. A sadly neglected building by Miklós Ybl, the neo-Renaissance **Unger House** (Unger ház) has fabulous fine old wooden tiles and a glazed first-floor colonnade. Further down on the same side on Ferenczy utca, you can see a small crenellated section of the **medieval wall of Pest**. Originally 2km long and 8m high, the walls gradually disappeared as the city was built up on either side, but fragments remain here and there – a larger freestanding chunk lurks in the courtyard of no. 21, if you get the chance to peep inside.

Back on the outer edge of Múzeum körút, you'll find the **Múzeum** at no. 12, which was one of the earliest coffee houses in Pest (not to be confused with the 24-hour café at no. 10). Its original frescoes and Zsolnay ceramic reliefs dating from 1885 still grace what has long since become a restaurant (see p.165).

Bródy Sándor utca

From Múzeum körút you can wander down **Bródy Sándor utca**, which runs along the garden of the Hungarian National Museum. The Renaissance-style mansion at no. 8 housed the lower chamber of the Hungarian Parliament from 1867 until its present building was completed, and is now home to the **Italian Institute**. Diagonally across the street at nos. 5–7 is the **Radio Building**, from which ÁVO guards fired upon students demanding access to the airwaves, an act which turned the hitherto peaceful protests of October 23, 1956 into an uprising against the secret police and other manifestations of Stalinism.

JOZSEFVÁROS AND FERENCVÁROS

N

Stadium District

Keleti Station

ⓂKEREPESI ÚT

BAROSS
TÉR

Keleti pu

**Police
History
Museum**

**Kerepesi
Cemetery**

ERZSÉBETVÁROS

WESSELÉNYI UTCA

Blaha Lujza tér Ⓜ

Ⓜ Deák tér

DOHÁNY UTCA

BLAHA LUJZA
TÉR Ⓟ

ÚT

LUTHER UTCA

II. JÁNOS PÁL
PÁPA TÉR

**Erkel
Theatre**

RÁKÓCZI

Astoria Ⓜ

②①

SZENTKIRÁLYI UTCA

PUSKIN UTCA

GYULAI PÁL UTCA

VAS UTCA

NÉPSZÍNHÁZ

(NAGYKÖRÚT)

Ⓜ II. János
Pál pápa tér

②

ALFÖLDI UTCA

TELEKI
TÉR

**ELTE
University**

③

Unger Ház

⑦

⑧⑨⑤

BRÓDY SÁNDOR UTCA

④⑥

**Gutenberg
tér**

②

Rákóczi
Tér

⑤

**Market
Hall**

**Italian
Institute**

MÚZEUM KÖRÚT

Radio Building

⑩

RÁKÓCZI
TÉR

MÁTYÁS
TÉR

JÓZSEFVÁROS

**National
Museum**

MÚZEUM UTCA

⑪

JÓZSEF UTCA

TAVASZMEZŐ UTCA

**Szabó
Ervin Library**

③④

Kálvin tér Ⓜ

MIKSZÁTH
KÁLMÁN TÉR

BAROSS UTCA

BAROSS UTCA

HORVÁTH
MIHÁLY TÉR

BAROSS UTCA

ÜLLÉS UTCA

KÁLVIN
TÉR

⑫

**Fountain
of Hungarian
Truth**

RÁDAY UTCA

LÓNYAY UTCA

JÓZSEF KÖRÚT

Fővám tér
Ⓜ

VÁMHÁZ KÖRÚT

PIPA UTCA

⑬

Great Market Hall

Budapest Music Center

⑮

**Museum of
Applied
Arts**

Corvin-negyed

**Corvin
Cinema**

**Paul Street
Boys**

PRÁTER UTCA

CORVIN SÉTÁNY

⑭

LEONARDO DA VINCI UTCA

TŐMŐ UTCA

**Botanical
Garden**

**Corvinus
University**

MÁTYÁS UTCA

KINIZSI UTCA

⑯

KISFALUDY UTCA

FUTÓ UTCA

**Cet
Building**

⑱

RAKTÁR UTCA

⑥

BÉKÉS TÉR

**Kilián
Barracks**

ÜLLŐI ÚT

**Trafó
Centre**

⑰

TŰZOLTÓ UTCA

**Holocaust
Memorial Centre**

VIOLA UTCA

**Natural
History Museum**

Klinikák
Ⓜ

KOZÁNYI SÁNDOR UTCA

ÜLLŐI ÚT

**Goethe
Institute**

⑲

FERENC KÖRÚT

LILIOM UTCA

PÁVA UTCA

TOMPA UTCA

**Nehru
Part**

BORÁROS
TÉR

MESTER UTCA

VASKAPU UTCA

FERENCVÁROS

Gellért-hegy ◄

PETŐFI HÍD

Ⓗ

JÓZSEF UTCA

IRINYI JÓZSEF UTCA

⑳

**Egyetemisták
Parkja**

**ELTE
University**

River Danube (Duna)

HALLER UTCA

SOROKSÁRI ÚT

VÁGÓHÍD UTCA

**National
Theatre**

**Ludwig
Museum**

**Palace
of Arts**

RÁKÓCZI HÍD

Budapest Park ▼

0   300
└──────────┘
metres

■ ACCOMMODATION

Atlas City Hotel	2
Atrium Fashion Hotel	1
Brody House	5
Casa de la Musica	4
City Hostel Pest	6
Mercure Museum	3

**● RESTAURANTS, CAFÉS,
& BARS**

A38	20
A Grund	14
Almárium	10
Amman	3
Borbiróság	13
Butter Brothers	15
Caffé Torino	8
Club 93	4
Corvintető	2
Csiga	5
Élesztő	17
Fülemüle	6
Jedermann	19
Jonás	18
Lumen	11
Monyo	12
Múzeum	9
Múzeum Cukrászda	7
Rengeteg RomKafé	17
Rosenstein	1
Tamp & Pull	16

● SHOPS

Fakopáncs	4
Iguana	3
Libra	2
Magyar Pálinka Háza	1

5

Hungarian National Museum

Magyar Nemzeti Múzeum • VIII, Múzeum körút 14–16 • Tues–Sun 10am–6pm • 1100Ft; audio-guide 750Ft • ☎ 1 327 7773, ⊕ hnm.hu

Like the National Library in the Royal Palace, the **Hungarian National Museum** was the brainchild of Count Ferenc Széchenyi (father of István), who donated thousands of prints and manuscripts to form the basis of its collection. Housed in a Grecian-style edifice by Mihály Pollack, it was only the fourth such museum in the world when it opened in 1847, and soon afterwards became the stage for a famous event in the **1848 Revolution**, when Sándor Petőfi (see box, p.44) first declaimed the *National Song* from its steps, with its rousing refrain "Choose! Now is the time! Shall we be slaves or shall we be free?" ("Some noisy mob had their hurly-burly outside so I left for home", complained the museum's director at the time.) Ever since, March 15 has been commemorated here with flags and speeches.

The basement and ground floor

The museum has two lower levels devoted to medieval and Roman stonework – the latter starring a second-century AD mosaic floor from a villa at Nemesvámos-Baláca in western Hungary.

The first floor

Most visitors make an immediate beeline for the darkened room to the left of the foyer, which displays the **coronation mantle**, allegedly donated to the Basilica of Székesfehérvár by King Stephen in 1031. Beautifully embroidered with gold thread, this exquisite silk robe was considered too fragile to be transferred to the Parliament building when the rest of the Coronation Regalia was moved there in 2000.

To the right of the foyer is the archeological exhibition, entitled **Between East and West**, which covers the pre-Hungarian peoples of the Carpathian Basin. Highlights of this outstanding hoard, roughly in chronological order, include animal figurines and anthropomorphic urns from the Copper Age, two magnificent bronze spoked wheels, and, from the Iron Age, a fine assortment of gilded helmets, many of which were unearthed from Március 15 tér. Winding up with the Avars – the last peoples here before the Magyars arrived in 804 AD – look out for a gorgeous 23-piece gold dinner service belonging to an Avar chieftain.

The second floor

The main exhibition upstairs traces **Hungarian history** from the Árpád dynasty to the end of Communism, starting to the left side of the rotunda at the top of the stairs. Room 1 contains Béla III's crown, sceptre and sword, and in room 2, there's a gilded reliquary bust of St László and a wall fountain from the royal palace at Visegrád (see p.136). Don't miss the ivory saddles inlaid with hunting scenes in room 3, the suit of armour of the child-king Sigismund II in room 5, or the huge carved Renaissance pew in room 6. Turkish weaponry and the ornate tomb of Count György Apafi in room 7 speak of the 150 years when Hungary was divided and its destiny decided by intriguers and warlords, including the Forgáchs and Nádasdys depicted in the oldest **portraits** in Hungary, hung in room 8 – except for the infamous "Blood Countess" Erzsébet Báthori, whose picture is kept in storage. As the widow of national hero Ferenc Nádasdy, charged with torturing six hundred women to death and reputedly bathing in their blood to preserve her beauty, she was walled up in her castle and the atrocity hushed up.

From here, proceed back across the rotunda to find the Reform era and the *belle époque*, covered in rooms 11–18. Here, too, you'll find **Beethoven's Broadwood piano**, which was subsequently acquired by Liszt, some of whose keepsakes are also on display. Following coverage of World War II, the last room is given over to the Communist era, featuring newsreel footage and such items as a radio set dedicated to Stalin's 70th birthday, a scaled-down model of the Stalin statue torn down by crowds in 1956, and kitsch tributes to János Kádár, who reimposed Communist rule with a vengeance, but later liberalized it to the point that his successors felt able to abandon it entirely.

Kálvin tér and around

Múzeum körút ends at **Kálvin tér**, a busy intersection with roads going to the airport, the east and westwards across the river. In 1956, street fighting was especially fierce here as insurgents battled tanks rumbling in from the Soviet base on Csepel Island. A freestanding section of the **medieval walls** of Pest can be found off Vámház körút in the courtyard of no. 16, if the door is open.

Ervin Szabó Library

Szabo Ervin Könyvtár • VIII, Szabó Ervin tér 1 • Mon–Fri 10am–8pm, Sat 10am–4pm, closed July, reduced hours in Aug • Free

It seems almost miraculous that the ornate reading rooms of the **Szabó Ervin Library**, on the corner of Baross utca, survived unscathed from the fighting in the surrounding streets in 1956. Built in 1887 by the Wenckheim family – who enjoyed a near-monopoly on Hungary's onion crop – the library has come through a thorough modernization in sparkling form. At the main entrance on Reviczky utca, you can ask at the information desk about visiting the fourth-floor reading rooms, reached by a lovely wooden staircase. Staff may ask you to register but will probably just wave you through. Otherwise, you could do worse than avail yourself of a coffee in the delightful atrium café.

Fountain of Hungarian Truth

Outside the library stands one of the few surviving monuments marking the hated Treaty of Trianon (see p.209): the so-called **Fountain of Hungarian Truth** (Magyar Igazság kútja). Erected in 1928, it honours the British press magnate Lord Rothermere, whose campaign against the treaty in the *Daily Mail* was so appreciated that he was offered the Hungarian crown. On June 4, the anniversary of the treaty's signing, nationalist and neo-Nazi groups gather to pay their respects.

To the Nagykörút and Keleti Station

Behind the library lies an atmospheric quarter of small squares and parochial schools; formerly shabby, it's now buzzing with cafés and bars popular with students. Having given a face-lift to **Mikszáth Kálmán tér** and much of Krúdy utca, the process of gentrification has crossed the **József körút** – one of the sleazier arcs of the Nagykörút – to embrace **Rákóczi tér**, the focus of street prostitution until it was outlawed in 1999. The square has one of Budapest's finest market halls, and the opening of the fourth metro line has brightened up the whole area.

The large square that lies up towards Keleti Station, **II János Pal pápa tér** (Pope John Paul II Square), was formerly known as **Köztársaság tér**, long associated with lynchings that were carried out in front of the Communist Party HQ here in 1956. The addition of a new metro station, alongside the reopening of the **Erkel Theatre**, Budapest's "second" opera house (named after the composer of the national anthem, Ferenc Erkel), has lent this square a pleasant air of respectability. A couple of blocks away lies **Keleti Station**, where the grittier side of life still prevails, though this is also much improved thanks to spruced-up Baross tér and new underpasses.

HIDDEN GEMS: JÓZSEFVÁROS AND FERENCVÁROS

Drinking craft beer on riverside terrace of Jonás See p.175

Szabó Ervin Library reading room See p.79

Jedermann jazz bar See p.181

Füvészkert Botanical Garden See p.84

Paul Street Boys statue See p.82

Islamic Art at the Museum of Applied Arts See p.82

Holocaust Memorial Centre See p.84

5

The Police History Museum

Rendőrség-Történeti Múzeum • VIII, Mosonyi utca 7 • Tues–Sat 9am–5pm • Free • ☎ 1 477 2183, 🕸 policehistorymus.com

To check on dodgy arrivals, the **police** used to patrol Keleti Station in threes ("One can read, one can write, and the third one keeps an eye on the two intellectuals", as the old joke had it). They are now trying to improve their public image in the **Police History Museum**, a couple of blocks from the station, its entrance marked by a sentry box. As you go in, ask for the English translation of the main displays to enjoy how they handle such awkward matters as the role of the police in the Communist period. To the left of the entrance is a display of uniforms and memorabilia going back to Habsburg times, while to the right is a sad display depicting a very 1960s-looking crime scene with a sign listing key points for trainee investigators, along with detailed descriptions of more crimes than you would ever want to read about.

Kerepesi Cemetery

Kerepesi temető • VIII, Fiumei út 16 • Cemetery daily: April & Aug 7am–7pm; May–July 7am–8pm, Sept 7am–6pm; Oct–March 7.30am–5pm • Free • **Funerary Museum** Kegyeleti Múzeum • Mon–Fri 9am–5pm • Free

Five minutes' walk from the Police History Museum, you'll find the **Kerepesi Cemetery** (also known as Nemzet Sírkert and Fiumei úti Sírkert). This is the Père Lachaise of Budapest, where the famous, great and not-so-good are buried. Vintage hearses and mourning regalia in the **Funerary Museum** near the main gates illuminate the Hungarian way of death and set the stage for the necropolis. In Communist times, Party members killed during the Uprising were buried in a special plot near the entrance and government ministers in honourable proximity to Kossuth, while leaders and martyrs who "lived for Communism and the People" were enshrined in a starkly ugly **Pantheon of the Working Class Movement**; some have been removed by their

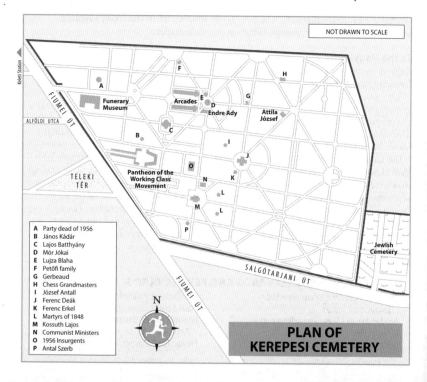

A Party dead of 1956
B János Kádár
C Lajos Batthyány
D Mór Jókai
E Lujza Blaha
F Petőfi family
G Gerbeaud
H Chess Grandmasters
I József Antall
J Ferenc Deák
K Ferenc Erkel
L Martyrs of 1848
M Kossuth Lajos
N Communist Ministers
O 1956 Insurgents
P Antal Szerb

NOT DRAWN TO SCALE

Keleti Station

FIUMEI ÚT

ALFÖLDI UTCA

Funerary Museum

Arcades

Endre Ady

Attila József

Pantheon of the Working Class Movement

TELEKI TÉR

Jewish Cemetery

SALGÓTARJÁNI ÚT

FIUMEI ÚT

N

PLAN OF KEREPESI CEMETERY

relatives since the demise of Communism, and all the old Communist sections are looking distinctly unkempt – in contrast to the area for 1956 insurgents. Party leader János Kádár – who ruled Hungary from 1956 to 1988 – rates a separate grave, heaped with plastic wreaths from admirers.

The florid **nineteenth-century mausoleums** of Hungarian historical giants Kossuth, Batthyány and Deák are quite extraordinary, though no less ostentatious is the mausoleum of József Antall, the first post-Communist prime minister of Hungary, who is honoured by a bizarre allegorical monument with riders on horseback struggling out from under a sheet.

Many of Hungary's **literary greats** also rate spots here, including twentieth-century poets Attila József (see p.53) and Endre Ady, and the writer Antal Szerb (see p.94), who has a very humble grave on the southern edge of the cemetery. Here, too, is the family tomb of Petőfi, though his own body was never found (see box, p.44). Other notables include the composer Erkel, the confectioner Gerbeaud and three chess grandmasters whose tombs are engraved with the chess moves that won them their titles.

Finally, don't miss the Art Nouveau funerary arcades, at the end of which (the novelist Jókai's mausoleums) is the tomb of the diva **Lujza Blaha**, the "Nation's Nightingale", whose effigy is surrounded by statues of serenading figures.

Jewish cemetery

Izraelita temető • VIII, Salgotarjáni út 6 • Mon–Fri & Sun 8am–2pm • Free

Next to Kerepesi lies an overgrown **Jewish cemetery**, with some beautiful Art Nouveau tombs of artists, politicians and industrialists, several designed by the brilliant architect Béla Lajta. That of **Manfred Weiss**, founder of the Csepel ironworks that once dominated the industrial island south of the city centre, is still maintained by Csepel's council, in gratitude and by way of apology for the fact that Weiss had to sign his factory over to the government in return for being allowed to leave Hungary with his family in 1944. The cemetery gates are on Salgótarjáni út, about ten minutes' walk from the main entrance to Kerepesi.

Ferencváros

Ferencváros was developed to house workers in the latter half of the nineteenth century, on the same lines as the more bourgeois Józsefváros. During the 1930s and 1940s, its population confounded Marxist orthodoxy by voting for the extreme right, who returned the favour by supporting the local football team **FTC** – popularly known as **"Fradi"** – which became the unofficial team of the opposition under Communism, subsequently known for its hooligan "ultras" (see p.192 for more on football).

Corvinus University

Budapesti Corvinus Egyetem • VIII, Fővám tér 8 • Trams #2, #47 and #49

Standing at the Pest end of Szabadság híd, the **Corvinus University of Budapest** makes a fine sight from Buda at night, reflected in the river, and adds to the liveliness of the area by day. The building was originally Budapest's main **Customs House** (Fővámház) – hence the name of the square and the adjoining section of the Kiskörút, **Vámház körút**. The university was named after Karl Marx during Communist times and is still sometimes called the Economics University.

Great Market Hall

Nagycsarnok • VIII, Fővám tér 1–3 • Mon 6am–5pm, Tues–Fri 6am–6pm, Sat 6am–3pm

The magnificent wrought-iron **Great Market Hall** was originally opened in 1897, though badly damaged in World War II and only properly restored in the late 1990s. Today, it's as famous for its ambience as for its produce, and ranks highly on many

5

tourists' list of things to see in Budapest. Downstairs, you'll find fresh fish, meat, fruit, vegetables and baked goodies, while the stalls along the right side are known to locals as "tourist row", thanks to the plethora of vendors selling paprika, Tokaj, foie gras and the like – you'll probably get better value elsewhere. Upstairs you'll find cheap stand-up food stalls and an excellent restaurant.

Around Üllői út

Extending for some 15km, which makes it Budapest's longest avenue, grey, polluted **Üllői út** isn't an obvious place to linger, but there's much to see within a few blocks' radius of the **Corvin negyed** metro station.

The Museum of Applied Arts

Iparművészeti Múzeum • IX, Üllői út 33–37• Tues–Sun 10am–6pm • Permanent collection 2000Ft • ☎ 1 456 5107, ⓦ imm.hu

The **Museum of Applied Arts** is the most flamboyant creation of Ödön Lechner, who strove to create a uniquely Hungarian form of architecture emphasizing the Magyars' Ugric roots, but was also influenced by Art Nouveau. Inaugurated by Emperor Franz Josef during the 1896 Millennial celebrations, it was given a rough reception, derided by some as "the palace of the Gypsy kings", thanks to its green-and-yellow-tiled dome, and a portico with ceramic Turkic motifs on an egg-yolk-coloured background. By contrast, the arcaded, all-white interior, with its glazed roof and elegantly arching girders, is reminiscent of Mogul architecture: at one time it was thought that the Magyars came from India.

Entitled **Collections and Treasures**, the permanent collection on the first floor is undoubtedly illuminating, but does take some getting through, with exhibits ranging from delicately carved eleventh-century ivory and medieval goldsmith works, to Hungarian folk ceramics and French furniture, though nothing comes close to the gilt copper and silver astronomical clock, commissioned by Emperor Maximilian II in 1566.

Better still is the **Islamic Art** exhibition; Ottoman-era carpets, exquisitely embroidered *dolmányok* (undercoats) and silk taffetas from Iran take their place alongside bejewelled gala saddles and ceremonial weapons, the latter items acquired mainly by way of trade with the Ottoman Turks – look out, too, for the beautifully painted wooden door panels from Syria. Temporary shows are also held on the ground floor.

Corvin köz

On the northeast corner of the Corvin negyed junction, duck into **Corvin köz**, the grand oval passage separating the **Corvin Cinema** from the surrounding flats, from which teenage guerrillas (some as young as 12) sallied forth to battle Soviet tanks in 1956. Since the fall of Communism, they have been honoured by a statue of a young insurgent outside the cinema. Its auditoriums are named after illustrious Hungarian actors or directors such as Alexander Korda – one of many Magyars who made it in Hollywood (see p.183).

Having renovated Corvin köz, developers have upped the stakes with the **Corvin Promenade** (Corvin sétány) – a mall and luxury apartment complex carving a path through the old blocks between Üllői út and Práter utca. Just around the corner from Corvin köz, you'll find a delightful statue of the **Paul Street Boys** – the heroes of Ferenc Molnár's eponymous 1906 novel – portraying the moment they are caught playing marbles in the yard of their enemies, the Redshirts. The most widely sold and translated Hungarian book ever, it's both a universal tale of childhood and a satire on extreme nationalism.

Kilián Barracks

If you're wondering how locals were able to fight so well in 1956, the answer lies across Üllői út from Corvin köz, where the Hungarian garrison of the **Kilián**

HUNGARIAN NATIONAL MUSEUM (P.78) >

5

Barracks was the first to join the insurgents, organizing youths already aware of street-fighting tactics due to an obligatory diet of films about Soviet partisans. It was in Budapest that the Molotov cocktail proved lethal to T-54s, as the "Corvin Boys" trapped columns in the backstreets by firebombing the front and rear tanks. Memorial plaques honour Colonel Pál Maleter and others who directed fighting from the Corvin Cinema.

The Holocaust Memorial Centre

Holokauszt Emlékközpont • IX, Páva utca 39 • Tues–Sun 10am–6pm • 1400Ft • ☎ 1 455 3333, ⓦ hdke.hu

One block past the Kilián Barracks, a right turn into Páva utca brings you to the **Holocaust Memorial Centre**, more chilling than the House of Terror (see p.60); think twice about bringing children here. Like Libeskind's Jewish Holocaust Museum in Berlin, the building is distorted and oppressive; darkened ramps resounding to the crunch of jackboots and the shuffle of feet lead to artefacts, newsreels and audiovisual testimonies relating the slide from "deprivation of rights to genocide".

From 1920 onwards, Jews in Budapest were increasingly stripped of their assets by right-wing regimes with the participation of local citizens, and Gypsies forced into work gangs. Under Admiral Horthy (there are some chilling photos of the Hungarian regent with Hitler), the interwar period was a time of increasingly repressive anti-Jewish measures, and the fate of both groups was effectively sealed in March 1944 following the German occupation. The section on pseudo-medical experiments makes for particularly grim reading, while the family stories and newsreel footage of the death camps after liberation are truly harrowing. Visitors emerge from the bowels of hell to find themselves within a glorious and sunlit Art Deco **synagogue**, built by Leopold Baumhorn in the 1920s, which has been restored and incorporated in the memorial centre, itself designed by István Mányi. There's a very pleasant on-site café here, and the bookshop is worth a quick browse too.

On your way back to the main road it's worth a detour on to Liliom utca to see another striking building – an old transformer plant turned into an outstanding contemporary arts centre, **Trafó** (see p.179).

The Natural History Museum

Magyar Természettudományi Múzeum • VIII, Ludovika tér 2 • Daily except Tues 10am–6pm • 1600Ft, 400Ft for dinosaur garden, 2000Ft for temporary displays • ☎ 1 210 1085, ⓦ nhmus.hu

A kilometre further down Üllői út just past the Klinikák metro stop, a left turn up Korányi Sándor utca brings you to the **Hungarian Natural History Museum**. Though slightly out on a limb, it's worth the hike, especially if you have children: the presentation is captivating, with lots of colour, wide-open spaces, interactive displays, explanations in English and, for the weary, benches made from huge tree trunks.

From the entrance hall, dominated by a whale skeleton, you walk through to a fantastic **underwater room**, which has colourful fish in sea- and freshwater aquariums – the mock seabed under the glass floor makes you feel as if you're walking on water. Upstairs are displays on animals and their Hungarian habitats, an Africa exhibition and a Noah's Ark that focuses on animals under threat and what Hungary is doing for the environment.

Botanical Garden

Fűvészkert • VIII, Illés utca 25 • Daily: April–Oct 9am–5pm; Nov–March 9am–4pm • 850Ft • ☎ 1 210 1074, ⓦ fuveszkert.org

Across the road from the Natural History Museum is a small **Botanical Garden**, established by the Eötvös Loránd University's faculty of medicine as long ago as 1771, before moving to its present site in 1847. Delightfully jungle-like, its main features are greenhouses, a pleasantly landscaped Japanese garden with ponds and streams, and a magnificent Palm House.

The Ferencváros riverbank

5

Taking the #2 tram down from the Corvinus University, you pass a striking development, locally known as **The Whale**, two old warehouses united by a huge waving glass roof to form a major retail and cultural centre; however, the project remains only partially complete owing to a fall-out between the developer and the City Hall. To the south of Petőfi híd, the bank is lined with hip office and flat developments, all the way down to two of Budapest's most important arts complexes near the Rákóczi híd.

The National Theatre

Nemzeti Szinház • IX, Bajor Gizi park • Ⓦ nemzetiszinhaz.hu • Tram #2 to Vágóhíd utca, or take the Csepel HÉV from Boráros tér one stop

Like something resembling a Ceauşescu folly, the **National Theatre** could have been plucked straight out of Bucharest, its exterior and environs strewn with random architectural references and statuary. The Classical facade is a replica of the frontage of the original theatre on Blaha Lujza tér, torn down to build the metro in 1964 – a Communist plot to undermine Hungary's identity, many said – which condemned the company to a dump in the backstreets of Pest while the debate continued as to where this national institution should be housed. A proposed move to Erzsébet tér never materialised and the theatre moved here in 2002.

Palace of Arts and Ludwig Museum

Művészetek Palotája • IX, Komor Marcell utca 1 • **Palace of Arts** Ⓣ 1 555 3001, Ⓦ mupa.hu • **Ludwig Museum** Kortárs Művészti Múzeum • Tues–Sun 10am–6pm, temporary exhibitions open till 8pm • 800Ft for permanent collection, 1300–2000Ft for temporary exhibitions • Ⓣ 1 555 3444, Ⓦ ludwigmuseum.hu

Across the way is the **Palace of Arts**, a vast edifice that is the home of the excellent Philharmonic Orchestra. Resembling a dull office block by day, it comes alive each evening with spectacular lighting and events – from classical and operatic works to popular and world music, jazz and dance. No expense has been spared to make this a top venue; particularly in the main Béla Bartók concert hall, whose acoustics are so sharp that some orchestras are said to dislike it, as you can hear their mistakes.

   The Palace also encompasses the **Ludwig Museum** or Museum of Contemporary Art, established in 1996 to build upon an earlier bequest by the German industrialist Peter Ludwig, prints and portraits of whom hang by the entrance to the main exhibition hall. There are some big-hitters on display here, notably **US Pop Artists** Warhol (*Single Elvis*) and Lichtenstein (*Vicki*), a trio of paintings by **Picasso**, including *Musketeer with a Sword* and *Matador*, and **Yoko Ono**'s glass-encased, pristine-white chess set entitled *Play it by Trust* – the artist's metaphor for the futility of war.

   Native and central/eastern European artists are well represented too, typically in such styles as Hyper-Realism and neo-Primitivism. Look out, too, for the occasional piece by **Judit Reigl**, perhaps Hungary's most famous contemporary artist, best known for her visceral surrealist/abstract works of art. The museum also hosts first class **temporary exhibitions** – so the permanent collection is not always on view.

MÁTYÁS CHURCH

The Vár and central Buda

The Vár (or Várhegy – Castle Hill) is Buda's most prominent feature. A 1500m-long plateau encrusted with bastions, mansions and a huge palace, it dominates both the Víziváros below and Pest, over the river, making this stretch of the river one of the grandest, loveliest urban waterfronts in Europe. Often referred to as the Várnegyed (Castle District), the hill is studded with interesting museums, from the National Gallery and the Budapest History Museum in the Royal Palace to the Golden Eagle Pharmacy and the Telephone Museum, but it's equally enjoyable just walking the streets and admiring such florid creations as the Mátyás Church and the Fishermen's Bastion, or exploring the World War II Hospital in the Rock and the surrounding nuclear bunkers and labyrinth of caves that lie beneath the hill.

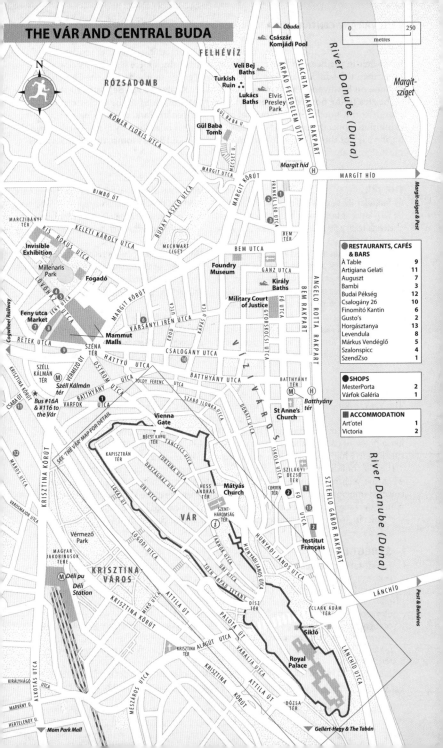

THE VÁR AND CENTRAL BUDA

0   250
metres

Óbuda

Császár Komjádi Pool

FELHÉVÍZ

River Danube (Duna)

Margit-sziget

Veli Bej Baths

Turkish Ruin

RÓZSADOMB

Lukács Baths

Elvis Presley Park

RÖMER FLORIS UTCA

Gül Baba Tomb

GÜL BABA U.

BÉCSI U.

MARGIT UTCA

Margit híd

MARGIT HÍD

Margit-sziget & Pest

BIMBÓ ÚT

BUDAY LÁSZLÓ UTCA

MARGIT KÖRÚT

FRANKEL LEÓ UTCA

SLACHTA MARGIT RAKPART

ÁRPÁD FEJEDELEM ÚTJA

1

BEM TÉR

3

MARCZIBÁNYI TÉR

KIS RÓKUS UTCA

KELETI KÁROLY UTCA

MECHWART LIGET

BEM UTCA

Invisible Exhibition

Millenáris Park

Fogadó

GANZ UTCA

Foundry Museum

Király Baths

Military Court of Justice

ANGELO ROTTA RAKPART

LÖVŐHÁZ UTCA

4
5

MARGIT KÖRÚT

FENY UTCA

VÁRSÁNYI IRÉN UTCA

6

FŐ UTCA

BEM RAKPART

Feny utca Market

7   8

ÉRÓD UTCA

KAPÁS UTCA

GYORSKOCSI UTCA

VÍZIVÁROS

Cogwheel Railway

RÉTEK UTCA

9

HATTYÚ UTCA

SZÉNA TÉR

CSALOGÁNY UTCA

10

BATTHYÁNY UTCA

BATTHYÁNY TÉR

SZÉLL KÁLMÁN TÉR

Mammut Malls

VÉRMEZŐ ÚT

OSTROM UTCA

Széll Kálmán tér

TOLDY FERENC UTCA

Batthyány tér

St Anne's Church

KRISZTINA KÖRÚT

CSABA ÚT

Bus #16A & #116 to the Vár

BATTHYÁNY UTCA

VÁRFOK

1

SZABO ILONKA UTCA

DONÁTI UTCA

ISKOLA UTCA

11

Vienna Gate

SEE 'THE VÁR' MAP FOR DETAIL

BÉCSI KAPU TÉR

TÁNCSICS UTCA

SZILÁGYI DEZSŐ TÉR

12

KAPISZTRÁN TÉR

FORTUNA UTCA

ORSZÁGHÁZ UTCA

HESS ANDRÁS TÉR

Mátyás Church

CORVIN TÉR

FŐ UTCA

MÁROS UTCA

VÁRMAJOR UTCA

VÁR

ÚRI UTCA

SZENT-HÁROMSÁG TÉR

2

13

ÚRI UTCA

LOVAS ÚT

i

2

Institut Français

Vérmező Park

LOGODI UTCA

TÁRNOK UTCA

ÚRI UTCA

HUNYADI JÁNOS UTCA

TÓTH ÁRPÁD SÉTÁNY

MAGYAR JAKOBINUSOK TERE

Déli pu Déli Station

KRISZTINA VÁROS

MIKÓ UTCA

ATTILA ÚT

DISZ TÉR

CLARK ÁDÁM TÉR

LÁNCHÍD

Pest & Belváros

KRISZTINA KÖRÚT

KRISZTINA TÉR

ALAGÚT UTCA

PALOTA ÚT

VÁRALJA UTCA

ATTILA ÚT

Sikló

River Danube (Duna)

MÉSZÁROS UTCA

KRISZTINA KÖRÚT

Royal Palace

LÁNCHÍD UTCA

KIRÁLYHÁGÓ UTCA

ALKOTÁS UTCA

MARVÁNY U.

HERTELENDY U.

DÓZSA TÉR

Mom Park Mall

Gellért-Hegy & The Tabán

RESTAURANTS, CAFÉS & BARS

À Table	9
Artigiana Gelati	11
Auguszt	7
Bambi	3
Budai Pékség	12
Csalogány 26	10
Finomító Kantin	6
Gusto's	2
Horgásztanya	13
Levendula	8
Márkus Vendéglő	5
Szalonspicc	4
SzendZso	1

SHOPS

MesterPorta	2
Várfok Galéria	1

ACCOMMODATION

Art'otel	1
Victoria	2

6

Between the castle and the river, the **Víziváros** is something of a quiet residential backwater in the heart of Buda, with a distinctive atmosphere but few specific sights other than the Lánchíd and the Sikló funicular at the southern end, the **Church of St Anne** on **Batthyány tér** in the middle, and the **Király and Veli Bej Baths** further up. The area to the **north of the Vár** has a variety of attractions in the backstreets off Margít körút, notably a lively **market** and the **Millenáris Park**, comprising an intriguing exhibition, concert venue and children's indoor and outdoor play areas. Further north, on the edge of the affluent Rózsadomb district, is **Gül Baba's tomb**, one of Budapest's most significant Turkish remnants.

ARRIVAL

THE VÁR

By funicular The simplest and most novel approach to the Vár is to ride up to the palace by the Sikló, a renovated nineteenth-century funicular that runs from Clark Ádám tér by the Lánchíd.

By bus From Pest, the most direct approach is to get bus #16 from Erzsébet tér across the Lánchíd to the lower terminal of the Sikló, or straight up to the Vár. From Széll Kálmán tér (on the red metro line #2) you can take buses #16, #16A or #116 from the raised side of the square, which all run through to Dísz tér.

On foot From Széll Kálmán tér head up Várfók utca or Ostrom utca to the Vienna Gate at the northern end of the Castle District. Walking from Batthyány tér via the steep flights of steps (*lépcső*) off Fő utca involves more effort, but the dramatic stairway up to the Fishermen's Bastion is worth the sweat. There are also stairs leading up from the southern end of the Vérmező on the western side of the hill.

Lift A passenger lift by the Lion Gateway of the Royal Palace provides direct access to and from Dózsa tér, on the western foot of the hill (Mon 6am–7pm, Tues–Sat 6am–9m, Sun 9am–6.30pm; 100Ft).

CENTRAL BUDA

Víziváros The red metro line and bus #16 are the best approach. For **Rózsadomb** trams #4 and #6 skirt the southern edge, running between Pest and Széll Kálmán tér.

The Vár

The Vár's striking location and its strategic utility have long gone hand in hand: Hungarian kings built their palaces here because it was easy to defend, a fact appreciated by the Turks, Habsburgs and other occupiers. The **Royal Palace** serves as a reminder of this past, rising like a house of cards at the southern end of the hill, as proud yet insubstantial as those who ruled there while Hungary's fate was determined by mightier forces.

The hill's buildings have been almost wholly reconstructed from the rubble of 1945, when the Wehrmacht and the Red Army battled over the hill while Buda's inhabitants cowered underground. This was the eighty-sixth time that the Vár had been ravaged and rebuilt over seven centuries, rivalling the devastation caused by the recapture of Buda from the Turks in 1686. It was this repeated destruction that caused the melange of styles

---

STREET LIFE

The **streets of the Vár** to the north of the palace still follow their medieval courses, with Gothic arches and stone carvings half-concealed in the courtyards and passages of eighteenth-century Baroque houses, whose facades are embellished with fancy ironwork grilles. For many centuries, residence here was a privilege granted to religious or ethnic groups, each occupying a specific street. This pattern persisted through the 145-year-long Turkish occupation, when Armenians, Circassians and Sephardic Jews established themselves under the relatively tolerant Ottomans. The liberation of Buda by a multinational Christian army under Habsburg command was followed by a pogrom and ordinances restricting the right of residence to Catholics and Germans, which remained in force for nearly a century. Almost every building here displays a stone *műemlék* (listed) **plaque** giving details of its history (in Hungarian), and a surprising number are still homes rather than embassies or boutiques – there are even a couple of schools and corner shops. At dusk, when most of the tourists have left, pensioners walk their dogs and toddlers play in the long shadows of Hungarian history.

characterizing the hill. Adding to the mix, the neo-Gothic **Mátyás Church** and **Fishermen's Bastion** are romantic nineteenth-century evocations of medieval glories, interweaving past and present national fixations. The plain exterior of the Royal Palace, an uninspiring reconstruction of the prewar behemoth that stood here, fails to evoke any such glory. Here, it's what is inside that matters: two major museums, the **Hungarian National Gallery**, and the **Budapest History Museum**, as well as the **National Széchenyi Library**.

Szentháromság tér

The obvious starting point is **Szentháromság tér** (Holy Trinity Square), the historic heart of the district, named after an ornate **Trinity Column** erected in 1713 in thanksgiving for the abatement of a plague; a scene showing people dying from the Black Death appears on the plinth. To the southwest stands the former **Town Hall**, Buda having been a municipality until its unification with Pest and Óbuda in 1873; note the corner statue of Pallas Athene, bearing Buda's coat of arms on her shield.

Mátyás Church

Mátyás templom • I, Szentháromság tér • Mon–Fri 9am–5pm, Sat 9am–1pm, Sun 1–5pm • 1200Ft, audio-guide 800Ft • Tickets from the office across the road by the Fishermen's Bastion • Mass is celebrated daily at 7.30am and 6pm, and on Sun at 10am (in Latin with a full choir), noon and 6pm • ☎ 1 355 5657, ⓦ matyas-templom.hu

Szentháromság tér's most prominent feature is the neo-Gothic **Mátyás Church** with its wildly asymmetrical diamond-patterned roofs and toothy spires. Officially dedicated to Our Lady but popularly named after "Good King Mátyás", the building is a late nineteenth-century recreation by architect Frigyes Schulek, grafted onto those portions of the original thirteenth-century church that survived the siege of 1686. Ravaged yet again in World War II, the church was laboriously restored by a Communist regime keen to show its patriotic credentials, and the transition to democracy in 1989–90 saw the sanctity of this "ancient shrine of the Hungarian people" reaffirmed.

As you enter the church through its twin-spired **Mary Portal**, the richness of the interior is overwhelming. Painted leaves and geometric motifs run up columns and under vaulting, while shafts of light fall through rose windows onto gilded altars and statues with stunning effect. Most of the **frescoes** were executed by Károly Lotz or Bertalan Székely, the foremost historical painters of the nineteenth century. The **coat of arms of King Mátyás** can

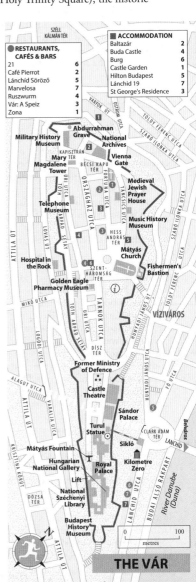

RESTAURANTS, CAFÉS & BARS

21	6
Café Pierrot	2
Lánchíd Söröző	5
Marvelosa	7
Ruszwurm	4
Vár: A Speiz	3
Zona	1

■ ACCOMMODATION

Baltazár	2
Buda Castle	4
Burg	6
Castle Garden	1
Hilton Budapest	5
Lánchíd 19	7
St George's Residence	3

THE VÁR

6

be seen on the wall to your left, just inside; his family name, Corvinus, comes from the raven (*corvus* in Latin) that appeared on his heraldry and on every volume in his famed Corvin Library.

Loreto Chapel

Beneath the south tower is the **Loreto Chapel**, containing a Baroque Madonna, while in the bay beneath the **Béla Tower** you can see two medieval capitals, one carved with monsters fighting a dragon, the other with two bearded figures reading a book. The tower is named after Béla IV, who founded the church, rather than his predecessor in the second chapel along, who shares a **double sarcophagus** with Anne of Chatillon. The tomb, originally located in the old capital, Székesfehérvár, 60km southwest of Budapest, was moved here after its discovery in 1848. Although Hungary's medieval kings were crowned at Székesfehérvár, it was customary to make a prior appearance in Buda – hence the sobriquet, the "Coronation Church".

Treasury

The Mátyás Church has a small collection of **ecclesiastical treasures** and relics, including the right foot of St János. The **crypt**, normally reserved for prayer, contains the red-marble tombstone of a nameless Árpád prince. Otherwise, climb a spiral staircase to the **Royal Oratory** overlooking the stained-glass windows and embossed vaulting of the nave; here votive figures and vestments presage a **replica of the Coronation Regalia**, whose attached exhibition is more informative about the provenance of St Stephen's Crown than that accompanying the originals, on display in Parliament (see p.54).

   Mass is celebrated in the Mátyás Church daily, on Sundays and public holidays. The church is also a superb venue for **concerts** during the festival seasons, and evening organ recitals throughout the year. These are listed on the church website, while tickets are available at the church itself or from any booking agency (see p.179).

Fishermen's Bastion

Halászbástya • 700Ft to go up to the upper level – tickets from the ticket office next door

After the Mátyás Church, the most impressive sight in the Vár is the **Fishermen's Bastion** just beyond. An undulating white rampart of cloisters and stairways intersecting at seven tent-like turrets (symbolizing the Magyar tribes that conquered the Carpathian Basin), it looks as though it was dreamt up by the illusionist artist Escher, but was actually designed by Schulek as a foil to the Mátyás Church. Although Fisherman from the Víziváros reputedly defended this part of the hill during the Middle Ages, the bastion is purely decorative. The **view** of Pest across the river, framed by the bastion, is only surpassed by the vistas from the terrace of Buda Palace, and the Citadella on Gellért-hegy. However, you might balk at paying the fee to climb to the upper level as the free view from the ground level is just as good.

Statue of King Stephen

Between the Fishermen's Bastion and the Mátyás Church, an equestrian **statue of King Stephen** honours the founder of the Hungarian nation, whose conversion to Christianity and coronation with a crown sent by the pope presaged the Magyars' integration into European civilization (see box, p.92). The relief at the back of the plinth depicts Schulek offering a model of the church to Stephen. Like the church and the bastion, his statue is reflected in the copper-glass facade of the **Budapest Hilton**, incorporating chunks of a medieval Dominican church and monastery on the side facing the river, and an eighteenth-century Jesuit college on the other, which bears a copy of the **Mátyás Relief** from Bautzen in Germany that's regarded as the only true likeness of Hungary's Renaissance monarch.

6

KING STEPHEN

If you commit just one figure from Hungarian history to memory, make it **King Stephen**, for it was he who welded the tribal Magyar fiefdoms into a state and won recognition from Christendom. Born Vajk, son of Grand Duke Géza, he emulated his father's policy of trying to convert the pagan Magyars and develop Hungary with the help of foreign preachers, craftsmen and merchants. By marrying Gizella of Bavaria in 996, he was able to use her father's knights to crush a pagan revolt after Géza's death, and subsequently received an apostolic cross and crown from Pope Sylvester II for his coronation on Christmas Day, 1000 AD, when he took the name Stephen (István in Hungarian).

Though noted for his enlightened views (such as the need for tolerance and the desirability of multiracial nations), he could act ruthlessly when necessary. After his only son Imre died in an accident and a pagan seemed likely to inherit, Stephen had the man blinded and poured molten lead into his ears. Naming his successor, he symbolically offered his crown to the Virgin Mary rather than the Holy Roman Emperor or the pope; ever since, she has been considered the Patroness of Hungary. Swiftly canonized after his death in 1038, **St Stephen** became a national talisman, his mummified right hand a holy relic, and his coronation regalia the symbol of statehood. Despite playing down his cult for decades, even the Communists eventually embraced it in a bid for some legitimacy, while nobody in post-Communist Hungary thinks it odd that the symbol of the republic should be the crown and cross of King Stephen.

Ruszwurm patisserie

Along the road from the Mátyás Church the tiny **Ruszwurm patisserie**, at Szentháromság utca 7, has been a pastry shop and café since 1827 and was a gingerbread shop in the Middle Ages. Its Empire-style decor looks much the same as it would have done under Vilmos Ruszwurm, who ran the patisserie for nearly four decades from 1884. Its two small rooms are invariably packed to the gills, but its delectable pastries are most definitely worth sampling (see p.170).

North along Táncsics Mihály utca

In the fifteenth century, when both Ashkenazi and Sephardic Jews lived here, **Táncsics Mihály utca** was known as Zsidó utca (Jewish Street). The Ashkenazi community was established in 1251 in the reign of Béla IV, but was completely wiped out when Buda was captured from the Ottomans in 1686. The Jews, who had fared well under Turkish rule, assisted in the defence of Buda, and those who had not fled or died in the siege were carted away as prisoners by the victorious Christian army. After several name changes, the street was renamed in 1948 after **Mihály Táncsics**, a radical Hungarian politician of the 1848 uprising who was imprisoned here. As it happens, Táncsics, though not Jewish, joined a Jewish platoon of the National Guard in protest against anti-Semitism. On the wall at no. 1, a plaque denotes the former British legation building where **Carl Lutz**, the Swiss vice-consul (see p.51), lived between 1942 and 1945.

Music History Museum

Zenetörténeti Múzeum • I, Táncsics Mihály utca 7 • Tues–Sun 10am–4pm • 600Ft • ☎ 1 214 6770, ⓦ zti.hu

The absorbing **Music History Museum** occupies the Baroque Erdödy Palace where Beethoven was a guest in 1800, and where Bartók once had a workshop before he emigrated. Indeed, an entire room is given over to Bartók's achievements in the form of photos, documents, manuscripts and folk songs he collected on his travels and which informed much of his work. No less fascinating is the assemblage of folk instruments from the eighteenth century onwards, including zithers, violins, a superb hurdy-gurdy, and that most Hungarian of instruments, the hammered dulcimer, or cimbalom, which was popularized in the mid-nineteenth century by Romani musicians.

Medieval Jewish Prayer House

Középkori Zsidó Imaház • I, Táncsics Mihály utca 26 • Wed–Sun: May–Oct 10am–5pm, Nov–April 10am–4pm • 600Ft • ⓦ btm.hu

Evidence of Buda's Jewish past can be found at no. 26, which contains a **Medieval Jewish Prayer House**. Around 1470, King Mátyás allowed the Jews to build a synagogue and appointed a Jewish council led by Jacobus Mendel; part of Mendel's house survives in the entrance to the prayer house. All that remains of its original decor are two Cabbalistic symbols painted on a wall, and though the museum does its best to flesh out the history of the community with maps and prints, all the real treasures are in the Jewish Museum in Pest (see p.64).

6

Bécsi kapu tér and the National Archives

At the end of Táncsics Mihály utca lies **Bécsi kapu tér**, named after the **Vienna Gate** (Bécsi kapu) that was erected on the 250th anniversary of the recapture of Buda. Beside it is the forbidding-looking neo-Romanesque **National Archives** building, distinguished by wildly colourful pyrogranite roof tiles from the Zsolnay factory. The archive holds the most important national historical resources – charters, plans, maps and the like (the oldest document dates from 1109) – as well as records pertaining to some of Hungary's most prominent families, such as the Eszterházys and Széchenyis. The building is not open for general admission, but guided tours are given on Mondays and Thursdays at 10am, 11am and 2pm.

Kapisztrán tér

The next square along is **Kapisztrán tér**, centred on the **Mary Magdalene Tower** (Magdolna-torony), whose accompanying church was wrecked in World War II. In medieval times this was where Hungarian residents worshipped (Germans used the Mátyás Church), so its reconstruction is occasionally mooted by nationalist politicians. Today the tower boasts a peal of ornamental bells that jingle through a medley composed by the jazz pianist György Szabados, including Hungarian folk tunes, Chopin *Études* and the theme from *Bridge over the River Kwai*.

Beyond the tower is a statue of **Friar John Capistranus**, who exhorted the Hungarians to victory at the siege of Belgrade in 1456, a triumph which the pope hailed by ordering church bells to be rung at noon throughout Europe. The statue, showing Capistranus bestriding a dead Turk, is aptly sited outside the Military History Museum.

Tóth Árpád sétány

Running along the western edge of the Vár is **Tóth Árpád sétány**, a promenade lined with cannons and chestnut trees, looking across to the Buda Hills. Just to the east of its northern end, past a giant **flagpole** striped in Hungarian colours, you'll find the symbolic **grave of Abdurrahman**, the last Turkish Pasha of Buda, who died on the walls in 1686 – a "valiant foe", according to the inscription.

The Military History Museum

Hadtörténeti Múzeum • I, Tóth Árpád sétány 40 • Tues–Sun: April–Sept 10am–6pm; Oct–March 10am–4pm • 1400Ft • ☎ 1 325 1600, ⓦ militaria.hu

At the northern end of Tóth Árpád sétány stands the entrance to the **Military History Museum**. Housed in a former barracks, the museum has an exhaustive display on Hungarian military history that starts upstairs with the period 1815–1918, covering the birth of the Honvéd (national army) and the 1848–49 War of Independence. The section covering 1918–48 has some harrowing pictures of two horrendous campaigns, the Italian front in World War I and the Russian front in World War II, and also covers the siege of Budapest at the end of the war and its aftermath – more misery for the Hungarians. Lovers of flags and uniforms will enjoy the display "One Thousand Years of Military Symbols". In the courtyard are post-Communist memorials to the POWs who never returned from the Gulag.

6

ANTAL SZERB

"Best of all I loved the Castle District. I never tired of its ancient streets." So speaks Mihály, the anti-hero of one of Hungary's most popular novels, *Journey by Moonlight* (*Utas és Holdvilág*), by **Antal Szerb** (1901–45). As Mihály recalls his Bohemian past, this enchanting book captures very strongly the Mittel Europa feel of the Vár. Brought up a staunch Catholic in an assimilated Jewish family, Szerb was a highly respected writer in the interwar period, writing histories of Hungarian and world literature and penning a series of short stories and novels that have been brilliantly translated into English (see p.221). Yet he was classified as Jewish in 1942 by the Third Jewish Law, and was shot in Balf, western Hungary on a forced march. Szerb turned down the chance to escape because he and two friends on the march had made a pact that they would either escape or die together. His grave can be found in Kerepesi Cemetery (p.80).

Unfortunately Hungarians like their thinkers to be weighty, and the underlying seriousness of Szerb's books is all too often dismissed on account of their wit and lightness of touch.

Országház utca

Running south from Kapisztrán tér towards Szentháromság tér, there's more to be seen on **Országház utca**, which was the district's main thoroughfare in the Middle Ages and was known as the "street of baths" during Turkish times. Its present name, Parliament Street, recalls the sessions of the Diet held in the 1790s in a former Poor Clares' cloister at no. 28, where the Gestapo imprisoned 350 Hungarians and foreigners in 1945. No. 17, over the road, consists of two medieval houses joined together and has a relief of a croissant on its keystone, from the time when it was a bakery. A few doors down from the old Parliament building, Renaissance graffiti survive on the underside of the bay window of no. 22 and a Gothic trefoil-arched cornice on the house next door, while the one beyond has been rebuilt in its original fifteenth-century form.

Úri utca

Úri utca (Gentleman Street) boasts historic associations, for it was at the former Franciscan monastery at no. 51 that the five Hungarian Jacobins were held before being beheaded on the "Blood Meadow" below the hill in 1795. As you walk down the street from Kapisztrán tér, notice the statues of the four seasons in the first-floor niches at nos. 54–56, Gothic sedilia in the gateway of nos. 48–50, and three arched windows and two diamond-shaped ones from the fourteenth and fifteenth centuries at no. 31. In the wall at no. 27 is a ventilation shaft for the secret hospital below.

Telephone Museum

Telefónia Múzeum • I, Úri utca 49 • Tues–Sun 10am–4pm • 500Ft • ☎ 1 201 8857

At Úri utca 49 is a wing of the Poor Clares' cloister that served as a postwar telephone exchange, before being turned into a **Telephone Museum**. It charts the development of telephone exchanges since their introduction to Budapest in the early 1900s, activating a noisy rotary one that's stood here since the 1930s – a quieter, more streamlined modern exchange still operates here. You're invited to dial up commentaries in English or songs in Hungarian, check out the webcam and internet facilities, and admire the personal phones of Emperor Franz Josef, Admiral Horthy and the Communist leader János Kádár.

The Hospital in the Rock

Sziklakórház • I, Lovas út 4/c – down the steps at the western end of Szentháromság utca and 50m to the right • Tues–Sun 10am–8pm; visits by guided tour only, every hour on the hour • 3600Ft • ☎ 70 701 0101, 🖰 sziklakorhaz.hu

Some six to fourteen metres beneath the Vár's streets lie 10km of galleries formed by hot springs and cellars dug since medieval times. In 1941, a section was converted into a military hospital staffed from the civilian Szent János hospital, which doubled as an air-raid shelter after the Red Army broke through the Attila Line and encircled Budapest in December 1944. In the 1950s, a nuclear bunker was added to the complex and was secretly maintained in readiness until 2000, a time capsule of the Cold War. Ramped throughout for wheelchairs and trolleys, its operating theatres contain 1930s military field X-ray and anaesthetic machines (used in the film *Evita* in 1996) and gory waxworks; bed-sheets in the wards were changed every fortnight until 2000.

The ventilation system is run by generators installed in the **nuclear bunker** built in 1953, with charcoal air-filters, a laboratory for detecting toxins, atropine ampoules to be injected against nerve gas, and an airlock fitted when the bunker was enlarged between 1958 and 1962. To preserve its secrecy, fuel was delivered by trucks pretending to "water" flowerbeds on the surface, via a concealed pipeline.

6

The Golden Eagle Pharmacy Museum

Arany Sas Patikamúzeum • Tárnok utca 18 • Tues–Sun 10.30am–5.30pm • 500Ft ☎ 1 375 3533, ⓦ semmelweis.museum.hu

South from Szentháromság tér towards the palace, the **Golden Eagle Pharmacy** was the first pharmacy in Buda, established after the expulsion of the Turks, and moved to its present site in the eighteenth century. Its original murals and furnishings lend authenticity to dubious nostrums, including the skull of a mummy used to make Mumia powder to treat epilepsy; there's also a reconstruction of an alchemist's laboratory, complete with dried bats and crocodiles, and other obscure exhibits such as the small, long-necked Roman glass vessel for collecting widows' tears. Notice the portrait of the Dominican nun pharmacist – it was common practice for nuns and monks in the Middle Ages to double up as apothecaries. The *Tárnok* coffee house, next door but one, occupies a medieval building with a Renaissance graffiti facade of red and yellow checks and roundels and, like the street, is named after the royal treasurers who once lived here.

Dísz tér

Both Tárnok utca and Úri utca end in **Dísz tér** (Parade Square), whose cobbled expanses are guarded by a mournful Honvéd memorial to the dead of 1848–49. To the south lies the scarred hulk of the old **Ministry of Defence**, to the east of which stands the **National Dance Theatre** (Nemzeti Táncszínház), which was a Carmelite church until the order was dissolved by Josef II; its conversion was supervised by Farkas Kempelen, inventor of a chess-playing automaton. It was here that the first-ever play in Hungarian was staged in 1790, and where Beethoven performed in 1800, as the plaque on the wall denotes. The last building in the row is the **Sándor Palace** (Sándor Palota), formerly the prime minister's residence, where Premier Teleki shot himself in protest at Hungary joining the Nazi invasion of Yugoslavia. It is now the residence of the country's president, a figurehead who is elected by Parliament rather than the electorate.

The Turul statue

Next door to Sándor Palace, the upper terminal of the **Sikló** funicular (see p.101) is separated from the terrace of the Royal Palace by stately railings and the ferocious-looking **Turul statue**– a giant bronze eagle clasping a sword in its talons, which is visible from across the river. In Magyar mythology, the Turul sired the first dynasty of Hungarian kings by raping the grandmother of Prince Árpád, who led the tribes into the Carpathian Basin. The Turul also accompanied their raids on Europe, bearing the sword of Attila the Hun in its talons. During the nineteenth century it became a symbol of Hungarian

---

HIDDEN GEMS: THE VÁR AND CENTRAL BUDA

Veli Bej Baths See p.197	**Pastries at the Ruszwurm Patisserie**
Sikló See p.101	See p.170
Sunset walk along Tóth Árpád	**Mesterporta CD shop** See p.190
sétány on western side of Castle	**Coffee in the Bauhaus foyer of the**
See p.93	**Átrium Theatre** See p.182

identity in the face of Austrian culture, but wound up being co-opted by the Habsburgs, who cast Emperor Franz Josef as a latter-day Árpád for the next millennium. Today, the Turul has been adopted as an emblem by Hungary's right-wing extremists.

From here, you can go through the wrought-iron gates and down some steps to the **terrace** of the palace, commanding a sweeping **view** of Pest and fine head-on views of Margit-Sziget. Beyond the souvenir stalls prances an equestrian **statue of Prince Eugene of Savoy**, who captured Buda from the Ottomans in 1686. The smaller bronze statues nearby represent **Csongor and Tünde**, the lovers in the play of the same name, by Vörösmarty.

The Hungarian National Gallery

Magyar Nemzeti Galéria • Royal Palace wings A, B, C and D • **National Gallery** Tues–Sun 10am–6pm, MNG Extra: 6–10pm first Fri of month • 1400Ft for permanent display (audio-guide 800Ft), 2400Ft for temporary shows, 2000Ft for MNG Extra • ☎ 1 201 9082, ⓦ mng. hu • **Habsburg crypt** Advance notice required - ask at the desk or ring ☎ 06 20 439 7408 • 600Ft

The biggest attraction in the Royal Palace is the **Hungarian National Gallery**, which is devoted to Hungarian art from the Middle Ages to the present. It contains much that's superb, but the vastness of the collection and the confusing layout can be fatiguing. Though all the paintings are labelled in English, other details are scanty. It's therefore worth taking the free guided tour in English (Thurs & Sat 11am). On one Thursday each month, the gallery stays open till 10pm for an evening of themed events, which consists of talks, tours and concerts.

The main entrance is on the eastern side of Wing C, overlooking the river, behind the statue of Eugene of Savoy. You'll need to give a couple of days' notice to see the separate **Habsburg crypt**, containing the tombs of several Habsburgs who ruled as palatines of Hungary until 1849.

Ground Floor

Through the shop to the left of the ticket office, a lovely **wooden ceiling** from a sixteenth-century church and marble reliefs of knightly tombs are the highlights of a **Medieval and Renaissance Lapidarium**. Between the two, doors on the left lead to the fantastic collection of fifteenth-century **Gothic altarpieces** and panels at the rear of Wing

---

A HISTORY OF THE ROYAL PALACE

As befits a former royal residence, the lineage of the **Royal Palace** (Királyi palota) can be traced back to medieval times, the rise and fall of various palaces on the hill reflecting the changing fortunes of the Hungarian state. The first fortifications and dwellings, hastily erected by Béla IV after the Mongol invasion of 1241–42, were replaced by the grander palaces of the Angevin kings, who ruled in more prosperous and stable times. This process of rebuilding reached its zenith in the reign of Mátyás Corvinus (1458–90), whose palace was a Renaissance extravaganza to which artists and scholars from all over Europe were drawn by the blandishments of Queen Beatrice and the prospect of lavish hospitality. The rooms had hot and cold running water, and during celebrations the fountains and gargoyles flowed with wine. After the Turkish occupation and the long siege that ended it, only ruins were left – which the Habsburgs, Hungary's new rulers, levelled to build a palace of their own.

From modest beginnings under Empress Maria Theresa (when there were a mere 203 rooms, which she never saw completed), the palace expanded inexorably throughout the nineteenth century, though no monarch ever dwelt here, only the Habsburg palatine (viceroy). After the collapse of the empire following World War I, Admiral Horthy inhabited the building with all the pomp of monarchy until he was deposed by a German coup in October 1944. The palace was left unoccupied, and it wasn't long before the siege of Buda once again resulted in total devastation. Reconstruction work began in the 1950s – you can see the contrast between the fancier prewar stonework in the Lion Courtyard and the tacky postwar version on the side overlooking the river. The interior also lacks the elegance of the prewar version, being designed to accommodate cultural institutions. However, one benefit of the reconstruction was that it revealed the medieval substrata beneath the rubble, which were incorporated into the new building.

D. Salvaged from churches great and small that escaped destruction by the Turks, some are artful and others rustic, but all are full of character and detail: notice the varied reactions expressed within the *Death of the Virgin* from Kassa (Kosice, a Slovakian centre of altar-painting) and the gloating spectators in the Jánosrét *Passion* in the second room. From the same church comes a *St Nicholas* altar as long as a limo and lurid as a comic strip, whose final scene shows cripples being cured by the saint's corpse. Also strange to modern eyes are *The Expulsion of St Adalbert*, who seems blithely oblivious to the

6

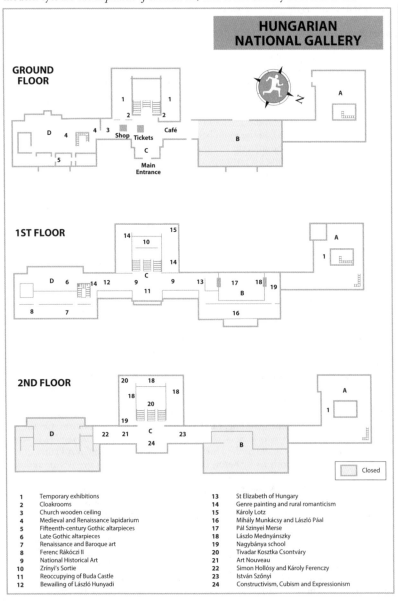

HUNGARIAN NATIONAL GALLERY

GROUND FLOOR

1 1
2 2
D 4 4 3 Shop Tickets Café
5 C
Main Entrance
B
A
N

1ST FLOOR

14 15
10
14
D 6 14 12 9 C 9 13 17 18 19
11 B
8 7 16
A
1

2ND FLOOR

20 18
18 18
18 20
19 C
D 22 21 23
24 B
A
1

Closed

1	Temporary exhibitions	13	St Elizabeth of Hungary
2	Cloakrooms	14	Genre painting and rural romanticism
3	Church wooden ceiling	15	Károly Lotz
4	Medieval and Renaissance lapidarium	16	Mihály Munkácsy and László Páal
5	Fifteenth-century Gothic altarpieces	17	Pál Szinyei Merse
6	Late Gothic altarpieces	18	Lászlo Mednyánszky
7	Renaissance and Baroque art	19	Nagybánya school
8	Ferenc Rákóczi II	20	Tivadar Kosztka Csontváry
9	National Historical Art	21	Art Nouveau
10	Zrínyi's Sortie	22	Simon Hollósy and Károly Ferenczy
11	Reoccupying of Buda Castle	23	István Szőnyi
12	Bewailing of László Hunyadi	24	Constructivism, Cubism and Expressionism

demolition of his church, and the woodcarving of *St Anthony the Hermit*, carrying a hill upon his back. The pointed finials on the high altar from Liptószentmária (Liptovská Mara in Slovakia) anticipate the winged altarpieces of the sixteenth century on the floor above. To get there without returning to the foyer, use the small staircase outside the doors to this section and turn left, left and left again at the top.

First floor

6

The **first floor** covers the widest range of art and is likely to engage you the longest. It picks up where the ground floor left off in the former Throne Room, where **late Gothic altarpieces** with soaring pinnacles and carved surrounds are displayed. Most of them come from churches now in Slovakia or Romania, such as the Annunciation altarpiece from Csíkmenaság (now Armaseni in Romania) or the homely St Anne altarpiece from Kisszeben (Sabinov, Slovakia), which looks like a medieval playgroup. On an altar from Berki (Rokycany, Slovakia), Mary Magdalene is raptured by angels as bishops are impaled, while another piece from Liptószentandrás (Liptovsky Ondrej, Slovakia) shows St Andrew clutching the poles for his crucifixion. Also look out for **The Visitation** by the anonymous "Master MS", in the anteroom, and the coffered **ceiling** from Gogánváralija (Gogan-Varolea, Romania), in the room behind the Kisszeben Annunciation altarpiece.

Many of the works in the adjacent section on **Baroque art** once belonged to Count Miklós Esterházy (including his portrait), or were confiscated from private owners in the 1950s. The prolific Austrian **Anton Maulbertsch**, who executed scores of altars and murals reminiscent of Caravaggio, is represented here by works such as *The Death of St Joseph*. On the back of one panel running across the room, don't miss **Ádám Mányoki**'s portrait of Ferenc Rákóczi II from 1712, a sober study of a national hero that foreshadowed a new artistic genre of **National Historical art** in the nineteenth century.

People coming up the **main stairs** from the ticket office will find, at the rear of the mid-floor landing, two vast canvases by **Peter Krafft**. *Zrínyi's Sortie* depicts the suicidal sally by the defenders of Szigetvár against a Turkish army fifty times their number; not a drop of blood spatters the melee, as Count Zrínyi leads the charge across the bridge. The other shows Franz Josef being crowned King of Hungary in equally slavish detail. Facing you in the large first-floor **atrium** is **Gyula Benczúr**'s *Reoccupying of Buda Castle*, whose portrayal of Eugene of Savoy and Karl of Lotharingia suggests a mere exchange of Turkish rulers for Habsburg ones, while *The Bewailing of László Hunyadi* by **Viktor Madarász** (hung off towards Wing D) would have been read as an allusion to the execution of Hungarian patriots after the War of Independence. At the other end, near Wing B, you'll find **Sándor Lilzen-Mayer**'s *St Elizabeth of Hungary* offering her ermine cape to a ragged mother and child, and two iconic scenes by **Bertalan Székely**: *The Battle of Mohács*, a shattering defeat for the Hungarians in 1526; and *The Women of Eger*, exalting their defiance of the Turks in 1552.

The remainder of the first floor illustrates other trends in nineteenth-century Hungarian art, namely genre painting, **rural romanticism** and Impressionism. On the Buda side of Wing C, *Thunderstorm on the Puszta* and *Horses at the Watering Place* evoke the hazy skies and manly world of the Hungarian "Wild West" – the Great Plain southeast of Budapest. Both are by **Károly Lotz**, better known for his frescoes around the city, such as in the Mátyás Church, Opera House and Parliament. Wing B devotes a section to works by **Mihály Munkácsy** and **László Paál**, exhibited together since both painted landscapes – though Paál did little else, whereas Munkácsy was internationally renowned for pictures with a social message (*The Last Day of a Condemned Man, Tramps of the Night*) and bravura historical works like *The Conquest* (in the Parliament building).

Impressionism was introduced to Hungary by **Pál Szinyei Merse**, whose models and subjects – such as in *A Picnic in May* – were cheerfully bourgeois. Nearby you'll find two luminous landscapes by the prolific **László Mednyánszky** – *Watering-place* and *Fishing on the Tisza* – and paintings from the **Nagybánya school**, an influential artists' colony in what is now Baia Mare in Romania. Look out for peasants discussing *The*

HUNGARY'S GREAT PAINTERS

They were two of Hungary's finest painters, living in the same age, yet the lives they led could not have been more different. While **Mihály Munkácsy** (1844–1900) was fêted for his work and buried like a national hero, his funeral attended by government ministers and his body lying in state in Hősök tere, **Tivadar Kosztka Csontváry** (1853–1919) died alone and unrecognized.

Munkácsy spent much of his life in Paris, but always declared himself Hungarian. He painted large dusty landscapes and pictures of peasants and outlaws as well as grand portrayals of Christ before Pilate. His realist style sold very well, but that financial success was his downfall, and he died of syphilis at the age of 56. Time has not been kind to his work, either: many canvases have suffered from his use of bitumen in mixing paint, which has caused them to darken and crack.

Trained as a pharmacist, Csontváry was 27 when a voice told him: "You will be the world's greatest *plein-air* painter, greater than Raphael." When he began to study painting at the age of 41, he did not belong to any school, and his canvases, simple yet expressive, display an extraordinary use of colour and light. Most of his work was completed in just six years – he painted his last work in 1909, overwhelmed by lack of recognition and schizophrenia. When Picasso saw an exhibition of his works in the 1940s he remarked: "And I thought I was the only great painter of our century."

6

Country's Troubles, by the school's guru, **Simon Hollósy**, who quit during a spiritual crisis; a cheerful *Drying the Laundry*, by his successor **Béla Iványi Grünwald**; and *Boys Throwing Pebbles*, by the school's most adept pupil, **Károly Ferenczy**.

There's more of their work on the next floor, off towards Wing D. Midway up the **stairs** hang three canvases by the visionary **Tivadar Kosztka Csontváry**, whose obsession with the Holy Land and the "path of the sun" inspired scenes such as *Pilgrimage to the Cedars in Lebanon* and the vast *Ruins of the Greek Theatre at Taormina*, with its magical twilight colours.

Second floor

The **second floor** covers **twentieth-century Hungarian art up to 1945**, starting with the vibrant **Art Nouveau** movement off to the right of the atrium. Pictures by **János Vaszary** (Golden Age) and **Aladár Körösfői Kriesch** (founder of the Gödöllő artists' colony – see p.147) are set in richly hand-carved frames, an integral part of their composition. **József Rippl-Rónai** was a pupil of Munkácsy whose portraits such as *Woman in a White-dotted Dress* went mostly unrecognized in his lifetime – they're now regarded as Art Nouveau classics. Here you'll also find Csontváry's magically lit *Coaching in Athens at the Full Moon*, and more works by Hollósy (*Rákóczi March*) and Ferenczy (*Morning Sunshine*).

Across the atrium, **István Szónyi**'s wintry *Burial at Zebegény*, and **József Egry**'s watery *St John the Baptist* have simple lines and muddy colours in common. Both belonged to a generation of artists whose sympathies were on the left in largely right-wing times: Constructivists such as **Béla Uitz**, Cubists **János Kmetty** and **Gyula Derkovits**, the Expressionist **Vilmos Aba-Novák** and the "Hungarian Chagall", **Imre Ámos** (who died in a Nazi death camp – see.p.132) are all represented in Wing C off the stairs.

Third floor

On the **third floor**, **Tamás Lossonczy**'s abstract-surrealistic *Cleansing Storm*, **Béla Kondor**'s whimsical *The Genius of Mechanical Flying* and a wire sculpture by Tibor Vilt portraying the awful fate of the peasant rebel leader Dózsa presage the section on **Hungarian art since 1945**. Exhibits are rotated to showcase the museum's collection of work by modern artists such as Endre Bálint, Attila Szűcs, Sándor Altorjai and Erzsébet Schaár. On fine days, visitors can ascend to the palace's **dome** for a **view** of the city.

The Mátyás Fountain

An archway just before the entrance to the National Gallery leads through a square flanked on three sides by the palace overlooking Buda to the west. Against the wall on the left stands the flamboyant **Mátyás Fountain**, whose bronze figures recall the legend of Szép Ilonka. This beautiful peasant girl met the king while he was hunting incognito, fell in love with him, and died of a broken heart after discovering his identity and realizing the futility of her hopes. The man with a falcon is the king's Italian chronicler, who recorded the story for posterity (it is also enshrined in a poem by Vörösmarty).

The Lion Courtyard

6

Down to the left past the Mátyás Fountain, a gateway guarded by lions leads into the **Lion Courtyard**, totally enclosed by further wings of the palace. To the right of the gateway entrance a passage leading to the passenger lift down to Dózsa György tér is lined with photos that bear witness to the grandeur of the prewar palace.

National Széchenyi Library

Országos Széchenyi Könyvtár • Royal Palace Wing F • Tues–Sat 9am–8pm, closed mid-July to late Aug • Reading room day-pass 1200Ft; passport or identity card required to apply • ☎ 1 224 3700, ⓦ oszk.hu

On the right-hand side of the Lion Courtyard is the **National Széchenyi Library** occupying the palace's nineteenth-century Ybl block, whose full size is only apparent from the far side of the hill, where it looms over Dózsa György tér like a mountain. The library was founded in 1802 on the initiative of Count Ferenc Széchenyi, the father of István (see box opposite). A repository for publications in Hungarian and material relating to the country from around the world, by law it receives a copy of every book, newspaper and magazine that is published in Hungary. The library hosts regular exhibitions from its collection of books and newspapers. You can only visit the reading room on guided tours or with a reader's pass. During library hours, one can use the passenger **lift** in the adjacent building by the Lion Gateway – open to all – which provides direct access to and from Dózsa tér, at the foot of the Vár.

Budapest History Museum

Budapest Történeti Múzeum • Royal Palace Wing E • Tues–Sun: March–Oct 10am–6pm; Nov–Feb 10am–4pm • 2000Ft, audio-guide1200Ft • ☎ 1 487 8871, ⓦ btm.hu

On the far side of the Lion Courtyard, the **Budapest History Museum** covers two millennia of history on three floors, and descends into original vaulted, flagstoned halls from the Renaissance and medieval palaces unearthed during excavations. It's worth starting with **prehistory**, to the left on the top floor, to find out about Paleolithic inhabitants of the area. The Avars, the nomadic precursors of the Magyars who overran the Pannonian Plain after the Romans left, are represented by some impressive items retrieved from their burial mounds, such as a gold bridle and stirrup fastenings in a zoomorphic style. Owing to the ravages inflicted by the Mongols and the Turks, there's little to show from the time of the Conquest on the first floor, and only a few artefacts from Hungary's medieval civilization (there is more in the medieval palace below). From the Turkish period there are some fine pots and metalwork, as well as Jewish gravestones, but most of this floor is occupied by the new display on **Budapest in Modern Times**, an exhibition giving insight into urban planning, fashions, trade and vices, from 1686 onwards. At the far end of the ground floor there is a fine display of **statues** from the late fourteenth century that were discovered in 1974.

The **remains of the medieval palace** are reached from the basement via an eighteenth-century cellar spanning two medieval yards on a lower level. A wing of the ground floor of King Sigismund's palace and the cellars beneath the Corvin Library form an intermediate stratum overlaying the cross-vaulted crypt of the **Royal Chapel** and a **Gothic Hall** where lute **concerts** are held. In another chamber are portions of red marble fireplaces and a massive portal carved with cherubs and flowers from the palace of King Mátyás. Emerging into daylight, bear left and up the stairs to reach yet another imposing hall, with a view over the castle ramparts.

The Sikló

Daily 7.30am–10pm, closed every other Mon • 1100Ft one-way, 1700Ft return; Budapest Card not valid

Between the Royal Palace and the Sándor Palace stands the upper station of the **Sikló**, a nineteenth-century **funicular** that takes you down to the river and the Lánchíd. Constructed on the initiative of Ödön Széchenyi, whose father built the bridge below, it was only the second funicular in the world when it was inaugurated in 1870, and functioned without a hitch until wrecked by a shell in 1945. The wooden carriages, replicas of the originals, are now lifted by an electric winch rather than a steam engine; they're divided into three sections at different heights to give as many people as possible a view (the bottom compartment gives the most unimpeded views). Capacity is limited, however, so in summer you can expect to queue to go up. In the small park at the foot of the Sikló stands **Kilometre Zero**, a zero-shaped monument from where all distances from Budapest are measured.

6

The Víziváros

Inhabited by Fisherman, craftsmen and their families in medieval times, the **Víziváros** ("Watertown"), between the Vár and the Danube, became depopulated during the seventeenth century, and was resettled by Habsburg mercenaries and their camp followers after the Turks were driven out. The following century saw the neighbourhood gradually gentrified, with solid apartment blocks meeting at odd angles on the hillside, reached by alleys which mostly consist of steps rising from the main street, **Fő utca**. Some of these are still lit by gas lamps and look quite Dickensian on misty evenings.

The Széchenyi Lánchíd

The majestic **Lánchíd** (Chain Bridge) has a special place in the history of Budapest and in the hearts of its citizens. As the first permanent link between Buda and Pest (replacing seasonal pontoon bridges and ferries), it was a tremendous spur to the country's economic growth and eventual unification, linking the rural hinterland to European civilization so that Budapest became a commercial centre and transport hub. The bridge symbolized the abolition of feudal privilege, as nobles (hitherto exempt from taxes) were obliged to pay the toll to cross it. It also embodied civic endurance, having been inaugurated only weeks after Hungary lost the 1849 War of Independence, when Austrian troops tried and failed to destroy it.

COUNT SZÉCHENYI

Count István Széchenyi (1791–1860) was the outstanding figure of Hungary's Reform era. As a young aide-de-camp he cut a dash at the Congress of Vienna and did the rounds of stately homes across Europe. While in England, he steeplechased hell-for-leather, but still found time to examine factories and steam trains, providing Bernard Shaw with the inspiration for the "odious Zoltán Karpathy" of *Pygmalion* (and the musical *My Fair Lady*). Back in Hungary, he pondered solutions to his homeland's backwardness and offered a year's income from his estates towards the establishment of a Hungarian Academy. In 1830 he published *Hitel* (Credit), a hard-headed critique of the nation's feudal society.

Though politically conservative, Széchenyi was obsessed with **modernization**. A passionate convert to steam power after riding on the Manchester–Liverpool railway, he invited Britons to Hungary to build rail lines and the Lánchíd. He also imported steamships and dredgers, promoted horsebreeding and silk-making, and initiated the dredging of the River Tisza and the blasting of a road through the Iron Gates of the Danube. Alas, his achievements were rewarded by a melancholy end. The 1848 Revolution and the short-lived triumph of the radical party led by his *bête noire*, Kossuth, triggered a nervous breakdown, and Széchenyi eventually shot himself. Today he is often referred to as "the greatest Hungarian" – though curiously it was Kossuth who originally called him this.

However, in 1945, the Wehrmacht dynamited all of Budapest's bridges in a bid to check the Red Army. Their reconstruction was one of the first tasks of the postwar era, and the reopening of the Lánchíd on the centenary of its inauguration (Nov 21) was heralded as proof that life was returning to normal, even as Hungary was becoming a Communist dictatorship. Today, the bridge is once again adorned with the national coat of arms rather than Soviet symbols. A positive development in recent years has been its closing to traffic for up to ten weekends over the summer for popular festivities.

The idea for a bridge came to **Count István Széchenyi** after he was late for his father's funeral in 1820 because bad weather had made the Danube uncrossable. Turning his idea into reality was to preoccupy him for two decades, and it became the centrepiece of a grand plan to modernize Hungary's communications. Owing to Britain's industrial pre-eminence and Széchenyi's Anglophilia, the bridge was designed by **William Tierney Clark** (who based it on his earlier plan for Hammersmith Bridge in London) and constructed under the supervision of a Scottish engineer, **Adam Clark** (no relation), from components cast in Britain. Besides the technical problems of erecting what was then the longest bridge in Europe (nearly 380m), there was also the attempt by the Austrians to blow it up – which Adam Clark personally thwarted by flooding its chain-lockers. He also dissuaded a Hungarian general from setting it alight in 1849.

Whereas Széchenyi died in an asylum, Clark settled happily in Budapest with his Hungarian wife. After his death, he was buried on the spot that now bears his name, though his remains were subsequently moved to Kerepesi Cemetery. Adam Clark also built the **tunnel** (*alagút*) under the Vár – another Széchenyi project – which Budapestis joked could be used to store the new bridge when it rained.

Szilágyi Dezső tér

Heading north from the Chain Bridge, you come to **Szilágyi Dezső tér**, a square infamous for the events that occurred here in January 1945. When Eichmann and the SS had already fled, the Arrow Cross massacred hundreds of Budapest's Jews and dumped their bodies in the river; an inconspicuous plaque commemorates the victims. From here, you can make a brief detour left up Vám utca, just north of the square, to see the **Iron Block**, a replica of a wooden block into which itinerant apprentices once hammered nails for good luck (the original is in a museum).

Batthyány tér

The main square and social hub of the Víziváros, **Batthyány tér** is named after the nineteenth-century prime minister, Lajos Batthyány, but it started out as Bomba tér (Bomb Square) after an ammunition depot sited here for the defence of the Danube. Today, it's busy with shoppers visiting the supermarket in an old market hall on the western side of the square, and commuters using the underground metro/HÉV interchange. On the southern side of the square is a **statue** of a stern-looking Batthyány standing on a bow of a ship, erected, rather belatedly, in 2008. The sunken two-storey building to the right of the market, meanwhile, used to be the *White Cross Inn*, where Casanova reputedly once stayed. Many of the older buildings in this area are sunken in this way owing to the ground level being raised several feet in the nineteenth century to combat flooding. The views across to the Parliament building from the square are superb.

Church of St Anne

The twin-towered **Church of St Anne** (Szent Anna templom), on the southern corner of Fő utca, is one of the finest Baroque buildings in Budapest. Commissioned by the Jesuits in 1740, it wasn't consecrated until 1805 owing to financial problems, the abolition of the Jesuit order in 1773, and an earthquake. During Communist times there were plans to demolish the building, as it was feared that the metro would undermine its foundations, but these, fortunately, came to nothing. Figures of Faith, Hope and Charity hover above the entrance, and in the middle of the facade St Anne cherishes the child Mary, while

God's eye surmounts the Buda coat of arms on its tympanum. The interior is ornate yet homely, the high altar festooned with statues of St Anne presenting Mary to the Temple in Jerusalem, accompanied by a host of cherubim and angels, while chintzy bouquets and potted trees welcome shoppers dropping in to say their prayers.

Military Court of Justice
Heading up Fő utca from Batthyány tér, on the left stands the hulking Fascist-style **Military Court of Justice** (Fővárosi Katonai Ügyészség), so big that it consumes an entire block. It was here that Imre Nagy and other leaders of the 1956 Uprising were secretly tried and executed in 1958, as indicated by the plaque on the wall facing the park. This square has now been renamed after Nagy, whose body lay in an unmarked grave in the New Public Cemetery for over thirty years (see p.124).

Király Baths
Király gyógyfürdő • II, Fő utca 84 • Daily 9am–9pm • ☎ 1 202 3688, ⓦ kiralyfurdo.hu • See p.196 for more details

Aside from its crumbling, muddy-green facade, you can identify the **Király Baths** by the four copper cupolas, shaped like tortoise shells, poking from its eighteenth-century facade. Together with the Rudas, this is the finest of Budapest's Turkish baths; the octagonal pool, lit by star-shaped apertures in the dome, was built in 1570 for the Buda garrison. The baths' name, meaning "king", comes from that of the König family who owned them in the eighteenth century.

Bem tér
Fő utca terminates at **Bem tér**, named after the Polish general Joseph Bem, who fought for the Hungarians in the War of Independence, and was revered by his men as "Father". A **statue of Bem** with his arm in a sling recalls him leading them into battle at Piski, crying "I shall recapture the bridge or die! Forward Hungarians! If we do not have the bridge we do not have the country." Traditionally a site for demonstrations, it was here that the crowds assembled prior to marching on Parliament at the beginning of the 1956 Uprising. In the northwest corner, at the junction of Frankel Leó utca, stands a Budapest institution, the *Bambi* – one of the few unreformed café-bars that retains its 1970s furnishings and no-nonsense waitresses.

Foundry Museum
Öntödei Múzeum • II, Bem utca 20 • Thurs–Sat 10am–2pm • 800Ft • ☎ 1 201 4370, ⓦ mmkm.hu

A century ago, the neighbourhood surrounding Bem tér was dominated by a foundry established by the Swiss ironworker Abrahám Ganz, which grew into the mighty Ganz Machine Works. The original ironworks only ceased operation in 1964, when it was turned into a **Foundry Museum**, which sits rather incongruously amidst the neighbouring flats and modern high-rises 200m up the hill from Bem tér. You can still see the old wooden structure and the foundry's huge ladles and cranes *in situ*, together with a quite superb collection of cast-iron stoves, tram wheels, lamp posts and other exhibits.

Széll Kálmán tér to Rózsadomb
The area immediately north of the Vár is defined by the scruffy transport hub of **Széll Kálmán tér** (Kálmán Széll Square). A former clay quarry that was turned into tennis courts between the wars, it was named in 1929 after Széll, a former finance and prime minister. Renamed **Moszkva tér** in 1951, it only regained its old name in 2011. To the north, the **Mammut mall** (fronted by a statue of the woolly beast) is a magnet for shoppers, as is the lively Fény utca **market** and the **Millenáris Park**. The park contains the long-standing tourist attraction of Gül Baba's tomb, on the lower slopes of Rózsadomb. Otherwise, Széll Kálmán tér is the place to catch buses to the Cogwheel Railway (see p.119) or the Farkasréti Cemetery (see p.122), as well as tram #4 or #6 to Pest.

Millenáris Park

Millenáris • II, Fény utca 20–22 • Indoor Play Centre daily 10am–6pm • 1590Ft • ☎ 1 336 4000, ⊛ millenaris.hu

The main attraction of the area is the **Millenáris Park**, the site of the former Ganz Machine Works behind the Mammut malls. Set around a small lake, the converted factory buildings and the landscaped park between them host indoor and outdoor concerts and theatre, as well as an interactive playhouse and a **playground** themed around a Hungarian folk tale. The main indoor play centre is in building G, the Fogadó.

6

Invisible Exhibition

Láthatatlan Kiállítás • Daily 10am–8pm • 1700Ft • ☎ 1 20 771 4236, ⊛ lathatatlan.hu

Over in building B, the marvellous **Invisible Exhibition** is one of Budapest's more unconventional attractions. Ostensibly aimed at educational groups, but open to individual visitors too, this was the first of several such centres to be opened (in 2007) throughout central/eastern Europe. Led by a blind or visually-impaired guide, the hour-long tour takes visitors on an interactive journey into darkness, with only touch, smell and sound to guide them. It's an experience that will unquestionably alter your perceptions of what it is to be blind.

Gül Baba's tomb

Gül Baba Türbe • II, Mecset utca 14 • Daily 10am–6pm • Free

The smoggy arc of **Margít körút** underlines the gulf between the polluted inner city and the breeze-freshened heights of Budapest's most affluent neighbourhood, **Rózsadomb** (Rose Hill). The hill is named after the flowers that were reputedly introduced to Hungary by a revered Sufi dervish, Gül Baba, the "Father of the Roses", who participated in the Turkish capture of Buda but died during the thanksgiving service afterwards. **Gül Baba's Tomb** is located through a grubby park and up some steps at the end of Mecset utca (Mosque Street), five minutes' walk uphill from Margít körút via Margít utca. Its octagonal shrine is adorned with Arabic calligraphy and Turkish carpets, and is surrounded by a colonnaded parapet, marble fountains decorated with tiles, and rose bushes.

Rózsadomb

The **Rózsadomb** itself is as much a social category as a neighbourhood: a list of residents would read like a Hungarian *Who's Who*. During the Communist era this included the top Party *funcionárusok*, whose homes featured secret exits that enabled ÁVO chiefs to escape lynching during the Uprising. Nowadays, wealthy film directors and entrepreneurs predominate, and the sloping streets are lined with spacious villas and flashy cars.

The baths

Lukács Baths Lukács Fürdő • II, Frankl Leó út 25–29 • Daily 6am–8pm • ☎ 1 326 1695, ⊛ lukacsbaths.com • **Veli Bej Baths** Veli Bej Fürdő • II, Árpád fejedelem útja 7 • Daily 6am–8pm • ☎ 1 438 8400 • **Császár Komjádi Pool** Császár Komjádi Uszoda • II, Árpád fejedelem útja 8 • Daily 6am–7pm • ☎ 1 212 2750 • See pp.169–197 for more details

Three noteworthy baths dominate the Buda bank of the Danube, north of the Margít híd. First up are the Neoclassical **Lukács Baths**, entered via an atmospheric drinking hall, beyond which lies a large complex of indoor and outdoor pools, whirlpools and the like; the Lukács is also renowned for its popular and raucous bath party nights. A little further up stand the sixteenth-century **Veli Bej Baths**, the oldest and largest of the city's Ottoman spa houses. After a lengthy restoration project, the Veli Bej have been restored to something like their former majesty, featuring a superb central cupola surrounded by four smaller domed pools, in addition to steam chambers, saunas and jacuzzis. Next door is the **Császár Komjádi Pool**, the venue for the first European swimming and water polo championships in 1926, and which today is still a training pool for Hungary's world-class water polo players.

LIBERATION MONUMENT, GELLÉRT-HEGY

Gellért-hegy and the Tabán

Gellért-hegy, a craggy dolomite hill rearing 130m above the embankment, is one area you'd be foolish to miss: it offers a fabulous view of the city from its imposing Citadella, and is as much a feature of Budapest's waterfront panorama as the Vár and the Parliament building. At its foot are two baths, the best known being the Gellért, with its Art Nouveau thermal baths and summer terrace, attached to the stately old hotel. North of Gellért-hegy is the Rudas, one of Budapest's most historic and magical Turkish baths. The second of these baths lies in the Tabán, Buda's former artisan quarter, though now with more roads than buildings; on its northern edge, however, you'll find the enlightening Semmelweis Medical Museum, as well as the Várkert Kioszk and Bazár.

ARRIVAL

Public transport to the district is plentiful: the new metro line #4 has stations at Gellért tér and Móricz Zsigmond körtér, while bus #7 and trams #47 and #49 from Pest serve these destinations too; tram #18 from Széll Kálmán tér and tram #19 from Batthyány tér via the Tabán serve the same points.

Gellért-hegy

Surmounted by the Liberation Monument and the Citadella, **Gellért-hegy** makes a distinctive contribution to Budapest's skyline. The hill is named after the Italian missionary Ghirardus (Gellért in Hungarian), who converted pagan Magyars to Christianity at the behest of King Stephen. After his royal protector's demise, vengeful heathens strapped Gellért to a barrow and toppled him off the cliff, where a larger-than-life **statue of St Gellért** now stands astride an artificial waterfall facing the Erzsébet híd, his crucifix raised as if in admonition to motorists.

The Gellért Hotel and Baths

Gellért Gyógyfürdő XI, Kelenhegyi út 4 • Daily 6am–8pm • ☎ 1 466 6166, ⟲ gellertbath.com • For more details, see p.196

At the foot of the hill, the graceful wrought-iron **Szabadság híd** (Liberty Bridge) links the inner boulevard of Pest to Szent Gellért tér on the Buda side, dominated by the Art Nouveau **Gellért Hotel**. Opened in 1918, it was commandeered as a staff headquarters by the Reds, the Romanian army, and finally by Admiral Horthy, following his triumphal entry into "sinful Budapest" in 1920 – in his eyes it was a decadent, Communist and, above all, a Jewish city. During the 1930s and 1940s, the hotel's balls were the highlight of Budapest's social calendar, when debutantes danced on a glass floor laid over its pool. The ostentatious domed **drinking fountain** in front of the hotel has been the source of some controversy: symbolizing the eight springs of Budapest, it was erected without planning permission, and the city authorities toyed with the idea of pulling it down before relenting.

The attached **Gellért Baths** (entered from Kelenhegyi út to the right of the main entrance, though hotel guests can go down in the lift in their bathrobes) are magnificently appointed with majolica tiles and mosaics, and a columned, Roman-style **thermal pool**, with lion-headed spouts. In the summer, visitors can also use the **outdoor pools**, including one with a wave machine, on the terraces behind the main baths.

The Cave Church (Pauline Welcome Centre)

Sziklatemplom (Pálos Fogadóközpont) • I, Szent Gellért rakpart 1 • Mon–Sat 9.30am–7.30pm but closed during 5pm service • 500Ft, which includes an audio guide • Service daily 8.30am, 5pm & 8pm and also Sun 11am

On the hillside opposite the *Gellért Hotel*, next to a **statue of St Stephen** with his horse, you'll find the **Cave Church**, where masses are conducted by white-robed monks of the Pauline order, the only religious order indigenous to Hungary. Founded in 1256, its monks served as confessors to the Hungarian kings until Josef II dissolved the order in 1773, though it was re-established 150 years later. The church itself was created in the 1930s to mark the return of the monks to Hungary, and functioned until the whole community was arrested by the ÁVO at midnight mass on Easter Monday, 1951, whereupon the chapel was sealed up until 1989.

Inside, a higgledy-piggledy warren of narrow corridors and small chambers eventually brings you to the nave, the most striking aspect of which is the **tiled altar** from the Zsolnay factory. To the rear of the nave, the tiny Polish Chapel is where Polish refugees sought sanctuary during World War II, while a relief commemorates Saint Maximilian Kolbe, who died at Auschwitz. Flickering candles and mournful organ music create a particularly eerie atmosphere during services.

The hillside behind, which still bears fig trees planted by the Turks, was covered in vineyards until a phylloxera epidemic struck in the nineteenth century; kids will enjoy the long tubular **slides** on the hotel-facing slopes.

The Liberation Monument and Citadella

Felszabadulási emlékmű • Bus #27 from Móricz Zsigmond körtér to the Busuló Juhász stop, followed by a 10min walk, or 20min walk up from the *Gellért Hotel* past the Cave Church

Whether you walk up or get there by bus, the **summit** of Gellért-hegy affords a stunning **panoramic view**, drawing one's eye slowly along the curving river, past bridges and monumental landmarks, and then on to the Buda Hills and Pest's suburbs, merging hazily with the distant plain. The best time to enjoy the view is early morning.

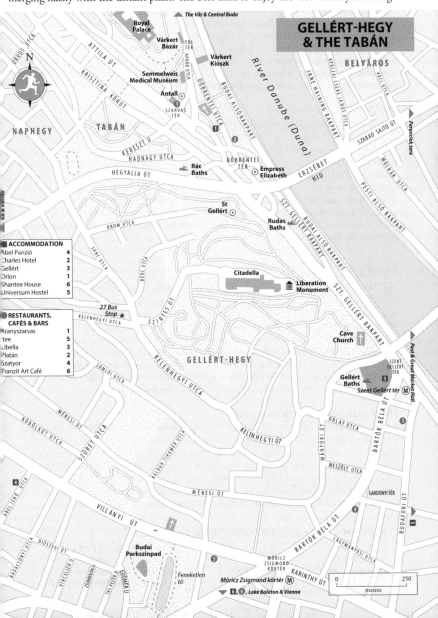

On the summit stands the **Liberation Monument**, a female figure brandishing the palm of victory over 30m aloft. There is a famous tale that the monument was originally commissioned by Admiral Horthy in memory of his son István (who was killed in a plane crash on the Eastern Front in 1942), and that, by substituting a palm branch for the propeller it was meant to hold and placing a statue of a Red Army soldier at the base, the monument was deftly recycled to commemorate the Soviet soldiers who died liberating Budapest from the Nazis. While the story may not be true, the monument's sculptor, **Zsigmond Kisfaludi-Strobl**, certainly succeeded in winning approval as a "Proletarian Artist", despite having previously specialized in busts of the aristocracy – and was henceforth known by his compatriots as "Kisfaludi-Strébel" (*strébel* meaning "to climb" or "step from side to side"). The monument survived calls for its removal following the end of Communism, but its inscription was rewritten to honour those who died for "Hungary's prosperity", and the Soviet soldier was banished to the Memento Park on the outskirts of Budapest (p.124).

7

The Citadella

The **Citadella** behind the monument was built by the Habsburgs to dominate the city in the aftermath of the 1848–49 Revolution; ironically, both its architects were Hungarians. When the historic Compromise was reached in 1867, citizens breached the walls to affirm that it no longer posed a threat to them – though in fact an SS regiment did later hole up in the citadel during World War II. Today it has been usurped by a private company, which charges visitors to set foot inside the walls (daily 9am–6pm; 1200Ft) and view an outdoor exhibition on the hill's history since the Celtic Eravisci lived here two thousand years ago; the recreation of a **Nazi bunker** in a concrete cellar is pretty dull – more interesting is the photo display on wartime Budapest.

The Tabán

The **Tabán** district, bordering the northern end of Gellért-hegy, chiefly consists of arterial roads built in Communist times on land left vacant by the prewar demolition of a quarter renowned for its drinking dens and open sewers. Traditionally this was inhabited by Serbs (Rác in Hungarian), who settled here en masse after the Turks were expelled, though in a typically Balkan paradox, some were present earlier, working in the Ottoman gunpowder factories which may have been the origin of the name Tabán (from *tabahane*, the Turkish for "armoury"). Thankfully, the slum-clearance and motorway building spared Tabán's historic Turkish baths, and its traditions of lusty nightlife are kept alive by summertime concerts in the park.

The Rudas Baths and drinking hall

Rudas Gyógyfürdő • I, Döbrentei tér 9 • Daily 6am–8pm, plus Fri & Sat night swimming 10pm–4am • ☎ 1 356 1010, ⊛ rudasfurdo.hu • See p.197 for more details; Rudas Ivócsarnok (drinking hall) • Mon, Wed & Fri 11am–6pm, Tues & Thurs 7am–2pm

The relaxing and curative effects of Buda's **mineral springs** have been appreciated for two thousand years, though it was the Turks who consolidated the habit of bathing and built proper bathhouses which function to this day. The **Rudas Baths**, in the shadow of Gellért-hegy, harbour a fantastic octagonal pool constructed in 1556 on the orders of Pasha Sokoli Mustapha. Bathers wallow amid shafts of light

---

HIDDEN GEMS: GELLÉRT-HEGY AND THE TABÁN

Cave Church See p.106	**Wallow in the Rudas Baths** See p.108
Várkert Bazar See p.110	**View from the Citadella** See p.107
Lounge in the 1930s Tranzit Art Café See p.170	**Semmelweis Medical Museum** See p.109
	Folk music at the Fonó See p.182

pouring in from the star-shaped apertures in the domed ceiling, surrounded by stone pillars with iron tie-beams and a nest of smaller pools for parboiling oneself or cooling down.

A short walk north of the Rudas Baths, by the grubby underpass beneath the road leading to the bridge, the **Drinking Hall** sells inexpensive mineral water from three nearby springs by the tumbler. Regular imbibers bring bottles or jerrycans to fill.

Statue of Empress Elizabeth

In the island of grass amid the swirl of roads leading to the Buda end of the bridge is a seated **statue of Empress Elizabeth** (1837–98), after whom the Erzsébet híd (Elizabeth Bridge) is named. The Austrian empress – she was also the Queen of Hungary – endeared herself to Hungarians by learning their language and refusing to be stifled by her crusty husband, Franz Josef. For more on the empress, see box, p.146.

The Rác Baths

Retaining an octagonal stone pool from Turkish times, the **Rác Baths** (Rác Gyógyfürdő) are tucked away beneath Hegyalja út, which leads uphill away from the bridgehead of the Erzsébet híd. At the time of writing, however, the baths remained closed pending redevelopment, though this has been going on for years. A cuboid **memorial stone** outside commemorates the 51st Esperanto Congress held in Budapest in 1966 – an event that would have been inconceivable in Stalin's day, when Esperanto was forbidden for conflicting with his thesis that the time for an international language had yet to come.

7

The Semmelweis Medical Museum

Semmelweis Orvostörténeti Múzeum • I, Apród utca 1–3 • Tues–Sun: mid-March to Oct 10.30am–6pm; Nov to mid-March 10.30am–4pm • 700Ft • ☎ 1 375 3533, Ⓦ semmelweis.museum.hu

Often overlooked by tourists, the **Semmelweis Medical Museum** contains a fascinating collection of artefacts relating to the history of medicine, with mummified limbs from ancient Egypt, and a shrunken head used by Borneo witchdoctors giving it an international dimension. Other exhibits – including a medieval chastity belt, trepanning drills, and a range of brutal-looking medical implements – bone saw, bullet extractor, dissection set – don't bear thinking about, frankly.

The museum is named after the eponymous nineteenth-century doctor who lived here until the age of five and is buried in the garden. Semmelweis helped save generations of women thanks to his work on puerperal fever (see box, p.110). Along with the many family portraits on display, there's one of Vilma Hugonai, Hungary's first woman doctor, and another of Kossuth's sister, Zsuzsanna, who founded the army medical corps during the War of Independence.

In the neighbouring room, the **Holy Ghost Pharmacy**, with its gorgeous, Baroque wood-carved fixtures and fittings, dates from 1786 and was transplanted here from Király utca.

Szarvas tér

Just around the corner from the Semmelweis Medical Museum is **Szarvas tér** (Stag Square), named after the eighteenth-century *Stag House* inn at no. 1, which today functions as the fabulous *Aranyszarvas* restaurant (see p.165). In between the museum and the restaurant stands a bust of **Dr József Antall** (1931–93), the first democratically elected prime minister of Hungary after the fall of Communism. For many years, while working as the director of the Semmelweis Museum, he had been dreaming of the chance to emerge from the political shadows, and as prime minister he skilfully ran his centre-right coalition to give Hungary a stable start, though his social conservatism was loathed by his opponents. He died in office and is buried in the Kerepesi Cemetery (see p.80).

DR IGNÁC SEMMELWEIS

Dr Ignác Semmelweis (1818–65) discovered the cause of puerperal fever – a form of blood poisoning contracted in childbirth, which was usually fatal. While serving in Vienna's public hospitals in the 1840s, he noticed that deaths were ten times lower on the wards where only midwives worked than on the ones attended by doctors and students, who went from dissecting corpses to delivering babies with only a perfunctory wash. His solution was to sterilize hands, clothes and instruments between operations – an idea dismissed as preposterous by the hospital, which fired him. Embittered, he wrote open letters to obstetricians, accusing them of being murderers, and was sent to an asylum where he died within a couple of weeks. Only after Pasteur's germ theory was accepted was Semmelweis hailed as the "saviour of mothers".

Ybl Miklós tér

Past the museum and by the riverbank on **Ybl Miklós tér** are two buildings designed in 1876 by Miklós Ybl (1814–91), the man behind the Opera House and other major works. To the left of the road stands the grand facade and terraces of the superbly renovated **Várkert Bazár**. Designed as the grand entrance to the Várkert, the park running up to the palace, with shops either side of the steps, the Bazár was never in the right location to attract business and by 1920 was occupied by artists' studios. After suffering damage in the war, it reopened in 1961 as a "youth park" and was one of the few places offering entertainment for the younger generation. Its outdoor pop concerts became legendary, but the crumbling building was forced to close in the 1980s, and numerous plans for redevelopment came to nothing. After years of decay, the Bazár finally reopened in 2014 as a multi-cultural complex incorporating exhibition rooms, restaurants and cafes, and a lush Renaissance garden.

Some insignificant-looking stones in the gardens behind (accessible from Szarvas tér) are actually Turkish gravestones. By the river across the road is the **Várkert Kioszk**, a former pumping station with an ornate interior and Ybl's statue standing in front.

Óbuda and Margít-sziget

Óbuda is the oldest part of Budapest, though that's hardly the impression given by the industrial sites and high-rises that dominate the district today, hiding such ancient ruins as remain. Nonetheless, it was here that the Romans built a legionary camp and a civilian town, later taken over by the Huns. Under the Hungarian Árpád dynasty, this developed into an important town, but in the fifteenth century it was eclipsed by the Vár. The original settlement became known as Óbuda (Old Buda) and was incorporated into the newly formed Budapest in 1873. The small but spruce old town centre is not much visited by tourists, which is a shame as it rates a clutch of very enjoyable museums. But to find the best-preserved Roman ruins, you'll have to go to the Rómaifürdő district, further out.

To the west, there is a pair of striking caves near the valley of Szépvölgy, a visit to which can be combined with the Kiscelli Museum, with its interesting collection of furniture and interior furnishings in a former monastery.

In the middle of the Danube, leafy **Margít-sziget** is a haven from the noise and pollution of the city. One of Budapest's favourite parks and summer pleasure-grounds, the island is part of its grand waterfront panorama – unlike shabby **Óbudai-sziget** just north which, like Cinderella, gets but one chance to have fun, by hosting Hungary's equivalent of Glastonbury, the **Sziget festival**, each August (see p.179).

ARRIVAL

Public transport The HÉV from Batthyány tér (see p.102) provides easy access to riverside Óbuda (get off at Szentlélek tér for Fő tér and the museums), or take #1 tram from northern Pest. For Margít-sziget, trams #4 and #6 stop at the southern entrance to the island, while bus #26 runs the length of the island itself. You can also reach Rómaifürdő and Margít-sziget on one of the ferries that zigzag up the river from Haller utca (see p.24).

Óbuda

After its incorporation within the city, **Óbuda** became a popular place to eat, drink and make merry, with garden restaurants and taverns serving fish and wine from the locality. Some of the most famous establishments still exist around **Fő tér**, the heart of eighteenth-century Óbuda, with its ornate Trinity Column; see p.166 for our pick of Óbuda's eating places.

Vasarely Museum

Vasarely Múzeum • III, Szentlélek tér 6 • Tues–Sun 10am–5.30pm • 800Ft • ☎ 1 378 7551, ⒲ vasarely.hu

The **Vasarely Museum** displays eyeball-throbbing Op Art works by Viktor Vasarely (1906–97), the founder of the genre, who was born in Pécs in southern Hungary, emigrated to Paris in 1930 and spent the rest of his life in France. Arguably, his most productive period was the 1950s and 60s, with his groundbreaking Black and White paintings, many of which are on display here (*Vega* and *Tau-Ceti* to name but two). You can also get a sense of his artistic development from earlier works, particularly as a graphic artist, when he gained numerous commissions from various publishing houses for advertising graphics.

Óbuda Museum

Óbudai Múzeum • III, Szentlélek tér 1 • Tues–Sun 10am–6pm • Entry 800Ft, information booklet 800Ft • ☎ 1 250 1020, ⒲ obudaimuzeum.hu

Round the corner from the Vasarely Museum, the excellent little **Óbuda Museum** charts Óbuda's development through the ages. Particular emphasis is given to the city's growth in the seventeenth century, which was inextricably linked to the Zichy dynasty, whose domain stretched from Óbuda all the way up to Szentendre. In the nineteenth century, as well as the local shipyard and porcelain factory, there were as many as three brickworks here; don't miss the wonderful display of brick stamps. Look out, too, for the twelfth-century Kalosca stone, depicting an angel alongside a bearded man – a fine example of Romanesque art. Reconstructed shops and kitchens – including a pre-electric fridge – from the early twentieth century, as well as a living room from the

---

HIDDEN GEMS: ÓBUDA AND MARGÍT-SZIGET

Varga Museum See p.114
Mosaics at Aquincum See p.115
Cool down at the Palatinus Lido
See p.197
Cycle around Margit-sziget See p.116

Party in Margit-sziget See p.172
Sziget Festival See p.179
Chill out at Fellini Római Kultúrbisztró
See p.176

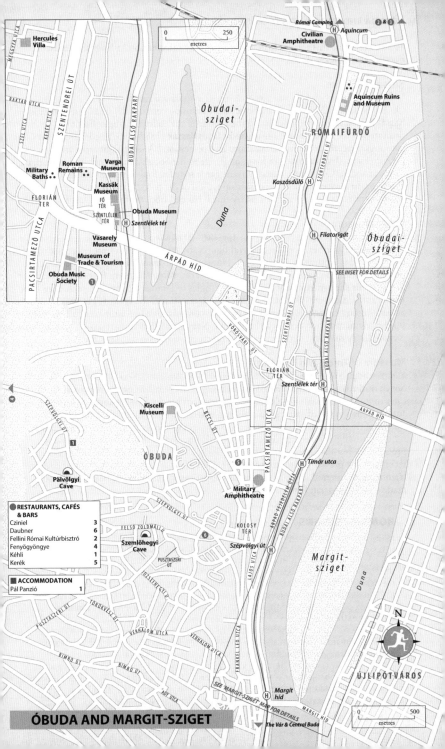

Hercules Villa

MEGYERI ÚT

RAKTÁR UTCA

SZÉL UTCA

KEREK UTCA

SZENTENDREI ÚT

BUDAI ALSÓ RAKPART

0   250
metres

Óbudai-sziget

Military Baths

Roman Remains

Varga Museum

Kassák Museum

FŐ TÉR

FLÓRIÁN TÉR

PACSIRTAMEZŐ UTCA

SZENTLÉLEK TÉR

Obuda Museum

(H) *Szentlélek tér*

Duna

Vasarely Museum

Museum of Trade & Tourism

Obuda Music Society ❶

ÁRPÁD HÍD

Római Camping ▲

❷ & ❸ ▲

(H) *Aquincum*

Civilian Amphitheatre ●

Aquincum Ruins and Museum

RÓMAIFÜRDŐ

SZENTENDREI ÚT

Kaszásdűlő (H)

(H) *Filatorigát*

Óbudai-sziget

SEE INSET FOR DETAILS

VÖRÖSVÁRI ÚT

SZENTENDREI ÚT

BUDAI ALSÓ RAKPART

FLÓRIÁN TÉR

Szentlélek tér (H)

ÁRPÁD HÍD

Kiscelli Museum

BÉCSI ÚT

Óbuda

PACSIRTAMEZŐ UTCA

❺

(H) *Timár utca*

SZÉPVÖLGYI ÚT

❹

❶

Pálvölgyi Cave

SZÉPVÖLGYI ÚT

Military Amphitheatre

ÁRPÁD FEJEDELEM ÚTJA

BUDAI ALSÓ RAKPART

FELSŐ ZÖLDMÁLI Ú.

❻

KOLOSY TÉR

Szépvölgyi út (H)

Margit-sziget

Duna

Szemlőhegyi Cave

PUSZTASZERI ÚT

LAJOS UTCA

RESTAURANTS, CAFÉS & BARS	
Cziniel	3
Daubner	6
Fellini Római Kultúrbisztró	2
Fenyőgyöngye	4
Kéhli	1
Kerék	5

ACCOMMODATION	
Pál Panzió	1

JÓZSEFHEGYI Ú.

TÖRÖKVÉSZ ÚT

PUSZTASZERI ÚT

VERHALOM UTCA

VERHALOM UTCA

BIMBÓ ÚT

BIMBÓ ÚT

FRANKEL LEO ÚT

N

ÚJLIPÓTVÁROS

0   500
metres

SEE MARGIT-SZIGET MAP FOR DETAILS

ÁDY UTCA

Margit híd

MARGIT HÍD

▼ *The Vár & Central Buda*

ÓBUDA AND MARGIT-SZIGET

1950s, complete this terrific little romp. The only information in English is a useful booklet at the ticket desk.

Kassák Museum

Kassák Múzeum · III, Fő tér 1 · Wed–Sun 10am–5pm · 600Ft · ☎ 1 368 7021, ⓦ kassakmuzeum.hu

On Fő tér itself, the run-down Baroque Zichy mansion contains the small but fascinating **Kassák Museum**. Located upstairs on the far side of the courtyard, the collection is dedicated to the Hungarian Constructivist **Lajos Kassák** (1887–1967) and features his paintings, magazine designs, publications and possessions. A self-taught artist and publisher who devoted much of his younger life to the Socialist cause (publishing work by Cocteau and Le Corbusier), Kassák's avant-garde style fell foul of regimes on both the left and right. In a selective form of censorship typical of the post-1956 Communist years, he was recognized as a writer but was pretty much banned from exhibiting his art from 1948.

Varga Museum

Varga Imre Múzeum · III, Laktanya utca 7 · Tues–Sun 10am–6pm · 800Ft · ☎ 1 250 0274

Whatever the weather, you'll see several figures sheltering beneath umbrellas just off Fő tér, life-sized sculptures by Imre Varga, Hungary's best-known living artist (now in his nineties), whose oeuvre is the subject of the nearby **Varga Museum**. Pathos and humour pervades his sheet-metal, iron and bronze effigies of famous personages, including Pope John Paul II, Liszt and Bartók. Varga's career has spanned the eras of "goulash Socialism" and democracy – evinced by state-commissioned monuments to Béla Kun (in the Memento Park, see p.124) and Imre Nagy (near Parliament; p.52). Today, Varga is more likely to paint, and there are several recent works on display here too.

Museum of Trade and Tourism

Magyar Kereskedelmi és Vendéglátóipari Múzeum · III, Korona tér 1 · Tues–Sun 10am–6pm · Free · ☎ 1 375 6249, ⓦ mkvm.hu

South of the bridgehead of the Árpád híd is another remnant of the old town that is even more isolated than Fő tér among the modern blocks. The **Museum of Trade and Tourism** was the world's first such museum when it opened in 1966, and today keeps a wealth of trade- and tourism-related relics, including shopfronts, merchandise and a series of nostalgia-inducing advertising boards promoting drink, food and tobacco products. A reconstructed sweet shop, stationer's and ironmonger's feature, as does a reconstructed prewar bedroom from the *Gellért Hotel* and specialized items of cutlery from the same period, such as asparagus clippers and a 25-bladed pocket knife, both made by a Hungarian firm.

ROMAN REMAINS

Roman soldiers had been in the region since the first century AD, but the larger settlement only came a century later, lasting until the fourth century. While Aquincum was the main civilian centre, the Romans' **military garrison** was to the south, and today its remains lurk in the concrete jungle of Óbuda's centre. On Flórián tér, 500m west of Fő tér, weathered columns rise next to a shopping plaza, while the old **military baths** (*thermae maiores*) are exposed in the pedestrian underpass beneath the Szentendrei út flyover. You'll also find the odd Roman wall protruding between the apartment blocks near Fő tér. The largest ruin is a **military amphitheatre** (*amfiteátrum*) which once seated up to 13,000 spectators, at the junction of Pacsirtamező utca and Nagyszombat utca, 800m further south – accessible by bus #86 or by walking 400m from Kolosy tér, near the Szépvölgyi út HÉV stop. (The remains of a **civilian amphitheatre** are by the Aquincum HÉV stop.)

A more elusive relic is the **Hercules Villa**, Meggyfa utca 19–21, north of Florian tér, which contained the **mosaic floor** of the centaur Nessus abducting Deianeira that can now be seen in the Aquincum Museum. A fragment of another mosaic remains *in situ*, featuring a delightfully rendered tiger and Hercules about to vomit at a wine festival.

Ruins of Aquincum

Aquincumi Múzeum • III, Szentendrei út 139 • Tues–Sun: ruins April–Oct 9am–6pm; museum opens at 10am; museum also open Nov–
March 10am–4pm • 1600Ft • ☎ 1 250 1650, 𝕎 aquincum.hu

North of Óbuda, the riverside factory belt merges into the **Rómaifürdő** (Roman Bath)
district, harbouring a campsite, a lido and the ruins of **Aquincum**. Originally a
settlement of camp followers spawned by the legionary garrison, Aquincum eventually
became a *municipium* and then a *colonia*, the provincial capital of Pannonia Inferior.
The **ruins** are visible from the Aquincum HÉV stop, from where a brief walk south
under the main-line rail bridge brings you to the site itself. Enough of the foundation
walls and underground piping survives to give a fair idea of the town's layout, with its
forum and law courts, its sanctuaries of the goddesses Epona and Fortuna Augusta, and
the *collegia* and bathhouses where fraternal societies met. Its bare bones are given
substance by an excellent **museum** and smaller exhibitions around the site. Its star
exhibit is the superb **mosaic** from the third century AD of Nessus abducting Deianeira,
whom Hercules had to rescue as one of his twelve labours. This originally consisted of
sixty thousand stones, selected and arranged in Alexandria before shipment to Europe.
Other highlights include a mummy preserved in natron, a cult-relief of the god
Mithras and a reconstructed water-organ. The **Floralia Festival** towards the end of May
sees theatrical performances, craft-making displays, mock gladiator battles and other
events staged here.

The caves

Bus #86 from Flórián tér or Batthyány tér, or bus #6 from Nyugati tér in Pest, from where you catch bus #65 five stops to the Pálvölgyi Cave,
or bus #29 four stops to the Szemlőhegyi Cave

The hills rising to the west of Óbuda feature a network of caves that are unique for
having been formed by thermal waters rising up from below, rather than by rainwater.
Two of the sites have been accessible to the public since the 1980s, with guided tours
only (some English spoken). In both cases, the starting point is **Kolosy tér** in Óbuda. As
the two caves are ten minutes' walk apart, it's possible to see them both within two and
a half hours if you start with the Szemlőhegyi Cave.

Pálvölgyi Stalactite Cave

Pálvölgyi cseppkőbarlang • III, Szépvölgyi út 162 • 45min tours hourly at quarter past the hour, Tues–Sun 10am–4.15pm • 1200Ft • ☎ 1
325 9505, 𝕎 palvolgyi.atw.hu

The **Pálvölgyi Stalactite Cave** is the more spectacular of the two labyrinths; part of the
longest of the cave systems in the Buda Hills, at around 29km, it is still being explored
by speleologists. It was discovered in 1904 by a quarryman searching for a sheep that
disappeared when the floor of the quarry fell in. Tours, on which you negotiate
hundreds of steps and dank constricted passages, start on the lowest level, which boasts
rock formations such as the "Organ Pipes" and "Beehive". From "John's Lookout" in
the largest chamber, you ascend a crevice onto the upper level, there to enter
"Fairyland" and finally "Paradise", overlooking the hellish "Radium Hall" 50m below.

Szemlőhegyi Cave

Szemlőhegyi barlang • III, Pusztaszeri út 35 • 40min tours hourly on the hour daily except Tues 10am–4pm • 1000Ft • ☎ 1 325 6001,
𝕎 szemlohegyi.atw.hu

Quite different from the Pálvölgyi Stalactite Cave is the **Szemlőhegyi Cave**, with less
convoluted and claustrophobic passages and no stalactites. Instead, the walls are
encrusted with cauliflower- or popcorn-textured precipitates. Discovered in 1930, the
cave has exceptionally clean air, and its lowest level is used as a respiratory sanatorium.
After the tour you can view a museum of cave finds and plans from all over Hungary.

For refreshment after the caves you should schedule in a stop at the *Daubner*
patisserie at Szépvölgyi út 29 (near Kolosy tér at the bottom of the hill), which does
some of the most delicious cakes in the city and attracts huge queues at weekends.

8

Alternatively, you can combine a visit to the Szemlőhegyi Cave with the Bartók Memorial House (see p.121) or the Kiscelli Museum.

The Kiscelli Museum

Kiscelli Múzeum • III, Kiscelli utca 108 • Tues–Sun: April–Oct 10am–6pm; Nov–March 10am–4pm • 1000Ft • ☎ 1 250 0304, ⓦ kiscellimuzeum.hu • Bus #165 from Kolosy tér or bus #160 from Batthyány tér

On a hillside above Óbuda, fifteen minutes' walk north of the Szemlőhegyi Cave, the **Kiscelli Museum** occupies a former Trinitarian monastery in a beautiful wooded setting. The museum's wide-ranging collection includes Baroque sculptures, craftsmen's tools, antique printing presses and the 1830 Biedermeier furnishings of the Golden Lion pharmacy, which used to stand on Kálvin tér. The blackened shell of the monastery's Gothic church makes a dramatic backdrop for exhibitions of contemporary art, classical **concerts**, animated film shows and other events.

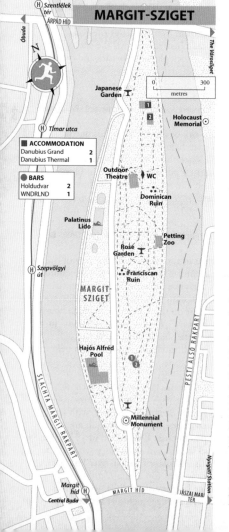

Margít-sziget

Trams #4 and #6 stop at the southern entrance on the Margít híd, and bus #26 runs down the middle of the island to and from the Árpád híd station on the blue metro line #3; Motorists can only approach from the north of the island, via the Árpád híd, at which point they must leave their vehicles at a paying car park. Near both entrances you can rent bikes, pedaloes and electric cars.

There's a saying that "love begins and ends on **Margít-sziget**", for this verdant island has been a favourite meeting place for lovers since the nineteenth century (though before 1945 a stiff admission charge deterred the poor). A royal game reserve under the Árpáds and a monastic colony until the Turkish conquest, today Margít-sziget has two public baths fed by thermal springs, an outdoor theatre and other amenities.

The island was named at the end of the nineteenth century after Princess **Margít** (Margaret), the daughter of Béla IV. Legend has it that he vowed to bring her up as a nun if Hungary survived the Mongol invasion, and duly confined the nine-year-old in a convent when it did. She apparently made the best of it, acquiring a reputation for curing lepers and other saintly deeds, as well as for never washing above her ankles. Beatification came after her death in 1271, and a belated canonization in 1943, by which time her name had already been bestowed on the **Margít híd**, built by a French company in the 1870s. Linking Margít-sziget to Buda and Pest, it's an unusual bridge in the form of a splayed-out V, with a short arm joined to the southern tip of the island. In November 1944, it was blown up by the Nazis, killing hundreds of people including the German sappers who had detonated the explosives by mistake.

The pools

Walking down from the tram stop on Margít híd, you are greeted by a Millennial Monument and a **fountain** that emits bursts of grand music. Further on, behind trees to the left, is the **Hajós Alfréd Pool** (known as the "Sport"; see p.196), named after the winner of the 100m and 1200m swimming races at the 1896 Olympics – hence the first modern Olympic swimming champion. Hajós (1878–1955) was also an architect and designed the indoor pool, but the main attractions here are the all-season outdoor 50m pool, where the national swimming team trains. Another swimming venue, the **Palatinus Strand** (see p.197), lies nearly a kilometre further north. With a monumental entrance from the 1930s, this lido can hold as many as ten thousand people at a time in numerous open-air thermal pools, complete with a water chute, wave machine and segregated terraces for nude sunbathing.

Ruins, zoo and gardens

Turning right off the road that runs northwards up the island before you get to the Palatinus, you'll come to the ruins of a **Franciscan church** from the late thirteenth century and, beyond that, the **petting zoo** (April–Oct daily 10am–6pm; free), where kids can enjoy llamas, peacocks, birds of prey and various waterfowl; pony rides are available too (500Ft). Walking north up the middle of the island takes you through the immaculately manicured **Rose Garden** and on up to the ruined **Dominican church and convent**. Just beyond here, in the shadow of the enormous Art Nouveau **water tower**, which rises some 66 metres, the **Outdoor Theatre** (Szabadtéri Színpad) hosts plays, operas, fashion shows and concerts during summer. The café here makes a convenient stop for a beer and a snack.

8

A short way northeast of the tower is a **Premonstratensian Chapel**, whose Romanesque tower dates back to the twelfth century, when the order first established a monastery on the island. The tower's fifteenth-century bell is one of the oldest in Hungary. Heading towards the northern tip, you can't miss the island's two hotels, the original, late nineteenth-century *Grand* and its ugly twin sister, the *Thermal*. Beside the latter is a pretty **Japanese Garden** with plants donated by the botanical gardens of Hokkaido University, and warm springs that sustain tropical fish and giant water lilies.

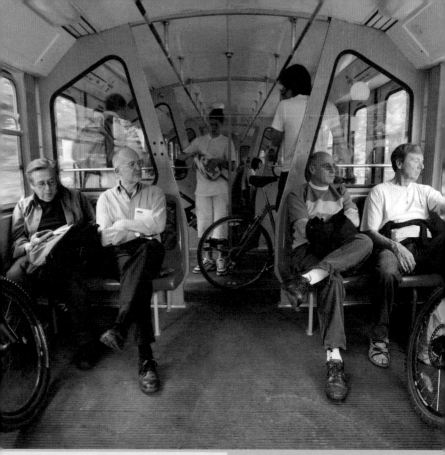

ON BOARD THE COG RAILWAY

The Buda Hills

A densely wooded arc around a sixth of Budapest's circumference, the Buda Hills are as close to nature as you can get within the city limits. The hills are a favourite place for walking in all seasons, with trails marked with the distance or the duration ("ó" stands for hours; "p" for minutes). While some parts can be crowded with walkers and mountain-bikers at the weekend, it's possible to ramble for hours during the week and see hardly a soul. The most rewarding destinations for those with limited time are the "railway circuit", using the Cogwheel and Children's railways and the chairlift, and the Bartók Memorial House. Further south is the Farkasréti Cemetery, noted for its architecture as well as the celebrated personages buried here.

ARRIVAL AND GETTING AROUND

By public transport Széll Kálmán tér is the easiest starting point for all the destinations in the hills, including all points along the railway circuit. The Cogwheel Railway is two stops away on tram #59 or #61 or bus #155 or #156; alight opposite the cylindrical *Budapest Hotel*; bus #155 goes on to the bottom of the Chairlift while tram #61 goes on to Hüvösvölgy. Bus #21 and #21A go up to Normafa; the #21 goes on to Csillebérc.

By bike Exploring the Buda Hills by trail-bike is a more ambitious option, if you've got a day to spare and the stamina. Velo-Touring (XI, Előpatak utca 1 ☏ 1 319 0571, ⓦ velo-touring.hu) rents 21-gear bikes (from €14/day; €100 deposit) and can advise on routes; its office is about 1km from Farkasréti Cemetery. Bikes can be carried on the Cogwheel (validate an extra ticket) and Children's railways (200Ft fee).

The railway circuit

This is an easy and enjoyable way to visit the hills that will especially appeal to kids. The whole trip can take under two hours if connections click, but you're better off taking your time and completing it over the course of a leisurely half-day.

The Cogwheel Railway

Fogaskerekűvasút, also designated tram #60 • Daily 5am–11pm • BKK fares and passes apply

The circuit begins at the lower terminal of the **Cogwheel Railway**, which was the third such railway in the world when it was inaugurated in 1874, and steam-powered until its electrification in 1929. Running every ten minutes or so, its cogs fitting into a notched track, the train climbs 300m over nearly 4km through the villa-suburb of **Svábhegy**; for the best view on the way up, take a window seat on the right-hand side, facing backwards.

The Children's Railway

Gyermekvasút • Tues–Sun June–Aug also Mon, trains go every 45–60min 9am–5pm • 600Ft to any mid-station, 700Ft from terminus to terminus • ⓦ gyermekvasut.hu

From the upper terminal on **Széchenyi-hegy**, it's a minute's walk to the **Children's Railway**. A narrow-gauge line built by Communist youth brigades in 1948, it's almost entirely run by 13- to 17-year-old members of the Scouts and Guides movement, enabling them to get hands-on experience if they fancy a career with MÁV, the Hungarian Railways company. Watching them wave flags, collect tickets and salute departures with great solemnity, you can see why it appealed to the Communists. The forty-minute ride along the full 11km length of the line is a delightful run through the wooded hills. In summer, they sometimes run heritage trains, pulled by a steam engine or vintage diesel loco, for which a 200Ft supplement is charged.

Normafa

The first stop along the Children's Railway route, **Normafa**, is a popular excursion centre with a modest **ski-run** and sledging slopes. Its name comes from a performance of the famous aria from Bellini's *Norma* given here by the actress Rozália Klein in 1840. A popular destination at the top of the slope is the *Rétes Büfé* (see p.170), a wooden shack that sells a range of delicious *rétes* strudel.

Csillebérc adventure playground

April–Sept daily 10am–6pm; Nov–March Sat & Sun 10am–5pm • 4200Ft, children 3200Ft • ☏ 1 274 5705, ⓦ kalandpalya.com

Right by the next stop, **Csillebérc**, there's a large wooded **adventure playground**, with tree-top walkways and a series of zip-wires of varying difficulty, though anyone attempting these must be over 100cm in height. Although not as challenging as the tree-top canopy at Visegrád (see p.137), it's tremendous fun. Moreover, on a hot day, the trees offer a refreshing shelter from the sun.

János-hegy

Alighting at **János-hegy**, two stops on from **Csillebérc**, you can either strike out down

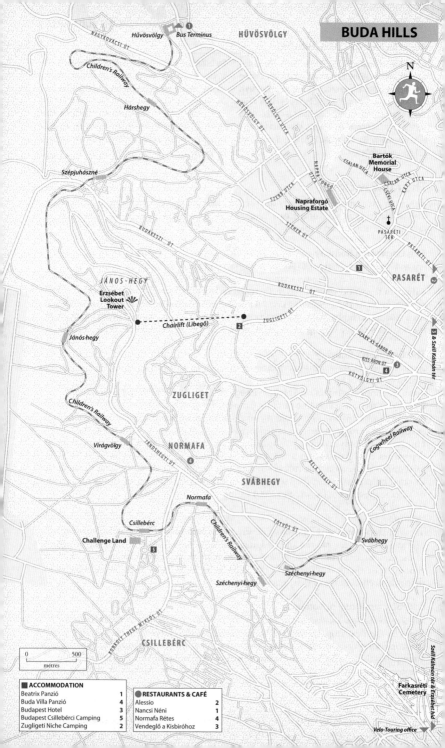

BUDA HILLS

HÜVÖSVÖLGY

NAGYKOVÁCSI ÚT

Hüvösvölgy

Bus Terminus

Children's Railway

Hárshegy

Szépjuhászné

BUDAKESZI ÚT

KÚTVÖLGY ÚT

ALSÓVÖLGY UTCA

SZENB UTCA

NAPRA FORGÓ

STÉHER ÚT

CSALÁN UTCA

CSÉV UTCA

KATÓ UTCA

Bartók
Memorial
House

PASARÉTI
TÉR

PASARÉTI ÚT

PASARÉT

Napraforgó
Housing Estate

JÁNOS-HEGY

Erzsébet
Lookout
Tower

Jánós-hegy

Chairlift (Libegó)

BUDAKESZI ÚT

ZUGLIGETI ÚT

SZARVAS GÁBOR ÚT

KISS ÁRON ÚT

KÚTVÖLGYI ÚT

ZUGLIGET

Children's Railway

Virágvölgy

JÁNOSHEGYI ÚT

NORMAFA

SVÁBHEGY

Normafa

Csillebérc

Challenge Land

Children's Railway

Normafa

Széchenyi-hegy

Széchenyi-hegy

Svábhegy

Cogwheel Railway

BÉLA KIRÁLY ÚT

EÖTVÖS ÚT

FORNACE THEGE MIKLÓS ÚT

CSILLEBÉRC

Farkasréti
Cemetery

Szél Kálmán tér & Erzsébet híd

& Szél Kálmán tér

Velo-Touring office

0   500
métres

■ ACCOMMODATION
Beatrix Panzió	1
Buda Villa Panzió	4
Budapest Hotel	3
Budapest Csillebérci Camping	5
Zugligeti Niche Camping	2

● RESTAURANTS & CAFÉ
Alessio	2
Nancsi Néni	1
Normafa Rétes	4
Vendeglő a Kisbíróhoz	3

through woods to the town of **Budakeszi**, from where bus #22 takes you back to Széll Kálmán tér, or make the steep twenty-minute climb from the station to the top of **János-hegy** (527m), the highest point in Budapest. The Romanesque-style **Erzsébet lookout tower** (daily 8am–8pm; free) on the summit offers a panoramic view of the city and the Buda Hills. The tower was designed by Frigyes Schulek, who also designed the Fishermen's Bastion – the similarity is clear. It takes its name from Empress Elizabeth, the Queen of Hungary (see box, p.146), who visited this spot in 1882 and came back on two other occasions.

By the buffet below the summit is the upper terminal of the **chairlift** or **Libegő**, meaning "floater" in Hungarian, which wafts you down over trees and gardens to the suburb of **Zugliget** (daily: May–Sept 9am–7pm; Oct–April 10am–3pm; closed every other Mon; 850Ft)

Hárshegy and Hűvösvölgy

Wild boar, which prefer to roam during the evening and sleep by day, are occasionally sighted in the forests above **Hárshegy**, one stop before the terminus at **Hűvösvölgy**. This is also a great place for **mushrooms** – most big markets, such as the Fény utca market by Széll Kálmán tér (see p.185) have stalls where you can get your mushrooms checked (*gombavizsgáló*). **Hűvösvölgy** (Cool Valley) is a vast suburb spreading into the hills and valleys beyond. It has always been a popular destination for Budapestis, trundling out on the old tram #56. Wicked tongues say that after the riots of 2006, the Socialist Party decided to change the numbering of the tram (with its connotations of 1956) to #61. The **Arts and Crafts bus terminus**, with its covered stairways leading to the train station, has been restored to its original elegance.

The Bartók Memorial House and Napraforgó utca

Bartók Béla Emlékház • II, Csalán utca 29 • Tues–Sun 10am–5pm, closed for three weeks in Aug • 1200Ft • ☎ 1 394 2100, 🌐 bartokmuseum.hu • Chamber music concerts 2000–3000Ft (includes entry to museum) are held here from Sept until June • Bus #29 from the Szemlőhegyi Cave to the Nagybányai út stop, or bus #5 from Ferenciek tere in Pest or Széll Kálmán tér to the Pasaréti tér terminus, and then a 10min walk uphill along Csévi utca (follow it round to the left at the first corner)

The **Bartók Memorial House**, located in a leafy suburb below Látó-hegy, was the residence of Béla Bartók, his wife and two sons from 1932 until their emigration to America in 1940, by which time Bartók despaired of Hungary's right-wing regime.

Now a museum, it keeps an extensive range of Bartók memorabilia, though there's very little by way of English translation or information: the three rooms on the second floor are much as they would have looked when Bartók lived here, with his piano, cupboards and writing desk, as well as the phonograph he used to make field recordings during his ethno-musical research trips to Transylvania with Zoltán Kodály. In the attic, you can also see folk handicrafts Bartók collected on his travels and the shirt cuff on which he wiped his pen-nibs when composing scores, many of which were completed here and are on show. The shop, meanwhile, sells CDs, books and scores of Bartók's music.

Napraforgó utca housing estate

II, Napraforgó utca • Signposted from Pasaréti tér, the terminus of bus #5: follow Pasaréti út until you reach a playing field and cross the bridge on the left

Before you return to Széll Kálmán tér from the Bartók Memorial House, it's worth a brief detour to see the delightful **Napraforgó utca housing estate**, built in 1931. Its 22 houses – designed by as many architects – embody different trends in Modernist architecture, from severe Bauhaus to folksy Arts and Crafts style. The houses are all occupied – you can't go in – but they have pretty much preserved their original look. For refreshment afterwards, head for the café in the listed 1930s **bus shelter** on Pasaréti tér. The shelter's curving horizontal form contrasts with the slender vertical lines of the

9

Franciscan Church of St Antal across the road – both were designed by the architect Géza Rimanóczy as a single project for the square.

Farkasréti Cemetery

Farkasréti temető • XII, Németvölgyi út 99 • Daily 7.30am–5pm • Free • Tram #59 from Széll Kálmán tér or bus #8 from Astoria in Pest

Two kilometres west of Gellért-hegy in the hilly XII district is the **Farkasréti Cemetery**, where a mass of flower stalls and funerary masons indicate that you've arrived. Among the ten thousand graves in the "Wolf's Meadow Cemetery" are those of **Béla Bartók** (whose remains were ceremonially reburied in 1988 following their return from America, where he died in exile in 1945); his fellow composer **Zoltán Kodály**; and the conductor **Georg Solti**, who left Hungary in 1939 to meet Toscanini and thus escaped the fate of his Jewish parents.

Less well known abroad are the actress Gizi Bajor, Olympic-medal-winning boxer László Papp and some infamous figures from the Communist era: Hungary's Stalinist dictator **Mátyás Rákosi** (as a precaution against vandalism, only the initials on his grave are visible), his secret police chief Gábor Péter (see box, p.61), and András Hegedüs, the Politburo member who asked the Soviets to crush the Uprising. Also look out for the many wooden grave markers inscribed in the ancient runic Székely alphabet – the Székely people now form roughly half of the Hungarian population of the Székely region in Transylvania, Romania.

However, the real attraction is the amazing **mortuary chapel** by architect Imre Makovecz – one of his finest designs, dating from 1975, which was used for his own funeral in 2011. Its wood-ribbed vault resembles the inside of a human ribcage, with a casket for corpses where the heart would be. Be discreet, as the chapel is in constant use by mourners. Visitors keen to see more of Makovecz's work should pay a visit to Visegrád (p.137), an hour's journey north of the capital.

MEMENTO PARK

The city limits

While the centre of Budapest is hardly short of attractions, it would be a shame to overlook some others out towards or just beyond the city limits. In Pest, the Railway History Park – where visitors can drive steam trains – is popular with Hungarian tourists, while the New Public Cemetery completes the roll call of illustrious Hungarian dead begun at Kerepesi. In Buda, the Memento Park, with its exiled Communist memorials, is the prime destination for foreigners, while children will enjoy both the Palace of Miracles and the Tropicarium, the former a "scientific playhouse", the latter with its sharks and rainforest creatures – leaving the Nagytétényi Castle Museum to devotees of stately homes. You can reach any of these places from the city centre within an hour.

Railway History Park

Magyar Vasúttörténeti Park • XIV, Tatai út 95 • Tues–Sun: April–Oct 10am–6pm • 1400Ft • Trains to Esztergom from Nyugati Station at 10.20am, 11.20am and 1.20pm stop at the museum's own station; a slower route is by bus #30 from Keleti Station or Hősök tere to the Rokolya utca stop, a short walk from the gates • ☎ 1 450 1497, ⓦ vasuttortenetipark.hu • See map p.5

The engagingly hands-on **Hungarian Railway History Park**, or Hungarian Railway Museum, lurks in the freight yards of the XIV district. Its roundhouse and sidings house over seventy locomotives and carriages from 1870 onwards, including the Árpád railcar that set the 1934 speed record from Budapest to Vienna in just under three hours, and a 1912 teak dining carriage from the *Orient Express*. Many of the museum's staff are ex-employees of MÁV (Hungarian State Railways), proud of a tradition inherited from the Royal Hungarian Railways. Here you can **drive** a steam train (1200Ft), luggage cart (600Ft) or engine simulator (800Ft), as well as operate a model railway (300Ft), and a turntable used for turning locomotives around (free). Worth looking out for are the special event days, when further activities are laid on, including the chance to ride a horse-drawn tram. The MÁV Nosztalgia office next to platform 10 at Nyugati Station can also give information.

New Public Cemetery and Jewish Cemetery

Új köztemető • X, Kozma utca 8–10 • Daily 8am–dusk • Free • Tram #28 or #37 from Népszínház utca, by Blaha Lujza tér • See map p.5 • Jewish Cemetery Izraelita temető • X, Kozma utca 6 • Mon–Fri & Sun 8am–2pm • Free • Last stop on tram #28 or #37 • See map p.5

The **New Public Cemetery** is located in the X district of Pest beyond the breweries of Kőbánya, near the end of one of the longest tram rides in town. This is Budapest's largest cemetery – reflecting the city's growth in the latter half of the nineteenth century – and it was in a remote corner that **Imre Nagy** and 260 others, executed for their part in the 1956 Uprising, were secretly buried in unmarked graves in 1958. Any flowers left at **Plot 301** were removed by the police until 1989, when the deceased received a state funeral on Hősök tere. The plot is 2km from the main gates on Kozma utca – but note that the minibuses that shuttle back and forth every twenty minutes only run between 9am and 3pm Tuesday to Friday. Near the graves, an ornate wooden gateway and headposts mark a mass grave now designated as a **National Pantheon** – as opposed to the Communist pantheon in Kerepesi (see p.80).

The **Jewish cemetery**, 700m up the road from the New Public Cemetery, is the burial place of Ernő Szép (author of *The Smell of Humans*, a searing Holocaust memoir), as well as many rabbis and industrialists. Beside the wall on Kozma utca stand the grand crypts of the Goldberger and Kornfeld manufacturing dynasties, and the dazzling blue-and-gold-tiled Art Nouveau tomb of shopkeeper **Sándor Schmidl**, designed by Ödön Lechner and Béla Lajta (who later became supervisor of Budapest's Jewish cemeteries).

Memento Park (Statue Park)

Szoborpark • XXII, Balatoni út • Daily 10am–dusk • 1500Ft; guided tours 1200Ft • ☎ 1 424 7500, ⓦ mementopark.hu • Memento Park bus goes from Deák tér bus stop with the Park logo by the old bus station at 11am, returning at 1pm (daily but Nov–March Sat–Mon only) for 4900Ft (including entry and a guided tour; tickets are purchased on the bus); alternatively, take metro line #4 to Kelenföld station, and then a Volán bus (not covered by BKV passes) towards Diósd-Érd • See map p.5

Fifteen kilometres southwest of the city centre, but easily the most popular site on the city's outskirts, the **Memento Park** (sometimes still known as the Statue Park) brings together 42 of the monuments that glorified Communism in Budapest, to celebrate its demise. Built in stages (1994–2004) as an "unfinished project" by architect Ákos Eleőd, the complex is an anti-temple to a bankrupt ideology. Visitors are greeted by a replica of the **Stalin grandstand**, from which Party leaders reviewed parades; the giant boots recall the 8m-high Stalin statue toppled in 1956. Beyond lies Witness Square, representing all those squares in Eastern Europe where people defied Communism; it's flanked by buildings with Socialist Realist facades. Of these, the **Barrack Hall** is used to screen *Life of an Agent*, a montage of ÁVO training films on how to bug or search premises and recruit informers. Across the way, the **Red Star Store** sells Lenin and Stalin candles, model Trabant cars and selections of revolutionary songs, which can be heard playing from a 1950s' radio set.

The park proper lies behind a bogus Classical facade framing giant statues of **Lenin**, **Marx** and **Engels**. Lenin's once stood beside the Városliget, while Marx's and Engels' are carved from granite quarried at Mauthausen, a Nazi concentration camp in Austria, later used by the Soviets. Inside the grounds, you'll encounter the **Red Army soldier** that guarded the foot of the Liberation Monument on Gellért-hegy, and dozens of other statues and memorials, large and small. Here are prewar Hungarian Communists such as Béla Kun (secretly shot in Moscow on Stalin's orders) and Jenő Landler (afforded a place in the Kremlin Wall); Georgi Dimitrov, hero of the Comintern; and the Lenin statue from outside the Csepel ironworks. Artistically, the best works are the **Republic of Councils Monument** – a giant charging sailor based on a 1919 revolutionary poster – and Imre Varga's **Béla Kun Memorial**, with Kun on a tribune surrounded by a surging crowd of workers and soldiers (plus a bystander with an umbrella).

Tropicarium and Palace of Miracles

Topicarium Campona Shopping Centre • XXII, Nagytétényi út 37–43 • Daily 10am–8pm • 2300Ft, children 1600Ft • ☎ 1 424 3053, ⓦ tropicarium.hu • Palace of Miracles • Daily 10am–8pm • 1950Ft, children 1550Ft • ☎ 1 814 8050, ⓦ csopa.hu • Bus #33 from Móricz Zsigmond körtér, or #114 and #214 from Kosztolányi Desző tér, or quicker is the main-line train from Deli Station to Budatétény • See map p.5

A must-see for kids, Budapest's **Tropicarium** is the largest aquarium-terrarium in Central Europe, covering three thousand square metres. Its saltwater section has an 11m-long glass tunnel for intimate views of sand, tiger and brown **sharks**, clownfish, triggerfish and wrasses; not to be missed is the shark feeding, which takes place every Thursday at 3pm. The freshwater part has piranhas, mouth-breeding cichlids from Africa's Great Lakes, and an outdoor pool to show fish lying dormant when it freezes over. Even better is the **mini-rainforest**, complete with macaws, marmoset monkeys, iguanas and alligators, kept steamy by a downpour with thunder and lightning effects every fifteen minutes.

Also here in the Campona Shopping Centre is the **Palace of Miracles**, another big draw for those with kids. With over a hundred interactive installations, this enormous playhouse is the brainchild of two Hungarian physicists and aims to explain scientific principles to 6- to 12-year-olds, using devices such as optical illusions, a bed of nails and a simulated low-gravity "moonwalk". The hands-on physics show is held four times a day.

Nagytétényi Castle Museum

Nagytétényi Kastélymúzeum • XXII, Kastélypark utca 9 • Tues–Sun 10am–6pm • 1000Ft, 1400Ft for temporary exhibitions • ☎ 1 207 0005, ⓦ nagytetenyi.hu • Bus #33 from Móricz Zsigmond körtér (30–45min) or the Tropicarium (15min) to the Petőfi utca stop; cross the road and follow Hugonnay utca down past the children's playground to the *kastély*; or main-line train from Déli Station to Nagytétény (20min) and then a 15min walk • See map p.5

Further out in the XXII district, the **Nagytétényi Castle Museum** is strictly for lovers of antique furniture. Though rendered as "castle" in English, "*kastély*" generally signifies a manor house or chateau without fortifications, which Hungarian nobles began building after the Turks had been expelled – in this case by converting an older, ruined castle into a Baroque residence. Nowadays, its 28 rooms display furniture from the Gothic to the Biedermeier epochs, owned by the Museum of Applied Arts; the most outstanding exhibit is a walnut-veneered refectory table from Trencsen Monastery.

ROYAL PALACE, GÖDÖLLŐ

Excursions from Budapest

The attractions in this chapter are all within an hour or so of the city. Foremost are three sites on the picturesque Danube Bend to the north of Budapest. Szentendre is a historic Serbian settlement and artists' colony with a superb open-air ethnographic museum. Further north, Visegrád boasts medieval ruins, splendid scenery, "organic" buildings and a tree-top zip-slide, while across the Danube from Slovakia, the cathedral town of Esztergom is steeped in history. While each site merits a full day (though don't go on a Monday, when most attractions are closed), you could cram two into one long day. On the other side of the Danube, Vác has a magnificent Baroque centre and some fascinating museums, or there's the former Habsburg palace at Gödöllő, where classical concerts are held all year round.

Szentendre

Szentendre (St Andrew), 20km north of Budapest, is both the most popular tourist destination in the vicinity of the capital and the easiest to reach. Despite a rash of souvenir shops, the centre remains a delightful maze of houses in autumnal colours, with secretive gardens and lanes winding up to hilltop churches, and plenty of museums and craft stalls; you should also allow at least a couple of hours for the open-air village museum outside town. Szentendre's location on the lower slopes of the Pilis Hills is not only beautiful, but ensures that it is one of the sunniest places in Hungary, making it a perfect spot for painters and artists – indeed, it was here, in the 1920s, that the town became a working **artists' colony**, and the links are just as strong today. Otherwise, the town retains a strong Serbian identity, thanks to the waves of refugees who settled here from the fourteenth century onwards.

Ferenczy Károly Museum

Ferenczy Károly Múzeum • Kossuth utca 5 • Tues–Sun 10am–6pm • 1500Ft • ☎ 1 20 779 6657, ⊕ femuz.hu

Heading up Kossuth utca from the HÉV and bus stations, you come to the splendid **Ferenczy** Károly **Museum**, which houses the oeuvre of the extraordinarily prolific Ferenczy family. Károly Ferenczy (1862–1917) pioneered Impressionism and *plein air* painting in Hungary, as beautifully demonstrated in works like *A Street in Nagybánya*. His elder son Valér swung towards Expressionism, while his two younger children, daughter Noemi, and son Beni, branched out into tapestries and sculpture respectively; Noemi's Communist-leaning tendencies are reflected in such works as *Bricklayers* and *Collective Society*; among Beni's many wonderful pieces, look out for the delightful *Playing Boys*.

11

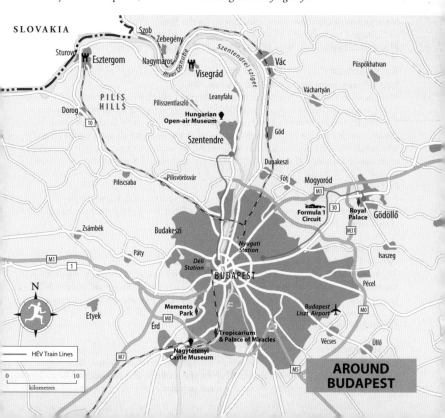

AROUND BUDAPEST

THE SERBIAN CONNECTION

Before artists moved in during the first decades of the twentieth century, Szentendre's character had been forged by waves of refugees from **Serbia**. The first followed the catastrophic Serb defeat at Kosovo in 1389; the second, the Turkish recapture of Belgrade in 1690, causing 30,000 Serbs and Bosnians to flee. Six thousand settled in Szentendre, which became the seat of the Serbian Church in exile. Prospering through trade, they replaced their wooden churches with stone ones and built handsome townhouses, but as Habsburg toleration waned and phylloxera (vine-blight) and floods ruined the local economy they trickled back to Serbia, so that by 1890 less than a quarter of the population was Serb.

11

Požarevačka Church

Kossuth utca 1• Daily noon–4pm, but opening times not reliable • 300Ft

Heading a little further up Kossuth utca, you'll encounter the first evidence of a Serbian presence just before the bridge over the Bükkos Stream in the form of an Orthodox church. Like many others in Szentendre, the slender **Požarevačka Church** was built from stone in the late eighteenth century to replace an older wooden structure in a grove of trees. The centrepiece of the interior is the Byzantine-style iconostasis, dating from 1742.

Marzipan Museum

Marcipán Múzeum • Dumtsa Jenő utca 12, entry from Batthyány utca • Daily 9am–7pm • 500Ft

Beyond the Bükkos Stream, and the Tourinform office, you're firmly into the tourist zone. First up is the chintzy *Múzeum Cukrászda* (see p.134), behind which lies the **Marzipan Museum** showcasing confections by the family firm Szabo, including portraits of Princess Diana, busts of Emperor Franz Josef and Sisi, and a model of the Hungarian Parliament. It's a bit naff, but good fun all the same.

Barcsay Collection

Barcsay Gyűjtemény • Dumtsa Jenő utca 10 • Wed–Sun 10am–5pm • 600Ft

Next door to the Marzipan Museum, the **Barcsay Collection** is dedicated to the work of Transylvanian-born Jenő Barcsay (1900–88), a long-standing resident and teacher at Szentendre's artists' colony. His dark, prewar canvases – mainly landscapes such as *Transylvanian Hills* and *Szentendre Streets* – give way to more abstract works after the war, while his later pieces included wall-length mosaics, tapestries and Quattrocento anatomical drawings, these last confirming his skills as a draughtsman.

Fő tér and around

At the top of Dumtsa Jenő utca, triangular **Fő tér** swarms with horse-drawn carriages and sightseers milling around an ornate **Plague Cross**, erected by the merchants' guild after Szentendre escaped infection in 1763.

Szentendre Gallery

Szentendrei Keptár • Fő tér 2–5 • Wed–Sun: May–Sept 10am–6pm, Oct–April 2–6pm

The square and surrounding streets are teeming with galleries of varying quality – the **Szentendre Gallery** (Szentendrei Keptár) on the east side of the square at nos. 2–5 mainly holds temporary contemporary art exhibitions, but sometimes features names such as István Szőnyi, the twentieth-century Hungarian painter much loved for his Danube Bend landscapes.

Kovács Ceramic Exhibition

Kovács Margit Kerámia Kiállítás • Past the Blagovestenska Church at Vastagh György utca 1 • Daily 10am–6pm • 1000Ft

Unjustly overlooked in the National Gallery, the sculptor and ceramicist Margit Kovács (1902–77) left a legacy that's by far the most popular of Szentendre's art collections.

SZENTENDRE

N

Hungarian Open-air Museum

MÉHÉSZ UTCA
HOLD UTCA
DARU PIAC
DEZSMA UTCA

Vinegrowers' Cross

DUNAKORZÓ

Szentendre I

River Danube

ZRINYI UTCA
ISKOLA UTCA
ANGYAL UTCA
BOGDÁNYI UTCA

DUNAKANYAR KÖRÚT

MARTINOVICS UTCA

Preobraženska Church

RÁKÓCZI UTCA

SZERB UTCA

Blue Dye Shop

Art Mill

Szentendre II

Skanzen Ház

BOGDÁNYI UTCA

Serbian Orthodox Ecclesiastical Art Collection

Belgrade Church

Szántó Memorial House

Lázár Cross

RÁKÓCZI UTCA

Czóbel Museum

ALKOTMÁNY UTCA

TEMPLOM TÉR

Vajda Museum

Imré Ámos-Margit Anna Museum

Parish Church

HUNYADI UTCA

Town Hall

BOGDÁNYI UTCA

Blagovestenška Church

Szentendrei sziget

FŐ TÉR

GÖRÖG UTCA

Plague Cross

Kovács Ceramic Exhibition

Szentendre Gallery

Peter-Paul Church

PÉTER-PÁL UTCA

Barcsay Collection

KUCSERA UTCA

DUMTSA JENŐ UTCA

Marzipan Museum

BÜKKÖS PART

PAPRIKABÍRÓ UTCA

Požarevačka Church

Bükkös Stream

DUNAKORZÓ

KOSSUTH UTCA

Ferenczy Museum

RÓMAI SÁNC KÖZ

PETŐFI UTCA

NAGY LAJOS
ŐRTORONY UTCA
ATTILA UTCA
DUNAKANYAR KÖRÚT
KOSSUTH UTCA

KERTÉSZ UTCA

VASÚTI VILLASOR

BOLGÁR UTCA

HÉV Terminal

Budapest

Bus Station

Budapest

● RESTAURANTS & CAFÉS

Aranysárkány	1
Görög Kancso	3
Mjam	2
Múzeum Cukrászda	5
Palapa	4

0 200
metres

The **Kovács Ceramic Exhibition** never fails to delight, the themes of legends, dreams, religion, love and motherhood giving her graceful sculptures and reliefs universal appeal. Her expressive, big-eyed statues are not particularly well known abroad, but in Hungary Kovács is honoured as one of the country's finest ceramicists.

Blagovestenska Church
Fő tér 4 (entrance on Görög utca) • Tues–Sun 10am–5pm • 400Ft

Looming over the north side of Fő tér, the **Blagovestenska Church** or Church of the Annunciation, is the most accessible of the town's Orthodox churches. Painted by Mihailo Zivkovic of Buda in the early eighteenth century, its icons evoke all the richness and tragedy of Serbian history. Look out for the tomb of a Greek merchant of Macedonian origin to the left of the entrance, and the Rococo windows and gate facing Görög utca (Greek Street). Next door to the church, a portal carved with emblems of science and learning provides the entrance to a former Serbian church school.

11 Templom tér and beyond

Off the opposite side of Fő tér to the Blagovestenska Church, an alley of steps ascends to **Templom tér**, a walled hilltop with a great view of Szentendre's rooftops and gardens.

Parish Church and Czóbel Museum
Szent János templom • Tues–Sun 10am–5pm, but opening times not reliable • Museum Czóbel Béla Múzeum • Tues–Sun 9am–5pm • 600Ft

Of medieval origin with Romanesque and Gothic features, the Catholic **Parish Church** was rebuilt in the Baroque style after falling derelict in Turkish times. The frescoes in its sanctuary were collectively painted by members of the town's artists' colony – among them Béla Czóbel (1883–1976), whose Bonnard-like portraits hang in the **Czóbel Museum** at no. 12, across from the church.

Belgrade Church and Serbian Orthodox Ecclesiastical Art Collection
Belgrád templom • Pátriáka utca 5 • April–Oct Tues–Sun 10am–6pm, but ask at the museum if the doors are locked • 600Ft • Ecclesiastical Collection Szerb Ortodox Egyháztörténeti Gyüjtemény • Mid-March to Oct Wed–Sun 10am–4pm; Nov to mid-March Fri–Sun 10am–4pm • 800Ft

North of Templom tér, the rust-red spire of the Orthodox cathedral or **Belgrade Church** rises above a walled garden on Alkotmány utca. Built during the late eighteenth century, it has a lavishly ornamented interior with icons depicting scenes from the New Testament and saints of the Orthodox Church. The old tombstones with Cyrillic inscriptions in the churchyard bear witness to a tale of demographic decline, echoed by the **Serbian Orthodox Ecclesiastical Art Collection** in the Episcopal palace, whose hoard of icons, vestments and crosses comes from churches in Hungary that fell empty after the Serbs returned to the Balkans and the last remaining parishioners died out.

Vajda Museum
Vajda Lajos Múzeum • Hunyadi utca 1 • Wed–Sun 10am–6pm • 600Ft

From the Belgrade Church you can follow Alkotmány utca back down towards Fő tér, passing another artist's legacy on Hunyadi utca. The upper floor of the **Vajda Museum** pays homage to Lajos Vajda (1908–41), whose playful fusion of Serbian, Jewish and Swabian traditions with Cubism and Surrealism gave way to anguished charcoal drawings in the years before his death in a Nazi labour camp.

Szántó Memorial House and Synagogue
Szanto Emlékház és Imaház • Hunyadi utca 2 • Tues–Sun 11am–5pm • Donations accepted

At the far end of Hunyadi utca the **Szántó Memorial House** was set up by the grandson of a Jewish couple who were among a 250-strong Jewish community in the town that was almost completely wiped out in the Holocaust. While Budapest has the second

largest synagogue in the world, this one is reputed to be the smallest; the documents and relics inside are few but they make a moving display

Bogdányi utca

Sloping gently downhill north from Fő tér, **Bogdányi utca** is packed with craft stalls and folk-costumed vendors – it's souvenir heaven if you like that kind of thing, though there are also some more interesting sights along the street's length.

Imre Ámos-Margít Anna Museum

Bogdányi utca 12 • Thurs–Sun 10am–10pm • 600Ft

The **Imre Ámos-Margít Anna Museum** commemorates the work of a painterly couple. Imre Ámos (1907–44) was a distinguished artist who was repeatedly called up on Jewish labour service from 1940 – painful excerpts from his diary are on display – where he died in 1944, and the museum presents some of his later works, including the disturbing *Apocalypse* series painted in the year of his death. Downstairs, his wife's works go from mellow prewar pictures to the uncomfortably bright and sometimes grotesque works she painted after the war.

Lázár Cross

Past the Ámos-Anna Museum, Bogdányi utca opens onto a square where the small iron **Lázár Cross** honours the Serb king Lázár, whom the Turks beheaded after the Battle of Kosovo. Lázár's body was buried here by the Serbs, before being taken back to Serbia in 1774. Between March and October, horse-drawn carriages can be rented on Bogdányi utca for rides round town (from 1000Ft per person for 30min); bargain hard. Nearby is Szentendre's proudest recent addition: a mobile **dam**, which has reconnected the town with its river allowing the removal of the old high embankment. Locals now keep their fingers crossed that it works.

Art Mill

Művészeti-Malom • Bogdányi utca 32 • Tues–Sun 10am–6pm • 1000Ft

Continuing along Bogdányi utca, the *Skanzen ház* at no. 28 is a bakery selling delicious produce made in the Open-Air Museum (see below). A short walk further on, the **Art Mill** is a converted watermill hosting installations and performance art events. A couple of doors up, at no. 36, admire the deep blue hues of clothes, tablecloths and bedspreads at the Kovács **Blue Dye Shop**, showcasing a traditional style of folk dyeing.

Preobraženska Church

At the end of Bogdányi utca the **Preobraženska Church**, on Vujicsics Tihamér tér, was erected by the tanners' guild in 1741–76, and its stoutness enhanced by a Louis XVI gate the following century. Though its lavish iconostasis merits a look, the church is chiefly notable for its role in the Serbian festival on August 19, when it hosts the Blessing of the Grapes ceremony, recalling Szentendre's past as a wine-producing centre. A few minutes' walk further on, the **Vinegrowers' Cross** was raised by a local guild and is fittingly wreathed in grapevines.

The Hungarian Open-Air Museum

Szabadtéri Néprajzi Múzeum • April–Oct Tues–Sun 9am–5pm; Nov to mid-Dec Sat & Sun 10am–4pm • 1800Ft; tickets for train inside museum 500Ft • ☎ 26 502 500 , ⓦ skanzen.hu • Buses leave from stand 7 at the Szentendre bus station.

Set in rolling countryside 4km north of town, the amazing **Hungarian Open-Air Museum** should not be missed. This museum is Hungary's largest outdoor museum of peasant architecture (termed a *skanzen*, after the first such museum, founded in a Stockholm suburb in 1891).

It takes at least two hours to tour the naturalistic village ensembles transported here from eight ethnographic regions of Hungary, representing rural life from the nineteenth century up until the 1920s and complete with dwellings, demonstrations of cottage industries and traditional breeds of livestock in barns. Each building has a custodian who can explain everything in detail, though usually only in Hungarian. The various areas are connected by a mini-railway, which makes it easier to cover the large site. Demonstrations of **crafts** such as pottery, weaving and boot-making occur in each section at weekends and during **festivals**, of which there are several throughout the year; these include the Pentecostal Games (end of May), a culinary Feast of the Soil (Aug 11), and two wine festivals (Sept & Nov).

Upper Tisza
Downhill to the right from the entrance, a village from the isolated **Upper Tisza** region in the northeast corner of the country reveals that the homes of the poorest squires were barely superior to those of their tenants, yet rural carpenters produced highly skilled work, such as the circular "dry mill", the wooden bell tower, and the Greek Catholic church (on a hilltop beyond). Past the Calvinist graveyard with its boat-shaped grave-markers, signs point you to the scant remains of a Roman village and on to the next region.

11

Northern Hungary
The following region takes you to the region northwest of Budapest: **Northern Hungary** includes an original stone house furnished in nineteenth-century style and recreates cave dwellings typical of the poorer parts of the region. You can also taste or get recipes for "Palóc" delicacies – the Palóc people being an ethnic Hungarian group retaining its own traditions, with a distinctive dialect to match.

The Uplands
Next comes the **Uplands** region, which on the map of Hungary is sandwiched between the two previous sections. This region includes the wine-growing area of Tokaj, where vineyards brought considerable privileges – and wealth, evident in the proud stone buildings from these market towns, with their stoves, well-stocked kitchens and, of course, wine cellars.

Bakony and Balaton Uplands
A short walk from the Uplands region brings you to a water-powered mill and grape-press; a washhouse and a fire station comprise the "centre" of a village from the **Bakony and Balaton Uplands**, where stone and hornbeam were used for building. The four neatly aligned dwelling houses reflect the varying financial standings of those living in the region in the early twentieth century.

Western Transdanubia
Across the stream and to the right, **Western Transdanubia** – on the Austrian border – was a poor region of clay soil and heavy rainfall, where houses were linked by covered verandas. Here, a schoolroom is equipped with benches, slates for writing on, a towel and basin for washing, and homespun schoolbags. The teacher's living quarters are at the other end of the building, separated by a kitchen with an apron chimney, where the smoke goes out of a hole in the roof.

Southern Transdanubia
Large adobe dwellings were typical of the wealthier, predominantly Protestant German and Hungarian villages in **Southern Transdanubia**, in the southwest of the country – their carved gateways big enough for haywains – but there are also wooden-framed thatched buildings typical of the more isolated areas. The region has a strong tradition of wine-making – it includes the areas of Szekszárd, which made the first Bull's Blood, and Villány – and you can see evidence of that here.

11

The Small Plain

The section representing the ethnic German communities of the **Small Plain**, in northern Transdanubia, seems far more regimented: neatly aligned whitewashed houses filled with knick-knacks and embroidered samplers bearing homilies like "When the Hausfrau is capable, the clocks keep good time". The village layout here is designed to show the diversity of the region: on one side of the street are stately brick buildings, while on the other are more humble dwellings with earth walls and thatched roofs.

The Great Plain

Large adobe dwellings were also typical of the market towns on the **Great Plain**. A Baroque cottage from Sükösd has its visitors' room or "clean room" laid out for Christmas celebrations with a nativity crib and a church-shaped box. Beyond the houses are stables and pastures for long-horned cattle and Rácka sheep, and a windmill built in 1888, its sails still operating.

ARRIVAL AND INFORMATION   SZENTENDRE

By train Szentendre is easily accessible by HÉV train from Batthyány tér metro station (every 20min 6.30am–10pm; 40min). BKK tickets (and Budapest Cards) are valid as far as the city limits (HÉV station: Békásmegyer), so you will need to buy a supplementary ticket to cover the remaining part of the journey, or show a BKK pass when buying a ticket at the station. The station is a 10min walk south of the town centre: cross Dunakanyar körút by subway and continue along Kossuth utca.

By bus Buses run from Budapest's Újpest-Városkapu bus station to Szentendre's bus station (30min), next to the HÉV station.

By boat Excursion boats sail from Vigadó tér at 10am and Batthyány tér at 10.10am, with an extra boat at 2pm in July & August (May–Sept Tues–Sun; 1hr 30min; 2000Ft; ☎ 1 484 4013, ⓦ mahartpassnave .hu) and dock at the Szentendre II landing near the heart of town.

Information Tourinform is at Dumsta Jenő utca 22 (June–Aug Mon–Fri 9.30am–7pm, Sat & Sun 9am–4pm; Sept–May Mon–Sat 9am–5pm, Sun 10am–2pm; ☎ 26 317 965, ⓦ szentendre.hu); there's disappointingly little info in English, but you can obtain a map of town and information on concerts and festivals.

EATING AND DRINKING

Szentendre has stacks of restaurants, though you'd do well to steer clear of those on and around Fő tér, which are heavily frequented by coach parties, and hence relatively pricey by Hungarian standards. You'll do better in the backstreets or on Dunakorzó (though it's no less crowded in summer), or in **cafés** on the periphery of the centre. The Serbian influence is particularly strong; look out for traditional dishes such as *pljeskavica* and *cevapi* (lamb and beef burgers or rissoles with diced onion, served in thick, soft pittas).

Aranysárkány Alkotmány utca 1a ☎ 26 311 670, ⓦ aranysarkany.hu. The long-standing and popular "*Golden Dragon*" serves Hungarian nouvelle cuisine in traditional, folksy surrounds; try the goose-liver wrapped in bacon with cognac (3900Ft) or the honeyed goose steak with red cabbage and mashed potatoes (3100Ft). Three-course menu 3800Ft. Booking advisable. Daily noon–10pm.

Görög Kancsó Dunakorzó 9 ☎ 26 303 178. A lively, affordable taverna down by the river, where you can park yourself at an outside table and tuck into Greek specialities like dolmades (stuffed vine leaves; 1190Ft), souvlaki (skewered meats and vegetables; 2590Ft), and pork tenderloin stuffed with feta cheese (1990Ft). Daily noon–midnight.

★**Mjam** Városház tér 2 ☎ 70 377 8178. Szentendre's standout restaurant, with innovative fusion menu of South

American, Asian and Caribbean cuisine; try the excellent Curacao burger, or the fish sausage and tempura. It's not especially cheap (mains 2600–4000Ft), but the weekday two-course lunch menu (1200Ft) is great value. Tues–Thurs & Sun 8am–10pm, Fri & Sat till 11.30pm.

Múzeum Cukrászda Dumsta Jenő utca 14. For afters or mid-morning refreshment, head to this chintzy café where coffee, cakes and ices have been served in the beautifully tiled salon since 1889. Cakes and confectionery to take away too. Daily 9am–8pm.

Palapa Dumsta Jenő utca 14a (entrance on Batthyány utca) ☎ 26 302 418. Dazzlingly colourful Mexican bar-restaurant with all the usual suspects (fajitas, enchiladas, tacos; all from 1700Ft), in addition to a great tapas menu (580ft each); there's a fine selection of cocktails too. Live music every Saturday at 7pm. Mon–Thurs & Sun noon–10pm, Fri & Sat till midnight.

Visegrád

Approaching **Visegrád** from Szentendre, the hillsides start to plunge and the river twists shortly before you catch first sight of the citadel and ramparts of the ancient fortified site whose Slavic name means "High Castle". The view hasn't changed much since 1488, when János Thuroczy described its "upper walls stretching to the clouds floating in the sky, and the lower bastions reaching down as far as the river". At that time, courtly life in Visegrád was nearing its apogee and the palace of King Mátyás and Queen Beatrice was famed throughout Europe. The papal legate Cardinal Castelli described it as a "paradiso terrestri", seemingly unperturbed by the presence of Vlad the Impaler, who resided here under duress between 1462 and 1475. Today, Visegrád is a mere village, where the ferry docks and a few bars and restaurants round the church are the hub of local life. Tourists tend to focus on the **historic sites** north of the centre: the

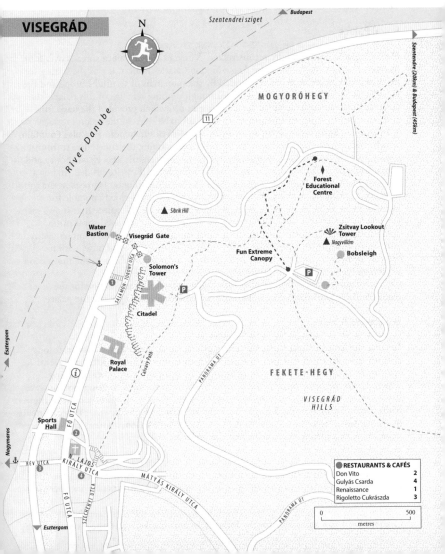

●RESTAURANTS & CAFÉS	
Don Vito	2
Gulyás Csarda	4
Renaissance	1
Rigoletto Cukrászda	3

Royal Palace and Solomon's Tower near the river, and the hilltop citadel. All the river sites are in easy walking distance of each other but you might prefer taking a bus up to the citadel, thus saving your energy for gung-ho **activities** in the **Visegrád Hills**.

The layout of the **ruins** dates back to the thirteenth century, when Béla IV began fortifying the north against a recurrence of the Mongol invasion, while the construction of a royal palace below the hilltop citadel was a sign of greater security during the reign of the Angevins. However, its magnificence was effaced by the Turkish conquest, and later mud washing down from the hillside gradually buried the palace entirely. Subsequent generations doubted its existence until archeologist János Schulek had a lucky break after searching in vain for years. At a New Year's Eve party in 1934, the wine ran out and Schulek was sent to get some more from the neighbours. An old woman told him to go down to the wine cellar, and there he found clues in the stones that convinced him the palace was there, beneath the surface.

Royal Palace

11 Királyi Palota • Fő utca 23 • Tues–Sun 9am–5pm • 1200Ft • ☏ 26 597 010, ⓦ visegradmuzeum.hu

Now excavated and tastefully reconstructed, Visegrád's **Royal Palace** spreads over four terraces. Founded in 1323 by the Angevin king Charles Robert, it was the setting for the Visegrád Congress of 1335, attended by the monarchs of Central Europe and the Grandmaster of the Teutonic Knights. Although nothing remains of this palace, the **Court of Honour** constructed for his successor Louis, which provided the basis for additions by kings Sigismund and Mátyás, is still to be seen on the second terrace.

A pilastered **Renaissance loggia** surrounds a replica of the famous **Hercules Fountain**, which cools the tiled, gilded uppermost storey, overlooking the court. The surrounding rooms house a voluminous display of exhibits, mainly ceramic vessels, weaponry and glazed stove tiles. On the third terrace, where Mátyás and Beatrice resided, stands a copy of the **Lion Fountain**, bearing his raven crest and standing on leg-rests in the form of sleepy-looking lions and dogs. The reconstructed chapel is chiefly notable for housing the red marble *Visegrád Madonna*, a Renaissance masterpiece that shows many similarities to the works of Italian Tomaso Fiamberti. The renovated royal suites, meanwhile, remain mostly bare, save for some superb-looking stoves complete with dark green ceramic tiles depicting various coats-of-arms. The bathhouse, with its underfloor heating, and the palace herb gardens, further contribute to the impression of courtly life.

If you've got kids, you can bet that they'll make an immediate beeline for the wonderfully colourful, medieval-themed playground directly opposite the palace.

Solomon's Tower

Salamon-torony • Salamon-torony utca • May–Sept daily 9am–5pm • 800Ft

Leaving the Royal Palace, turn right along Fő utca and then follow Salamon-torony utca up through a fortified gate to reach **Solomon's Tower**. Named after an eleventh-century Hungarian king once thought to have been imprisoned here after being deposed, this mighty hexagonal keep is buttressed on two sides by unsightly concrete slabs. Inside, various exhibits can be found from the palace, including a copy of the white Anjou Fountain of the Angevins. From the top of the tower you can see ramparts plunging down from the Citadel to the riverside **Water Bastion**, a squat, long-derelict structure with a fortified arch spanning the highway.

The Citadel

Fellegvár • Mid-March to April & Oct daily 9.30am–5pm; May–Sept daily 9.30am–6pm; Nov to mid-March Sat & Sun 9.30am–4pm • 1800Ft • You can come from the rear gate of Solomon's Tower (40min), or an easier climb (20min) via the Calvary footpath behind Visegrád's church

Dramatically sited on a crag above Solomon's Tower, Visegrád's thirteenth-century **Citadel** served as a repository for the Hungarian crown jewels until they were stolen by a treacherous maid of honour in the fifteenth century. Following the last major rebuilding work later that same century, the castle was occupied by the Turks, then the Habsburgs, before falling into decay. It's now only partly restored but mightily impressive nonetheless, commanding a superb view of the Börzsöny Mountains across the Danube. Come for this and not the two rather dull **museums** devoted to medieval hunting, fishing, punishment and torture; in fact, so comical are the waxworks, they probably are actually worth visiting. Otherwise, there are outdoor displays of **archery** and **falconry** in the summer.

The Visegrád Hills

A popular rambling spot with fantastic views, the densely wooded **Visegrád Hills** offer great walks and views, and for thrill-seekers there is the chance to zip through the tree tops or go bobsleighing.

Zsitvay lookout tower

Zsitvay-kilátó • 10am–6pm: May–Oct daily; Nov–April Sat & Sun • 400Ft

Four hundred metres up the road from the Citadel car park, paths radiate from another car park. One leads up to the **Zsitvay lookout tower** on the top of the highest hill on the Danube Bend, Nagy-Villám (Great Lightning; 377m), with wonderful views as far as Slovakia.

Bobsleigh

Bobpálya • March Mon–Fri 11am–4pm, Sat & Sun 10am–5pm; April & Sept–Oct Mon–Fri 10am–5pm, Sat & Sun 10am–6pm; May–Aug Mon–Fri 9am–6pm, Sat & Sun 9am–7pm; Nov–Feb daily 11am–4pm; closed on rainy days • 450Ft for one run • ☎ 26 397 397, ⓦ bobozas.hu

Just downhill from the higher car park are two **bobsleigh** runs, where kids of all ages (and adults) can whizz down a couple of 1km-long chutes on either the summer bobsled or the Alpine Coaster; note that these may be closed on rainy days, when the sleds' brakes are ineffective, so it's best to call ahead.

Fun Extreme Canopy

Canopy pálya • March–Oct Tues–Sun 10am–6pm • 4000Ft • Trips require a minimum of four people, max twenty; individuals who turn up can be put with a group, but it's wiser to book ahead; ages 12 and over only • ☎ 20 661 7873, ⓦ canopy.hu

More thrilling than the Bobsleigh is the **Fun Extreme Canopy**, inspired by the tree-top walkways in Costa Rica's Monteverde Cloud Forest National Park. Eleven platforms, 14m high, are linked by wires to form an amazing zip-ride through the forest, which takes about forty minutes to complete, sliding at speeds of up to 50km an hour. Guides, safety harnesses and helmets are provided; nerve rather than strength is needed. The zip-wire's upper terminus is by the *Nagyvillám Vendéglő*, on the far side of the car park from the bobsleigh. Riders end up on a lower hill, Mogyoróhegy, from which they can return by minibus or walk up through the woods to Nagy-Villám.

The Imre Makovecz buildings

Two hundred metres along from the lower terminus of the Fun Extreme Canopy stand a couple of iconic wooden buildings by **Imre Makovecz** (1935–2011), the Hungarian guru of "organic architecture". After creating the breathtaking crypt at Farkasréti Cemetery (p.122), he was branded a troublemaker for his outspoken nationalism and "exiled" to Visegrád's forestry department, where he acquired a following by teaching summer schools on how to construct buildings using low-tech methods and materials such as branches and twigs. In the 1980s he built here a campsite **restaurant** with a roof like a nun's wimple, and the yurt-like, turf-roofed **Forest Education Centre** (in the centre of town, he also built a **Sports Hall** resembling a Viking church), before being allowed to work elsewhere and given the honour of designing the Hungarian Pavilion

11

FESTIVALS

Each year (usually on the second weekend in July), Visegrád hosts the **International Palace Games**, an orgy of medieval pageantry featuring jousting and archery tournaments, craft workshops, a street fair, and plenty of eating and drinking, most of which is held in the grounds of the Royal Palace and surrounding streets; tickets for the jousting start at around 1600Ft; check ⓦpalotajatekok.hu for more information.

During the second half of June, the **Danube Bend Summer Games** see sports, musical and cultural events in all the villages between Szentendre and Visegrád; for details, visit ⓦdunakanyar.org.

---

at the 1992 Seville Expo. Though Makovecz's work was by this point widely acclaimed, his lavish use of wood vexed some environmentalists, and his dabbling in right-wing politics made his call for a return to a "real" Hungarian style of building somewhat suspect.

11

ARRIVAL AND INFORMATION

VISEGRÁD

By bus Bus #880 leaves from stand 7 at Budapest's Újpest Városkapu terminal (every hour; 1hr 25min) and stops at various points along the main road between the town and the river, including in front of the tourist office and by the local ferry stop (at the bottom of Rév utca), before running on to Esztergom.

By boat Given the majestic scenery of the Danube Bend, arriving by river is far more scenic. The boat leaves Budapest's Vigadó tér at 10am and Batthyány tér at 10.10am (May–Sept Tues–Sun; 3hr 30min; 3000Ft; ☎1 484 4013, ⓦmahartpassnave) and docks by the pier at the

end of Rév utca.

By hydrofoil A much quicker way (just one hour) is the hydrofoil, which leaves Vigadó tér at 9.30am (May–Sept Sat & Sun; 4000Ft). The landing stage is by the highway, just below Solomon's Tower.

Information The excellent local tourist office is located along the main road, in front of the Royal Palace (May–Oct daily 9am–7pm; Nov–Feb Tues–Sat 10am–4pm); this is by far the best place to go for any information on sightseeing on the Danube Bend.

EATING AND DRINKING

Don Vito Fő utca 83 ☎26 397 230. The town's most enjoyable restaurant, this stylish pizzeria features three brightly decorated rooms and a long wooden bar themed on *The Godfather*, with wood-fired pizzas (1890Ft) named accordingly; Pizza Michael Corleone and Pizza Consigliere to name but two. It's also the best place in town to drink, with occasional live music to boot. Daily noon–11pm.

Gulyás Csárda Nagy Lajos király utca 4 ☎26 398 329. This 1980s-style inn right in the centre of Visegrád does hearty, traditional Hungarian and German dishes at very

affordable prices (mains 1700Ft), and also has a sunny beer garden. Daily noon–11pm.

Renaissance Fő utca11 ☎26 398 081. A medieval-themed restaurant mainly frequented by coach parties, where diners can feast on the likes of venison in red wine (3500Ft) served in ceramic bowls while wearing a cardboard crown and being serenaded by a lute-player. Daily noon–11pm.

Rigoletto Cukrászda Rév utca 13 ☎20 590 4970. Sweet and welcoming little daytime café doling out strong coffee, cakes and cookies alongside a delicious selection of ice creams. Daily 10am–6pm.

Esztergom

Beautifully situated in a crook of the Danube facing Slovakia, **Esztergom** is dominated by its basilica, whose dome is visible for miles around – a richly symbolic sight, as it was here that Prince Géza and his son Vajk (the future king and saint Stephen) brought Hungary into the fold of Christendom. Even after the court moved to Buda following the Mongol invasion, Esztergom remained the centre of Catholicism until the Turkish conquest, and resumed this role in the 1820s – as the poet Mihály Babits (who lived here) remarked, "this is the Hungarian Rome". Persecuted in the Rákóczi era but increasingly tolerated by the regime from the 1960s onwards, the Church regained much of its former property and influence under Christian governments in the post-Communist era, making Esztergom an obligatory stop for politicians in election year.

Despite the town's current problems (see box, p.140), Esztergom makes an ideal day-trip, combining historic monuments and small-town charm in just the right doses, with the bonus of being within strolling distance of the Slovak town of Štúrovo (Párkány in Hungarian).

Esztergom consists of an upper town beside the basilica, the waterfront Víziváros below it with its magnificent Turkish remains, and a sprawling lower town separated from the island of Prímás-sziget by a tributary of the Danube.

The basilica

Cathedral • Daily 8am–6pm • Free • **Crypt** • Daily: March–Oct 9am–5pm, Nov–Feb 10am– 4pm • 200Ft • **Cupola** • April–Oct daily 9.30am–5pm (closed in bad weather) • 700Ft • **Treasury** • Daily: March–Oct 9am–5pm, Nov to mid-Jan 10am–4pm • 900Ft • ☎ 33 402 354, ⓦ bazilika-esztergom.hu

Built upon the site of the first cathedral in Hungary, where Vajk was crowned as King Stephen by a papal envoy on Christmas Day 1000 AD, Esztergom's **basilica** is the

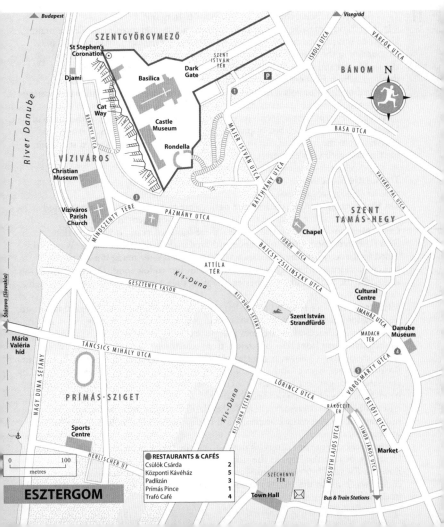

RESTAURANTS & CAFÉS

Csülök Csárda	2
Központi Kávéház	5
Padlizán	3
Prímás Pince	1
Trafó Café	4

ESZTERGOM

THE BATTLE OF ESZTERGOM

In 2010, Ezstergom was crippled by an extraordinary political stalemate when the Fidesz mayor was roundly defeated by an independent candidate but would not admit defeat. He finally vacated his office, but the Fidesz-controlled town council refused to cooperate with the new mayor in any way. It then emerged that the town was massively in debt, but Fidesz did not help the new mayor take any steps. Even the Prime Minister, who had spoken about the symbolic importance of the town, has refused to admit Fidesz's mistakes, while the local people despaired at the crisis that by the end of 2011 had decimated local services and left the centre of town looking very neglected. At the time of writing, the stalemate continued and the town remains a strangely forlorn place.

11

largest in the country, measuring 118m in length and 40m in width, and capped by a dome 100m high. Representing a thousand years of faith and statehood, it was begun in 1822, and completed József Hild in 1869, an occasion for which Liszt composed *Gran Mass* (Gran being the German name for Esztergom).

Its nave is on a massive scale, clad in marble, gilding and mosaics, while the main altarpiece was painted by the Venetian Michelangelo Grigoletti, based on Titian's *Assumption* in the Frari Church in Venice. More architecturally impressive, though, is the lavish, red and white marble **Bakócz Chapel** (below the relief of Christ on a donkey), whose Florentine altar was salvaged from the original basilica that was destroyed by the Mongols. Off to the right is the **treasury** (*kincstár*), an overpowering collection of bejewelled crosiers, vestments and kitsch papal souvenirs.

The spooky **crypt** (*krypta*), with its seventeen-metre-thick walls, bears the tomb of Cardinal Mindszenty (see box opposite), amongst other grand mausolea; another stairway from the nave leads up to the **cupola**, reached by three hundred steps and offering a superb view of Esztergom.

The Castle Museum

Vármúzeum • Tues–Sun 10am–6pm • 900Ft

On higher ground 30m south of the basilica are the red-roofed, reconstructed remains of the palace founded by Prince Géza, now presented as the **Castle Museum**. A royal seat for almost three hundred years, it was here that Béla III entertained Philip of France and Frederick Barbarossa on their way to the Third Crusade, while the Renaissance prelate János Vitéz made it a centre of humanist culture, where Queen Beatrice spent her widowhood. Despite being sacked by the Turks and twice besieged before they were evicted in 1683, enough survived to be excavated in the 1930s.

The main entrance is round to the left on the courtyard: past archeological finds and visualizations of the palace in various epochs, you reach the best part of the museum, the royal suite. Traces of the frescoes that once covered every wall can be seen in the vaulted living hall from Béla III's reign, from which stairs ascend to the study of Archbishop Vitéz – known as the **Hall of Virtues** after its allegorical murals. Beyond lies the **royal chapel**, whose Gothic rose window and Romanesque arches were executed by craftsmen brought over by Béla's French wives, while the reconstructed tower offers a panoramic view of Esztergom and the river.

Returning to the courtyard, there is a lapidarium and a further section of the museum, where you can see archeological finds and a less enthralling collection of weapons.

From the basilica, you can walk down the slope that descends to the Kisvonat terminus, or take the steps at the side down to the former primate's wine cellars – now the *Prímás Pince* restaurant – and the monumental **Dark Gate**. This imposing tunnel was built in the 1820s as a short cut between church buildings on either side of the hill.

CARDINAL MINDSZENTY

When the much-travelled body of **Cardinal József Mindszenty** was finally laid to rest with state honours in 1991, it was a vindication of his uncompromising heroism – and the Vatican realpolitik that he despised. As a conservative and monarchist, Mindszenty had stubbornly opposed the postwar Communist takeover, warning that "cruel hands are reaching out to seize hold of our children, claws belonging to people who have nothing but evil to teach them". Arrested in 1948, tortured for 39 days and nights, and sentenced to life imprisonment for treason, Mindszenty was freed during the Uprising and took refuge in the US Embassy, where he remained for the next fifteen years – an exile in the heart of Budapest.

When the Vatican struck a deal with the Kádár regime in 1971, Mindszenty had to be pushed into resigning his position and going to Austria, where he died in 1975. Although his will stated that his body should not return home until "the red star of Moscow had fallen from Hungarian skies", his reburial occurred some weeks before the last Soviet soldier left, in preparation for Pope John Paul II's visit. Nowadays the Vatican proclaims his greatness, without any hint of apology for its past actions.

11

The Víziváros

At the northern end of the parapet overlooking the Danube is the striking **white statue** of the crowning of St Stephen. Nearby, the stairs of the precipitous **Cat Way** (or Cat Stairs – Macskaút or Macskalépcső) offer a dramatic way down from the heights, and provide a splendid view of the river and Štúrovo. At the bottom lies the **Víziváros**, a Baroque enclave of churches and seminaries – and the most magnificent Turkish relic.

Oziceli Hacci Ibrahim Djami

Oziceli Hadzsi Ibrahim Dzsami • Berényi utca 18 • Tues–Sun 10am–5pm

To the right at the bottom of the Cat Way, at the northern end of Berényi utca, lies the fascinating **Oziceli Hacci Ibrahim Djami** – a seventeenth-century mosque. Built on what was then the northern edge of the Ottoman Empire, this is a rare example of a two-storey *djami* – the only other ones are in Bosnia. The mosque was later turned into a granary, and many of its original features have been very well preserved, including a partly restored minaret. The lower floor is even more remarkable: squeezed between the city wall and the castle hill, the *djami* was built over the medieval road that led to the gate in the city walls. You can walk down the excavated road and out of the gate, on the outside of which stands a tablet commemorating the victory of Suleiman I: when the Turks besieged Esztergom in 1543 they broke through this gate and discovered that the well inside supplied water for the castle. With their water cut off, the Hungarians surrendered.

Christian Museum

Keresztény Múzeum • Mindszenty tér 2 • March–Nov Wed–Sun 10am–5pm • 900Ft • ☎ 33 413 880, ⓦ christianmuseum.hu

Walking back from the mosque past the Cat Way, you come to the wedge-shaped plaza named after Cardinal Mindszenty. Next to the Italianate Baroque **Víziváros Parish Church** stands the old Primate's Palace, which now houses the **Christian Museum**. This is Hungary's richest hoard of religious art, featuring the largest collection of Italian prints outside Italy; Renaissance paintings and woodcarvings by German, Austrian and Hungarian masters; and some beautiful Orthodox icons from Russia and Serbia. Don't miss, either, the unique wheeled, gilded catafalque once used in Easter Week processions.

Prímás-sziget

From Mindszenty tér, you can cross a bridge to **Prímás-sziget** (Primate's Island), a popular recreation spot separated from the mainland by the narrow Kis-Duna (Little Danube). Lined with chestnut trees and weeping willows, Gesztenye fasor and Kis-Duna sétány form a lovely shady promenade frequented by lovers and anglers.

Mária Valéria híd

Further west along Táncsics Mihály utca, the reconstructed **Mária Valéria híd** links Esztergom with Slovak Štúrovo (also signposted as Párkány, its Hungarian name), five minutes' stroll across the river. Blown up by retreating Germans at the end of World War II, the bridge was left in ruins until an agreement to rebuild it was finally signed in 1999 after years of bilateral negotiations, with the European Union footing the bill. It seems only fair that EU citizens can **walk into Slovakia** with barely a flourish of their passports – other nationalities may need visas. Bring your passport anyway.

The lower town

From Prímás-sziget, it's an easy walk into the lower town, which has borne the brunt of the town's ongoing problems – as evidenced by the numerous boarded-up buildings. Largely devoid of life, the area's civic focus is the sprawling, pedestrianized **Széchenyi tér**, framed by an imposing **Town Hall** with Rococo windows that once belonged to Prince Rákóczi's general, János Bottyán. It's markedly quieter than nearby Rákóczi tér, the hub of everyday life with its supermarkets, banks and outdoor **market** running off along Simor János utca. Stop for cake and coffee at the Art Nouveau *Központi Kávéház* (see opposite) on the corner of Vörösmarty utca before exploring the backstreets beyond.

Danube Museum

Duna Múzeum • Kölcsey utca 2 • Daily except Tues: May–Oct 9am–5pm; Nov–April 10am–4pm; closed Jan • 700Ft • ⓦ dunamuzeum.hu

The **Danube Museum** mounts a visitor-friendly exhibition on the history and hydrology of Hungary's great rivers, the Danube and the Tisza. Interactive models, videos and a children's section explain the principles of fluid hydraulics, regulating rivers and disaster relief during floods, which are not uncommon on this stretch of the Danube; the most recent floods occurred in 2013, comfortably beating previous record levels.

Szent Tamás-hegy

To get a final overview of the lower town, walk up Imaház utca past a flamboyant, Moorish-style edifice that was once Esztergom's synagogue and is now a **Cultural Centre** (Művelődési Ház) with a variety of programmes. Shortly afterwards you'll find a flight of steps leading to **Szent Tamás-hegy** (St Thomas's Hill), a rocky outcrop named after the English martyr Thomas à Becket. A **chapel** was built here in his honour by Margaret Capet, whose English father-in-law, Henry II, prompted Thomas's assassination by raging "Who will rid me of this turbulent priest?" Even after her husband died and Margaret married Béla III of Hungary, her conscience would not let her forget the saint. The existing chapel (postdating the Turkish occupation) is fronted by a trio of life-size statues representing Golgotha.

ARRIVAL AND INFORMATION
ESZTERGOM

By train The train station is 1km south of town and linked to the centre by bus #1 and #5, or it's a 15min walk.

By bus Buses run from Budapest's Újpest Városkapu terminal via Szentendre and Visegrád (#880 hourly from stand 7; 2hr) or from the Árpád híd terminal via Dorog, west of the Pilis Hills (#800 every 30min from stand 6; 1hr 15min), a less scenic but faster route (both routes cost 950Ft). Arriving from Visegrád, get off near Basilica Hill rather than riding on to the bus station in the south of town.

By boat The boat leaves Budapest's Vigadó tér at 9am and takes five hours (May–Aug Tues–Sun, Sept Sat only; 2500Ft; ⓦ mahartpassnave.hu); it returns at 4.30pm, taking 3hr 30min to get back downriver.

By hydrofoil The 9.30am hydrofoil (May–Sept Sat & Sun; 5000Ft; 1hr 30min; ⓦ mahartpassnave.hu) from Budapest ties up at Prímás-sziget, a 15min walk from the centre.

Information There is no tourist office in the town, but you can get information inside the *Prímás Pince* on Szent István tér (Mon–Sat 10am–10pm, Sun 10am–5pm; ☎ 33 541 965).

EATING AND DRINKING

Csülök Csárda Batthyány utca 11–13 ☎ 33 412 420. Popular with tourists and locals alike, the reasonably priced

"Knuckle Inn" serves hearty Hungarian, Czech and German food, including a myriad of knuckle-contrived dishes

(2500Ft), as well as the likes of goose-liver pie and smoked ox tongue. Daily noon–10pm.

Központi Kávéház Vörösmarty utca 2 ☎33 520 570. A stylishly revamped Art Nouveau patisserie-cum-chocolatier in the centre of town, whose fabulous coffee and delectable cakes you'll find difficult to resist; there's a chocolate museum upstairs too. Daily 9am–8pm.

Padlizsán Pázmány Péter utca 21 ☎33 311 212. A hive of activity in the otherwise quiet Vizíváros district, this well-regarded restaurant offers crisp, modern cooking, like pork fillet with onion cake and roast potatoes (2500Ft); dine out on the pleasant stone-cobbled courtyard. Daily noon–10pm.

Primás Pince Szent István ter ☎33 541 965. Despite being completely hammed up for the tourist hordes, the cavernous bowels of the former primate's wine cellars – all brick-vaulted ceilings and neat rows of thick tables – are an enjoyable place to tuck into solid national grub. Mon–Sat noon–10pm, Sun noon–5pm.

Trafó Vörösmarty utca. Popular little bar in an old electrical substation on a small triangular square across the road from the Danube Museum: the terrace under the trees is a particularly lovely spot to kick back with a coffee or glass of wine. Mon–Sat 7am–2am, Sun 8am–midnight.

Vác

The town of **VÁC**, 40km north of Budapest, has a worldlier past than its sleepy atmosphere suggests, allowing you to enjoy its architectural heritage in relative peace. Its bishops traditionally showed a flair for self-promotion, like the cardinals of Esztergom, endowing monuments and colleges. Under Turkish occupation (1544–1686), Vác assumed an oriental character, with seven mosques and a public *hammam*, while during the Reform Era it was linked to Budapest by Hungary's first rail line (the second continued to Bratislava). In 1849 two battles were fought at Vác, the first a victory for the town over the Austrian army, followed a few months later by a defeat in July 1849 when the town was captured; the battles are commemorated by a bright green **obelisk** by the main road from Budapest, shortly before you enter the town. More recently Vác became notorious for its prison, which has one of the toughest regimes in the country and was used to incarcerate leftists under Admiral Horthy and "counter-revolutionaries" under Communism.

Március 15 tér and St Michael's Church crypt

Crypt Szent Mihály Altemplom • Március 15 tér • April–Oct Thurs & Fri 10am–2pm, Sat & Sun 10am–6pm • 300Ft

One of the most eye-catching squares in the entire country, **Március 15 tér** is a perfect triangular wedge framed by a handsome melange of sunny, pastel-coloured Baroque and Rococo buildings. At the heart of the square are the excavated ruins of **St Michael's Church**, developed piecemeal since its thirteenth-century origins. What you see now – foundation walls, sections of nave and parts of a crypt – dates mainly from the eighteenth century; the crypt itself can be visited in summer.

Memento Mori (Ignác Tragor Museum)

Memento Mori (Tragor Ignác Múzeum) • Március 15 tér 19 • Tues–Sun 10am–6pm • 1000Ft • ☎30 555 7620

The Baroque style evolved into a fine art in Vác, as evinced by the gorgeous decor of the **Dominican church** – also known as the White Friars' Church (Fehérek temploma) – on the south side of the square. During renovation work in 1994, the church crypt was rediscovered, unearthing some remarkable finds, not least 262 corpses (166 of which were positively identified) that had been preserved in a state of mummification owing to the crypt's microclimatic conditions. Three of the mummified corpses (a male, female and infant) – dating from the eighteenth century – can be seen in the **Memento Mori** display in a chilly medieval wine cellar near the church.

Also retrieved from the bodies were an immaculately preserved assortment of clothes and other burial accessories (including crucifixes, which were traditionally placed in the hands of the deceased), alongside their colourfully painted wooden coffins – typically, the adult coffin would be painted brown or dark blue, and the child's coffin green and white.

Diocesan Treasury

Székesegyházi kincstár • Marcius 15 tér 4 • May–Oct Wed–Fri 2–6pm, Sat & Sun 10am–6pm • 500Ft

On the northeast side of the square, the **Diocesan Treasury** is housed in the former Bishop's Palace (Nagyprépostí palota). It was built for Bishop Kristóf Migazzi (1714–1803) who erected Vác's cathedral and the Baroque **Town Hall** across the square, its gable adorned with two prostrate females bearing the coats of arms of Hungary and of Migazzi himself. During his years as Bishop of Vác (1762–86), this ambitious prelate was the moving force behind the town's eighteenth-century revival, impressing Empress Maria Theresa sufficiently to make him Archbishop of Vienna. Meanwhile his former palace was converted into Hungary's first Institute for the Deaf and Dumb in 1802. Downstairs is a collection of church treasures and displays on local diocesan history and architecture. But it is worth persevering and going upstairs, where restoration work has uncovered fabulous Rococo frescoes from two periods of the eighteenth century in four of the rooms, one with a winter garden scene, another decorated with fruit and flowers.

Museum Hall

Értéktár • Köztársaság út 19 • May–Oct Thurs & Fri 10am–2pm, Sat & Sun 10am–6pm • 400Ft, joint ticket with the crypt 500Ft

Two doors along from the Treasury – the main square turns seamlessly into Köztársaság út – is the **Museum Hall**, which has a delightful display of works by the popular Hungarian children's illustrator Gyula Hincz (1904–86). The museum is also covered by a combined ticket that includes the St Michael's crypt (see p.143).

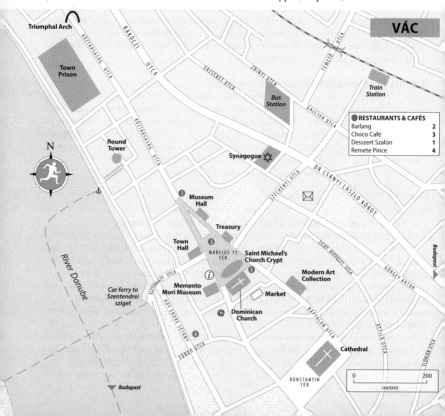

The cathedral

Székesegyház • Konstantin tér • April–Nov Mon–Sat 10am–noon & 1.30–6pm, Sun 7.30am–7pm

A short walk down Káptalan utca brings you to the lively **market** (Mon–Sat 8am–2pm) selling flowers, fruit and vegetables. Pressing on along the road you come to the back of Vác's **cathedral**. Chiefly impressive for its gigantic Corinthian columns, Migazzi's church is a temple to self-esteem more than anything else. Its Neoclassical design by Isidore Canevale was considered revolutionary in the 1770s, the style not becoming generally accepted in Hungary until the following century. Migazzi himself took umbrage at one of the frescoes by Franz Anton Maulbertsch, and ordered *The Meeting of Mary and Elizabeth*, above the altar, to be bricked over. His motives for this are unknown, but one theory is that it was because Mary was depicted as being pregnant. The fresco was only discovered during restoration work in 1944. From the cathedral you can head along Múzeum utca to Géza király tér, the centre of Vác in medieval times, where there's a Baroque **Franciscan church** with a magnificent organ, pulpits and altars.

Along the waterfront

11

From the Franciscan church you can follow the road down to the **riverside promenade**, József Attila sétány, where the townsfolk of Vác walk on summer weekends and evenings. The northern stretch of the promenade, named after Liszt, runs past the **Round Tower**, the only remnant of Vác's medieval fortifications.

The prison

Beyond the dock for ferries to Budapest and Esztergom rises the forbidding hulk of the town's **prison** (*fegyház*). Ironically, the building was originally an academy for noble youths, founded by Maria Theresa. Turned into a barracks in 1784 – you can still see part of the older building peering awkwardly above the blank white walls of the prison – it began its penal career a century later, achieving infamy during the Horthy era, when two Communists died here after being beaten for going on hunger strike to protest against maltreatment. In October 1956 a mass escape occurred. Thrown into panic by reports from Budapest where their colleagues were being "hunted down like animals, hung on trees, or just beaten to death by passers-by", the ÁVO guards mounted guns on the rooftop, fomenting rumours of the Uprising among prisoners whose hopes had been raised by snatches of patriotic songs overheard from the streets. A glimpse of national flags with the Soviet emblem cut from the centre provided the spark: a guard was overpowered, locks were shot off, and the prisoners burst free.

Triumphal Arch

The **Triumphal Arch** (Kőkapu or Diadalív) flanking the prison was another venture by Migazzi and his architect Canevale, occasioned by Maria Theresa's visit in 1764. Migazzi initially planned theatrical facades to hide the town's dismal housing (perhaps inspired by Potemkin's fake villages in Russia, created around the same time), but settled for the Neoclassical arch, from which Habsburg heads grimace a stony welcome.

ARRIVAL AND INFORMATION   **VÁC**

By train There are regular services from Nyugati Station to Vác – the *zonázó* trains are the faster ones. From the train station, at the northern end of Széchenyi utca, it's a 10min walk down to Március 15 tér.

By bus Buses go from Ujpest Városkapu bus station in Budapest every half-hour and take 55min. They arrive at Szent István tér, a few minutes closer to the main square than the train station.

By ferry The boat leaves Budapest's Vigadó tér at 9am (May–Aug Tues–Sun, Sept Sat only; 1500Ft; Ⓦ mahartpassnave.hu) and takes two hours to make the journey upriver (the return is at 6.30pm and takes 1hr 30min back down to Budapest). Disembarking at the landing stage for ferries from Budapest, you can see the prison and triumphal arch to the north; head south along the promenade and the town centre is on the left.

Tourist office The helpful Tourinform, at Március 15 tér 17 (Mon–Fri 9am–5pm, Sat & Sun 10am–noon; ☏ 27 316 160, Ⓦ tourinformvac.hu), has all the information you need.

EATING AND DRINKING

Barlang Marcius 15 tér ☎ 27 315 584. Down some steps in the very centre of the square, the *Barlang* is a friendly, neon-lit cellar restaurant with red leather seating, serving a cracking range of pizzas. In summer it opens up its large outdoor terrace up above. Daily 11am–10pm.

Choco Café Marcius 15 tér 20. Here at this cosy cafe, you can mull over a long menu of chocolate drinks in every conceivable flavour, such as almond, cinnamon, and orange and nutmeg. Mon–Thurs & Sun 9am–9pm, Fri–Sat 9am–10pm.

Desszert Szalon Köztársaság út 21 ☎ 20 390 3367. Also known as *Mihályi László Cukrászda* – László is the award-winning confectioner who produces a toothsome selection of the most perfectly formed cakes in this tiny, salon-like place. Outdoor terrace in summer. Daily 10am–7pm.

Remete Pince Fürdő lépcső 3 ☎ 27 302 199. Located out by the town's lido, this is the town's best restaurant, an elegant but not too pricey brick-vaulted cellar with candle-topped tables and wrought-iron chairs, while the flower-bedecked terrace is lovely in warmer weather. The food, meanwhile, ranges from roast goose with braised red cabbage (2900Ft) to grilled pike-perch with king prawns (3400Ft). Daily noon–10pm.

11 | Gödöllő

The small town of **Gödöllő** boasts a former Habsburg summer palace and a famous artists' colony, but being 30km northeast of Budapest rather than on the Danube Bend, it gets far fewer tourists than Szentendre, despite a reliable HÉV service from Örs Vezér tere (the terminus of the red metro line #2) that means you can enjoy an evening concert and return easily to the capital afterwards.

The Royal Palace

Királyi Kastély • Daily: April–Oct 10am–6pm; Nov–March 10am–5pm • 2200Ft; last tickets sold 40min before closing; audio-guide 800Ft • ☎ 28 410 124, ⦿ kiralyikastely.hu

The **Royal Palace** was commissioned by a confidante of Empress Maria Theresa's, Count Antal Grassalkovich, and designed by András Mayerhoffer, who introduced the Baroque style of mansion to Hungary in the 1740s. The palace suffered as a result of both world wars, being commandeered as a headquarters first by the Reds and then by the Whites in 1919–20, and pillaged by both the Nazis and the Red Army in 1944. One wing was later turned into an old people's home, while the rest was left to rot until 1985, when the restoration of the palace finally began. The work gathered pace after the palace was chosen as the venue for Hungary's EU presidency in 2011.

Pick up a plan of the palace's 26 rooms in the ticket office. The formal **state rooms**, reached by a grand staircase, precede the private apartments used by Emperor Franz Josef and his wife Elizabeth – his decorated in grey and gold, hers draped in her favourite colour, violet. Sisi, as she was known, stayed two thousand nights in the

SISI, THE FRIEND OF HUNGARY

One of the most popular historical figures in Hungary today is **Empress Elizabeth** (1837–98), the beautiful wife of the Austrian Emperor Franz Josef. She might seem a strange choice, given that her husband crushed the Hungarians in 1848, but that may be the clue to the bond that developed between the empress and Hungary. She loathed life in the Viennese court and was none too attached to the emperor either, and Budapest came to represent a refuge for her. She also avoided staying in the empty Royal Palace in Budapest, preferring to spend her time in the palace in Gödöllő and a villa in the Buda Hills near the Jáno-shegy (p.119). The Hungarians called her Sisi (pronounced see-see) and she pleaded their cause in Vienna. There were even rumours of affairs with the Hungarian statesman Count Gyula Andrássy.

Sisi's later years were blighted by tragedy – the death of her siblings and the suicide of her son Rudolf at Mayerling – before she herself was stabbed to death by an anarchist in 1898 in Switzerland. Mourned throughout Hungary, she became the focus of a cult that outlasted all attempts to stifle it under Communism.

palace at Gödöllő, preferring it to Vienna. While her possessions are reverentially displayed – right down to a horseshoe from her stallion – there's no sign to identify the secret staircase that she had installed as a means of getting some privacy in a relentlessly public life.

Temporary exhibitions are held in the Rudolf and Gizella wings, while the **Riding Hall** (Lovárda), which hosted the EU presidency, is used for exhibitions and concerts. The **Baroque Theatre** (Barokk színház) that Count Grassalkovich established in a side-wing (used for only two weeks each year when he was in residence), the **Royal Hill Pavilion** (Királydombi pavilion) and **Baths** (Fürdő) in the large park that stretches behind the Palace are occasionally open to individual visitors. The baths were last enjoyed by Admiral Horthy, who used Gödöllő as a holiday home from 1920 till 1944, installing a swimming pool and an air-raid shelter; this can only be visited on a guided tour, though these are normally reserved for groups only. Musical and cultural programmes are staged within the palace throughout the year.

Gödöllő Town Museum

Gödöllői Városi Múzeum • Szabadság tér 5 • Tues–Sun 10am–6pm • 600Ft • ☎ 28 422 002

Back across the main road and the HÉV tracks and down to the right, the delightful **Gödöllő Town Museum** focuses on the **Gödöllő Artists' Colony**. Founded in 1901, the colony was inspired by the English Pre-Raphaelites and the Arts and Crafts movement of William Morris and John Ruskin, whose communal, rural ethos it took a stage further. Members included Aladár Körösfői-Kriesch, who wrote a book about Ruskin and Morris, and Sándor Nagy, whose home and workshop may eventually become a separate museum. There was a strong tradition of weaving in the artists' colony – here at least the lack of English captions is no obstacle to enjoyment. The museum's other displays include good exhibitions of regional history, including mock-up rooms illustrating the life of the Gödöllő estate; the displays on hunting and the Gödöllő scout troop should not detain you too long.

ARRIVAL AND INFORMATION

GÖDÖLLŐ

By train HÉV trains from Örs Vezér tere (every 30min) take about 50min to reach Gödöllő; get off at the Szabadság tér stop, bang opposite the palace. BKK tickets (and Budapest Cards) are valid as far as the city limits, so you will need to buy a supplementary ticket to cover the remaining part of the journey, or show a BKK pass or ticket when buying a ticket at the station or on the train.

Tourist booth There's a Tourinform booth inside the palace (Tues–Sun: Nov–March 10am–4pm; April–Oct 10am–5pm; ☎ 28 415 402, ⊚ gkrte.hu).

EATING AND DRINKING

Solier Café Dózsa György utca 13 ☎ 20 396 5512. Set in a modern block on the corner of Kossuth Lajos utca, some 300m north of the HÉV station, *Solier* serves up the best meals and cakes in town; the wide repertoire of food includes duck breast with sesame tempura (3100Ft). Mon–Sat 8am–10pm, Sun 10am–9pm.

Sulyán Cukrászda Szabadság tér 8 ☎ 28 416 536. In the big square behind the Gödöllő Town Museum, this is a popular place for cakes, ices and coffee. Outside tables in summer. Daily 9am–7pm.

Accommodation

Budapest's accommodation is improving all the time, both in terms of availability and quality, though the downside is that prices are in many cases on a par with most Western Europe capitals. The city is flush with high-end hotels, typically around the Belváros and up in the Vár (Castle District), which includes the burgeoning trend for flashy boutique hotels where style is big but the rooms are often small. That said, there's still a decent spread of affordable three-star hotels out beyond the main downtown areas. Pensions are an even cheaper alternative, often with much the same facilities as small hotels, while the city is bursting with hostels. If you're on a tight budget, your safest bet is a private room, though these are getting harder to find – the trend nowadays is for self-contained studio flats or apartments rented through internet-based companies.

All hotels are **star-rated**, though this is not always an accurate guide to the standard or ambience of a place. Some of the newer, smaller hotels have facilities that belie their star rating, while some of the more luxurious establishments can be disappointingly bland with an impersonal feel. Budapest is awash with well-run and well-equipped youth hostels, many of which now offer smart en-suite private rooms to go alongside the traditional large dorm. You'll see them all over the place, though you're best off avoiding any that advertise themselves just as "hostel" and stick to those listed in this guide. Some represent the cheapest form of accommodation in the city, while others are more expensive than private rooms. While it's unlikely that you'll come to Budapest to **camp**, there are a few year-round possibilities over on the Buda side.

ESSENTIALS

Reservations It's advisable to book a room during high season (roughly May–Oct). Otherwise, rooms are most in demand at Christmas, New Year, and during the Spring and Autumn Festivals in March/October respectively, when many hotels ramp up the rates; unless you're here for the Grand Prix in early August, you may wish to avoid the city then, as most hotels double their prices. Also during August, many hostels get booked up months in advance for the Sziget Festival – here, too, most up their rates. Even so, it should always be possible to find somewhere that's reasonably priced, if not well situated.

Booking a room Aside from booking a room directly (either by phone or online), there are several online accommodation sites. w hotelinfo.hu lists the city's hotels and pensions and has information about Hungary Card discounts, but doesn't allow you to make bookings. To book online, try the following: w budapesthotelreservation .hu, w destinationbudapest.hu or w hotels.hu. Agencies in Budapest that can arrange accommodation include: Ibusz V, Aranykéz utca 4–6, ☎ 1 501 4910, w ibusz.hu (Mon–Fri 9am–5pm), and Vista Visitor Center VI, Paulay Ede utca 7–9 ☎ 1 429 9735, w vistahungary.com (Mon–Fri 9am–5.30pm).

Prices Accommodation rates are usually quoted in euros; where prices are given in forints, we have followed suit, but note that you can always pay in forints. Rates given in our reviews reflect the typical cost of a double or twin room in high season. That said, rates fluctuate wildly according to both season and demand, and you can find some terrific deals, particularly in some of the top-end hotels – indeed, book early enough and out of season, and you'll often find prices much lower than the ones given here. The cheapest rooms in a three-star hotel or pension go for between €50–70, while you'll typically pay upwards of €100–120 for a room in a four-star or design hotel. Beyond this, in many of the five-star establishments, you're often entering the realms of the stratospheric. Hostel dorm beds vary between €10 and €15, with a double room (with shared facilities) going for around €35–40, while a private double room in a hostel costs about €45. Note that some hotels do not include twenty percent VAT (*Áfa*) and three percent tourist tax in quoted prices, so check before you commit yourself.

Internet Nearly all the hotels listed here have internet access, and the majority of these have wi-fi. Access is usually free, although a handful of places still charge. In any case, it's always best to check first.

12

HOTELS AND PENSIONS

The greatest choice of accommodation, particularly hotels and hostels, is in **Pest**, which is where you'll also find the greatest concentration of restaurants and bars – though you will have to contend with more traffic noise. The grand hotels that lined the riverbank were all destroyed during World War II, and while their replacements – such as the *Marriott* and *InterContinental* – offer fantastic views, they don't have quite the same elegance. Going in the other direction, there are plenty of hotels along and beyond the Nagykörút (the larger ring road) and up towards City Park. Across the water, **Buda** offers more restful possibilities, especially within the Castle District where there are several first-rate hotels, with more along the riverfront. It's on this side of the river, too, that you'll find Budapest's most appealing pensions, notably up in the **Buda Hills**, which is within easy reach of Széll Kálmán tér. In this city of baths, it's no surprise that several of the big hotels offer **spa packages**: the *Gellért* and the *Danubius* (on Margit-sziget) hotels were built next to springs, while several other five-star hotels in the centre have luxury spa complexes.

THE BELVÁROS

Astoria V, Kossuth utca 19–21 ☎ 1 889 6000, w danubiushotels.com/astoria; map p.38. Four-star vintage hotel which has given its name to the major junction in central Pest on which it's located, though fortunately all the windows are soundproofed. The two categories of room available (standard and classic) differ little by way of facilities, but the latter are larger and markedly more pleasing on the eye. Wi-fi costs extra in the rooms. The hotel's coffee house (see p.168) and bar is a popular meeting point. **€140**

Bohém Art V, Molnár utca 35 ☎ 1 327 9020,

> ### TOP 5 COOL HOTELS
> **Brody House** see p.152
> **Buda Castle** see p.152
> **Gerlóczy** see p.150
> **La Prima Fashion** see p.150
> **Baltazár** see p.152

12

ⓦ bohemarthotel.hu; map p.38. Hip four-star boutique hotel in a former paper factory close to the Danube with bright art and cosy rooms. The sixty rooms squeezed into the building come in different sizes, from apartments and family suites to superior rooms, with baths, to the very compact classic rooms with showers. All rooms are dominated by large prints covering whole walls. €100

Buddha-Bar V, Váci utca 34 ☎1 799 7300, ⓦ buddhabar.com; map p.38. If you thought the exterior of *Buddha-Bar* was grand enough, step through the doors and see the striking black and red decor inside. Pest's new luxury chill-out zone is housed in one of the palaces that form the gateway to the Erzsébet Bridge. The 102 rooms have high ceilings and state of the art fittings, from heated mirrors to remote control toilet-bidets, while the corner apartments have huge family-size baths. The windows are well soundproofed, though you may prefer a room away from the main road. The bar has a DJ continuing the chill-out theme, and the restaurant also gets good marks. €160

Cosmo Fashion V, Váci utca 77 ☎1 799 0077, ⓦ cosmohotelbudapest.com; map p.38. Despite its location smack-bang in the heart of tourist central, the tall, slender *Cosmo* is well insulated against the passing traffic. The deep purple, black and pink furnished rooms might be a bit much for some tastes, but there's no disputing the level of comfort on offer. Breakfast is taken in the adjoining Italian restaurant. €120

Estilo Fashion 83 Váci utca 83 ☎01 799 7170, ⓦ estilohotelbudapest.com; map p.38. Although sited along the city's busiest pedestrianised street, this smart retreat is surprisingly restful, while the bold blue, red and white striped colour theme running throughout the hotel is rather more tasteful than it sounds. €90

★**Gerlóczy** V, Gerlóczy utca 1 ☎1 501 4000, ⓦ gerloczy.hu; map p.38. Above the café of the same name, the nineteen elegant *Gerlóczy* rooms all lead off a spiral staircase topped by a coloured glass skylight. The rooms are colour themed according to floor (grey, blue, red and yellow-green from the bottom upwards), though all have similar fixtures and fittings – high doors and ceilings, parquet flooring and gorgeous, brass-fitted bathrooms, some with clawfoot tubs, some with showers only. Two rooms have small balconies looking out over the square (€110). Free minibar. One of the best value-for-money places in the city, especially if you can nab one of the slightly cheaper attic rooms. €95

Kempinski Corvinus V, Erzsébet tér 7–8 ☎1 429 3777, ⓦ kempinski-budapest.com; map p.38. Flashy five-star establishment on the edge of the Belváros holding more than three hundred rooms. Luxurious to a fault, the rooms are fitted with handsome beige and black Art Deco furnishings, and a host of mod cons to boot. The hotel's comprehensive leisure facilities include a spa, indoor pool and a gym, and there's also the fabulous *Nobu* restaurant. €350

La Prima Fashion V, Piarista utca 6 ☎1 799 0088, ⓦ laprimahotelbudapest.com; map p.38. A stone's throw from the Elizabeth Bridge, this sparkling fashion hotel oozes sophistication, from the smart lobby to the plush rooms decorated in fetching turquoise and chocolate brown colours. The cool factor extends to the oversized wall mirrors embedded with TVs, and designer bathrooms with walk-in showers. €140

Le Méridien V, Erzsébet tér 9–10 ☎1 429 5500, ⓦ lemeridien-budapest.com; map p.38. Originally built for the Adria insurance company at the turn of the twentieth century, this building housed the police headquarters in the Communist years until it was totally gutted and reopened as a luxury hotel. It's magnificently furnished throughout, with a pronounced French influence manifest in grand sofas, big chests and wall-length mirrors, and beautifully tiled marble bathrooms. €400

Peregrinus V, Szerb utca 3 ☎1 266 4911, ⓦ peregrinushotel.hu; map p.38. Low-key, university-owned place on a quiet backstreet in central Pest, whose 25 rooms (including six singles and two apartments) are spacious, light-filled and come with TV, radio and writing tables – the last provided to meet the needs of visiting academics. €90

Zara Boutique V, Só utca 6 ☎1 577 0700, ⓦ zarahotels .com; map p.38. Four-star boutique hotel off the bottom of Váci utca, close to the Main Market Hall. Although by no means large, the rooms are impressive, with smart, dark furniture set against hardwood flooring and light, design-papered walls. Double and twin-bedded rooms in equal measure, and all with showers. €190

LIPÓTVÁROS AND ÚJLIPÓTVÁROS

★**Four Seasons** V, Széchenyi tér 5–6 ☎1 268 6000, ⓦ fourseasons.com/budapest; map p.48. A magnificent restoration of this Budapest landmark has produced an unprecedented level of luxury in the city; the rooms have Art Nouveau-style fittings (even down to the beautiful radiators) and are excellently equipped; those overlooking the Danube naturally have the best aspect. The *Gresham* restaurant, which also acts as a coffee house, is excellent – drinks are also served in the bar in the wonderful glass-roofed Peacock Passage – and the service throughout the hotel is superlative. €310

Starlight Suiten V, Mérleg utca 6 ☎1 484 3700, ⓦstarlighthotels.com; map p.48. Amazingly good value given its location near the Lánchíd (right behind the *Four Seasons*), with 54 immaculate and incredibly roomy suites. Each has a kitchenette with a microwave, two televisions (one in each room), a sofa and a writing desk. Facilities include a sauna, steam bath and fitness rooms. €199

TERÉZVÁROS AND ERZSÉBETVÁROS

Benczúr VI, Benczúr utca 35 ☎1 479 5650, ⓦhotelbenczur.hu; map p.58. Large, modern and functional hotel on a leafy street off Andrássy út offering three categories of room; boxy, no-frills standard rooms, eco rooms, which are renovated standard rooms (most have a/c and some are designated smoking rooms) and bigger, brighter superior rooms which come with showers – several also have a balcony. Some of the superior rooms are anti-allergen and have disabled access. There are also some apartments for families. Breakfast included. €60

Casati VI, Paulay Ede utca 31 ☎1 343 1198, ⓦcasatibudapesthotel.com; map p.58. The new management has given the old *Pest Hotel* a new name and a striking facelift but has kept the old features of this historic apartment block – such as the eighteenth-century bared walls in the bar area. The lively decorations by young Hungarian artists in the public spaces of the hotel might not be to all tastes, but the 25 rooms themselves are calmer, coming in four styles, according to your mood. Most of the generously sized, gracefully furnished rooms face inwards over a balconied courtyard crawling with greenery, which is also where breakfast is served. Gym and sauna in the basement. €95

City Comfort Apartments VI, Benczúr utca 19 ☎0670 375 6228, ⓦcitycomfortapartments.com; map p.58. Situated in a leafy street next to the Chinese embassy, in a modern block round a small courtyard, the *City Comfort* offers spacious, simply furnished self-catering one- and two-bedroom apartments complete with a living room, TV, big twin beds and a small kitchen with two electric rings; no a/c, however. There are also two small doubles. A good-value option. Doubles €35, apartments €50,

Continental Hotel Zara V, Dohány utca 42–44 ☎1 815 1000, ⓦcontinentalhotelbudapest.com; map p.58. Occupying the old Hungária bathhouse, this towering Secessionist edifice has been superbly restored. From the shiny lobby, with its magnificent glass-panelled ceiling, to the sumptuous Art Deco rooms, the place oozes class. The spa centre, meanwhile, is as swish as any in Budapest, though its real selling point is the rooftop garden with a sparkling little pool offering views across the city. €120

Corinthia Grand Royal VII, Erzsébet körút 43–49 ☎1 479 4000, ⓦcorinthiahotels.com; map p.58.

Opened as the *Grand Hotel Royal* in 1898, the *Corinthia* and its concierges enjoy the idea that this is the inspiration for Wes Anderson's celluloid *Grand Budapest Hotel*. The imposing building was used as offices for some forty years, and it took a major rebuilding project – only the facade is original – to turn out four hundred or so rooms with such unbridled luxury. Many look out onto the main boulevard, though a good number face inwards, overlooking the splendid, marble-tiled atrium. The centrepiece of the hotel's Royal Spa complex is a stunning pool. €125

easyHotel VI, Eötvös utca 25/a ☎1 411 1982, ⓦeasyhotel.com; map p.58. Decent location near Oktogon with the same approach as easyJet, where cheapness and simplicity rule. The a/c rooms have one bright orange wall and come in two sizes: small (7–9 square metres, enough room for a bed and your bag, as long as it's not too big); and standard, which has slightly more space and even a couple of hooks. The en-suite shower/toilets have the feel of an airplane cubicle, and, in true Easy style, you pay for everything else, such as TV, internet and breakfast. There are two larger rooms with disabled access on the ground floor. Bookable online only, rooms start at around €19 according to demand, but are usually €60–70

K&K Opera VI, Révay utca 24 ☎1 269 0222, ⓦkkhotels .com; map p.58. Opulent, and expensive, four-star hotel that really trades on its location right by the Opera House. Most of its two-hundred-plus rooms are of average size, but they are supremely comfortable; around half have baths, the others showers, some walk-in. €225

★**Mamaison Hotel Andrássy** VI, Andrássy út 111 ☎1 462 2100, ⓦmamaison.com; map p.58. Housed in a fine Bauhaus building up near the Városliget (but with easy access to the Belváros), *Mamaison* offers luxury accommodation without the corporate feel. The rooms, some of which have a balcony, are beautifully appointed in silvery-grey tones offset with splashes of red, while bathrooms feature turquoise and cream patterned tiles. Try and bag one of the rooms away from busy Andrássy út. The tree-shaded terrace is a lovely spot to take in the first meal of the day (€15). €89

Medosz VI, Jókai tér 9 ☎1 374 3001, ⓦmedoszhotel .hu; map p.58. Overlooking a leafy square near Oktogon, the three-star hotel's location, good prices and the helpful staff make this a popular choice. Operating till 1989 as a trade union hostel – its exterior betrays its past – the *Medosz* still has simply furnished but pleasant rooms. Most rooms have baths and those with showers benefit from overlooking the quieter courtyard. The lower floors have family rooms sleeping up to six people, while the ninth floor rooms have small balconies. The four new rooftop Panorama apartments (€119) have terraces with breathtaking views. €69

12

Mirage Fashion VI, Dózsa György út 88 ☎1 462 7070, ⊛miragehotelbudapest.com; map p.58. Despite its location fronting a busy thoroughfare, this hotel – occupying a splendid nineteenth-century villa – is superbly sited, being just a short walk from both the metro and the many attractions of the Városliget. The rooms are amply sized, stylishly furnished and represent terrific value. €75

Radisson Blu Béke VI, Teréz körút 43 ☎1 889 3900, ⊛radissonblu.com/hotel-budapest; map p.58. Large, vintage hotel in a handy location on the Nagykörút near Nyugati station. The rooms are smooth without being spectacular, though other facilities include a pool, sauna and gym, underground garage and an agreeable café on the ground floor. If you're passing, take a look at the corner facade, which is distinguished by a nineteenth-century mosaic of St George and the Dragon. €100

Soho V, Dohány utca 64 ☎1 872 8292, ⊛sohohotel.hu; map p.58. The visual assault begins in the Pop Art-inspired lobby, and continues through to the small but snappily designed rooms, decked out in cool reds, greys and blacks, and sporting Swedish hardwood flooring, bamboo-covered walls and glass-partitioned bathrooms. A filling American-style buffet breakfast rounds things off. €125

Star Inn VI, Dessewffy utca 36 ☎1 472 2020, ⊛starinnhotels.com; map p.58. This rather non-descript glass and brick building does little to inspire, but the rooms concealed within are fresh and contemporary; deep-red walls, white armchairs and low-slung beds. The location and price makes this a very respectable option. €50

JÓZSEFVÁROS AND FERENCVÁROS

Atlas City VIII, Népszinház utca 39–41 ☎1 299 0256, ⊛atlashotelbudapest.com; map p.77. There are few frills about this solid three-star hotel, located in a slightly down-at-heel neighbourhood ten minutes' walk from Blaha Lujza tér. However, the rooms are perfectly adequate, it's fairly priced, and you'll get a friendly welcome. Triples and quads available too. €60

★**Atrium Fashion** VIII, Csokonai utca 14 ☎1 299 0777, ⊛hotelatrium.hu; map p.77. This otherwise glum-looking street has been given a welcome dollop of colour, thanks to this cleverly conceived hotel. The focal point of the building is a gloriously sunny atrium, encircled by state-of-the-art rooms with floor-to-ceiling windows, built-in flat-screen TVs, and bits of artwork; some rooms have tubs, others have showers. €60

★**Brody House** VIII, Bródy Sándor utca 10 ☎1 266 1211, ⊛brodyhouse.com; map p.77. A fabulously hip and award-winning retreat accommodating eight individually styled rooms and three apartments in what was once the home of the Hungarian Prime Minister. The

relaxed, shabby-chic style of the reception and lounges (at the top of the hotel, on the second floor – no lift) is continued throughout – the recycling of fittings in the furniture is great fun. It also has a members' club, the *Brody Studios*, not far from Oktogon, which stages concerts and shows, and where guests can have lunch. Breakfast €8. €90

★**Lavender Circus** V, Múzeum körút 37 ☎0670 417 7763, ⊛lavendercircus.com; map p.77. Eccentric little "hostel" (actually more a budget hotel as there are no dorms) opposite the National Museum with a very individual touch – the owner Ádám has spent the past six years designing the rooms – expect vintage furniture, goldfish tanks and satirical artwork gracing the walls. The pricier ones on the second floor have en-suite bathrooms and kitchenettes. Reception is on the third floor (no lift). No breakfast. Doubles from €33

Mercure Museum VIII, Trefort utca 2 ☎1 485 1080, ⊛mercure.com; map p.77. Having established itself in an imaginatively transformed Pest apartment block on a quiet street behind the National Museum, the *Mercure* has expanded into the next-door block. The newer half is sleek and modern in design, but the older, Italian-flavoured part has more appeal, set around a glass-roofed courtyard. The rooms, which have a mix of baths and showers, aren't big, but it's a friendly place and in a good location. There's a small Wellness centre in the basement and the hotel also holds its own permanent art gallery. €120

THE VÁR AND THE VÍZIVÁROS

Art'otel I, Bem rakpart 16–19 ☎1 487 9487, ⊛artotels.com; map p.87. Boutique hotel that combines eighteenth-century buildings – comprising beautiful, spacious rooms with original doors and high ceilings – with a modern wing overlooking the river, offering marvellous views; here, too, the rooms are well equipped and come with funkily designed bathrooms, most with shower. €115

★**Baltazár** I, Országház utca 31 ☎1 300 7051, ⊛baltazarbudapest.com; map p.89. Family-run boutique hotel that has become a firm favourite with travellers since it opened in 2013. Its location is superb, next to the National Archives at the northern end of the Vár. Like the nearby eateries *21* and *Café Pierrot*, which are run by the same people, the hotel is stylishly presented, and its showy eleven rooms – inspired by the likes of Vivienne Westwood, Andy Warhol and Keith Haring – are kitted-out with antique furniture and luxury products. Breakfast €10–15. €137

Buda Castle I, Úri utca 39 ☎1 224 7900, ⊛budacastlehotelbudapest.com; map p.89. Located midway along one of the quieter streets in the Vár, this fifteenth-century merchant's house has been superbly converted into a handsome design hotel. The rooms –

which are essentially mini suites – are of the highest order, constructed around a small grassy courtyard, which is where guests can also take breakfast. The place is impeccably staffed too. **€200**

Burg I, Szentháromság tér 7–8 ☎ 1 212 0269, ⓦ burghotelbudapest.com; map p.89. Anonymous white-brick building right in the heart of the Castle District, opposite the Mátyás Church. The 26 rooms are nothing out of the ordinary, but most of them have a great view, overlooking the bustling main square and church. **€90**

★**Castle Garden** I, Lovas út 41 ☎ 1 224 7420, ⓦ hotelcastlegarden.hu; map p.89. Friendly modern four-star just below the Castle walls, a short walk down from the Bécsi kapu. The 39 rooms are light and airy, and the superior rooms have terraces and great views. They have connecting rooms for families, and one room with disabled access. The hotel's restaurant is excellent, and there's also a wellness centre with a jacuzzi. It's a refreshingly understated place, and it offers unbeatable value. Breakfast €10. **€79**

Hilton Budapest I, Hess András tér 1–3 ☎ 1 889 6600, ⓦ hilton.com; map p.89. By the Mátyás Church in the Vár, with superb views across the river, this top hotel incorporates the remains of a medieval monastery, where summertime concerts are held in the former church. Luxurious to a fault, the rooms veer between classic and modern, and it's worth paying the extra for a room with river view. **€220**

Lánchíd 19 I, Lánchíd utca 19 ☎ 1 419 1900, ⓦ lanchid19hotel.hu; map p.89. Located by the Chain Bridge, as its name suggests, this award-winning design hotel includes such features as an exterior facade of moving panels and suspended glass walkways leading to artfully conceived rooms, each of which has been individually themed – for example on a wedding or a film. Breakfast €13. **€135**

★**St George's Residence** I, Fortuna utca 4 ☎ 1 393 5700, ⓦ stgeorgehotel.hu; map p.89. Variously a medieval inn, art school and law court, this fabulous building has been tastefully restored to become one of the city's most characterful hotels; the 26 sumptuously decorated suites, all furnished in Grand Empire style, are priced according to size but all essentially comprise a bedroom, bathroom (some with jacuzzi), and living room with a study corner and kitchenette. A fine location and cheerful, obliging staff make this a first-class stopover. **€129**

★**Victoria** I, Bem rakpart 11 ☎ 1 457 8080, ⓦ victoria .hu; map p.87. Small, super-friendly hotel on the embankment directly below the Mátyás Church. The neat, a/c rooms are handsomely furnished and there are big windows through which you can soak up the excellent views of the Lánchíd and the river. **€99**

GELLÉRT-HEGY AND THE TABÁN

★**Ábel Panzió** XI, Ábel Jenő utca 9 ☎ 1 209 2537, ⓦ abelpanzio.hu; map p.107. There are few more enjoyable pensions in Budapest than this graceful, early-1900s villa situated in a quiet, leafy street 20min walk from the Belváros. It boasts ten rooms of charming simplicity (none has TV, but all have wi-fi), a drawing room where you can watch TV or listen to music, and a delightful garden and terrace for further relaxation. A popular place so advance booking is essential. **€50**

Charles XI, Hegyalja út 23 ☎ 1 212 9169, ⓦ charleshotel.hu; map p.107. On the hill up from the Erzsébet híd on the main road to Vienna, this friendly apartment hotel was one of the first of its kind in the city. It has a wide range of studios and apartments (with double or twin beds, bath or shower) all of which come with a decently equipped kitchen; those facing the inner yard are better, as the road is very busy. Bikes available for rent. **€65**

Gellért XI, Szent Gellért tér 1 ☎ 1 889 5500, ⓦ danubiushotels.com/gellert; map p.107. There's no escaping the magnificence of this Art Nouveau building, which also incorporates one of the city's largest, most popular bath complexes. Once inside, there's a rather stiff atmosphere about the place, though the rooms are impressive enough, if overpriced; try and bag one facing the river, some of which also have a balcony. Hotel guests receive one free entry to the pools, and 50% discounts after that. Wi-fi in rooms costs extra. **€160**

Orion I, Döbrentei utca 13 ☎ 1 356 8583, ⓦ bestwestern-ce.com/orion; map p.107. Small modern block in the Tabán district, at the foot of the Vár. The thirty rooms are simply furnished (with space for a small writing desk) and the bathrooms are pretty cramped, but it's reasonably priced and in a useful location, across the river from the Belváros and a tram ride from the baths. Guests can also make use of a sauna. **€79**

ÓBUDA AND MARGIT-SZIGET

Danubius Grand and Danubius Health Spa Resort XIII, Margit-sziget ☎ 1 889 4752, ⓦ danubiushotels .com; map p.116. Both hotels are at the northern end of the island and provide a very wide range of spa facilities from mud spas to massages, as well as medical and cosmetic services from pedicures to plastic surgery. Rates include access to the thermal baths, pool, sauna, gym and other facilities. The *Grand* is the island's original, *fin-de-siècle* spa hotel; rooms here have period furniture, balconies and high ceilings. The *Health Spa Resort* is the big modern one, with balconies offering views over the island. Wi-fi free in public areas. Some rooms have disabled access. Rooms in both **€200**

Pál Panzió III, Pálvölgyi köz 15 ☎ 0630 312 9351; map p.113. Four double rooms in this small, welcoming

12

12

pension, situated right on the edge of the Buda Hills near the Pálvölgy Stalactite Cave. €40

THE BUDA HILLS

★**Beatrix Panzió** II, Szehér út 3 ☎1 275 0550, ⓦbeatrixhotel.hu; tram #61; map p.120. Friendly pension in the villa district northwest of Széll Kálmán tér, keeping 22 good-sized rooms with modern amenities. There's a bar on the ground floor, while you're quite likely to find yourself attending one of the grill and goulash parties held in the landscaped garden. €60

Budapest II, Szilágyi Erzsébet fasor 47 ☎1 889 4200, ⓦdanubiushotels.com; map p.120. Cylindrical tower facing the Buda Hills, opposite the lower terminal of the Cogwheel Railway, 500m from Széll Kálmán tér. The three hundred a/c rooms are functional as opposed to fancy, but there's lots of window space and the views over the city from the upper floors are excellent. There's a sauna, fitness room and business centre too. Wi-fi free in public areas. €90

★**Buda Villa Panzió** XII, Kiss Áron utca 6 ☎1 275 0091, ⓦbudapansio.hu; bus #155; map p.120. Up in the hills above Széll Kálmán tér, this comfortable and friendly pension has ten personable rooms, a bar in the lounge on the first floor, and a small garden that's perfect for relaxing in after a day's sightseeing. €58

HOSTELS

Most hostels offer a combination of same- and mixed-sex dorms, in addition to private rooms (singles or doubles) at much the same price as hotel or pension accommodation. Student dormitories – many of them located in the university area south of Gellért-hegy – are open during July and August only. As well as the year-round *Marco Polo Hostel*, the Mellow Mood group (☎1 413 2062, ⓦhostels.hu) runs a couple of excellent summer hostels and also handles some of the university accommodation open during the summer. Staff at the office in Keleti Station (see p.21) can make bookings and organize transport to their hostels from the station. You can't be sure of getting a bed in the hostel of your choice in summer without **booking** in advance. Note that many of Pest's hostels are in residential blocks – exceptions being *Marco Polo* and *City Hostel Pest* – therefore rowdy guests are generally frowned upon. Most hostels have wi-fi, as well as laundry facilities (for which there's usually a charge of around €5).

PEST

Astoria City VII, Rákóczi út 4.III.27 ☎1 950 6480, ⓦastoriacityhostel.com; map p.58. On the third floor (with a lift), this is a pleasant, well-run hostel in the heart of the city, with two eight-bed dorms, two six-beds, as well as quads, triples and doubles, some en suite. One of the six-bed dorms overlooks a quiet inner courtyard, the others to the noisy main road. They also have apartments in the same block, and rooms a few doors along. Dorm beds (includes breakfast) €14, double rooms €40

★**Casa de la Musica** VIII, Vas utca 16 ☎0670 373 7330, ⓦcasadelamusicahostel.com; map p.77. Colour is the watchword at the sparky *Casa*, located in a super spot and within easy walking distance of the Belváros and the Seventh District bars. Brightly painted stripes adorn the exterior walls, a theme echoed in the retro-styled dorms, which sleep four to twelve people, and double rooms. The reception is up on the second floor (no lift), and the rooms are on the second and third floors. The complex is arranged in a U-shape looking down onto a smart wood-decked terrace, where you'll find a bar and an inflatable swimming pool (in summer). Breakfast €3. Dorms €9, doubles €28

Caterina VI, Teréz körút 30.III.28 ☎1 269 5990, ⓦcaterinahostel.com; map p.58. Long-established hostel located above the Művész cinema near the Oktogon, and although it's on the third floor with no lift, the small setup gives it a friendly feel. There are rooms of five and six beds, as well as doubles and singles – the best ones are those looking on to the courtyard rather than the busy road. Price includes breakfast. Dorms €8, doubles €25

City Hostel Pest IX, Ráday utca 43–45 ☎0620 443 2883, ⓦcityhostels.hu; map p.77. Large summer-only hostel on this buzzing street has rooms of two to seven beds – you pay for rooms rather than beds – with and without shower facilities. Open July & Aug. Doubles €26

★**Home-Made Hostel** VI, Teréz körút 22 ☎1 302 2103, ⓦhomemadehostel.com; map p.58. As homely as its name suggests, this is a gem of a hostel, and its location, on the first floor near Oktogon, isn't bad either. The brilliantly conceived, rustically styled dorms (a four-, six- and eight-bed) feature household accoutrements (radios, typewriters, sewing machines) stuck to the walls, alongside patchwork rugs, paper lamps and random scattered suitcases. There are also two cosy double rooms, one with a loft space, the other with a bathroom, and a cute little kitchen which guests are free to use. Dorms €13, doubles €42

Marco Polo VII, Nyár utca 6 ☎1 413 2555, ⓦmarcopolohostel.com; map p.58. Very large, busy and popular hostel close to Blaha Lujza tér, with simply

---

TOP 5 HOSTELS AND CAMPING

Home-Made see p.154
Case de la Musica see p.154
Shantee House see p.155
Marco Polo see p.154
Zugligeti Camping see p.155

PRIVATE ROOMS AND APARTMENTS

The budget option is a **private room**, bookable through the agencies listed below or the likes of airbnb, booking.com, etc. You'll also find people touting rooms outside the metro station on Deák tér and the nearby Tourinform office, and less commonly at the train stations. However, while getting a room this way may be cheaper, the chances are that you'll be located further out from the centre; in any case, check first.

Depending on location and amenities, **prices** for a double room start at around 6000Ft a night, 7500Ft with a bathroom, while a one-bedroom apartment costs upwards of 8000Ft, two-bedrooms from 13,000Ft. For stays of less than four nights, there's usually a thirty-percent surcharge, though this is sometimes only applicable on the first night. These days most of the rooms and apartments are inside or near the Nagykörút – or in Buda close to the Vár. Families might enjoy the Szent István Park area (the inner XIII district just beyond the Nagykörút), which has plenty of playgrounds and green space.

Self-contained **studio** flats or **apartments** are available to rent through agencies such as Ibusz, Vista or small To-Ma agency at V, Nádor utca 20 (Mon–Fri 9am–noon, Sat & Sun 9am–5pm; ☎ 1353 0819, ⓦ tomatour.hu), and internet-based companies such as Budapest Lets (ⓦ budapestlets.com), a UK-Hungarian venture managing about forty well-equipped properties, from one-room studio flats on Ráday utca to three-bedroom luxury apartments in the city centre.

furnished four- and twelve-bed dorms with bunks, as well as triple, twin and single rooms; all rooms except dorms are en suite and have a TV. Wi-fi on the ground floor and in the courtyard. Breakfast €3. Dorms €13, doubles €60

BUDA

Universum XI, Kruspér u. 2-4 ☎ 1 209 4883, ⓦ erik-apartments.hu; tram #47 or #49 from Deák tér to Gárdonyi tér stop; map p.107. Close to the Gellért Baths, with basic one-, two-, three- and four-bed rooms, all with showers but shared toilets. There's also wi-fi access and a basic kitchen for guests' use. The sister hostel, the *Martos*, is just round the corner. Open July & Aug only. Dorms €12 single room is €16

Shantee House XI, Takács Menyhért utca 33 ☎ 1 385 8946, ⓦ shanteehouse.com; tram #49 or bus #7 to Karolina út stop; map p.107. The old *Back Pack Hostel* has been given a new name and a transformation, but the essence is the same: it's a charming forty six-bed hostel about 20min from the centre, with perky rooms holding four to eleven beds, as well as doubles, some ensuite. The cool vibe continues in the common-room area and garden, where guests can chill out in one of the hammocks or under the gazebo. You can also sleep in the yurt in the garden. The staff also provide lots of information on the city, and organize trips into the hills and to the caves. Dorm beds €14, double rooms €40, ensuite €46 garden yurt €10

12

CAMPING

Budapest's **campsites** are generally well equipped and pleasant, with trees, grass and sometimes even a pool. They can get crowded between June and September, when smaller places might run out of space. It is illegal to camp anywhere else, and the parks are patrolled to enforce this. The campsites listed here are all in Buda, since the Pest ones are not very inviting. Expect to pay around €20 per night for two people and a tent and around €25 for a basic two-bed bungalow.

Csillebérci Camping XII, Konkoly Thege Miklós út 21 ☎ 1 395 6527, ⓦ csilleberciszabadido.hu; bus #21 from Széll Kálmán tér to the Csillebérc stop or bus #21A to Normafa, then a short walk; map p.120. Large, well-equipped site up in the Buda Hills, with space for over a thousand campers and a range of bungalows. Open all year.

Római Camping III, Szentendrei út 189 ☎ 1 388 7167, ⓦ romaicamping.hu; map p.113. Huge site beside the road to Szentendre in Rómaifürdő (25min by HÉV from Batthyány tér), with space for 2500 campers. They also

have wooden bungalows, and the price includes use of the neighbouring Rómaifürdő lido. Open all year.

Zugligeti Niche Camping XII, Zugligeti út 101 ☎ 1 200 8346, ⓦ campingniche.hu; map p.120. At the end of the #155 bus route from Széll Kálmán tér, opposite the chairlift up to János-hegy, this is a small, terraced ravine site in the woods with space for 260 campers and good facilities, including a pleasant little restaurant occupying the former tram station at the far end. A substantial breakfast is included in the price. Open all year.

Restaurants

The Budapest dining scene is developing at a hectic pace, with new restaurants opening all the time. However, where once all the new places were aimed squarely at those with an expense account, the new kids on the block are food trucks and street food joints bringing in exciting global flavours, retro bistros that look back to the Sixties or the Thirties, and quality sandwich bars. Amidst it all has come a general rise in standards – *Borkonyha* being the latest winner of a Michelin star. Despite the occasional tourist trap in the Vár, Buda offers some terrific eating possibilities, with a handful of world-class restaurants; *21*, *Vendéglő a KisBiróhoz* and *Csalogány 26* to name but three. Inevitably, Pest has a much wider range of places, with the largest concentration to be found within the Nagykörút, and the likes of *Laci Pecsenye* and *Café Kör* leading the way.

13

Many offer terrific value for money, and Budapest rates well when compared to dining out in capital cities elsewhere in Western Europe. **Meat** takes centre stage, more than ever, cooked on shiny open grills, while there is a new focus on quality and ingredients. Moreover, the renaissance in Hungarian **wine** is now being reflected in Budapest's restaurants, and you'll find superb wine lists in many places – indeed, some restaurants deem the quality of the wine to be as important as the food. Another sign of the times has been the proliferation of lemonades on the menu – there seems to be a rivalry for the most unusual flavours.

Hungarians have welcomed the **street food** revolution with open arms, whether it is magnificent burgers – locally made, not industrial fast-food – or small authentic Thai and Vietnamese eateries, which have greatly increased the choice for **vegetarians**. Of course the other joy of street food is that you can eat quickly and informally. The emphasis on quality is nowhere more apparent than in the new sandwich bars, which pride themselves both on their bread and the interesting combinations they put inside. Another feature is a growing awareness of **allergens**, and an increasing number of places in central Budapest will alert you to gluten-free and other diet-sensitive foods.

Where no **website** is given below, you'll often find the places on Facebook.

ESSENTIALS

Prices and payment While Budapest is not the bargain gastronomic destination it once was, you can still eat out handsomely here without breaking the bank. Generally speaking, a two-course meal in most half-decent restaurants will set you back anywhere between 3000Ft and 4000Ft (€10–14) a head, while dining at the very top end will cost somewhere in the region of 5000–7000Ft (€18–23). A number of the smarter restaurants also offer tasting menus, which, if you have the time and inclination, are a great way to sample a range of varied dishes; however, they usually go from 7000Ft (€23). Credit and debit cards are now widely accepted (*Café Kör* being one exception) though not necessarily in cheaper places, so check in advance if this is how you wish to pay.

Reservations While few restaurants in Budapest require you to make a reservation, it's best to do so at the more fashionable end of the market, especially if you're really determined to eat somewhere in particular.

Opening hours Restaurants are generally open 11am or noon to 10 or 11pm, though those that serve breakfast – of which there are an increasing number – will open around 8am. Most restaurants are open daily, though

HUNGARIAN CUISINE

For foreigners, the archetypal Magyar dish is still goulash – historically the basis of much **Hungarian cooking**. The ancient Magyars relished cauldrons of this *gulyás* (pronounced "gou-yash"), a soup made of potatoes and whatever meat was available, which was later flavoured with paprika and beefed up into a variety of stews, modified over the centuries by the various foreign influences which helped diversify the country's cuisine. Hungary's Slav visitors probably introduced native cooks to yogurt and sour cream – vital ingredients in many dishes – while the influence of the Turks, Austrians and Germans is apparent in a variety of sticky pastries and strudels, as well as in recipes featuring sauerkraut or dumplings. There's a lot of fish, too – fish soup (*halászlé*) is one of the national dishes, a marvellously spicy *bouillabaisse* in the right hands – but it's worth remembering that landlocked Hungary's fish, such as the very bony carp and the more palatable catfish, all come from lakes and rivers – anything else will be imported. For a glossary of **food and drink terms** see p.225.

Traditionally, Hungarians take their main meal at **lunchtime**. While some restaurants offer a bargain set menu (*napi menü*) – some places call them business lunches – the majority of places are strictly à la carte. The menu (*étlap*) usually kicks off with **cold and hot starters** (*hideg* and *meleg előételek*), **soups** (*levesek*) and then the **main courses** (*főételek*) – sometimes divided into meat (*hús*) and fish (*hal*). These are followed by vegetables (*zöldségek*), salads (*saláták*) and sometimes pasta (*tészták*). Finally, there are the desserts (*édességek* or *desszertek*). Bread is provided automatically, on the grounds that "a meal without bread is no meal". **Drinks** are under the heading **italok** – or may be on a separate drinks or wine menu (*itallap* or *borlap*). If you don't want a full meal, you might just order a filling soup, such as a fish or bean soup like *Jókai bableves*.

13

quite a few do close on Sundays; some of the top-end establishments, such as *Zona* and *Csalogány 26*, also close on Mondays.

Menus It's unusual now to find any establishment that doesn't have a menu in English, although dishes chalked up on a blackboard may not have a translation. Menus should clearly state whether there is a service charge (typically ten or twelve percent) or not, but if you're not sure, ask before ordering. If you're with children it's always worth asking whether there's a kids' menu, or whether they're able to knock up a small portion (*kisadag*).

Smoking The smoking ban that came into being in 2012 is strictly enforced indoors. Now it is the terraces and garden areas that are the haunts of smokers.

A warning The days of waiters in Budapest overcharging or making "mistakes" with your bill are largely gone. However, you should still be on your guard; avoid any establishment that doesn't display its prices (either food or drink), and don't be at all shy about querying the total amount if you think it looks suspect. One particularly annoying practice is waiters touting for business, which is a highly conspicuous activity along Váci utca.

THE BELVÁROS

FAST FOOD AND SNACKS

★**Al-Amir** V, Petofi Sándor utca 18 ☎1 266 0662, ⓦal-amir.hu; map p.38. This highly popular Syrian restaurant has been moving round the city over the years, but the latest incarnation is as good as ever. One of the best places for vegetarians in the city, with its range of salads and fresh ingredients, – and also a wide range of Middle Eastern meat dishes, all at very moderate prices. Mains from 1400Ft. No alcohol. Daily 10am–11pm.

Belvárosi Disznótoros V, Károlyi utca 17 ☎0670 602 2775 ⓦtinyurl.com/oxfg8or; map p.38. Meat galore in the " Downtown Pig Feast", a stand-up retro lunch bar that's the perfect place to taste traditional Hungarian dishes such as pig's trotters and tripe stew. It's modelled on an old-style butcher's shop – there's even a butcher's counter at the back – and even has old-style surly staff. They also have delicious sausages, black pudding, and salads, but not the sort to lure in vegetarians. Mon–Fri 8.30am–7pm, Sat 11am–7pm.

★**Jacques Liszt** V, Apáczai Csere János utca 7 ☎0630 428 2232 ⓦfacebook.com/jacquesliszt; map p.38. Small rough-hewn bakery café near Vigadó tér that serves some of the best bread in town – the name is a joke: to a Hungarian it sounds like "bag of flour". Misi the baker leads an Italian baking team in producing delicious sandwiches, quiches, pastries and cakes, which you can also eat at the couple of tables. They serve coffee as well as caramel and chocolate milk. Mon–Fri 8am–7pm, Sat 8am–2pm.

Tako Café V, Petőfi Sandor utca 7 ☎0630 200 3270; map p.38. Bright central joint offering freshly squeezed juices, fruit smoothies and shakes, and crisp, colourful salads, alongside more traditional meaty fare. Sit down or takeaway. Daily 8am–7pm.

★**Vapiano** V, Bécsi utca 5 ☎1 411 0864 ⓦvapiano.hu; map p.38. Fast food Italian-style, and what style it is; excellent pizzas, pastas and salads made with fresh ingredients before your eyes. Collect a card as you enter, place your order at the counter and the meal will appear in minutes; your purchases are recorded on the card which is

---

BREAKFAST OF CHAMPIONS

A nation of early risers, Hungarians traditionally have a calorific **breakfast** (*reggeli*). Commonly, this includes cheese, eggs or salami together with bread and jam, washed down with coffee; in rural areas it's often accompanied by a shot of *pálinka* (brandy) to "clear the palate" or "aid digestion". While we're not suggesting that you should start the day with a brandy, quite a few city-centre restaurants offer breakfast menus, from the standard coffee-and-croissant option to French toast with ham and cheese, or Viennese sausages with mustard. Breakfast favourites include *Café Kör*, *Gerlóczy* and *Ket Szerescen*, *Szendzsó*, *Briós* and *Sarki Fűszeres*. For the best caffeine hit try the new-wave coffee bars (see p.168) – where superb coffee with good pastries is an irresistible combination.

   Sunday brunch remains popular, offering an all-you-can-eat buffet for a fixed price. Brunch at *Gundel* is a great way to taste its cuisine without the usual formality, though it will still set you back 6800Ft; most of the top hotels also lay on a spread. Prices can be slightly higher there, but most of the hotels have children's play areas. Brunch usually starts around 11am and lasts till about 3pm; booking is advisable.

TOP 5 FOR BREAKFAST

Brios see p.159

SzendZso see p.165

Most see p.174

Sarki Fűszeres see p.159

Café Alibi see p.159

then handed to the cashier as you leave. Pasta and pizzas 1390–2390Ft, salads 900–1900Ft. Mon–Thurs & Sun 11am–11pm, Fri & Sat till midnight.

RESTAURANTS

Café Alibi V, Egyetem tér 2 ☎ 1 317 4209, ⓦ cafealibi .hu; map p.38. Breakfast place popular with students at the nearby university – which helps to keep the prices down a little. The coffee is wonderful and surprisingly cheap – they roast their own in the contraption near the entrance – and their signature omelette with mushrooms and basil (1290Ft) is hard to beat. Later in the day it takes on a bistro feel, offering the likes of duck breast with tagliatelle (2790Ft). Daily 8am–11pm.

Gerlóczy V, Gerlóczy utca 1 ☎ 1 501 4000, ⓦ gerloczy .hu; map p.38. This atmospheric corner café on quiet Károly Kammermayer tér gets packed at lunchtime with office staff popping in for a quick bite – the two-course

(1500Ft) and three-course (1950Ft) set lunch menus are good value – but it's equally enjoyable for breakfast or a steaming cappuccino. Daily 7am–11pm.

★ **Sonka Arcok** V, Kecskeméti utca 2 ☎ 1 794 6137, ⓦ sonkaarcok.hu; map p.38. There is meat aplenty in "Ham Faces", an stylish and popular eatery with a buzzy atmosphere and an extensive menu. The Catalan ham and cheese platter is a big starter (3250Ft for two persons), and the veal paprika stew is delectable (1645Ft). They have a two-course lunch menu for 1150Ft. Sun–Wed 11am–midnight, Thurs–Sat 11am–2am.

Trattoria Toscana V, Belgrád rakpart 13 ☎ 1 327 0045, ⓦ toscana.hu; map p.38. On the Danube riverfront near Szabadság Bridge, this is a favourite spot for authentic Italian cuisine at reasonable prices, and with appealing faux-Tuscan surroundings. The atmosphere is relaxed despite the smart business clientele. Mains 3000–5000Ft. Daily noon–midnight.

LIPÓTVÁROS AND ÚJLIPÓTVÁROS

FAST FOOD AND SNACKS

Briós V, Pozsonyi út 16 ☎ 1 789 6110, ⓦ brioskavezo .hu; map p.48. Early birds should pay a visit to this sweet little neighbourhood café for its cracking breakfast menu (900–1800Ft) – American pancakes, French toast with ham and cheese, and their "omelette for hangovers" with bacon, sausage and cheese are just some of the tempters. If visiting later in the day, try a duck breast baguette (1200Ft). Those with children will love this place as there's a dedicated kiddies' menu and a small play area upstairs, so you might be able to drink your coffee in peace. Daily 7.30am–10pm.

★ **Delibaba** V, Nádor utca 19 ☎ 0630 250 5169, ⓦ delibaba.hu; map p.48. Some of the best sandwiches in town come from Delibaba, whose baguettes and rolls have delicious fillings such as *caponata* (grilled aubergine), grilled squash and duck liver. The desserts are fabulous too and all the ingredients are carefully sourced – as are the beers and coffee . Mon–Fri 7am—7pm, Sat 9am–2pm.

Hummus Bar V, Október 6 utca 19 ☎ 1 354 0108, ⓦ hummusbar.hu; map p.48. You'll find Hummus Bar outlets in seven places in central Budapest, two of which are completely vegetarian. This branch serves up plates of falafel (1500Ft as a main course) and hummus and fresh salad (1400Ft), as well as meaty versions with chicken

breast or chicken liver (1500Ft). Mon–Fri 11.30am–10pm, Sat–Sun noon–10pm.

Sarki Fűszeres XIII, Pozsonyi út 53-55 ☎ 1 238 0600, ⓦ sarkifuszeres.hu; map p.48. Trendy deli bistro with a Thirties feel on the northern side of Szent István Park, where you can join the locals chatting away over breakfast. The excellent deli selection of fine hams and cheeses serves the basis for tasty sandwiches, but the coffees, pastries and lemonades should not be missed. Mon–Fri 8am—8pm, Sat 8am–3pm.

RESTAURANTS

★ **Borkonyha** V, Sas utca 3 ☎ 1 266 0835, ⓦ borkonyha.hu; map p.48. The third Budapest restaurant to earn a Michelin star, and the most appealing of the three. You're greeted by the sight of a beautiful, gleaming bar stacked high with bottles of excellent Hungarian wine: more than two hundred are on offer, with just shy of fifty varieties sold by the glass. The food is no less exciting – expect suckling pig carpaccio, rabbit with rosemary and savoy cabbage, and lemon cake with gorgonzola ice cream. Mains 4000–7000Ft. Mon–Sat noon–midnight.

★ **Café Kör** V, Sas utca 17 ☎ 1 311 0053, ⓦ cafekor .com; map p.48. Local favourite round the corner from the Bazilika, with tightly packed tables but a very relaxed feel. Its grilled meats (predominantly chicken but also turkey and duck) are excellent, as are the salads and specials of the day – the roasted pike-perch in garlic is always a favourite – and the wine list is reliably strong. Moreover, this place has retained its traditionally high standards of service. Mains 2000–4300Ft. Booking advised. Cash payment only. Mon–Sat 10am–10pm.

TOP 5 FOR FINE-DINING

Bock Bisztró see p.162
Borkonyha see p.159
Café Kör see p.159
Csalogány 26 see p.166
Lacipecsenye see p.160

13

Csarnok V, Hold utca 11 ☎1 269 4906 ⓦcsarnokvendeglo.hu; map p.48. Down-to-earth Hungarian restaurant that used to serve the workers at the market a few doors along; despite a slightly more upmarket clientele these days, its unpretentious feel is still very much in evidence, with faded wood-panelled walls and red-and-white-check tablecloths. The food, too, is honest-to-goodness fare, such as veal paprika stew and pickled shank of smoked pork (1600Ft). Daily 10am–10pm.

Firkász XIII, Tátra utca 18 ☎1 450 1118, ⓦfirkasz.hu; map p.48. Done up like a journalists' haunt from the turn of the last century – witness the walls covered in newspaper cuttings and the rows of empty wine and *pálinka* bottles – *Firkász* serves decent traditional Hungarian dishes along the lines of crispy roast pork and goose leg with cabbage. The resident pianist tinkles his way into action nightly at 7pm. Mains 2500–5000Ft. All-you-can-eat-and-drink menu for 12,700Ft. Daily noon–midnight.

Govinda V, Vigyázó Ferenc utca 4 ☎1 267 7631 ⓦgovinda.hu; map p.48. This Hare Krishna vegetarian restaurant has been serving up its dhals and pakoras for twenty years. The inexpensive set meals range from 990 to 1900Ft, all accompanied by the whiff of soporific incense. The sister restaurant *Govinda* at V, Papnövelde utca 1 near Ferenciek tere is vegan. Mon–Sat noon–9pm.

★**Kispiac** V, Hold utca 13 ☎1 269-4231 ⓦkispiac.eu; map p.48. Small and very popular bistro right by the market hall behind the US Embassy. The small menu, displayed on blackboards, is meat-dominated, and the grill is kept busy. You can get grilled duck, steak and sea bass, or there is tripe for the adventurous. They make their own breads and jams too. There are a few outside tables – and further afield, a sister branch in the 1930s bus shelter at Pasaréti tér in northern Buda. Mains 2000–4000Ft. Booking essential. Mon–Sat noon–10pm.

★**Lacipecsenye** V, Sas utca 11 ☎0670 370 7474, ⓦlacipecsenye.eu; map p.48. The sure-footed chef, Lajos, has produced another winner in the city centre – if it can survive the pressure of its prime tourist location, right in front of the Bazilika. The focus at Lacipecsenye – "barbeque" – is meat, cooked on the huge grill, and you can buy it by the yard (the spare ribs go for 10,000Ft a metre). The menu has a strong Hungarian flavour, with favourites such as bone marrow on toast and veal stew with noodles. Two-course lunch menu 2450Ft, tasting menus from 6900Ft for three courses, kids' menu 2200Ft. Mains 2000–4000Ft. Daily 11am–midnight, Tues–Sun 11am–10.30pm.

Pomo D'Oro V, Arany János utca 9 ☎1 302 6473, ⓦpomodorobudapest.com; map p.48. An established fixture on the Budapest dining scene, this split-level trattoria also rates highly among the city's Italian community. The wood-burning oven turns out excellent pizzas from 1800Ft, and the pastas and risottos (2500–5000Ft) are also exceptional, although if you're only here once, seek out the charcoal grill (3000–4500Ft). A surprisingly varied selection of wines rounds things off beautifully. Daily noon–midnight.

Pozsonyi Kisvendéglő XIII, Pozsonyi út 18 ☎1 787 4877 ⓦfacebook.com/PozsonyiKisvendeglo; map p.48. Atmospheric local joint with filling Hungarian dishes. The tables are in booths, which makes for a very cosy feel. Small terrace on the pavement in the summer. Booking advisable on Friday evenings – the only day they serve *sólet*, and you need to book that too. Mains 1400–2500Ft, lunch menu 850Ft. Daily 10am–midnight.

VEGETARIAN BUDAPEST

Compared to yesteryear, **vegetarians** are much better catered for, though exclusively *vegetáriánus* restaurants are still thin on the ground in Budapest. *Govinda*, with its Indian food, two branches of the *Hummus* Bar chain and the vegan *Ganga* are some of the best options. The new Thai and Vietnamese restaurants have brought a welcome breadth to a quite limited palette, alongside the Middle Eastern cuisine found in *Al-Amir* and *Amman*.

Elsewhere, there's a growing understanding of the concept – you're less likely to get told that noodles with bacon is okay because bacon is not real meat. Many restaurants now include one or two vegetarian options on the menu – most popularly *sült zöldségek* (roasted vegetables). Still, in more traditional places your choice might restricted to a diet of vegetables and cheese fried in breadcrumbs known as *rántott gomba* (with mushrooms), *rántott karfiol* (cauliflower), or *rántott sajt* (cheese). *Gomba paprikás* (mushroom paprika stew) is also fine, though check if it has been cooked in oil rather than in lard. Alternatively there are eggs – fried (*tükörtojás*), soft-boiled (*lágy tojás*) or scrambled (*tojásrántotta*) – or salads, though Hungary has traditionally been weak in this department, despite the excellent produce you see in the markets.

13

TERÉZVÁROS AND ERZSÉBETVÁROS

FAST FOOD AND SNACKS

Bors VII Kazinczy utca 10 ⓦfacebook.com /BorsGasztroBar; map p.58. Delicious soups, pastas and baguettes at the "Pepper" gastrobar next to the Szimpla. The soft drinks come in appealing combinations, too, such as mint and raspberry. The queues can be long here, and there are no tables – just a handful of seats round the walls. Baguettes start at 540Ft. Cash only. Mon–Sat 11.30am–9pm.

Butcher's Kitchen VII, Klauzál utca 11–13 ☎30 448 1758 ⓦfacebook.com/ahenteskonyhaja; map p.58. It's not just meat on offer at the *Butcher's Kitchen*. If the smoked sausage isn't to your taste, try the scrumptious beetroot and camembert sandwich. You can perch on a stool amid the minimalist décor inside, or there are tables on the wide pavement out front. Sandwiches from 1300Ft. Mon–Wed & Sun 11am–11pm, Thurs 11am–1am, Fri–Sat 11am–3am.

Falafel VI, Paulay Ede utca 53 ☎1 705 7142 ⓦfacebook falafel.hu; map p.58. Budapest's most popular falafel joint for years (hopefully the new owners who took over in 2014 won't change the formula); you just pay your money and stuff your pitta breads as full as you can. Seating upstairs. Mon–Fri 10am–8pm, Sat 10am–6pm.

Frici Papa VII, Király utca 55 ☎1 351 0197 ⓦfricipapa .hu; map p.58. The plastic-covered tables give a fair indication of what to expect, and this no-nonsense place (which includes the waiters) certainly won't win any awards for refinement, but if it's cheap, no-frills grub you're after, look no further. A menu of grilled or fried chicken with chips, beef and mushroom goulash, and not much else, all for under 1000Ft. Daily 11am–10pm.

Ganga VI, Bajcsy-Zsilinszky út 25 ☎06 20 886 1795 ⓦon facebook.com; map p.58. One of the growing band of vegetarian restaurants, *Ganga* knocks up uncomplicated but tasty dishes such as spiced potatoes and lasagne. The two-course menu for 1090Ft makes for an excellent deal. Mon–Fri 8am–10pm, Sat noon–10pm.

Kádár Étkezde VII, Klauzál tér 10 ☎1 321 3622; map p.58. Local stalwart in the heart of the old Jewish quarter, with its red and white checked tablecloths and autographed photos on the walls. The menu has traditional (non-kosher) specialities such as roast goose leg with red cabbage and "broken" potatoes and – on Saturdays – *sólet*. Mains from 1500Ft. You pay at the door as you leave – tips should be given directly to the waitresses. Mon–Sat 11.30am–3.30pm; closed mid-July to mid-Aug.

La Pizza di Mamma Sofia VI, Király utca 20 ☎1 266 0444 ⓦfacebook.com/lapizza.hu; map p.58. The long queues are proof enough of this pizza joint's popularity. It's right by the Goszdu udvar, and is always full of partygoers waiting for a slice (from 300Ft) on their way to and from the nearby bars. The range of toppings may be small but it includes nutella (450Ft a slice), and the bases are wonderfully thin. Hardly enough room to swing a pizza dough, let alone sit down. Wed & Sun 11am–1am, Thurs–Sat 11am–4am.

★**Montenegrói Gurman** VII, Rákóczi út 54 ☎0670 434 9898 ⓦmnggurman.com; map p.58. Fans of the traditional Balkan grill should make this place their first port of call. Gut-busting portions of succulent *Čevapčići* (spiced mincemeat rissoles) and *pljeskavica* (hamburger style patty) served with spicy paprika and *lepinja* (doughy bread), and all washed down with a bottle of Slovenian Laško beer. It's open around the clock, so just the job for post-drink munchies. Daily 24hr.

Sonkapult VII, Rumbach Sebestyén utca 7 ☎0630 943 7073 ⓦsonkapult.hu; map p.58. Start your day at the "Ham Counter" breakfast spot, just off Dob utca where the emphasis is on quality. Sandwiches (from 700Ft) are made with local produce and the soft drinks are organic. It also sells craft beers, wine, and stronger stuff. Pride of place is a shiny red 1972 ham slicer in the corner – there is room for that and a couple of armchairs, and that is about it. Mon–Wed 8am–6pm, Thurs–Fri 8am–midnight, Sat 10am–midnight.

RESTAURANTS

2Spaghi VII, Gozsdu udvar ☎0670 222 3701 ⓦtinyurl .com/jwnlw38; map p.58. Superb fresh pasta joint run by two Italians located at the quieter end of the udvar near Dob utca. Service is fast and the food has an authentic feel to it – you can buy to take home too. Mains from 1500Ft. Mon–Thurs 11am–10pm, Fri–Sat 11am–1am, Sun 11am–6pm.

★**Bock Bisztró** VII, Erzsébet körút 43–49 ☎1 321 0340, ⓦbockbisztro.hu; map p.58. Located within the *Grand Corinthia Hotel*, *Bock* takes its name from one of Hungary's top vintners, József Bock, and its stock includes many labels that you won't find elsewhere in the city. It's a great place to eat, both classy (check out the cork-filled glass tables) and relaxed, with friendly staff and beautifully crafted food; if you don't fancy a full-blown meal, try something from the tapas menu, such as duck tongue salad or oven-roasted beetroot. Tapas 1400Ft, mains 3000–4400Ft. Booking advised. Mon–Sat noon–midnight.

Café Bouchon VI, Zichy Jenő utca 33 ☎1 353 4094, ⓦcafébouchon.hu; map p.58. A real neighbourhood stalwart, and popular with the nearby opera-going crowd, *Café Bouchon* is a cracking place. The Art Deco furnishings look fab, the Hungarian/French-fused cuisine (Tokaj grape salad with walnuts and Camembert); Hungarian sausage with goose-liver pâté is first class, and the place is serviced by friendly, knowledgeable staff. Mains 2600–5000Ft. Mon–Sat 11am–11pm.

Cirkusz VII, Dob utca 25 ☎1 786 4959 ⓦfacebook .com/cirkuszbudapest; map p.58. Stylish, airy café in

13

TOP 5 CHEAP EATS

Delibaba see p.159
Funky Pho see p.163
Kisüzem see p.174
Montenegrói Gurman see p.162
Vapiano see p.158

the old Jewish quarter with high ceilings and a spacious feel. The chicken breast with lentils (1800Ft) is excellent, as is the beetroot chocolate cake. And don't forget the coffee – wonderful stuff, as you might expect when they roast their own and have a champion barista. Mon–Wed 9.30am–11pm, Thurs–Sat 9.30am–1am, Sun 9.30am–5pm.

Dang Muoi VI, Nagymező utca 51 ☎ 06 30 955 2548 ⓦ vietnamietterem.hu; map p.58. Small and very appealing Vietnamese bistro with a very authentic feel, created by Dang and Muoi, a Vietnamese couple who met in Budapest. They work to their own recipes of *Pho*, the noodle soup and national dish of their homeland. Soups from 1000Ft. Perfect place for the reviving snack after a late-night drinking session. Mon–Thurs 10am–10pm, Fri– Sun 10am–midnight.

Fausto VII, Dohány utca 5 ☎ 1 269 6806, ⓦ fausto.hu; map p.58. Chef Fausto DiVora has unfailingly maintained standards at his elegant Italian restaurant in Dohány utca for more than twenty years. You can choose between the bistro-like osteria (lunch menus 2900Ft) on one side – sample dish: turkey ossobuco with herbed mash – and the more formal restaurant (three-course lunch menus for 5000Ft) on the other where you'll find a mean swordfish steak with black spaghetti and pistachios (7500Ft). Mon–Sat noon–11pm.

★**Félix Hélix** VII, Kazinczy u. 52/b ☎ 0630 416 6959, ⓦ felixhelix.hu; map p.58. Located on the walk between Kazinczy utca and Holló utca - but it is easy to miss this small eatery as it doesn't shout about itself. That's partly the appeal of the place, squeezed in amid the brash bars in the middle of Seventh District partyland. The Irish-Egyptian duo behind it turn out a marvellous range of foods that you won't get anywhere else, such as cucumber soup with goat's milk and Moroccan-style beef with couscous. There is occasional music, and you'll find backgammon boards up in the gallery. Two-course lunch 900Ft. Mon–Fri 9am–3pm, 6pm–1am, Sat–Sun 3pm–1am.

★**Funky Pho** VI, Mozsár utca 7 ☎ 0670 251 2980, ⓦ funkypho.hu; map p.58. Set up by András and Éva after they worked out east and learnt from top chefs in Vietnam, *Funky Pho* is a rarity in Budapest. Unlike most other places it serves up food from South Vietnam, as well as other Asian cuisines. The menu is MSG-free (there is some in a jar on the counter if you are hankering after it) and appeals to a younger Vietnamese generation. The Funky team have won

awards for their sustainability, and their food – try their *pho* and summer rolls – is delicious, too. Mains from 1090Ft. Mon–Sat 11.30am–10pm.

Il Terzo Cerchio VII, Dohány utca 40 ☎ 1 354 0788, ⓦ ilterzocerchio.hu; map p.58. The Third Circle of Dante's hell was full of gluttons, and this handsome Florentine-run pizzeria has its share. Pizzas aside (from 2000Ft), there's superb risotto (3450Ft) and pasta, where seafood is a speciality – try the pennette with a spicy octopus sauce (2900Ft) or gnocchi with salmon with rocket pesto (2850Ft). It's popular with Italian visitors, which must be a good sign. Daily noon–11.30pm.

★**Kazimir** VII, Kazinczy utca 34 ☎ 1 798 5747, ⓦ kazimir.hu; map p.58. Popular large café-bar in the middle of the Seventh district that is welcoming throughout the day. They serve very good breakfasts – omelettes start at 1090Ft – and have a two-course lunch menu for 1090Ft. Specialities include duck leg (2890Ft) and the popular Jewish dish *sólet* (2590Ft). There is a courtyard terrace, and live music on Friday evenings. Daily 8am–4am.

★**Két Szerecsen** VI, Nagymező utca 14 ☎ 1 343 1984, ⓦ ketszerecsen.com; map p.58. Buzzy place nicely secreted away just off Andrássy út, that's good for coffee and breakfast (8–11am) or full-blown supper. The most appealing aspect, though, is the tapas menu (veg, meat and seafood), which can be taken individually or as an assortment. A varied mains menu includes salmon steamed in white wine, and a Thai green curry. Mains 1900–3000Ft. Mon–Fri 8am–midnight, Sat & Sun 9am–midnight.

Kis Parázs VII, Kazinczy utca 7 ☎ 0670 517 4550 ⓦ parazspresszo.com; map p.58. At last you can get authentic Thai food in Budapest, and at a very reasonable price. Delicious curries and pad thai served up in a small restaurant across the road from the *Szimpla* bar. Another branch is close by at VII, Király utca 53. Mains 1500–2000Ft. Mon–Sat 11am–10pm.

Klassz VI, Andrássy út 41 ☎ 1 413 1545 ⓦ klasszetterem.hu; map p.58. *Klassz* means "super", which describes this strikingly decorated restaurant-cum-wine bar to a tee. Typical staples include pork tenderloin with sweet potato purée and roast *Mangalica* (a fatty Hungarian pork) with gratin potatoes – while links with the Budapest Wine Society ensure a choice of top Hungarian vintages, most of which are available by the glass. It's small, extremely popular and does not take reservations. Mains 3000–5500Ft. Daily 11.30am–11pm.

Kőleves VII, Kazinczy utca 37-41, ☎ 1 322 1011, ⓦ kolevesvendeglo.hu; map p.58. This relaxed restaurant in the heart of the Jewish quarter is named "Stone Soup" in reference to the fairytale about making soup in a time of scarcity. Instead you'll find classic Central European Jewish

13

dishes, as well as Hungarian specialities. There is a terrace at the back, and a garden bar, *Kőleveskert*, next door for summer nights. They do breakfasts too. Booking advisable. Mains 2000-3000Ft and a menu of the day 1000–1250Ft. Daily 8am–midnight.

★**Krizia** VI, Mozsár utca 12 ☎1 331 8711, Ⓦristorantekrizia.hu; map p.58. All the pasta at this refined Italian restaurant is made here on the premises, as is the delicious prosciutto, resulting in a long list of well-thought-out creations like fettuccine with porcini mushrooms and prawns or tortelloni stuffed with goose liver and truffle sauce. There's also a daily "From the Market" menu, sourcing local ingredients, and a dedicated truffle menu, which, not surprisingly, comes at a price. The three-course lunch menu is good value at 1500Ft. Mains 2800–6800Ft. Mon–Sat noon–3pm & 6.30pm–midnight.

M VII, Kertész utca 48 ☎1 322 3108, Ⓦmetterem.hu; map p.58. This small boho-style bistro is just the spot for a low-key evening dalliance. The small menu changes daily and can throw up some surprises; rabbit kidneys, as well as the more enticing duck breast with wild mushroom risotto, and shoulder of rabbit in garlic and thyme with ratatouille are what you can expect. Mains 2800–3500Ft. Tues–Sun 6pm–midnight.

Menza VI, Liszt Ferenc tér 2 ☎1 413 1482, Ⓦmenzaetterem.hu; map p.58. Few places on this lively square merit much consideration – at least where food is concerned – but *Menza* is one of them. The stylish retro decor, and very affordable retro-influenced Hungarian dishes, such as *hagymás rostélyos* (braised steak piled high with onions) and *kolozsvári töltött káposzta* (stuffed cabbage) seem to evoke nostalgic memories among the locals. The two-course lunch menu is terrific value at 1090Ft. Mains 2300–4900Ft. Daily 10am–midnight.

Spinoza VII, Dob utca 15 ☎1 413 7488, Ⓦspinozahaz .hu; map p.58. In the heart of the old Jewish quarter, this popular restaurant has a very cultured feel – not least because the small theatre at the back has performances and readings every night, including a Jewish evening of music and food on Fridays. It has a big menu, including salads and sandwiches, alongside Hungarian favourites such as goose leg with red cabbage and potatoes (2750Ft), and on the soft drinks menu are elderflower and lavender lemonades. Lunch menu 950Ft. Daily 8am–11pm.

★**Zeller Bistro** VII, Izabella utca 36-38 ☎0630 651 0880 Ⓦon facebook.com; map p.58. Boho-chic meets rustic simplicity in this superb and very popular basement restaurant. There's an appealing thoughtfulness behind the place: guests are welcomed with elderflower champagne, and this and much of what you eat and drink is the proprietor's own produce. The enticing seasonal menu is Hungarian with a twist, such as the roasted lamb with smoked cheese polenta. It's a great place for families too – pencils and papers await on all tables and there's a children's corner with books and toys. Mains 2000–4000Ft. Booking essential. Tues–Sat noon–3pm, 6–11pm.

THE VÁROSLIGET

RESTAURANTS

Bagolyvár XIV, Állatkerti körút 2 ☎1 468 3110, Ⓦbagolyvar.com; map p.69. Sister to the *Gundel*, the "Owl's Castle" offers traditional Hungarian family-style cooking at far lower prices. Housed in an intriguing Károly Kós-style building, it aims to recreate the atmosphere of the interwar middle-class home in its menu. Its classic dishes include chicken paprika with dumplings and poppyseed cake with cherry sauce. Mains 3500–5000Ft, three-course lunch menu 3400Ft. Daily noon–11pm.

Gundel XIV, Állatkerti körút 2 ☎1 889 8100, Ⓦgundel.hu; map p.69. Budapest's most famous restaurant – opened in 1910 – may have lost some of its lustre in the face of the city's gastronomic revolution, but it remains something of an institution. The menu is, predictably enough, very expensive, but the range and quality of food, alongside the ornate surroundings and impeccable service, will ensure a unique experience. Formal dress is not compulsory, but smart attire is preferred. Mains 6600Ft. The all-you-can-eat Sunday brunch (11.30am–3pm; 6800Ft) remains hugely popular. Booking advised. Daily noon–4pm & 6.30pm–midnight.

INTO THE HUNGARIAN KITCHEN

Budapest's **cookery courses** are not just about how much paprika to add to your *halászlé*, and when is a goulash not a *gulyás*. It is also a primer in Hungarian culture. Courses often begin with a visit to a market to give an insight into the main pillars of the Hungarian kitchen – their love of pickling everything and how to use every inch of a pig – before the cooking proper begins followed by a sit-down meal to enjoy it. You will also learn what wines go with what – and that Hungarian reds are often best served chilled. One of the best courses is Chef Parade (☎1 210 6042 Ⓦchefparade.hu), which has well-equipped kitchens and an informal, fun attitude.

JÓZSEFVÁROS AND FERENCVÁROS

13

FAST FOOD AND SNACKS

Amman VIII, Rákóczi út 29 ☎ 1 338 2429, ⓦ amman.hu; map p.77. Spacious Middle Eastern self-service restaurant that gets very good marks from locals. It has a wide selection of dishes, such as creamy chicken with turmeric and vegetables and rhubarb mousse, and its good range of salads makes it ideal for vegetarians, too. Mains from 1200Ft. Mon–Sat 9am–midnight, Sun 10am–11pm.

Caffè Torino VIII, Bródy Sándor utca 2 ☎ 0630 303 9466 ⓦ on facebook.com; map p.77. Just across the road from the National Museum, the *Torino* is a very Italian basement café bar serving panini, quiches, pasta (from 890Ft), as well as cheesecake and other cakes. Mon–Fri 8am–5pm, Sat 9am–3pm.

Butter Brothers Bakery IX, Lonyay utca 22 ☎ 0620 978 6868 ⓦ butter-brothers.com; map p.77. A congenial place to start the day, *Butter Brothers* is a small bright café shop with a couple of tables and a few stools, with a cheery team serving coffee and excellent pastries. They also bake their bread, and their milk is delicious. They have a small lunch menu, and sandwiches. Mon–Fri 7am–7pm, Sat 8am–1pm.

RESTAURANTS

★Borbíróság IX, Csarnok tér 5 ☎ 1 219 0902, ⓦ borbirosag.com; map p.77. The marvellous "Wine Court" offers one of the most affordable and enjoyable introductions to modern Hungarian cuisine anywhere in the city. The menu is by no means exhaustive, but that doesn't detract from what is an exceptional medley of dishes; try the Hortobagy pancake for starter, followed by grilled duck liver

with caramelized fruits, and if there's still space, get stuck into a portion of cottage cheese dumplings. The wine list, on the other hand, will leave you completely spoilt for choice, with some of Hungary's finest vintners represented. Mains 2200–5000Ft. Mon–Sat noon–11.30pm.

Fülemüle VIII, Kőfaragó utca 5 ☎ 1 266 7947, ⓦ fulemule.hu; map p.77. Popular and relaxed family-run restaurant a few minutes' walk from Rákóczi út, serving typical dishes of middle-class secular Jewish Budapest: *sólet* (beans), goose soup with matzo dumplings, and duck leg with cabbage and "broken" potato. Mains 2500–5000Ft. Mon–Thurs & Sun noon–10pm, Fri & Sat noon–11pm.

Múzeum VIII, Múzeum körút 12 ☎ 1 267 0375, ⓦ muzeumkavehaz.hu; map p.77. This grand nineteenth-century restaurant, adorned with Lotz ceiling frescoes and Zsolnay tiles, is another old-school venture working hard to retain standards in the face of stiff competition. For the most part, it succeeds, with a line-up of core Hungarian classics like breaded Mangalica pork chops with mashed potato, and grilled goose liver with Tokaji Aszú cream. Mains 3300–7000Ft. Mon–Sat 6pm–midnight.

★Rosenstein VIII, Mosonyi utca 3 ☎ 1 333 3492, ⓦ rosenstein.hu; map p.77. Don't be put off by the dingy location, in an anonymous side street near Keleti Station: the family-run *Rosenstein* offers a most satisfying dining experience. Give yourself plenty of time to digest the menu, where you'll discover dishes as diverse as wild boar *ragout* with forest mushrooms, leg of wild hare, and breaded calf's foot with tartar and chips. Booking advised. Mains 3000–4500Ft. Mon–Sat noon–11pm.

THE VÁR, CENTRAL BUDA AND THE TABÁN

FAST FOOD AND SNACKS

Finomító Kantin II, Varsányi Irén utca 33 ☎ 0630 871 9588, ⓦ finomito.com; map p.87. Friendly small and smoky burger bar that has a big local following, lying in a quiet street running down from Széna tér. All the ingredients are carefully sourced – these are burgers made with care. Also serves vegetarian burgers, three different soups, sandwiches and home-made lemonade. Mon–Sat 11.30am–8pm.

Gusto's II, Frankel Leó utca 12 ☎ 1 316 3970; map p.87. Near the Buda end of the Margít híd, a charming little bar serving salads and cold dishes, but you can put together your own plateful from a range of hot dishes in the Daily Deal (990Ft). The bar is famed for its tiramisu (650Ft). Mon–Fri 10am–10pm, Sat 10am–4pm.

SzendZso II, Frankel Leó utca 11 ☎ 0630 992 8006, ⓦ szendzso.hu; map p.87. Cosy breakfast joint at the Buda end of Margit híd, where you squeeze past the locals to get to your table. Ham and eggs (900Ft) and baguettes from 1300Ft, and the coffee is excellent. Weather

permitting, you can sit at the long table outside. Mon–Fri 7.30am–7.30pm, Sat 7.30am–3.30pm.

RESTAURANTS

★21 I, Fortuna utca 21 ☎ 1 202 2113, ⓦ 21restaurant .hu; map p.89. Perhaps the pick of the restaurants in the Vár, the *21* has an elegant and modern feel (and a wonderful terrace) while the food is fresh, contemporary Hungarian fare superbly cooked and beautifully presented. Mains 3000–5000Ft. Booking advised. Daily noon–midnight.

Aranyszarvas I, Szarvas tér 1 ☎ 1 375 6451, ⓦ aranyszarvas.hu; map p.107. Not in the most promising of locations, at the junction of several busy roads, the "Golden Deer" is, nevertheless, a fine restaurant, rustling up superb flavours like duck breast with orange carrot and pak choi. Mains 3000–4000Ft. Booking advised. Daily noon–11pm.

Café Pierrot I, Fortuna utca 14 ☎ 1 375 6971, ⓦ pierrot.hu; map p.89. A rare elegant hangout in the

13

late Communist era, *Pierrot* remains an important fixture more than thirty years after opening. The interior has an almost retro feel – with one eye on the 1980s perhaps – the walls adorned with images of actors and musicians like De Niro and Depeche Mode. Alternatively take a seat out in the handsome vaulted corridor, which leads through to a pretty garden terrace. Mains 3800–5000Ft. Booking advised. Daily 11am–midnight.

★**Csalogány 26** I, Csalogány utca 26 ☎1 210 7892, ⓦcsalogany26.hu; map p.87. Notwithstanding the very ordinary location and occasionally muted atmosphere, this is undoubtedly one of Budapest's finest restaurants. It's neither showy nor prohibitively expensive, and the small menu, which changes regularly according to the whim of the chef, contains some wonderfully executed dishes; expect creations like glazed rabbit leg with veg ragout, scallop with corn risotto and rice pudding with red-fruit ice cream. Mains 4000–5000Ft, but the portions aren't that big, so it's worth going for a four-course menu for 9000Ft or even the eight-course one for 13000Ft. Booking advised. Tues–Sat noon–3pm & 7–10pm.

Horgásztanya I, Fő utca 27 ☎1 212 3780, ⓦhorgasztanyavendeglo.hu; map p.87. Nets and other maritime paraphernalia are strung along the walls in this enjoyable fish restaurant that has remained unchanged for many years. The fish soups are served in generous (mug or kettle) portions, while freshwater fish dominate:

pike-perch, carp, catfish and trout. Mains from 2500Ft. Daily noon–midnight.

Márkus Vendéglő II, Lövőház utca 17 ☎1 212 3153 ⓦmarkusvendeglo.hu; map p.87. Close to Széll Kálmán tér, this is a great no-frills option after a long walk in the Buda Hills. Large portions of traditional Hungarian dishes, including an excellent *Jókai bableves* (a filling, smoky bean soup for just 1000Ft) and various stuffed turkey dishes. Daily noon–midnight.

Vár: A Speiz I, Hess András tér 6 ☎1 488 7416, ⓦvara speiz.hu; map p.89. Just across the road from the *Hilton* hotel, the distinguished "pantry" has a homely yet smart feel, with half a dozen huge hams (from Spain, Italy and Hungary) dangling temptingly near the entrance. The schnitzels here are outstanding – there is a special breadcrumbed section of the menu. Mains 3000–5000Ft. Daily noon–11pm.

Zona I, Lánchíd utca 7–9 ☎30 422 5981, ⓦzonabudapest.com; map p.89. In his new sleek riverfront restaurant chef Krisztián Huszár presents an intriguing mix of Japanese and Basque dishes with a Hungarian touch on his small but pricey menu. Mangalica pork sausage, marinated cockles and artichokes (4900Ft), saddle of lamb, Atlantic shrimps and asparagus (7500Ft). The wine list, however, is large – drawing on wines from around the world. Two-course lunch 2800Ft, five-course dinner 14,900Ft. Tues–Sat noon–3pm & 7–11pm, during the summer open evenings only.

ÓBUDA AND THE BUDA HILLS

RESTAURANTS

Alessio II, Pasaréti út 55 ☎1 275 0049, ⓦcafealessio .hu; map p.120. Elegant local Italian restaurant and pizzeria place ten minutes out from Széll Kálmán tér on the #5 bus. The chicken breast with goat's cheese is superb, as is the veal saltimbocca. The excellent pizzas start from 1600Ft – they also deliver orders. Mains 2500–5000Ft. Daily 9am–midnight.

Kéhli III, Mókus utca 22 ☎1 368 0613, ⓦkehli.hu; map p.113. One hundred years ago this was the favourite haunt of one of Hungary's great gourmands, the turn-of-the-century writer Gyula Krúdy, and today the *Kéhli* still serves the dishes he loved, such as beef soup with bone marrow on garlic toast. Set in one of the few old buildings in Óbuda to survive the 1960s planning blitz, it's a big place and does attract large groups, but there are plenty of local regulars, too; eat your fill to the accompaniment of a lively Hungarian Gypsy band (Tues– Sun). Mains 2000–4500Ft. Daily noon–midnight.

Kerék III, Bécsi út 103 ☎1 250 4261, ⓦkerekvendeglo .hu; map p.113. There is an unchanging feel to the "Wheel", a small 100-year old restaurant in southern Óbuda – if the new management in 2014 preserves its character. It serves traditional Hungarian food, such as *bableves füstölt csülökkel* (bean soup with smoked pork knuckle) and *vasi pecsenye*

(pork marinated in garlic and milk) at very reasonable prices. No haute cuisine here, just locals out for a meal. *Srámli* (accordion) music is provided by a couple of old musicians (Mon–Sat from 6pm), and there's outside seating in summer. Mains 1300–2500Ft. Daily noon–11pm.

Náncsi Néni II, Ördögárok út 80 ☎1 397 2742, ⓦnancsineni.hu; map p.120. Popular family restaurant with a large leafy terrace out in Hűvösvölgy fifteen minutes' walk from the terminus of tram #61. Excellent, well-cooked Hungarian specialities such as cold strawberry soup, *lecsó* and duck cooked in orange. The large garden has a children's playground to one side. Mains 2000–3500Ft. Daily noon–11pm.

★**Vendéglő a KisBíróhoz** XII, Szarvas Gábor út 8/d ☎1 376 6044, ⓦvendegloakisbirohoz.hu; map p.120. The Bock empire has produced another superb restaurant, this time in Buda, a fifteen-minute ride on bus #155 up from Széll Kálmán tér. The name is a play on the name of the wizard chef, Lajos Bíró, who produces Hungarian food with a modern twist, such as lamb in a nettle sauce or duck breast with ginger and kohlrabi. It doesn't come cheaply (even the butter is 300Ft) but it is worth the journey: the portions are huge and the wines – from the Bock vineyard and elsewhere – are superb. Mains 3700–6400Ft. Tues– Sun noon–11pm.

CÉNTRÁL KÁVÉHÁZ

Cafés and patisseries

Daily life in Budapest has long been punctuated by the consumption of strong black coffee and the city's coffee houses (*kávéház*) rival those of Prague and Vienna for sheer grandeur and deferential service. The days of writers, journalists and the odd revolutionary using them as unofficial "offices" has long gone, but they are still full of character and a hit with locals and tourists alike. The global trend towards artisan coffee and hip baristas has also arrived with a vengeance. New-wave coffee bars (*kézműves kávézók*) have sprung up across the city, in designer premises – and often with English names. Tea-lovers won't be short-changed either, with several fine tea houses around the city.

Any caffeine quest should begin with the grand old stalwarts of the coffee-house world such as the *Centrál Kávéház* and *Gerbeaud*. In contrast, the new coffee bars dotted around the centre of the city such as *Espresso Embassy* and *Tamp & Pull* are cosy little affairs with a handful of tables. Most coffee houses also have counters stocked with scrumptious, beautifully crafted **cakes and pastries** like brightly coloured macaroons, *dobos torta*, *rétes* and *flódni*. Otherwise head straight to the nearest **patisserie** (*cukrászda*) for a delicious helping of sugar and carbs. Hungarians love their **ice cream**, too, and there are several excellent parlours dotted around the city.

14

THE BELVÁROS

Café Astoria V, Kossuth utca 19 ☎1 889 6000; map p.38. Dating from the turn of the last century the *Astoria* hotel's coffee house-bar has retained much of its old charm, even if some of the old glitz has faded; oversized chandeliers, dusty pale tableclothes and red velvet seating combine to make this a still-popular meeting place. Daily 7am–11pm.

★**Centrál Kávéház** V, Károlyi Mihály utca 9 ☎1 266 2110; map p.38. In its heyday, the decades around World War I, this large coffee house was a popular venue in Budapest's literary scene. After many years as a dowdy university club, it was restored to its former grandeur and today stands as the city's most sophisticated café. Good coffee (450–700Ft) and an immaculate selection of cakes (650–750Ft), which are cheaper than at many other places in the Belváros. They also have a full menu for meals. Daily 8am–midnight or 1am.

Fekete V, Múzeum körút 5 ⓦfeketekv.hu; map p.38. Just down the Astoria junction, *Fekete* is typical of the hip *kézműves* bars, with equal emphasis on design and good

coffee. It's little more than a hole in the wall, but it turns out excellent flat whites, lattes and delicious hot chocolate. It has a couple of tables out on the pavement. Mon–Fri 7.30am–6.30pm, Sat 9am–4pm.

Gerbeaud V, Vörösmarty tér 7 ☎1 429 9000 ⓦgerbeaud.hu; map p.38. Another Budapest institution, *Gerbeaud* has been a fixture on this square since 1858. The gilded salon is magnificent, though most people park themselves outside on the massive terrace, one of the best in the city. But be warned, this is very much tourist-central, with prices that reflect this; coffee will set you back 800–1200Ft. Daily 9am–9pm.

Szamos Gourmet Ház V, Váci utca 1 ☎0630 233 3412 ⓦszamosmarcipan.hu; map p.38. Housed in the former Stock Exchange, this is the flagship café of the Szamos empire that was built in marzipan but now extends much further. The entrance is round the corner on Vörösmarty tér. Next to the elegant café is also a chocolate-making workshop where you can sign up for three-hour courses. Daily 9am–9pm.

LIPÓTVÁROS

Bedő Ház V, Honvéd utca 3 ☎1 269 4622; map p.48. Housed in a gem of a building just north of Szabadság tér, the café shares the same space as the Museum of Hungarian Art Nouveau, though it's hard to tell where one begins and the other ends, such is its pleasantly cluttered nature. A quiet place, and with a fairly modest range of drinks and pastries, it is, nevertheless, a delightful spot for a coffee break if you're in the neighbourhood. Mon–Fri 8am–7pm, Sat 9am–5pm.

★**Espresso Embassy** V, Arany János utca 15 ☎0630 864 9530 ⓦespressoembassy.hu; map p.48. One of the larger of the new-wave coffee bars – the interior, with its bare brick vaulting, is by the same team that designed two of the new metro stations. The coffee is exquisite – several members of the barista team have won awards – and don't miss the cheesecake and pastries, too. Mon–Fri 7.30am–7pm, Sat 9am–7pm.

Europa V, Szent István körút 7 ☎1 312 2362; map p.48. Large and perennially busy coffee house a short stroll from the Margit híd, with lots of seating, including a

segregated, salon-style room. Both the coffee and cake is first-rate, though nothing tops the delicious, and very generously sliced, *rétes* or *flódni*. Daily 9am–8pm.

Madal XIII, Hollán Ernő utca 3 ☎1 796 6287, ⓦmadalcafe.hu; map p.48. New-wave coffee bar with a spiritual side – it was inspired by the Indian philosopher Sri Chinmoy, whose childhood name was Madal. Coffee aficionados will feel at home here. The friendly capped baristas take their beans very seriously and occasionally run workshops on making the perfect filter coffee. You can also get soy, vegan chocolate and macaroons. In summer there's a terrace in the pedestrian street out front. Mon–Fri 7.30am–8pm, Sat 9am–11.30am.

Szalai V, Balassi Bálint utca 4 ☎1 269 3210; map p.48. One of the few remaining old-style cake shops in Budapest, serving pastries baked on the premises. Beneath its large gilt-framed mirrors are a few tables where the regulars watch the world pass by. Daily except Tues 9am–7pm, Nov–April closed Mon.

TERÉZVÁROS AND ERZSÉBETVAROS

★**À Table** VII, Wesselényi utca 9 ⓦatable.hu; map p.58. One of a chain of French-style cafés that are an

excellent place to start the day. Delicious coffees, sandwiches and pastries – the pistachio croissants are

TOP 5 FOR COFFEE

Centrál see p.168
Espresso Embassy see p.168
Mai Manó see p.169
Ruszwurm see p.170
Tamp & Pull see p.169

mouth-watering – and you can also get delectable bread for picnics. Order from the counter before you sit down. Other branches are in V, Arany János utca 16, and at II, Retek utca 6, next to the Mammut mall by Széll Kálmán tér. Mon–Fri 7am–7pm, Sat–Sun 8am–6pm.

Chocodeli VI, Csengery utca 48 ⓦfacebook.com/chocodeli.bonbondiveki; map p.58. A small café with just a couple of tables just across the road from the House of Terror and a few doors along from the Hunyadi tér market hall. Its *raison d'etre* is of course chocolate – served in drinks and cakes – but they also serve very good coffee and soft drinks such as home-made lemonades. Daily 8am–8pm.

Coffee Cat VI, Ó utca 44 ☎1 708 0170 ⓦcoffeecat.hu; map p.58. One of the cheapest and friendliest of the new cafés, with delicious coffee, a wide selection of good teas and great sandwiches and baguettes with unusual fillings. Mon–Fri 7.30am–4pm, Sat 8am–8pm.

Eco Café VI, Andrássy út 68; map p.58. Welcoming little organic café with sweet little countrified tables and cushioned seating, serving up a small selection of very reasonably priced sandwiches, salads and cakes; it also does a nice line in freshly baked breads. Mon–Fri 7am–8pm, Sat & Sun 8am–8pm.

Fröhlich VII, Dob utca 22 ☎1 266 1733; map p.58. Excellent kosher patisserie 5min walk from the Dohány utca synagogue, with sweet wrought-iron garden-bench-like seating and red and orange painted walls. Specialities include the best *flódni* (apple, walnut and poppyseed cake) in the city. Mon–Fri 9am–4pm, Sun 10am–6pm; closed Sat & Jewish holidays.

★**Mai Manó** VI, Nagymező utca 20 ☎1 269 5642; map p.58. One of the more agreeable spots in the theatre quarter,

this small café underneath the Mai Manó Photography Museum retains a cutesy interior with patterned tables and images splayed across the walls, as well as a convivial outdoor terrace. A perfect place to stop, either for a pastry and breakfast or a late-night drink. Daily 10am–1am.

Művész VI, Andrássy út 29 ☎1 352 1337; map p.58. There's an air of faded grandeur in this coffee house that's as notable for its decor – deep leather seating, chandeliers and gilt – as it is for its coffee and cakes. Mon–Sat 9am–10pm, Sun 10am–10pm.

My Little Melbourne VII, Madách Imre út 3 ☎0670 394 7002, ⓦmylittlemelbourne.hu; map p.58 & map p.38. Superb artisan coffee made by award-winning – but not always the most cheery – baristas, and excellent pastries make this a perfect place for a quick breakfast. Inspired by their Australian travels, Dia and Peti were pioneers when they opened this minuscule place – if you want to sit, there is a small gallery with a few tables. Mon–Fri 7am–7pm, Sat–Sun 8am–5pm.

New York Café VII, Erzsébet körút 9 ☎1 886 6111; map p.48. This opulent coffee house was a popular haunt of writers in the early 1900s. Restored as part of the *Boscolo* hotel, it has lost none of its magnificence, and the service is first class, but exorbitant prices mean it has struggled to win back its place among today's impoverished intelligentsia. Daily 9am–midnight.

Podma Café VI, Podmaniczky utca 14 ☎1 302 2696; map p.48. Tea has really yet to catch on in Budapest, but this unassuming, two-floored café is a good place to start. Row upon row of teas from around the world are lined up in old-fashioned tins on the lovely mahogany shelves, and while you're here, you may as well grab a home-made cookie too. Mon–Fri 8am–10pm Sat 10am–10pm.

Zokni VII, Dohány utca 1/b ☎1 785 6765; map p.48. "Socks" is an unlikely name for a coffee bar – it was the owner's nickname from his taxi-driving days, but the barista knows his stuff, and the cakes, if they are fresh, are delicious. Stands right across the road from the Great Synagogue, so very handy for sightseeing. Tues–Fri 10.30am–8pm, Sat & Sun till 8.30pm.

14

JÓZSEFVÁROS AND FERENCVÁROS

Múzeum Cukrászda VIII, Múzeum körút 10 ☎1 338 4415; map p.77. Friendly hangout which makes for a good spot to rest up at after digesting the nearby National Museum, or when you have been partying into the early hours. Open daily 24hr.

Rengeteg RomKafé IX, Tüzoltó utca 22 ☎0620 321 0229, ⓦfacebook.com/Rengeteg; map p.77. Congenial cellar café underneath the *Élesztő* beer bar in a former glass factory near the Corvin negyed. The teddy bears, sewing machines and bric-a-brac covering the brick walls and every surface give the place a very homely feel, and you can relax in armchairs. There's a huge range of teas, as well as coffee

and hot chocolate, all fairly sourced, and home-made biscuits and savoury snacks. Daily 10am–10pm.

★**Tamp & Pull** IX, Czuczor utca 3 ☎0630 668 3051, ⓦtamppull.hu; map p.77. Students at the University across the road flock to this minute craft coffee bar, where the expert baristas in the cosy *Tamp & Pull* serve superb "third-wave" coffee – they also run courses on making and tasting the stuff. The board on the wall tells you about the beans of the day: where they are from, who grew them and at what altitude. The pastries and sandwiches are delicious too. Mon–Fri 7am–7pm, Sat 9am–6pm, Sun noon–4pm.

THE VÁR AND CENTRAL BUDA

Artigiana Gelati XII, Csaba utca 8 ☎1 212 2439; map p.87. A couple of minutes up the road from Széll Kálmán tér, this parlour has been concocting fine ice cream for more than twenty years. A magical assortment of wondrous flavours, such as beetroot, cherry and chilli, and lavender and rosemary, served up in cones or cups. It also has lactose- and sugar-free *gelati*. Tues–Fri 10.30am–8pm, Sat & Sun till 8.30pm.

Auguszt II, Fény utca 8 ☎1 316 3817 ⓦauguszt cukraszda.hu; map p.87. Five generations have been continuing the *Auguszt* patisserie tradition since 1870, with mainly the women of the family at the helm. They certainly produce some of Budapest's finest cakes, and you can enjoy them upstairs or on the terrace out the back. The branch at V, Kossuth Lajos utca 14-16 in the Belváros is open Monday too. Tues–Fri 10am–6pm, Sat 9am–6pm.

Budai Pékség XII, Maros utca 23-25 ☎1 375 5284; map p.87. A great bakery with a couple of tables that serves sandwiches, cakes, pastries, coffees and surprisingly delicious milk. It is also handy for picnics in the hills – the bread is excellent, and you can get delicious aubergine and garlic spreads. The sister outlet, *Budai Pékség II*, at Vársányi Irén utca 21, just below Széna tér, also sells excellent ice cream. Mon–Fri 7am–7pm, Sat 7am–1pm.

Levendula II, Fény utca, underneath the market ⓦlevendulafagylaltozo.hu; map p.87. This new parlour chain serves some of the best ice cream in town. Flavours include nutella, coconut, lavender (*levendula* in Hungarian), and more intriguingly, camembert. You'll also find outlets at V, Vámház körút 6, opposite the Great Market Hall, and at V, Szent István körút 21, near the Margít híd. Daily 11am–9pm.

Marvelosa I, Lánchíd utca 13 ☎1 201 9221 ⓦmarvelosa.eu; map p.89. Overlooking the riverside park between the Lánchíd and restored Várkert Bazár, this sweet little café feels like a very personal creation. The art on the walls is by the daughter of Ági néni, who presides over the proceedings. The artistic links continue in the menu and at the tables which each bear an artist's name rather than a number. They also serve full meals throughout the day. Tues–Sat 10am–10pm, Sun 10am–6pm.

Ruszwurm I, Szentháromság utca 7 ☎1 375 5284; map p.89. Near the Mátyás Church in the Vár, this diminutive Baroque coffee house can be so packed that it's almost impossible to get a seat in summer. Still, it's definitely worth seeking out for its coffee and cakes, the pick of which is its mouth-watering *rétes* (strudel). Daily 10am–7pm.

GELLÉRT-HEGY

Itee I, Villányi út 12 ☎1 279 1133; map p.107. Charming, just below street level teahouse with lots of jaunty seating areas either side of the main lounge, whose main feature is a miniature goldfish pond. Although tea is very much the speciality here – over eighty types kept fresh in bright red tins – there are lots of other beverages to mull over. Mon–Fri 1–11pm, Sat & Sun 3–11pm.

★**Tranzit Art Café** XI, Bukarest utca 3 ☎1 209 3070, ⓦ tranzitcafe.com; map p.107. Friendly alternative café in the fabulous Bauhaus-style ex-bus station behind Kosztolányi Dezső tér. It's a very relaxed space where you can lounge around on sofas, with a children's play area in one corner. They have salsa evenings and film screenings outside in summer. You can get a lunch menu for 1,200Ft, and they serve toasted sandwiches and burgers throughout the day. Mon–Fri 9am–11pm, Sat–Sun 10am–11pm.

ÓBUDA

Czniel III, Nánási út 55 ☎1 240 1188; map p.113. Large, popular café just north of the Roman ruins at Aquincum, with excellent ice creams and chestnut *puree*. A good place to bring children too, as it has its own play area, and handy if you've been on the riverbank enjoying the bars and restaurants on the Római-part or want to head further out from Aquincum. Daily May–Sept 9am–10pm, Oct–April 9am–7.30pm.

Daubner III, Szépvölgyi út 50 ☎1 335 2253 ⓦdaubnercukraszda.hu; map p.113. It is a trek to get to this patisserie in Óbuda, but the place is always crowded, especially at weekends, when people will patiently queue up for its delicious cakes, such as the plum slipper (*szilvás papucs*) or pumpkin-seed scone (*tökmagos pogácsa*). The Daubner family have sold the business, but the quality should hold. Mon–Sat 9am–7pm.

THE BUDA HILLS

Normafa Rétes XII, Eötvös utca 59, Normafa ⓦnormafaretes.hu; map p.120. The *Rétes Büfé* hut at the top of the Buda Hills by the old tree where Bellini's aria was sung (see p.119) is a place of pilgrimage for families, walkers and (in winter) skiers who flock to the hills. You can expect to queue for the excellent *rétes* on fine days. The same crowd run the *Rétes Kert* across the road and the *büfé* at the top of the Libegő. Summer 9am–8pm, winter 10am–4pm.

SZIMPLAKERT, ERZSÉBETVAROS

Bars and clubs

Trendy, traditional or bohemian – whatever you're after in Budapest, you're likely to find it. Rather than being focused on one central zone, the drinking scene is fairly diffuse, albeit heavily skewed towards Pest. Party central is the VII district, where you'll find the pick of the ruin bars, Budapest's home-grown drinking trend. In the Belváros, Erzsébet tér has leapfrogged Liszt Ferenc tér as the in-place to meet and hang out, while the outdoor bars on Margit-sziget and at various spots along the Danube do a roaring trade in the summer. For a slightly quieter night the pleasantly chilled area around the newly pedestrianized Kecskeméti utca and the Károly kert are reliable bets. What's more, the focus on quality that has transformed the city's restaurants and cafés can be found here, too, in the new wine and craft beer bars.

Budapest's **ruin bars** (*romkocsma*) have been a firm favourite with visitors for several years. *Szimplakert* and *Instant* have turned into very established enterprises, but the bohemian feel keeps on spreading across the Seventh and Eighth Districts. Once a deserted series of courtyards between Király and Dob utca, **Gozsdu udvar** is now packed with places to eat and drink, and newer venues such as *Lumen* and *Kisüzem* to continue the dilapidated arty tradition. For alfresco boozing you'll find several **outdoor summer bars** at the southern end of Margit-sziget, two very successful ones at the Városliget, while up the Danube on the Római-part the *Fellini Római Kultúrbisztró* offers a more relaxed vibe.

The **wine bar** (*borozó*) scene has changed markedly recently, as the growing interest in provenance, backed by a passionate belief in promoting Hungarian wine, has led to the emergence of sophisticated bars with clued-up staff. *Doblo* and *Kadarka* are fine examples, but you can still find the more traditional Hungarian wine bars that are mainly working men's watering holes offering humble snacks such as *zsíros kenyér* (bread and dripping with onion and paprika).

15   **Beer** has long lived in the shadow of wine in Hungary. However, the emergence of microbreweries has sparked a new curiosity in the humble hop and specialist beer bars (*söröző*) such as *Élesztő*, *Jónás* and *Monyó* are attracting a new generation of discerning drinkers.

The **club** scene is especially varied in the summer, when it expands into several large outdoor venues, and there are also regular events held in the thermal baths such as the old Turkish Rudas and the big outdoor Széchenyi, or in sites further out of town (advertised via promotional posters). DJs to look out for include Palotai and Mango and anything with the Tilos Rádió stamp on it. Another interesting new fad is the slam poetry craze, which you can catch all over town.

ESSENTIALS

Opening hours Most places open around lunchtime and stay open until well after midnight, unless otherwise stated, though bars in residential areas have to close their terraces at 10pm. Summer-only bars usually announce their openings (generally in May) via a Facebook page.

Costs Note that the warnings about rip-offs in restaurants (see p.158) apply equally to bars. Most bars do not take credit cards. Expect to pay 500–1000Ft upwards to get into a club.

Transport There is a good network of night buses (see p.24) that can help you make your way home, taxis are easy to flag down, and the streets are generally safe.

Smoking The smoking ban is strictly enforced indoors, but generally you can smoke on terraces and garden areas.

THE BELVÁROS

Csendes Létterem V, Ferenczy Isván utca 5 ☎0630 727 2100, ⓦfacebook.com/csendesvintagebar map p.38. Just down the road from Astoria junction, this bar's wacky decoration, chandeliers and bare brick walls have made it a popular destination for students at the university across the road (attracted in part by its vast range of spirits). Its sister bars, *Kis Cserfes* spills out on to the pavement in front the delightful Károly kert. Mon–Fri 10am–2am, Sat 2pm–2am, Sun 2pm–midnight.

Ibolya V, Ferenciek tere 5 ☎1 788 1944, ⓦibolyaespresso.hu; map p.38. An old favourite with local students, the *Ibolya* preserves a wonderfully retro feel

---

BOTTOMS UP!

Hungarian has a variety of tongue-twisting ways to **toast** fellow drinkers. *Egészségedre!* ("Your health") is the most common, but it's usually said to one person whom you know well. To a group, you might use *Egészségetekre!*; if your acquaintance is more formal, it would be *Egészségére!* To a friend, a simple *Szia!* is fine.

Clinking glasses of **beer** used to be frowned upon, as it was said that this was how the Austrians celebrated the execution of the Hungarian generals in 1849; the "right" Hungarian way was to bang your glass on the table before raising it to your lips. These days, though, people say that there was a 150-year time limit on that taboo, and clinking beer-glasses is back.

with its neon street sign, plastic seats and surly waiters. Even the snacks have stayed the same – *melegszendvics* (toasted sandwiches) and peanuts. Football matches are shown out on the terrace. Mon–Thurs 8am–1am, Fri 8am–3am, Sat 11am–3am, Sun noon–1am.

★ **Tip Top Bar** V, Kecskeméti utca 3; ☎ 0670 333 2113, ⓦ facebook.com; map p.38. It's a long, seven flights of stairs up to this laid-back rooftop bar, but the view at the top makes the cocktails even more enjoyable. To soak up your drinks you can get bagels and sandwiches. Quiet live music or DJ, Thurs–Sat. Entry from the street is through the bar on the ground floor (its name changes) to the stairs at the back. Booking advisable. May–Oct daily 4–11pm, Nov–April Wed–Sat 4–11pm.

LIPÓTVÁROS

Drop Shop V, Balassi Bálint utca 27 ☎ 0630 345 3739, ⓦ dropshop.hu; map p.48. An excellent wine bar at the Pest end of the Margít Bridge where the stock is dominated by imported wines, but interestingly its Hungarian wines draw mainly on the smaller producers such as Gizella pince. You can lounge around on the sofas tasting the delicious snacks – or you can buy to take out, as the slightly strange name suggests. Not as cheap as the relaxed interior might suggest. Daily 11am–midnight.

Tokaji Borozó V, Falk Miksa utca 32 ☎ 1 269 3143, ⓦ facebook.com; map p.48. Old-style cellar wine bar serving wines from the Tokaj region in northeast Hungary – though this is not top-end stuff – as well as snacks such as *lepcsánka* (potato pancakes) and *zsíros kenyér* (bread and dripping). Mon–Fri noon–9pm.

TERÉZVÁROS AND ERZSÉBETVÁROS

Amigo Bar VII, Hársfa utca 1 ☎ 1 352 1424, ⓦ amigobar.hu; map p.58. A fun time is guaranteed at this rockabilly haunt, with three floors crawling with 1950s nostalgia, right down to the bartenders with their pompadour quiffs. Live music (Sept–May) takes place down in the cellar bar, which otherwise has a fabulous jukebox and three immaculate red-clothed pool tables. Mon–Fri 3pm–3am, Sat 6pm–4am.

Cafe Bobek VII, Kazinczy utca 53 ☎ 1 322 0279, ⓦ bobek.hu; map p.58. Named after a Communist rabbit, this is one of the district's more discreet *kerts*, the sort of place where you could happily linger for hours. The venue is divided between a cosy covered terrace, with cushioned benches, leather sofas, and pink-and-white lanterns, and an adjoining garden spilling over with trees and plants. There also a very creditable food menu to hand if you decide to stay just that little bit longer. Mon–Thurs 1pm–midnight, Fri & Sat 3pm–2am.

Castro Bistro VII, Madách Imre tér 3 ☎ 1 215 0184, ⓦ facebook.com/castrobistro; map p.58. Located on a rather dull square, this casual, cheery bar with a misleadingly Cuban name nevertheless draws a mixed crowd of Hungarians and foreigners. It's nothing particularly fancy, but the boho-style decor, good beer, and Serbian-style meats, keep people coming back. Mon–Thurs 11am–midnight, Fri & Sat 11am–1am, Sun 2pm–midnight.

Csak a Jó Sör VII, Kertész utca 42 ☎ 0630 251 4737, ⓦ csakajosor.hu; map p.58. Small bar that is more of a shop with a few tables, but it's a must for craft ale lovers as the name "only good beer" suggests. As it's run by a true devotee, Gergely, you'll find five beers on tap, Hungarian

15

RISING FROM THE RUINS

Now synonymous with Budapest nightlife, the city's first ruin bars (*romkocsma*) were guerrilla-like ventures, turning condemned buildings and crumbling courtyards into hip summer drinking spots. Decorated with graffiti and collages, the first wave of bars also put on entertainment in the form of music, film-screenings and poetry readings. Once the authorities forced out a *romkocsma* it would simply take its name elsewhere: at the start of the summer word would spread where the latest incarnations of the *Szóda*, *West Balkan* and *Mumus* would be. This purely nomadic existence began to change when councils began to realize the commercial potential of the bars, not least in attracting tourists. With a relaxation in attitudes places such as *Szimpla* and *Kuplung* began to open year-round and focus on turning a profit. While this has caused some inevitable commercialization most bars retain an undeniable wackiness, and the opening of *Rácskert*, for example, hints at a return to the anarchic spirit.

TOP 5 RUIN BARS

Café Bobek see p.173   **Instant** see p.174
Most see p.174   **Rácskert** see p.175
Szimplakert see p.175

15

TOP 5 OUTDOOR VENUES

Fellini Római Kultúrbisztró see p.176
Kertem see p.176
Mika Tivadar see p.174
Tip Top Bar see p.173
WNDRLND see p.177

and imported, and more than two hundred by the bottle. Mon–Sat 2pm–9pm.

Doblo VII, Dob utca 20 ☎1 20 398 8863, ⓦ budapestwine.com; map p.58. *Dobló* is a classy, though far from pretentious, wine bar, which looks all the better for its exposed brickwork. Some two hundred varieties of Hungarian wine are available by the glass, each costing between 850–1400Ft – and the meat and cheese plates are delicious. Wine-tasting sessions (45min) from 4500Ft. Live music Wed and Thurs. Mon–Fri 2pm–2am, Sat 5pm–3am, Sun 5pm–1am.

Fekete Kutya VII, Dob utca 31 ☎0620 580 3151, ⓦ facebook.com/feketekutja; map p.58. Friendly Seventh-district bar run by a mother and son team just off Kazinczy utca. The couple of tables under the arcade in front are good places to people watch. Its Hungarian tapas are delicious (3 dishes for 1200Ft). Mon–Fri 7.30am–7.30pm, Sat–Sun 7.30am–3.30pm.

Garzon VII, Wesselényi utca 24 ☎0630 438 7788, ⓦ facebook.com as Garzon Café; map p.58. Another thoughtfully contrived bar, *Garzon* takes its cue from the 1970s. The whole space is fitted out to resemble an apartment from that era; gaudy wallpaper, household appliances plastered to the walls, and a corner kitchen complete with checked tablecloth and red-and-white enamel tiles. The beer and the music are pretty decent too. Mon–Thurs 4pm–2am, Fri–Sat 4pm–3am, Sun 4pm–midnight.

Instant VI, Nagymező utca 38 ☎1 311 0704, ⓦ instant.co.hu; map p.58. Big-hitting ruin bar whose moniker, "The Enchanted Forest", suits it well; surveying the vast central courtyard are herds of rabbits suspended in mid-air, a cat-woman-sphinx figure and other fantastical creatures. Meanwhile, some twenty rooms (many bizarrely themed), half a dozen bars and three dance floors lend the place a rollicking party vibe. Daily 4pm–6am.

Kadarka VI, Király utca 42 ☎1 266 5094, ⓦ facebook .com/kadarkabar; map p.58. Taking its name from the distinctive Hungarian grape, this colourful modern wine bar has a youthful appeal. It's mainly Hungarian wines on offer, and at reasonable prices. You can also buy bottles to take away. Their food is as good as the wine – with snacks as well as light meals. Daily 4pm–midnight.

Kiadó VI, Jókai tér 3 ☎1 331 1955, ⓦ facebook.com /kiadokocsma; map p.58. The polar opposite of the type

of bar to be found across Andrássy út on Liszt Ferenc tér, *Kiado* has few pretensions, with its laid-back feel, small tables and cosy gallery. Full bar menu available too. Mon–Fri 10am–1am, Sat & Sun 11am–1am.

★**Kisüzem** VII, Kis Diófa utca 2 ☎1 781 6705, ⓦ facebook.com/Kisuzem; map p.58. Small bohemian bar on the corner of Klauzál tér, that stands out from the Seventh-district crowd with its unpretentious feel, avant-garde art, good music and delicious cheap food (a bowl of chili con carne for just 950Ft). Live music on Thurs, silent movies on Sun. Mon–Wed & Sun noon–2am, Thurs–Sat noon–3am.

Központ VII, Madách Imre út 5 ☎1 783 8405, ⓦ facebook.com/kozpontbudapest; map p.58. Stylish bar at the entrance to the Seventh district that is a favourite meeting place for media folk. In the daytime the "Centre" feels more like a relaxed café with its big window seats, but it turns livelier later as the music and the crowds arrive. Good salads and sandwiches. Mon–Fri 8.30am–1am, Sat 4pm–2am, Sun 4–11pm.

Kuplung VI, Király utca 46 ☎0630 755 3527, ⓦ facebook.com/Kuplung; map p.58. This one-time motorcycle repair shop (the name means "clutch") is accessed via a graffiti-splattered corridor leading into a concrete courtyard masked with weirdly painted murals. A lime-green-coloured bar runs the length of one side, while the remaining space is taken up with simple wooden bench seating, table football (*csocsó*) and ping-pong. Mon–Thurs & Sun 3pm–2am, Fri–Sat 4pm–5am.

Lokál VII, Dob utca 18 ☎1 352 4198, ⓦ lokalbar.hu; map p.58. In true ruin bar style, a ramshackle interior design and a chilled courtyard, where a grill operates in summer. Electro swing on the dance floor on Fri–Sat. Mon–Wed 5pm–midnight, Thurs–Sat 5pm–4am.

Mika Tivadar VII, Kazinczy utca 47 ☎0620 965 3007, ⓦ mikativadarmulato.hu; map p.58. One of the busiest bars on Kazinczy utca, with a large summertime garden next door, good food and great music on the stage at the back. The name comes from the owner of the factory that once stood here. Mon–Wed 5pm–midnight, Thurs 5pm–3am, Fri–Sat 5pm–5am.

★**Most** VI, Zichy Jenő utca 17 ☎0670 248 3322, ⓦ mostjelen.hu/most; map p.58. Another of the major ruin bars, though a little more clean-cut, this massive complex centres around a bistro-like lounge, to the side of which is a small bar and stage, where there is regular live music. In May the brick wall at the back is ceremoniously knocked down, opening up an enormous gravel-bedded garden. *Most* is also one of the better *kerts* for food, and is especially popular for its breakfasts and brunches (1690Ft). Mon–Wed & Sun 10am–2am, Thurs–Sat 10am–5am.

★**Pótkulcs** VI, Csengery utca 65b ☎1 269 1050,

ⓦpotkulcs.hu; map p.58. There's not much by way of a sign on the tatty metal door, but go through and you'll find yourself in a verdant yard, with the bar straight ahead, and a room with sofas and table football off to the left. The "Spare Key" is a laid-back kind of place with a reputation built largely on the strength of its live music programme, ranging from klezmer and Roma bands to underground, folk and jazz. Mon–Wed & Sun 5pm–1.30am, Thurs–Sat 5pm–2.30am.

PRLMNT VII, Teréz Körút 62 ☎1 911 0901, ⓦprlmnt .hu; map p.58. Flashy club in a hundred-year-old cinema down the road from Nyugati station. The black and gold auditorium has a state-of-the-art sound system and is a glorious setting for clubbing and live acts (Hungarian and British). Mon–Tues & Sun noon–midnight, Wed–Thurs noon–2am, Fri–Sat noon–5am.

Rácskert VIII, Dob utca 40 ☎1 321 0816, ⓦfacebook .com/racskert; map p.58. One of the newer ruin bars, behind the railings (*rács*) of an old car park that hopes to recapture the iconoclastic spirit of the late 1990s. Run by the man behind the first ruin garden in the city, the much mourned Rácskert. On Fridays, two worlds collide as a

traditional folk band plays to the cool kids. Mon–Wed & Sun 4pm–midnight, Thurs–Sat 4pm–4am.

Szimplakert VII, Kazinczy utca 14 ☎0620 261 8669, ⓦszimpla.hu; map p.58. Occupying a former stove factory, this is the grandaddy of *romkocsma* bars. The darkened corridor feeds a warren of graffiti-strewn, junk-filled rooms, beyond which is the main, partially canopied, courtyard with bars on three sides and an old Trabant for seating. There's free live music (jazz, rock, retro, funk) most nights of the week. Although there's a fair old din here at night, it makes a delightful refuge by day. Farmers' market held here every Sunday. Mon–Sat noon–3am, Sun 9am–3am.

Szóda VII, Wesselényi utca 18 ☎1 461 0007, ⓦfacebook.com/szodabar; map p.58. As enjoyable in winter as it is in summer, this hip bar behind the main synagogue sports super-cool retro stylings in the form of red leather seating, odd bits of furnishings, and cartoon strips for wallpaper. Between Wednesday and Sunday, enthusiastic groovers move downstairs to catch the latest DJ tunes. Mon–Thurs 5pm–3am, Fri–Sat 5pm–5am.

15

JOZSEFVÁROS AND FERENCVÁROS

A Grund VIII, Nagy Templom utca 32 ☎0620 583 6712, ⓦagrund.hu, map p.77. Occupying the whole of a derelict house, a short trek from the centre, *A Grund* is a fabulous party place where you can count on something happening most nights of the week, with DJs, live acts and football screenings. The focal point of the complex is a slick, bare-brick bar with side rooms and sofas, outside of which lies a neatly landscaped terrace with grass and gravel walkways. There is an outdoor grill at the back, and even an excellent children's playground by the entrance. Mon–Fri 11am–4am, Sat 4pm–4am.

Corvintető VIII, Blaha Lujza tér 1–2, entrance on Somogyi Béla utca, ☎0620 378 2988 ⓦcorvinteto .hu; map p.77. For some of the best night-time views of Budapest, head on up to the inspired rooftop bar atop the Communist-era Corvin department store. A 30m-long bar keeps happy folk going until the very early hours, while the floor below hosts DJs and the occasional band. You take a lift on the left-hand side of the building. Daily 6pm–6am.

Csiga VIII, Vásár utca 2 ☎0630 613 2046, ⓦfacebook .com/cafecsiga; map p.77. An artsy, mellow atmosphere prevails at the appealing *Csiga* corner café, which remains the drinking venue of choice in the increasingly hip area around Rákóczi tér. Stripped wood flooring, mezzanine seating and big windows set the scene for a daytime or evening chillout. The food is excellent too – the two-course lunch menu is 1000Ft. Daily 10am–midnight.

★**Élesztő** IX, Tüzoltó utca 22 ☎0670 233 5052, ⓦelesztohaz.hu; map p.77. Housed in a former glass

factory near the Corvin negyed, "Yeast" is one of the best places in town to try Hungarian artisan beers, with no less than twenty on tap. You can soak up the booze with cheese scones, peanuts, sausages and other snacks. There's seating out in the courtyard, ruin-bar style – and ambitious plans to develop the rest of the space with a brewing school and a hostel make this a place to watch. Daily 3pm–3am.

★**Jedermann** IX, Ráday utca 58 ☎0630 406 3617, ⓦjedermann.hu; map p.77. *Jedermann*, at the bottom of Ráday utca, scores top marks on all counts: it's a relaxed bar, has good food (two-course lunch for 890Ft), and puts on excellent jazz on Wed and Sat. It's popular with local students for its cheap breakfasts (coffee 210Ft) and you can lounge about on a terrace at the back. As a bonus, it's attached to the Goethe Institute, which has a lively cultural programme. No credit cards. Daily 8am–1am.

Jonás IX, CET building (Bálna) ☎0670 930 1392, ⓦfacebook.com/jonaskezmuvessorhaz; map p.77. Craft beer bar at the southern end of the "Whale" on the Pest riverbank. Eight beers on tap, and also craft *pálinka*, wine and soft drinks. The terrace has great views over the river (though no table service). Occasional live music. Mon–Thurs 9am–midnight, Fri–Sat 9am–2am, Sun 9am–11pm.

★**Lumen** VIII, Mikszáth Kálmán tér 3 ☎1 781 5156, ⓦfacebook.com/lumen.kavezo; map p.77. A wonderfully bohemian little bar that is fizzing with ideas. You can choose from craft beers on tap, freshly roasted coffee – it was the first place in town to roast its own – and the mainly vegetarian salads, soups and sandwiches. It is also a gallery, and has music too: free jazz on Tuesdays, folk on Fridays. The terrace spreads out into the popular square. Mon–Fri 8am–midnight, Sat 10am–midnight, Sun 10am–10pm.

Monyo IX, Kálvin tér 7 ☎ 0670 415 7835, ⓦ monyo.hu;

map p.177. Small bar with friendly staff who will enthusiastically lead you through their stock of Hungarian craft beers, both on tap and by the bottle. Light snacks only. Mon–Wed noon–midnight, Thurs–Fri noon–2am, Sat 5pm–2am.

THE VÁROSLIGET

Dürer Kert XIV, Ajtosi Dürer sor 19–21 ☎ 1 789 4444, ⓦ durerkert.com; map p.69. One of the big party venues that Budapest seems to excel in, attracting a young crowd with its concerts and DJs, and indoor and outdoor dance floors, table football and big screens. If you like it buy the t-shirt. Daily 5pm–5am.

★**Kertem** XIV, Olaf Palme sétány 3 ☎ 0630 225 1399, ⓦ kertemfesztival.hu; map p.69. "My Garden",

located in the middle of the Városliget, is great place to lounge away the summer. It's popular with families by day, with children playing around on the grass, while at night it is always packed. Cheap drinks, good music and a very busy grill produces the perfect accompaniment for those long lazy evenings. Note that by the end of the summer the grassy expanse gets pretty dusty. May–Sept daily 11am–4am.

THE VÁR AND CENTRAL BUDA

★**Bambi** I, Frankel Leó utca 2–4 ☎ 1 212 3171, ⓦ facebook.com/bambieszpresszo; map p.87. One of the few surviving Socialist-Realist bars, complete with stern waitresses, and old men chatting and playing dominoes on red plastic-covered tables. It's all straight honest fare, omelettes and toasted sandwiches, and none of your fancy coffee here: it is just black, with milk or with cream. Mon–Fri 7am–10pm, Sat & Sun 9am–10pm.

Lánchíd Söröző I, Fő utca 4 ☎ 1 214 3144, ⓦ lanchidsorozo.hu; map p.89. Handily placed at the Buda end of the Lánchíd, this chilled little bar is a quiet

place in daytime, frequented by tourists and the odd regular, but by sundown the mood is more animated. The owner is a serious music fan, as the randomly scattered instruments, gig posters, and photos of him with Robert Plant, BB King et al on the walls testify. Daily 11am–1am.

Szalonspicc II, Lövőház utca 17 ☎ 0630 861 9006, ⓦ szalonspicc.hu; map p.87. Excellent wine, friendly staff and tasty mini-burgers at this small bar on a buzzy pedestrianized street close to Széll Kálmán tér. The pavement terrace is standing-room-only in summer. Mon–Sat noon–midnight, Sun 2–10pm.

GELLÉRT-HEGY AND THE TABÁN

Libella XI, Budafóki út 7 ☎ 1 209 4761, ⓦ facebook.com/libellakavezo; map p.107. Friendly, agreeably down-at-heel spot near the *Gellért Hotel*, which is popular above all with the student crowd from the nearby Technical University. Bar snacks, chess and draughts seem to keep those that pop by satisfied. Mon–Fri 8am–1am, Sat 4pm–1am.

Platán I, Döbrentei tér ☎ 0620 361 2287; map p.107. This amicable bar's location under the plane tree near the

river, and with outdoor tables, guarantees a steady stream of visitors. Daily 10am–10pm.

Szatyor XI, Bartók Béla út 36 ☎ 1 279 0290, ⓦ szatyorbar.com; map p.107. A typical Budapest mix here of bar and culture, colourfully exotic decoration, settees to lounge on in the gallery, good Hungarian fare on a full menu, and a strong student presence from the nearby Technical University. Mon–Fri noon–1am, Sat–Sun 2pm–1am.

ÓBUDA AND MARGIT-SZIGET

Fellini Római Kultúrbisztró III, Kossuth Lajos üdülőpart 5-6, Római-part ☎ 1 279 0290, ⓦ tinyurl.com/cfsndv5; map p.113. The best of the string of open-air bars lining the riverbank north of Óbuda. You can sit on the shore on deckchairs enjoying the regular live music,

films and other cultural programmes. Take the HÉV train from Batthyány tér to Rómaifürdő and it's a 10min walk down to the river. May–Sept, Mon–Fri 3–11pm, Sat–Sun 10am–midnight.

Holdudvar XIII, Margit-sziget ☎ 1 236 0155, ⓦ facebook.com/holdudvaroldal; map p.116. While the northern end of the island has the grand hotels, the southern end has the summer bars. Located about ten minutes' walk from the Margit Bridge end of the island, *Holdudvar* is smarter of the two bars in the old Casino building. Here, you can relax under the trees and enjoy music, dancing and films. The main bar is huge and service should be fairly quick even on busy nights. May to Sept,

---

TOP 5 CRAFT BEER BARS

Csak a Jó Sör see p.173
Élesztő see p.175
Jónás see p.175
Lumen see p.175
Monyó see p.176

HUNGARIAN WINE

Hungary's **wines** have come a long way in recent years, though they are still under-appreciated in the global market. In general, the country's climate favours whites, especially crisp and floral varieties, but its reds are also delicious and offer more complexity and variation.

Many of the grape varieties used in Hungarian wines will be familiar, even if their Hungarian names are less so, but there are also some indigenous grapes that are worth trying. Among **reds**, alongside the well-known Cabernet Franc and Cabernet Sauvignon and others, the Kadarka yields a light, spicy, cherry-coloured wine that has undergone a revival in the past decade. It is a common ingredient in **Bikavér**, the well-known Hungarian **Bull's Blood wine** from Eger and Szekszárd. Alongside the familiar **whites** of Sauvignon Blanc and Olaszrizling (Italian Riesling) are Irsai Olivér, which produces a floral, aromatic wine, and Cserszegi Fűszeres, which has a slightly smoother, spicier flavour, as well as the crisp dry Furmint and Hárslevelű (lime or linden leaf), which produce some of Hungary's finest bottles in Tokaj and Somló. Another grape found in Somló is Júhfark, "sheep's tail", said to have desirable results if drunk on your wedding night. Hungary's **rosés** have improved markedly in recent years, benefiting from a good balance of fruit without being too sweet.

Although Hungary has twenty-two official wine regions, the best producers are concentrated in a few areas. Alongside the big established vintners, it is the smaller cellars (*pince*) that are producing the most exciting wines. Below is a brief introduction to the main regions and some of the best labels (★) to look out for.

Lake Balaton to the southwest of Budapest has five different regions where whites dominate. ★Huba Szeremley, Jásdi, Otto Légli and Mihály Figula.

Eger is one of the big wine regions, in the north. ★Vilmos Thummerer, St. Andrea, Nimród Kovács, Bolyki and Tamas Pók. One to avoid: Egri Csillag, a lame marketing attempt to produce a white version of the famed Bikavér.

Etyek-Buda is a smaller region that produces mainly white wines. It is perhaps best known for its sparkling wines in the Budafok cellars. Etyek, lying 30km west of Budapest, has some excellent wines and is easy to visit. Four times a year crowds flock out to its wine and food festival(ⓦetyekipiknik .hu). ★Törley (for sparkling), Etyeki Kúria and Nyakas Pince.

Szekszárd is strong on reds, especially Kadarka. ★Ferenc Vesztergombi, Takler, Tamás Dúzsi, Péter Vida, Németh János, Zoltán Heimann, and Adrian Bösz.

Somló is the smallest region, based around a hill west of Balaton whose volcanic soil produces fascinating results, just as it does around Tokaj; this is a crisp yet rich wine with a minerally character, and it found favour with Queen Victoria. ★ Béla Fekete, Imre Györgykovács, Kolonics.

Tokaj is famed for its incredibly sweet Aszú wines, but the drier Furmint and the fragrant Hárslevelű (lime or linden leaf), less cloying than the Aszú, are the real surprise. ★Royal Tokaj, Disznokő, Oremus and Szepsy (whose wines are brilliant but very pricey), Gizella pince, Erzsébet pince, Kikelet, Vayi and Berger Zsolt.

Villány, near the Croatian border, was the first region to make its name after 1989. It is strong on reds, but its rosés are also good. ★ József Bock, Attila Gere and Tiffán, Vylyan and Sauska, and the smaller names, Jackfall, Ruppert and Balázs Hárságyi.

TOP 5 WINE BARS

Doblo see p.174
Kadarka see p.174
Szalonspicc see p.176

Drop Shop see p.173
Kis Csendes see p.172

15

Mon–Wed & Sun 11am–midnight, Thurs–Sat 11am–4am.
WNDRLND XIII, Margit-sziget ☎0670 775 5667, ⓦwndrlnd.hu; map p.116. On the other side of the Casino building from *Holdudvar*, "Wonderland" has a far more laid-back feel, and no one dresses up to come here. It

has been described as pop-up bar meets ruin pub meets artist workshop, or as "Narnia without the wardrobe" – it is certainly a bizarre mix. On weekend afternoons it has a great family atmosphere, as people bring the kids along. May to Sept, Mon–Thurs 4pm–2am, Fri 4pm–4am, Sat 1pm–4am, Sun 1pm–2am.

EDITORS PERFORM AT THE SZIGET FESTIVAL

Arts and entertainment

Hungary's cultural pedigree is strong, and this is reflected in both the diversity of performers and quality of productions available on any given night in Budapest. Music is a Hungarian forte, and there's a huge depth of talent, particularly in classical, folk, jazz and world music. Its rhythms and vigour make Hungarian folk music very accessible, and you can catch its different forms, played by skilled bands in venues large and small, accompanying large ensembles on the big stage, or in the more informal setting of the "dance house". The city also boasts some magnificent concert halls, cinemas and theatres, many worth visiting for their architecture alone. The Spring Festival in March and the Café Budapest Contemporary Arts Festival in October showcase some of the finest in both Hungarian and international cultural talent.

ESSENTIALS

Concert season The season for the main opera, theatre and concert halls runs from mid-September to the end of May. During the summer most concerts are in open-air venues (see p.180).

Tickets and reservations The best place for tickets is at the venues themselves where you'll avoid paying booking fees on top. Otherwise try Ticket Express, VI, WestEnd Centre, next to Info desk, Mon–Fri 11am–7pm, Sat 11am–4pm ☎ 0630 303 0999, ⓦ eventim.hu; Jegymester ⓦ jegymester.hu (ticket collection only at VI, Bajcsy-Zsilinszky út 31, 1st floor); Ticketportal, VI, Bajcsy Zsilinszky út 49, Mon–Fri 10am–6pm ☎ 1 302 2942, ⓦ ticketportal .hu; Cultur-Comfort VI, Paulay Ede utca 46, Mon–Fri 10am–6pm ☎ 1 322 0000, ⓦ cultur-comfort.hu; Rózsavölgyi record shop V, Szervita tér 5 ☎ 1 266 8337.

Prices Attending any kind of performance in Budapest needn't cost an arm and a leg. A decent seat at the opera or for a classical music concert will set you back anywhere between 3000–5000Ft, although you can bank on paying at least double that for the big international names. Theatre and dance performances are slightly cheaper at around

2000–4000Ft. Rock or pop concerts range from 1000Ft for local bands up to 30,000Ft for stadium gigs by superstars, while a gig at the Budapest Jazz Club will cost 1400–2500Ft. Cinema tickets typically cost 1500–1900Ft, with cheaper prices on a cinema's discount day (*kedvezményes nap*).

Listings The best online listings are provided by ⓦ xpatloop.com, ⓦ funzine.hu and ⓦ muzsikalendarium .hu, the latter covering classical music events in English – they also publish in the free monthly *Koncert Kalendárium*, available from ticket offices, while the listings magazine *Funzine* can be found in bars. Many gigs and concerts by both local and international bands are publicized on posters around town – particularly around Deák tér, Ferenciek tere and the Astoria underpass. The most comprehensive cinema listings appear in the *mozi* section of the free Hungarian weekly *Pesti Est*. Note that the times of shows are cryptically abbreviated: *n8* or *1/4 8* – short for *negyed 8* – means 7.15pm; *f8* or *1/2 8* (*fél 8*) means 7.30pm; and *h8* or *3/4 8* (*háromnegyed 8*) means 7.45pm. "*Mb.*" indicates the film is dubbed – as many are – and *fel.* or *feliratos* means that it has Hungarian subtitles.

ARTS AND CULTURAL CENTRES

16

The venues listed below are used for a variety of concerts and other entertainment events. Bear in mind that many arts centres close for the summer.

★**A38** XI, Pázmány Péter sétány ☎ 1 464 3940, ⓦ a38 .hu. Housed on a boat that was reputedly given to Hungary in return for writing off the Ukrainian debt and is moored on the Buda side of the river, just below Petőfi híd. One of the best venues in Budapest, it has a separate admission charge for each of its three decks, where top international and Hungarian performers play rock, jazz, folk and world music.

Jurányi II, Jurányi utca 1 ☎ 0670 777 2533, ⓦ juranyihaz.hu. New alternative cultural centre in a former school building just down the road from Széll Kálmán tér presenting exhibitions, theatre and dance. The café is recommended for its laid-back feel.

Millenáris Park II, Kis Rókus utca 16–20 ☎ 1 336 4000, ⓦ millenaris.hu. Complex of buildings near Széll Kálmán tér which has music, theatre and dance shows. In summer,

concerts are held on the park's outdoor stages.

★**Palace of Arts (Művészetek palotája – Müpa)** IX, Komor Marcell utca 1 ☎ 1 555 3000, ⓦ mupa.hu. This substantial complex on the riverbank in southern Pest (15 mins on tram #2 from Vigadó tér) has one of the best concert halls in Europe, as well as a theatre and museum. As the show window for the capital's culture scene, it sees a superb range of concerts, attracting the top international classical, jazz and world music orchestras and acts. Box office Mon–Fri 1–6pm, Sat & Sun 10am–6pm.

Trafó IX, Liliom utca 41 ☎ 1 215 1600, ⓦ trafo.hu. A dynamic contemporary arts centre in a former transformer station, it pulls in full houses with its strong roster of dance, theatre and music, by Hungarian and foreign artistes. Contemporary art gallery and a good bar too. Box office daily 4–8pm. Closed July & Aug.

MUSIC FESTIVALS

Budapest stages several terrific music festivals throughout the year. The big one is the week-long **Sziget festival** (ⓦ sziget.hu/fesztival), held on Óbudai (or Hajógyári) sziget north of Margit-sziget, in mid-August. Now established as one of Europe's largest and most vibrant music events, it draws the very biggest names in rock, pop and world music. It's great value, too, with day tickets costing around €50, and weekly tickets €199 (if bought in advance). Going by public transport, you take the HÉV from Batthyány tér to the Filorigát stop and follow the crowds across the bridge to the island. Slightly less crowded is the bus from Deák tér and the boats from Batthyány tér or Jászai Mari tér, at the Pest end of the Margít híd.

CHURCH AND OPEN-AIR CONCERTS

Quite a few places of worship in Budapest regularly host concerts, among them the church on **Kálvin tér** (see p.79); the **Lutheran Church** on Deák tér (see p.44; the programme includes free performances of Bach before Easter, details of which are posted by the church entrance); and the **Dohány utca synagogue** (see p.63). The **Mátyás Church** on Várhegy (see p.90) stages choral or organ recitals on Fri and Sat between June and Sept (from 8pm), and less frequently the rest of the year.

There is a summer season of concerts at open-air venues, including the outdoor stage on Margit-sziget (see p.117), the **Dominican Yard** of the *Hilton* hotel (see p.153) in the Castle District, the courtyard of the **Pest County Hall** (Pesti Vármegyeháza, V, Városház utca 7, see p.39) and the **Vajdahunyad Castle** in the Városliget (see p.72), though the music most of these venues offer is fairly mainstream.

CLASSICAL MUSIC, OPERA AND BALLET

The city offers a wide variety of performances, with several concerts most nights, especially during the Budapest Spring Festival and the Contemporary Arts jamboree in the autumn, when you can bank on a roll call of world-class artists pitching up. Most opera productions are in Hungarian, a custom introduced by Gustav Mahler when he was director of the Opera House, which remains Budapest's principal venue. One genre that has long appealed to the Hungarian spirit is **operetta**, with Hungarians making a major contribution to the turn-of-the-century Viennese tradition through composers such as Ferenc Lehár and Imre Kálmán. Lehár's *The Merry Widow* and Kálmán's *The Csárdás Princess* still draw the crowds with their combination of grand tunes, extravagant staging and romantic comedy in the suitably over-the-top Operetta Theatre.

16

★**Bartók Memorial House (Bartók Emlékház)** II, Csalán utca 29 ☎1 394 2100, ⓦbartokmuseum.hu. Concerts – not just of the music of Bartók – are held in the villa where the composer used to live, most on Fri at 6pm but also on other days. Tickets are either included in the entry fee or are up to a modest 2500Ft. Tues–Sun 10am–5pm or until start of concert.

Budapest Music Center IX, Mátyás utca 8 ☎1 216 7894, ⓦbmc.hu. Great acoustics in this new chamber music venue just south of the Great Market Hall. Box office Tues–Sun 9am–9pm, Sat–Sun open from two hours before start of concert.

Bartók National Concert Hall (Bartók Béla Nemzeti Hangversenyterem) in the Palace of Arts. The home of the Hungarian National Philharmonic Orchestra has superb acoustics and attracts world-class performers, not just in the classical arena. Box office daily 10am–6pm or until start of concert.

Budapest Operetta Theatre (Budapesti Operettszínház) VI, Nagymező utca 17 ☎1 312 4866, ⓦoperett.hu. The magnificently refurbished home of Hungarian operetta, where you can enjoy works by Lehár and Kálmán, as well as modern musicals. Box office Mon–Fri 10am–7pm, Sat & Sun 1–7pm.

Erkel Theatre (Erkel Színház) VIII, János Pál papa tér 30 ☎1 332 6150, ⓦopera.hu. Large concert hall fresh from a major restoration, with magnificent Bauhaus-style interior that presents opera and ballet on its vast stage. Box office Tues–Sat 11am–5pm, Sun 4pm, or until start of performance.

★**Music Academy (Zeneakadémia)** VI, Liszt Ferenc tér 8 ☎1 342 0179, ⓦzeneakademia.hu. The Liszt Music Academy – founded by Ferenc Liszt in 1875 – has just undergone a total refurbishment, restoring the original look of the interior and vastly improving the acoustics, air-conditioning and seats (which no longer creak). The magnificent gold-covered Nagyterem (Great Hall) and the smaller Sir Georg Solti Chamber Hall have regular concerts of a very high standard. Daily 11am–6.30pm or until start of concert.

Óbuda Music Society (Óbudai Társaskör) III, Kiskorona utca 7 ☎1 250 0288, ⓦobudaitarsaskor.hu. Small concert hall on the edge of the housing estates south of the Árpád híd in Óbuda. The quality of performance is impressive, and big local ensembles such as the Liszt Chamber Orchestra, Budapest Strings and Auer String Quartet are based here. Also stages some jazz concerts. Daily 9am–7pm.

Old Music Academy (Régi Zeneakadémia) VI, Vörösmarty utca 35 ☎1 322 9804 ⓦlisztmuseum.hu. Performances by young musicians every Saturday morning, in the concert hall of the Liszt Memorial Museum. Mon–Fri 10am–6pm, Sat 9am–5pm.

Opera House (Magyar Állami Operaház) VI, Andrássy út 22 ☎1 332 7914, ⓦopera.hu. Home to both the Hungarian State Opera and Hungarian National Ballet companies, it is one of the grandest venues in town, with its gilded frescoes and three-tonne chandeliers. The productions don't always live up to the setting, though the singers and orchestra can be scintillating. With tickets at

600–15,000Ft for most shows, and up to 20,000Ft for the best ones, you're almost guaranteed a good-value night out. The box office is inside the main doors or, if they are closed, round on the left-hand side of the building in Dalszínház utca. Mon–Sat 11am–5pm, Sun 4–7pm.

Thália Theatre (Thália Színház) VI, Nagymező 22 ☎ 1 331 0500, ⊕ thalia.hu. On Budapest's "Broadway", the Thália hosts operas and musicals, as well as theatre and dance. Box office Mon–Thurs 10am–6pm, Fri 10am–5pm.

Vigadó V, Vigadó tér 1 ⊕ vigado.hu. Another fabulously decorated hall, dating from 1865, this is the oldest of the major concert venues, attracting names such as Liszt, Brahms and Debussy. It is open again after a long and costly restoration, and no expense will be spared to make sure big names perform here. Daily 10am–7.30pm.

POP, ROCK AND JAZZ

Budapest is one of the main stops in Central/Eastern Europe for touring international bands, while every Hungarian **band** worth its amplifiers will play the capital. Apart from the venues listed below, performances are also held at the cultural centres listed on p.179. A number of bars host live music, such as *Instant*, *Corvintető*, *Dürer Kert* and *Simplakert*, plus some of the places listed on p.179.

A38 XI, Pázmány Péter sétány ☎ 1 464 3940, ⊕ a38.hu. Top international and Hungarian performers play rock, folk, world music and jazz – it is strong on experimental free jazz.

Akvárium V Erzsébet tér. Launched as a new venue in 2014, the *Aquarium* is less alternative and more hip than the old Gödör club that operated here, but with big names on its programme, the authorities clearly want it to succeed. You'll understand the name "Aquarium" when you're sitting in the bar area, with the light coming through the artificial lake above your head.

Almárium VIII Horánszky utca 5 ☎ 0620 928 9302, ⊕ almariumbisztro.hu. Low-key jazz venue with a pleasant covered courtyard where you can eat well and enjoy jazz concerts Wed–Sat.

★**Budapest Jazz Club** XIII, Hollán Ernő utca 13 ☎ 1 267 2610, ⊕ bjc.hu. The high quality of acts ensures a terrific atmosphere at Budapest's premier jazz club. There are regular themed jazz evenings and weekly late-night jam sessions on Friday and Saturday. Mon–Sat 4pm–midnight

Budapest Park IX, Soroksári út 60 ☎ 0630 702 2919 ⊕ budapestpark.hu. The largest outdoor venue in the city just beyond the *Palace of Arts* in southern Pest, with Hungarian and international acts. April–Sept. Booking office Mon–Sat 1–8pm or until end of concert.

Gödör Klub VII, Central Passage, Király utca 8 ☎ 20 201 3868, ⊕ godorklub.hu. After nine years in Erzsébet tér this alternative cultural centre moved to smaller premises up the road, where it plays host to jazz, folk, alternative Hungarian pop and Roma acts. Mon–Sat 6pm–2am

Jedermann IX, Ráday utca 58 ☎ 0630 406 3617, ⊕ jedermann.hu. Popular venue where the jazz is often avant-garde, concerts on Wed, Sat and some other days, including monthly appearances by the masterful Mihály Dresch, all under the watchful eye of Hans, the saxophonist who runs the show. No credit cards. Daily 8am–1am.

IF Kávézó IX, Ráday utca 19 ☎ 1 299 0694, ⊕ ifkavezo .hu. *IF* offers a particularly exciting programme of jazz, and you can count on something happening most nights of the week.

★**Opus Jazz Club** V, Mátyás utca 8 ☎ 1 216 7894, ⊕ opusjazzclub.hu. Part of the new arts venue, the Budapest Music Center, the *Opus* is a brilliant venue with two levels: the lower level, for performers and connoisseurs, and the upstairs section, where you can chat quietly. The acoustics are highly praised, and the food isn't pricey. Concerts Wed–Sat from 9pm. Booking office Mon–Tues 11.30am–5pm, Thurs–Fri 11.30am–midnight, Sat 7pm–midnight.

FOLK MUSIC AND DANCE

Hungarian folk music and dancing underwent a revival in the 1970s, drawing inspiration from Hungarian communities in Transylvania, regarded as pure wellsprings of Magyar culture. The movement still exists today, and has been extended to other cultures – you'll also see adverts for Greek (*görög*), Slav, Irish and other dance houses. Visitors are welcome to attend

16

BUDAPEST JAZZ

When it comes to **jazz** (or *dzsessz*, as it is sometimes becomes in Hungarian), don't be fooled by the small number of regular venues in Budapest. The country boasts some brilliant jazz musicians, such as the pianists Béla Szakcsi Lakatos and Kálmán Oláh and the experimental guitarist Gábor Juhász. It is worth looking out for the **Harmonia Jazz Workshop** (**Harmonia Jazz Műhely**), which holds regular sessions at the **Budapest Jazz Club**. There are also occasional jazz concerts in the *kert* bars.

the gatherings and learn the steps; see ⓦtanchaz.hu for more. Apart from the places detailed below, performances take place at the *Music Academy*, the *Palace of Arts* and the *A38*, the venues listed on p.179 and in some of the *kert* bars such as the *Rács Kert*.

Aranytíz Cultural Centre V, Arany János utca 10 ☎1 354 3400, ⓦaranytiz.hu. The dancefloor is packed on Saturday nights from late September through to early June, with dance teaching from 7pm; the children's session begins at 5pm. As the evening rolls on, a jamming session often develops with other bands joining in. The cultural centre's programme includes Hungarian and international theatre performances and jazz concerts, too.

★ **Fonó Music Hall (Fonó Budai Zeneház)** XI, Sztregova utca 3 ☎1 206 5300, ⓦfono.hu. The best place to catch regular folk music, this is a lively international folk and world music venue, four stops south of Móricz Zsigmond körtér on tram #18 or #47. Every Wednesday evening there's a dance house led by Tükrös, Pál Szalonna and his band and others. Box office opens one hour before performances.

Hungarian Heritage House (Hagyományok Háza) I, Corvin tér 8 ☎1 225 6049 ⓦheritagehouse.hu. Folk dance in the more formal setting of the state ensemble on the big stage, just down the road from Batthyány tér.

RS9 Theatre VII, Rumbách Sebestyén utca 9 ☎1 269 6610. Small cellar theatre on the edge of the VII district, where you can catch folk evenings Tues & Wed.

CINEMA

Hollywood blockbusters dominate Budapest's mainstream **cinemas**, though the city has a small chain of art-house cinemas that specialize in the latest releases and obscure European films – *angol* indicates a British film, *lengyel* Polish, *német* German, *olasz* Italian, and *orosz* Russian. In the summer some of the outdoor bars, such as *Holdudvar* on Margit-sziget, have weekly open-air film screenings, while there are also summer outdoor and drive-in cinemas on the edge of town.

16

Cirko-gejzir V, Balassi Bálint utca 15–17 ☎1 269 1915, ⓦcirkofilm.hu. One of the best alternative cinemas, with a regular selection of movies from around the globe. They have English subtitles for some Hungarian films. Cheaper tickets on Mon and Tues.

Corvin Budapest Film Palace (Corvin Filmpalota) VIII, Corvin köz 1 ⓦcorvin.hu. This glitzy multiplex, near the Corvin negyed metro, is a good place to catch the latest foreign releases, and it also hosts the Hungarian Film Festival. Cheaper tickets on Wednesday.

Puskin V, Kossuth Lajos 18 ☎1 459 5050, ⓦartmozi .hu. Complex of three cinemas in the centre of town, with a large café attached. The coffered ceiling of the turn-of-the-century main screen is magnificent. Cheaper tickets on Mon.

★ **Toldi** V, Bajcsy-Zsilinszky út 36–38 ☎1 459 5050, ⓦartmozi.hu. Next door to Arany János utca metro station, the two-screen Toldi is one of the more dynamic alternative cinemas in town. Decent bar too. Cheaper tickets on Thurs.

Uránia National Film Theatre (Uránia Nemzeti Filmszínház) VIII, Rákóczi út 21 ⓦurania-nf.hu. With its magnificent Venetian-Moorish decorations, this might seem a strange choice of location for Budapest's main showcase of Hungarian films. But it was in this cinema, built in the 1890s as a dance hall, that the first Hungarian feature film was shot in 1901. While its programme is international, it places special emphasis on local films, and is the principal venue for the annual Titanic film festival. Cheaper tickets on Mon.

THEATRE AND CONTEMPORARY DANCE

Hungarians show great sophistication when it comes to building theatres: take the splendid mass of the **Vígszínház** up the road from Nyugati Station, or the **New Theatre** near the Opera House. The **National Theatre** attracted heavy criticism for its strange design when it opened in 2000, but perhaps one day it will be lauded. However what's performed inside is more disappointing: productions tend to be conservative in style – a situation reinforced by the government, who insist that Hungarian drama should be given more room and denounce the theatre world as being dominated by the "queer lobby". **Alternative theatre** *is* worth seeking out, however, particularly for visitors as music and dance play a greater part than language here. One Hungarian group that has received considerable critical acclaim abroad is Krétakör, while other names to look out for are László Hudi, Pál Frenák, Béla Pintér, Viktor Bodó and the Hoppart company. Two exciting names in **dance** are Réka Szabó, who runs the Tünet (Symptom) group, and Krisztián Gergye. And finally, Hungary has a strong puppet tradition and the shows in the two **puppet theatres** will appeal to adults and children alike.

Atrium II, Margít körút 55 ☎1 317 9338, ⓦatriumfilmszinhaz.hu. Fabulous Art Deco cinema that is now a venue for theatre – including some performances in English – and dance. The café in the foyer is a great place to people-watch. Box office daily 10am–8pm.

HUNGARY ON FILM

Hungarians have an impressive record in film, and many of the Hollywood greats were **Hungarian émigrés** – Michael Curtiz, Sir Alex Korda, George Cukor, and actors Béla Lugosi, Tony Curtis and Leslie Howard to name but a few. In the Communist years Hungarian film continued to make waves, with Miklós Jancsó, Károly Makk, István Szabó, Márta Mészáros and others directing films that managed to say much about the oppressive regime in spite of its restrictions. Now the main constraint on film-makers is chronic underfunding, one exception being István Szabó, who seems to have no problem with funding, though critics have not been impressed by his recent films.

Alongside established names such as Béla Tarr, the master of the slow, stark and very long take, younger directors who have attracted international recognition include Kornél Mundruczó, with his *White God* (*Fehér Isten*), Péter Bergendy, with his 1950s thriller *The Exam* (*A vizsga*), and Ádám Császi, whose debut film *Land of Storms* (*Viharsarok*) was released in 2014.

Budapest is a popular **location** both for its looks and its cheapness, for films, such as *Hercules* and *Strike Back*. It served as Buenos Aires in *Evita*, as Berlin in *The Boy in the Striped Pyjamas*, as Moscow in *A Good Day to Die Hard* and as Paris in the *Maigret* TV series, where the view towards the Basilica down Lázár utca behind the Opera House acts as the view of the Sacré-Coeur. But it also serves as itself: the American documentary *Divan* by Pearl Gluck captures some of the characters and atmosphere of the old Jewish quarter in its interviews.

DVDs, most of them subtitled, have made Hungarian films much more accessible, making it possible to enjoy classics such as Géza Radványi's *Valahol Európában* (1947) and Zoltán Fábri's *Körhinta* (1955). See p.190 for DVD shops.

16

★**Budapest Bábszínház** VI, Andrássy út 69 ❶1 342 2702, ⓦbudapest-babszinhaz.hu. Budapest Puppet Theatre has a lot of shows for adults – masked grotesqueries or renditions of Bartók's *The Wooden Prince* and *The Miraculous Mandarin* and Mozart's *Magic Flute*. Open all year. Box office daily 9am–6pm.

Katona József Theatre V, Petőfi Sándor utca 6 ❶1 266 5200, ⓦkatonajozsefszinhaz.hu. The best of the established theatres, with a talented company and good productions. Box office Mon–Fri 11am–7pm, Sat–Sun 4–7pm, open till 9pm when shows are running.

Kolibri Pince VI, Andrássy út 77 ❶1 353 4633, ⓦkolibriszinhaz.hu. Puppet shows and live performances for adults as well as children at three venues (see p.199 for the other two); this is the best one for grown-up performances. Closed early June–Aug.

MU Színház XI, Körösy József utca 17 ❶1 209 4014, ⓦmu.hu. Alternative theatre venue that is particularly strong on dance, and also hosts the odd jazz concert.

★**National Dance Theatre (Nemzeti Táncszínház)** I, Színház utca 1–3 ❶1 201 4407, ⓦnemzeti tancszinhaz.hu. Housed in the old Castle Theatre in Buda – until it has to find a new home in about 2016 when the government requisitions the building – the national company performs everything from classical ballet to contemporary dance. Box office Mon–Thurs 10am–6pm, Fri 10am–5pm.

National Theatre (Nemzeti Színház) IX, Bajor Gizi park 1 ❶1 476 6868, ⓦnemzetiszinhaz.hu. The proud flagship of Hungarian theatre. Some shows are in English, put on by local troupes. Box office Mon–Fri 10am–6pm, Sat & Sun 2–6pm.

Szkéné Színház XI, Műegyetem rakpart 3 ❶1 463 2451, ⓦszkene.hu. A small theatre housed in the main building of the Technical University near the *Gellért Hotel*, this has been an alternative venue for many years, dating back to the bad old days of Communism. Box office opens one hour before performances.

SHOPPING IN THE GREAT MARKET HALL

Shopping

The capital's streets have been transformed in recent years by the mushrooming of international chain stores and the opening of modern shopping malls. However, there are numerous small retailers that preserve local crafts and traditions as well as backstreet shops recently colonised by young fashion designers. Budapest also has a set of distinguished market halls (*vásárcsarnok*) dating from the late nineteenth century, where the displays of cured meats and paprika are a fine introduction to the national cuisine. You can also spend a happy afternoon stocking up on Tokaj and Bull's Blood at the city's growing number of wine sellers. The city's cultural strengths are also reflected in the many bookshops and music shops across town.

One feature of old Budapest that has survived is its **artisan shops**: whether it's the small jewellery workshops such as Wladis, the quirky brush shop in Dob utca and the old craftsmen and workshops in the backstreets inside the Nagykörút, or the growing number of young designers whose work is deservedly attracting attention. Look out for Emilia Anda, Use and Je Suis Belle, whose clothes range from the trendy to the avant-garde and the eccentric. One event worth catching is the Wamp design market (ⓦwamp.hu); taking place every month on Erzsébet tér, it showcases the work of emerging Hungarian designers, with some one hundred vendors selling everything from clothes and jewellery to home decor.

It has taken a while, but at last there is a far wider choice of **souvenirs** to take home from Budapest that extends beyond the folk tat sold in the Vár. You can find some chic Hungarian accessories and clothes in Rododendron or Insitu; while the city's markets and small shops such as Hercserli offer excellent local produce – jams, sausages, honey and the like.

ESSENTIALS

Shopping areas The main shopping areas are located to the south of Vörösmarty tér in central Pest, in particular in and around pedestrianized Váci utca, which has the biggest concentration of glamorous and expensive shops, as well as branches of popular Western stores. It is also, however, full of tourist tat. The nearby Deák Ferenc utca has been jazzed up as "Fashion Street" and attracted names such as Sisley, Tommy Hilfiger and Benetton, but also young Hungarian designers like Nanushka. The main streets radiating out from the centre – Bajcsy-Zsilinszky út, Andrássy út and Rákóczi út – are other major shopping focuses, as are the Nagykörút (especially between Margit híd and Blaha Lujza tér) and the Kiskörút. Shops in the Vár are almost exclusively given over to providing foreign tourists with folksy souvenirs such as embroidered tablecloths, hussar pots and fancy bottles of Tokaj wine.

Opening times Most shops are open Monday to Friday between 10am and 6pm, and Saturday until 2pm, with food stores generally operating from 8am to 6 or 7pm. Some shops in the centre of the city have extended hours on Saturdays, while the malls are open roughly 10am to 8pm every day, but close around 6pm on Sunday. However, quite a few places are closed at weekends, so it is worth checking beforehand. The sale of tobacco is now restricted to "national tobacco shops" (*nemzeti dohánybolt*), which have frosted glass windows that make them look like pornography outlets. It's useful to recognize that "Azonnal jövök" or "Rögtön jövök" signs on shop doors both mean "back shortly".

MARKETS

Belvárosi (Hold utca) V, Hold utca 13; map p.48. Right behind the American Embassy, this fine nineteenth-century market hall still has some smallholders selling their produce. Mon 6.30am–5pm, Tues–Fri 6.30am–6pm, Sat 6am–2pm.

Bio-piac XII, Csörsz utca 18; map p.87. Organic market spreading around the Mom Cultural Centre (Mom Művelődési Központ), up the road from the Mom Park Mall. Great range of produce, especially in summer – the peaches, tomatoes and peppers are so much better than supermarket fare. There is also a playground for children. Sat 6.30am–1pm.

Fény utca II, Lövőház utca 12; map p.87. Popular market that has survived a transfer to a modern setting. Fruit and veg stalls on the street-level floor, and meat and cheese counters on the top floor, alongside one of the best *lángos* kiosks in town – a popular stand-up snack of fried dough eaten with garlic, sour cream, cheese or all three together. The nearby café seves excellent coffee Mon–Fri 6am–6pm, Sat 6am–2pm.

★ **Great Market Hall** IX, Vámház körút 2; map p.77. By the Szabadság híd at the bottom end of Váci utca, the Nagycsarnok is the largest and finest market hall of them all, as well as being the most expensive. Fruit, veg, meat and cheese counters galore, as well as bakers, confectioners and endless paprika stalls, though it's all rather hammed up for the tourists. Mon 6am–5pm, Tues–Fri 6am–6pm, Sat 6am–3pm.

Hunyadi tér VI, Hunyadi tér; map p.58. Another of the old market halls, free of any modernization with stalls full of colourful produce spilling out into the square in front. Mon 7am–5pm, Tues–Fri 7am–6pm, Sat 7am–2pm.

Lehel Csarnok XIII, Lehel tér; map p.48. Large, popular market housed in an ugly, wacky market hall designed by the former dissident László Rajk – whatever you think of the exterior, it's a lively place inside with lots of small stalls. Mon–Fri 6.30am–6pm, Sat 6.30am–2pm, Sun 6am–1pm.

★ **Szimplakert** VII, Kazinczy utca 14 ⓦszimpla.hu; map p.58. The weekly farmers' market in the ruin bar courtyard has a particularly villagey feel, with the stallholders and shoppers exchanging banter. You can get sausages, cakes, bread, honey, jams, cheeses – with cheese

17

17

making and other workshops – and maybe a hen or two. But it is still the *Szimpla*, so there is music too. Sun 9am–2pm.

FLEA MARKETS

Ecseri market (Használtcikk piac) XIX, Nagykőrösi út; bus #84E from the Határ út metro stop on the blue line, or bus #54 from Boráros tér by Petőfi híd; map p.5. On the southeast edge of the city, this has become a well-known spot for tourists – and for ripping them off (you'll need to bargain hard). Stalls sell everything from bike parts and jackboots to peasant clothing and hand-carved pipes, with a few genuine antiques among the tat. The food on offer is fairly basic. Mon–Fri 8am–4pm, Sat 6am–3pm, Sun 9am–1pm.

Gardrób Second Hand and Vintage Clothing VII, Király utca 8; map p.58. The idea behind this "community market" in the Central Passage outside the *Gödör Klub* is that anyone can take a table and sell off their old clothes, bags and accessories. So join the locals and spot those gems. Sat11am–4pm.

Petőfi Csarnok XIV, Zichy Mihály utca 14; map p.69. A weekend flea market in and around the "Pecsa", the ugly cultural centre on the edge of the Városliget, this is smaller than Ecseri, and less established. Lots of the wares are junk, but there are some good bargains too. 150Ft entry. Sun 8am–2pm.

MALLS

Mammut II, Lövőház utca 2–6 ☎1 345 8020, ⓦmammut.hu; map p.87. Close to Széll Kálmán tér, and next to Fény utca market, this is actually two malls linked by a pedestrianized bridge. Amid the 330 shops, there's a cinema, fitness centre, squash courts, children's play area and nappy-changing room. Mon–Sat 10am–9pm, Sun 10am–6pm.

Mom Park XII, Alkotás utca 53 ☎1 487 5500, ⓦmompark.hu; tram #61; map p.87. One of the more relaxed Buda malls up the road from Déli Station, and with more than seventy shops, a cinema, playhouse and fitness centre. Mon–Sat 10am–8pm, Sun 10am–6pm.

WestEnd City Center VI, Váci út 1–3 (next to Nyugati Station) ☎1 238 7777, ⓦwestend.hu; map p.48. Past the grand indoor waterfall cascading down at the southern entrance, you'll find the city's busiest mall, with over 400 shops (including lots of familiar brand-name stores), cinema and a huge food court. Mon–Sat 10am–9pm, Sun 10am–6pm.

ANTIQUES

Falk Miksa utca, running south off Szent István körút, near the Pest end of the Margit híd, is known as Budapest's "Street of Antiques", and is where you'll find the biggest collection of **antique stores** and galleries. Three or four times a year the street holds an evening festival of music, entertainment and, of course, antiques. Most antique specialists should be able to advise on what you can export from the country and how to go about it. Several shops organize **auctions**; the best months for these are April, May, September and December – check the free hotel magazine *Where Budapest* for dates. Another good source of antiques are the flea markets listed above, though you'll need to be wary about parting with large sums of money, as stallholders can charge hugely inflated prices.

BÁV V, Bécsi utca 1–3 ☎1 429 3020; map p.38. The biggest of numerous BÁV outlets in the city, this store specializes in paintings, jewellery and other treasures. BÁV is primarily an auction house, and it holds regular auctions here. Mon–Fri 10am–6pm, Sat 10am–2pm.

Budapest Poster Gallery V, Falk Miksa utca 28 ☎0630 662 7274, ⓦbudapestposter.com; map p.48. Superb stock of original vintage posters from between 1885 and 1990, with some fine Communist-era propaganda posters, such as one for the 1955 Tractor Day, but there are some choice film and commercial ones too. Prices from 10,000Ft.

The gallery is on the sixth floor (ring bell #61 at the street entrance). Appointment only.

Judaica VII, Wesselényi utca 13 ☎1 354 1560; map p.58. Down the road behind the Dohány utca synagogue, and offering Jewish books, pictures and artefacts. It also organizes occasional auctions. Mon–Thurs 10am–6pm, Fri 10am–3pm.

Sóos Foto VII, Wesselényi utca 10 ☎1 460 0036 ⓦsoosfoto.hu; map p.58. An excellent place to pick up some fine junk and secondhand photographic goods. Mon–Fri 9am–5pm, Sat 10am–1pm.

ART AND PHOTOGRAPHY

ACB VI, Király utca 76 ☎1 413 7608, ⓦacbgaleria.hu; map p.58. Contemporary fine arts with a friendly, well-informed management, up the road from the Music Academy. Tues–Fri 2–6pm, Sat noon–4pm or by appointment.

★**Deák Erika Galéria** VI, Mozsár utca 1 ☎1 201 3740, ⓦdeakgaleria.hu; map p.58. Contemporary Hungarian art gallery off Andrássy út. Wed–Fri noon–6pm, Sat 11am–4pm.

Knoll VI, Liszt Ferenc tér 10 ☎1 267 3842,

GREAT MARKET HALL (P.185) >

17

ⓦknollgaleria.hu; map p.58. Run by the Viennese gallery owner Hans Knoll, this was the first private gallery in the city when it opened in 1989. Since then, it has built up a strong reputation, with shows by Hungarian and foreign contemporary artists. Tues–Fri 2–6.30pm, Sat 11am–2pm.

★**Mai Manó Galéria** VI, Nagymező utca 20 ☎1 473 2666 ⓦmaimano.hu; map p.58. Located on the first floor within the Hungarian House of Photography, this delightful little gallery/shop stocks contemporary and old Hungarian photographs, cards and books. Daily 11am–7pm.

Várfok Galéria I, Várfok utca 11 ☎0630 562 2772, ⓦvarfok-galeria.hu; map p.87. The best known of the three small galleries just off Széll Kálmán tér, the gallery was founded in 1990 and displays work by the younger generation of Hungarian avant-garde artists. Tues–Sat 11am–6pm.

BOOKS AND MAPS

Hungarians are a literary bunch and Book Week, held in the capital each June, is a long-awaited event. If it's old books and prints you want, one of the best places to head for is Múzeum körút, where there are numerous **secondhand bookshops** (*antikvárium*) clustered opposite the Hungarian National Museum. Larger stores often have a café attached and sell a range of English-language titles.

Alexandra VI, Andrássy út 39 ☎1 484 8000, ⓦalexandra.hu; map p.58. Occupying the magnificent Paris Deparment store, this is the flagship store of the chain, with three vast floors of browsing; the English language section – with lots of good Hungarian fiction – is to the rear of the ground floor. While here, it'd be remiss not to visit the sumptuous coffee salon in the Lotz Hall on the first floor. Its branch by the Dohány utca synagogue at Károly körút 3 has a secondhand section upstairs as well as a pleasant covered rooftop café. Both branches daily 10am–10pm.

★**Bestsellers** V, Október 6 utca 11 ☎1 312 1295, ⓦbestsellers.hu; map p.48. Budapest's oldest and best English-language bookshop, with thousands of titles; English and Hungarian literature, travel and reference, academia and children's books, as well as newspapers and magazines. Staff are friendly and can order books in. Mon–Fri 9am–6.30pm, Sat 10am–5pm, Sun 10am–4pm.

CEU bookshop V, Zrinyi utca 12 ☎1 327 3096; map p.48. Just around the corner from Bestsellers, and attached to the Central European University, this has mainly academic books, though there is a comprehensive selection of Hungarian literature in English. Mon–Fri 10am–7pm, Sat 11am–3pm.

★**Írók Boltja** VI, Andrássy út 45 ☎1 322 1645; map p.58. On the premises of the prewar *Japán* coffee house, the beautiful "Writers' Bookshop" has a wide range of Hungarian fiction in translation in the gallery upstairs, and a good selection of photography, art and architecture books and Hungarian DVDs in the main part of the shop. You can drink coffee and read at the tables in the front or in the gallery. Mon–Fri 10am–7pm, Sat 11am–7pm (July & Aug Sat 11am–3pm).

Központi Antikvárium V, Múzeum körút 13–15; map p.77. Large secondhand bookshop with some antiquarian books and prints, plus maps. Mon–Fri 10am–6pm, Sat 10am–2pm.

Libra VIII, Kölcsey utca 1 ☎1 483 0659; map p.77. General fiction, history and the like – and a small café in which to mull it all over. The other branch across the road has language teaching books only. Mon–Fri 8am–7pm, Sat 9am–2pm.

★**Massolit Books** VII, Nagy Diófa utca 30 ☎1 788 5292; map p.58. Peaceful secondhand bookshop/café where you can relax over your favoured tome. The café, which has eco-friendly coffee and tea and good brownies, opens out onto a courtyard garden at the back. Strong on – but not restricted to – foreign-language literature and Jewish studies. Hosts exhibitions and readings. Mon–Sat 10am–8pm, Sun noon–8pm.

Térképkirály VI, Bajcsy-Zsilinszky út 21; map p.58. Range of maps and guidebooks across the road from Arany János utca metro station. There is another map shop at no. 37 up the road, Földgömb-Térkép, if you can't find what you want here. Mon–Fri 10am–6.30pm.

CLOTHES AND SHOES

Many of the hottest new Hungarian designers don't have their own shops as yet so check their websites for stockists: **Je Suis Belle** (ⓦjesuisbelle.hu), **Use** (ⓦuse.co.hu), **Juhos Janka** (jewellery; ⓦjuhosjanka.com) and **Anh Tuan** (bags; ⓦanh-tuan.com).

Emilia Anda V, Galamb utca 4 ☎0630 933 9746, ⓦandaemi.com; map p.38. One of the most highly regarded Hungarian couturiers, Anda designs classy day and evening wear for women, and a range of jewellery including chunky rings and beautiful pendants. Mon–Fri 11am–6pm, Sat 11am–2pm.

Gardrob VI, Király utca 42 ☎1 317 1627; map p.58. Locals swear by this small shop as a great source of

17

secondhand clothes and bags. Mon–Fri 10am–7pm.

Iguana VIII, Krúdy Gyula utca 9 ☎ 1 317 1627; map p.77. A packed, colourful shop selling all kinds of 1950s, 1960s and 1970s retro – clothes, bags, music, sunglasses and jewellery. Mon–Fri 10am–6pm, Sat 10am–2pm.

Ludovika VII, Rumbach Sebestyén utca 15; map p.58. Vintage and modern women's clothes and bags by a variety of Hungarian designers, in a friendly setting on the edge of the VII district. Mon–Fri noon–8pm, Sat noon–6pm.

Manier VI, Hajós utca 12 ☎ 1 354 1878, ⓦ manier.hu; map p.58. Zany, appealing clothes by Anikó Németh; the designs have calmed down from the Baroque early days but they retain plenty of inventiveness. Mon–Sat 11am–7pm.

Nanushka V, Deák Ferenc utca 17 ☎ 1 202 1050, ⓦ nanushka.hu; map p.38. The Hungarian-born designer Sandra Sandor stands up well against the big international names on "Fashion Street". Mon–Fri 11am–9pm, Sat 11am–8pm.

Retrock VII, Anker köz 2 ☎ 0630 472 3636, ⓦ retrock .com; map p.38. An extensive collection of clothes and jewellery, both vintage and new, as well as by young Hungarian designers, just off Deák tér. Mon–Fri 11am–9pm, Sat 11am–8pm.

Tisza Shoes VII, Károly körút 1 ☎ 1 266 3055; map p.58. This Hungarian brand of trainers is an unlikely survivor of the Communist era, and the shop at the Astoria junction, Tisza Cipő, has won an international reputation for the hipness of the shoes. Mon–Fri 10am–7pm, Sat 9am–1pm.

Valéria Fazekas V, Váci utca 50 ☎ 1 337 5320; map p.38. Another of the more creative places on the lower part of Váci utca, this small shop produces delightful hats, some wacky and some very wearable, as well as clothes – the silk jackets look great. Mon–Fri 10am–6pm, Sat 10am–4pm.

Vass V, Haris köz 2 ☎ 1 318 2375; map p.38. The most established of several fine shoemakers along this street, this traditional outfit, just behind Ferenciek tere, has been producing handmade shoes to order and ready-to-wear since 1978. Mon–Fri 10am–6pm, Sat 10am–2pm.

JEWELLERY AND SOUVENIRS

Brush Shop VII, Dob utca 3; map p.58. A wonderful little place: every kind of brush you can think of in this very traditional artisan's shop. Mon–Fri 10am–6pm, Sat 10am–1pm.

★**Haas & Czjzek** VI, Bajcsy-Zsilinszky út 23 ☎ 1 311 4094, ⓦ porcelan.hu; map p.58. This lovely shop, dating back to 1792, offers a full selection of Hungarian porcelain, including Hollóháza, Alföld and Zsolnay, and some glassware. Mon–Fri 10am–7pm, Sat 10am–3pm.

Herend V, József nádor tér 11 ☎ 1 317 2622) & VI, Andrássy út 16 (☎ 1 374 0006) ⓦ herend.com; map p.58. Very fancy – some would say twee – and expensive porcelain from the Herend factory in western Hungary, as collected by the likes of Queen Victoria. Both shops Mon–Fri 10am–6pm, Sat 10am–2pm.

★**Holló Folk Art Gallery** V, Vitkovics Mihály utca 10 ☎ 1 317 8103; map p.38. This beautiful early nineteenth-century shop near the Astoria is a very pleasant place in which to browse wares such as intricately iced gingerbread figures, and wooden furniture, boxes, eggs and candlesticks, all hand-painted with bird, tulip and heart folk motifs. Ring bell to enter. Mon–Fri 10am–6pm (closed 1–1.30pm), Sat 10am–2pm.

Insitu V, Múzeum körút 67 ☎ 1 266 3080, ⓦ insitu.hu; map p.77. In the courtyard of the beautiful Unger Ház, Insitu is a design shop full of clever ideas, and has some souvenirs with a difference, such as T-shirts bearing the Hungarian alphabet. Mon–Fri 10am–7pm, Sat 10am–3pm.

Intuita V, Váci utca 67; map p.38. Amid the tourist tat at the main market hall end of Váci utca, this shop stands out for its quality Hungarian pottery and jewellery. Intuita 2, just along the road, is the place to go for hats and bags. Both Mon–Fri 10am–6pm, Sat 10am–2pm.

Magma V, Petőfi Sándor utca 11 ☎ 1 253 0277, ⓦ magma.hu; map p.38. Wide range of stock by local designers, including funky bags and cushion covers decorated with Hungarian rare breeds – puli dogs and long-horned cattle – and with Budapest-related designs that make ideal souvenirs. Mon–Fri 10am–7pm, Sat 10am–3pm.

★**Ómama Bizsúja** V, Szent István körút 1 ☎ 1 312 6812, ⓦ omamaantik.hu; map p.48. A tiny treasure-trove of a shop, crammed full of jewellery at the Pest end of the Margit híd – it is on the left as you walk in from the street. In among the more glitzy costume jewellery are some stunning Deco-style pieces and good-quality paste. They have a larger shop with more clothes at the Buda end of the bridge at XII, Frankel Leó 7. Mon–Fri 10am–6pm, Sat 10am–1pm.

★**Rododendron** V, Semmelweis utca 19 ☎ 0670 419 5329 ⓦ rododendronart.com; map p.38. Books, toys and accessories by thirty local artisans, such as a delightful design on T-shirts and bag with a pyramid of Hungarian rare breeds. Mon–Fri 10am–7pm, Sat 10am–4pm.

Wladis Galéria V, Falk Miksa utca 13 ☎ 1 354 0834, ⓦ wladisgaleria.hu; map p.48. Founded by a lecturer at the Applied Arts College the workshop produces very appealing chunky silver jewellery at a price: rings from 20,000Ft and earrings from 29,000Ft. Mon–Fri 10am–6pm, Sat 10am–2pm.

17

MUSIC AND FILM

Kodály Zoltán Zeneműbolt V, Múzeum körút 21; map p.38. Scores of CDs and secondhand Hungarian classical records, opposite the Múzeum Cukrászda. Good jazz and folk section, and they sell sheet music too. Mon–Fri 10am–6pm, Sat 9am–1pm.

Kultúr Barlang VII, Kertész utca 42–44; map p.58. The "Culture Cave" has one of the best selections of DVDs of Hungarian films around – and next door Laci Bácsi's record shop has thousands of rock, pop, blues and jazz records. Mon–Fri 11am–6pm.

★**MesterPorta** I, Corvin tér 7 ☎ 1 4202 3859; map p.87. The outlet for Etnofon Records, one of the most active publishers of Hungarian and other folk music, has a great range of CDs, instruments and sheet music. The other half of the shop is given over to folk crafts to fill your case with pots and embroideries. You'll find it a tram stop down from Batthyány tér. Tues–Sat 10am–6pm.

Rózsavölgyi Music V, Szervita tér 5 ☎ 1 318 3500; map p.38. Long-established record shop with a knowledgeable staff, near Vörösmarty tér. Classical music on the ground floor, rock and folk downstairs. It has a concert ticket office at the back, and is good for sheet music as well. Mon–Fri 9.30am–7pm (Wed 10am), Sat 10am–5pm.

★**Wave** VI, Révay köz 1 ☎ 1 269 0754; map p.58. Cool, independent shop off the bottom of Bajcsy-Zsilinszky út, with wall-to-wall vinyl and racks of CDs; mainly indie-rock, but also strong on underground, folk and Roma. It also sells tickets to concerts. Mon–Fri 11am–7pm, Sat 11am–3pm.

TOYS

★**Fakopáncs** VIII, Baross utca 46 ☎ 1 337 0992, ⊛ fakopancs.hu; map p.77. A massive array of wooden puzzles, toys and models, and sweet little cotton finger puppets, in the wonderful "Woodpecker" shop, near the junction of Baross utca and the Nagykörút. It has smaller outlets at József körút 50 and Erzsébet körút 23. Mon–Fri 10am–6pm, Sat 9am–1pm.

★**Játékszerek anno** VI, Teréz körút 54 ☎ 1 302 6234; map p.58. Gorgeous little shop with beautifully made reproductions of toys and games from the turn of the last century, including wooden tops, kaleidoscopes, and a spectacular wind-up duck on a bicycle. Mon–Fri 10am–6pm, Sat 9am–1pm.

Játék Udvar VII, Nagydiófa utca 24 ☎ 1 215 6864; map p.58. The three small rooms of this toyshop are packed with models, books, puzzles, puppets, craft activities and games – mainly secondhand, but also some new. Mon–Fri 10am–6pm.

FOOD, WINE AND PÁLINKA

Bamo VII, Dob utca 16 ☎ 70 632 2771; map p.58. On the edge of the Jewish quarter, a couple of minutes' walk from the Dohány utca synagogue, this is one of the few shops in Budapest selling kosher Hungarian and imported wines and foods. Mon–Thurs 8am–8pm, Fri 8am–6pm, Sun 10am–4pm.

Bio ABC V, Múzeum körút 19; map p.38. Stacks of great organic products in this large store opposite the National Museum; natural oils, organic fruits, juices and teas, pastas, pulses and herbal medicines. Mon–Fri 10am–7pm, Sat 10am–2pm.

★**Bortársaság** V, Vécsey utca 5 ☎ 1 269 3286, ⊛ bortarsasag.hu; map p.48. The largest branch of what's become the major distributor of Hungary's leading producers, with excellent wines and knowledgeable staff. There are three more outlets in the centre: Batthyány utca 59 (up the hill from Széll Kálmán tér), Lánchíd utca 5 and Ráday utca 7. Vécsey utca branch Mon–Fri 10am–8pm, Sat 10am–7pm.

★**Hecserli** V, Szerb utca 15 ☎ 0670 253 9868, ⊛ hercserli.hu; map p.38. The perfect place to pick up presents with its wide selection of Hungarian produce – sausages, oils (the pumpkin oil is spectacular), honey, jams and more. Mon–Fri 10am–7pm, Sat 10am–4pm.

In Vino Veritas VII, Dohány utca 58–62 ☎ 1 413 0002, ⊛ borkereskedes.hu; map p.58. Friendly store close to Blaha Lujza tér, with an excellent range of wines, including a beautiful Baroque cabinet stocked with some vintage bottles of Tokaj. Mon–Fri 9am–8pm, Sat 10am–6pm.

Kézműves Csemege IX, Ráday utca 7; map p.77. The 'Artisan Grocery' has a fine selection of Hungarian bottled beers from local microbreweries, as well as some wines and *pálinkas*. Mon–Fri 10am–8pm, Sat 9am–7pm.

Magyar Pálinka Háza VIII, Rákóczi út 17 ☎ 1 338 4219; map p.77. A vast and dazzling range of flavours going far beyond the conventional pear and apricot *pálinkas* to include elderflower, quince, paprika and many more. Mon–Sat 10am–2pm.

Malatinszky V, József Attila utca 12 ☎ 0620 969 4170, ⊛ malatinszky.hu; map p.38. Tucked away just off the main street, this delightful small shop has a concentrated selection of excellent wines from Villány and Tokaj. Mon–Fri 10am–6pm, Sat–Sun 10am–7pm.

★**Rózsavölgyi Chocolates** V, Királyi Pál utca 6 ☎ 0630 814 8929, ⊛ rozsavolgyi.com; map p.38. Perhaps the best chocolates in the city are from this little shop just off Egyetem tér. Mon–Fri 10.30am–1pm, 1.30–6.30pm, Sat noon–6pm.

ICE-SKATING IN THE VÁROSLIGET

Sports and activities

Hungarians are passionate about sport and the country possesses a far greater sporting pedigree than most people appreciate. The Olympics, above all, have been a source of outstanding triumph, which is all the more surprising given the country's size and resources; the men's waterpolo team, in particular, has achieved extraordinary success. Budapest's major annual sporting event, bar none, is the Formula 1 Grand Prix, with the other main spectator sports being football and, to a lesser degree, horse racing – though years of underfunding and mismanagement have brought the last two nearly to their knees. Other activities that are popular with visitors are the "escape rooms", in which Hungarians lead the field, and cooking courses (see p.193).

FOOTBALL

Hungary's great footballing days are long past – the golden team of the 1950s that beat England 6–3 in 1953 and reached the World Cup Final in 1954 with stars such as Ferenc Puskás and József Bozsik is a world away from today's national squad, which hasn't qualified for a major tournament since 1986. However, the football-obsessed Prime Minister Viktor Orbán dreams of turning the nation's fortunes round, and is pumping money into the sport. New stadiums are springing up across the country – including in the village of Orbán's birth, Felcsut, where a population of 1,800 now has a 3,500-seater stadium, a folly that was opened with great splendour in 2014. In spite of his efforts, the national team shows no signs of improvement, while the domestic league is terribly weak, with clubs struggling along with little or no money, and their best players continuously sold off to clubs in other countries. While **international matches** are held at the 56,000-capacity Puskás Ferenc Stadium – which is currently undergoing redevelopment – club football in Budapest revolves around the turf of four main teams (listed below), though in recent years, the domestic league has been dominated by Debrecen in eastern Hungary. The **season** runs from late July to late Nov and late Feb to mid-June. Most matches are played on Saturday afternoons, with tickets costing 800–2500Ft; you can find fixtures online.

Ferencváros (aka FTC or Fradi) IX, Üllői út 129 📞1 215 6025, 🌐ftc.hu; Népliget metro. Fradi is the biggest club in the country and almost a national institution, though success has been harder to come by in recent times. Its supporters, dressed in the club's colours of green and white, are the loudest presence at international matches too. The club has long had right-wing ties: this was the fascists' team before the war, and some of its supporters preserve its reputation for thuggishness and anti-Semitism. It plays at the newly redeveloped 25,000-capacity Albert Flórián Stadium next to the road towards the airport.

MTK VIII, Salgótarján utca 12–14 📞1 333 8368, 🌐mtkhungaria.hu; tram #37 from Blaha Lujza tér. Fradi's big local rival, "Em-tay-kah" – as it is popularly known – has traditionally had strong support among the Jewish community. Second only to Ferencváros in terms of the number of domestic league titles won, and despite being the last Budapest side to win the league (in 2008), these days MTK are consistently a middle-ranking side in the top tier. MTK's Hidegkuti Nándor Stadium (capacity 12,700) was the setting for scenes in the film *Escape to Victory*.

Újpest IV, Megyeri út 13 📞1 231 0088, 🌐ujpestfc.hu; four stops on bus #30 from Újpest Központ metro station. Formed in 1885, Újpest have traditionally been one of the powerhouses of Hungarian football, enjoying particularly golden periods in the 1930s – when it supplied half of the Hungarian national team that were runners-up in the 1938 World Cup – and the 1970s, when they reached the semi-finals of the European Cup in 1974. Known as the Lilák (Purples) – after the club colours – Újpest play at the 13,000 all-seater Szusza Ferenc Stadium north of the city.

Honvéd XIX, Puskás Ferenc utca 1–3 📞1 357 6738, 🌐honvedfc.hu; Six stops on bus #42 from Határ út metro station. Founded as Kispest in 1904, they assumed the mantle of the army team in 1949, and their name was changed to Honvéd. Their glory days of the 1950s owed much to having the likes of Puskás, Kocsis and Bozsik (the backbone of the Mighty Magyars) in their side. The 1980s was another hugely successful decade, but since then the team has yo-yoed between the top two divisions. Honvéd play at the 7,200-capacity Bozsik József Stadium, southeast of the centre.

HORSE RACING

Horse racing was introduced from England by Count Széchenyi in 1827 and flourished until 1949, when flat racing (*galopp*) was banned by the Communists. For many years punters could only enjoy trotting races, but in the mid-1980s flat racing resumed. **Betting** operates on a tote system, where your returns are affected by how the odds stood at the close of betting. The different types of bet comprise *tét*, placing money on the winner; *hely*, on a horse coming in the first three; and the popular *befutó*, a bet on two horses to come in either first and second or first and third. Winnings are paid out about fifteen minutes after the end of the race.

Kincsem Park X, Albertirsai út 2–6; Pillangó utca on the red metro, and then either walk or catch #100 bus. Flat racing takes place here on Sundays from April to November; trotting – *ügető*, where the horse is harnessed to a light carriage – is all year round, mostly on Sat. Races are advertised in *Fortuna* magazine. Both types have a devoted and excitable following, which makes attending the races entertaining; the atmosphere at the tracks is informal, but photographing the racegoers is frowned upon, since many attend unbeknownst to their spouses or employers.

FORMULA 1

The Hungarian Grand Prix usually takes place at the end of July or beginning of August at the purpose-built Formula One racing track, the Hungaroring, at Mogyoród, 20km northeast of Budapest. First held in 1986, it has managed to retain its place on the lucrative F1 calendar ever since, and has been guaranteed the event until 2016. Tickets (book far in advance) are available from Ostermann Forma-1, V, Apáczai Csere János utca 11, third floor (☎ 1 266 2040 ⓦ gpticketshop.hu). A day pass starts at €80, with a weekend pass costing anything between €90 and €500. You can reach the track by special buses from the Árpád híd bus station; trains from Keleti Station to Fót, and then a bus from there; or by HÉV train from Örs vezér tere to the

TOP 5 HUNGARIAN SPORTS STARS
Aladár Gerevich (fencing)
Ferenc Puskás (football)
Katalin Kovács (kayaking)
László Papp (boxing)
Tamás Kásás (water polo)

18

Szilasliget stop, which is 1800m northeast of Gate C.

ACTIVITIES

Canoeing Taking a canoe or kayak out on the Danube can be exhilarating – you just have to remember to head upstream first. The Béke Boathouse (Béke Csonakház) is a 10min walk from the Rómaifürdő HÉV station (or take bus #34 to the door from the Árpád híd station) at III, Rómaipart 51–53 ☎ 1 388 9303. Open April to mid-Oct.

Caving Óbuda offers the opportunity to explore a couple of fascinating cave systems (see p.115). You can walk round them without any special equipment, or you can go on more adventurous visits with Caving under Budapest (☎ 0620 928 4969, ⓦ barlangaszat.hu). The group leads two- to three-hour tours – you don't need caving experience, but you do need to be fit and fairly agile, as you'll be climbing on walls and squeezing through passageways. You are given helmets, headlights and overalls. English-speaking tours (6000Ft) are on Mon, Wed and Fri afternoons and start at the Pálvölgyi Stalactite Cave. The Hungarian Association of Speleologists, at the Szemlőhegyi Cave (☎ 1 346 0495, ⓦ barlang.hu) can put you in touch with groups exploring caves in the Buda Hills and elsewhere in Hungary.

Escape rooms The dilapidated apartment blocks of Budapest have spawned a new craze: locking people in a room and leaving clues and challenges for them to work out how to escape in sixty minutes. Luckily help is at hand if you can't work it out. It is ideal for team building and stag parties. There are several venues for this kind of slightly warped fun, including Parapark, the first of the breed, VIII, Vajdahunyad utca 4 ☎ 0620 986 9196, ⓦ parapark.hu, and Claustrophilia, VII, Erzsébet körút 8

☎ 0630 724 2274, ⓦ claustrophilia.hu.

Fitness centres and gyms Most of the larger hotels and some of the shopping malls have them – they are properly regulated, unlike some of the backstreet ones, and are open to non-residents.

Ice-skating During winter, there's skating at the City Park ice rink by Hősök tere in the Városliget (mid-Nov to Feb Mon–Fri 9am–1pm & 4–8pm, Sat & Sun 10am–2pm & 4–8pm); entry costs around 1500Ft, and skates can be rented. Or there's the Buda Ice Rink (Budai Jégpálya) at Széna tér in Buda (Oct–April daily 8am–10pm); entry 1400Ft, skates can be rented.

Skiing If it's a snowy winter, you can ski at Normafa in the Buda Hills, best reached on bus #21A from Széll Kálmán tér. Equipment can be rented from Suli Sí by the entrance of the Császár Komjádi pool at II, Árpád Fejedelem utca 8 (☎ 1 212 0330, ⓦ sulisi.hu), or Bikebase at VI, Podmaniczky utca 19 (daily 9am–7pm; ☎ 1 269 5983, ⓦ bikebase.hu), where the friendly staff can advise you on other places to ski.

Squash (Fallabda) Try City Squash Club, II, Marczibányi tér 13 (☎ 1 336 0408, ⓦ squashtech.hu; court rental 2500Ft/hr), 5min walk from Széll Kálmán tér; or Mammut Squash, on the fourth floor of the nearby Mammut Mall I (☎ 1 345 8093, ⓦ mammutsquash.hu; court rental 2500Ft/hr).

Tennis Courts can be booked all year round at the Városmajor Tennis Academy in Városmajor Park, near Széll Kálmán tér (☎ 1 202 5337 ⓦ teniszbudapest.hu) and at the Sziget Club at the southern end of the Margít Island (☎ 1 329 3147 ⓦ szigetklub.hu). Racquets are available for rent.

GELLÉRT BATHS

Baths and pools

With more than a hundred springs offering an endless supply of hot water at temperatures of up to 76°C, Budapest is deservedly known as a spa city, and visiting one of the many baths is an unmissable experience. Housed in some of Budapest's finest buildings, the baths are impressive in their own right, while the thermal waters are reputed to cure myriad ailments – and of course there's the swimming itself. The baths are an important social hub too. As you admire the light filtering through the dome in the Rudas, watch chess players ponder strategies in the outdoor pool of the Széchenyi or peer through the mists in the steam rooms of the Gellért, there's a real sense of being part of a tradition that has lasted centuries. That history of indulgence has been given a new twist in recent years with the advent of night-time parties at the baths.

There are three types of bath: *gyógyfürdő*, a **thermal bath** in its original Turkish form, as at the Rudas and Király, or the magnificent nineteenth-century settings of the Gellért and Széchenyi; *uszoda*, a proper swimming pool such as the Sport; and *strand*, a lido in a verdant setting, such as the Palatinus. Most baths are divided into a **swimming** area and a separate section for **steam baths** (*gőzfürdő* or the *göz*, as they are popularly known). The smaller Rudas, Veli Bej and Király baths are first and foremost steam baths, with saunas and pools fed by thermal springs. In the larger baths, such as the Gellért and Széchenyi, you can alternate between brisk dips in the swimming pool and leisurely soaks in the steam section.

The Budapest bathing experience can be a little daunting, as little is written in English once you are inside – though in baths that are popular with tourists such as the Széchenyi the attendants speak much more English and are well-equipped to guide lost tourists through the system. However, the basic system of attendants and cabins is the same in most steam baths and swimming pools, and once you get the hang of the rituals, a visit to the baths becomes most rewarding. The website ⓦspasbudapest.com has general information on all the main baths. At present the **night-time parties** take place on Saturdays in the Széchenyi (May–Sept) and Lukács Baths (Oct–April), where you can enjoy laser discos, music and films in a most unusual setting (ⓦspartybooking .com, tickets €25–40), but it is worth keeping an eye out for raves at other venues. The thermal baths are not recommended for **children under 14,** and baths such as the Veli Bej, which are purely thermal, will not allow them in. Similarly, some baths insist that only potty-trained (*szobatiszta*) babies are allowed in the water.

19

A ROUGH GUIDE TO BATHING

Tickets A standard ticket purchased from the ticket office (*pénztár*) gets you into the pools as well as the sauna and steam rooms; you'll often have the choice between changing in a communal room and using a locker

---

BATHHOUSE BACKGROUND

Even though the sulphurous content of Budapest's waters mean that they don't always smell very pleasant, their therapeutic qualities have long been exploited. The earliest remains of baths here date back to the Bronze Age, and a succession of invaders have since capitalized on the benefits of the healthy waters. The **Romans**, who appreciated a good bath, set up camp along the banks of the Danube – you can see the ruins of their bathhouses in Óbuda. After their arrival from the east, the **Hungarian tribes** also recognized the value of the thermal springs, as testified by the remnants of a hospital bathhouse from 1178 found near the Lukács.

During their occupation, the **Ottomans** played a vital role in the development of Budapest's baths – the precept, under Islamic law, for washing five times a day before prayers is thought to have engendered a popular bathing culture here. The oldest baths that survive today are the Turkish baths on the Buda side of the river: built in the late sixteenth century, the Király and the Rudas baths have preserved their original layout, with a central bathing pool surrounded by smaller pools that lie below the old Turkish cupolas.

The next **golden age of bathing** occurred in the late nineteenth and early twentieth centuries, as a fashion for spas swept across Europe. Budapest's existing baths were dressed up in a new magnificence, and splendid buildings such as the neo-Baroque Széchenyi Baths in the Városliget and the Art Nouveau Gellért Baths were erected. During the **Communist era**, the baths were as popular as ever – a place to meet and gossip in the murky mists – but they suffered prolonged neglect. In recent years, however, major investments have seen the buildings restored and their facilities upgraded by way of new features such as whirlpools – Budapest's baths are now far more salubrious places to visit. And it's not just people who have benefited from the thermal waters. The success of the hippopotamus-breeding programme at Budapest Zoo is thought to be partly due to the constant supply of hot water from the Széchenyi Baths across the road – the hippos clearly benefit from wallowing in lovely thermal pools. The hot springs also saved them during the bitter winter siege of the city in 1944–45, when most of the zoo's other animals died in the freezing temperatures.

(*szekrény*), or a slightly more expensive cubicle (*kabin*) – the latter gives you more privacy and, in the mixed-sex baths, this allows couples to change together. At the *pénztár* you also pay for any other treatments, such as massages and pedicures that you want during your visit.

Costs Entrance prices are around 2500–3500Ft on weekdays, though expect to pay 200–400Ft more at weekends; cabins cost around 400Ft more; individual prices are given under each bath listing. There are also discounts in most places if you go before 8am or after 4-6pm. Everything you need can be rented at all baths – costs are typically: swimsuit (1100Ft), bathrobe (1100Ft), towel (700Ft), sheet (700Ft) and hat (300Ft – though it is cheaper to buy one if you go more than once). You have to pay deposits of between 1500 and 10,000Ft for each item. It's usual to tip the attendant a couple of hundred forints. Supplementary tickets will buy you a massage (*masszázs*), a soak in a private tub (*kádfürdő*) or a mud bath (*iszapfürdő*) – a list by the office will detail the available services.

What to bring In all baths bring flip-flops if you have them, as well as your own soap and shampoo; in the steam baths, you don't need a towel as you're given a sheet to dry yourself with. In many pools, bathing caps (*uszósapka*) are compulsory: in the Széchenyi, they're only required in the middle of the three outdoor pools (the one reserved for swimming proper); go in without a cap and you'll be whistled at by the attendant and told to get out. The best advice is not to take valuables to the baths, but in practice that is not always possible. Most baths do have safes

(*értékmegőrzés*), but in some, such as the Lukács, these are small and will not hold a handbag.

Getting changed Most – though not all – baths have the same system for entry and getting changed. Bath staff are now much more helpful – especially at places such as the Széchenyi – in showing foreign visitors what to do and telling them treatments are available. At the *pénztár* you'll be given tickets for any treatments and a plastic "wrist watch" that lets you through the turnstile into the baths and also locks your locker or cabin (don't lose it or you'll need to cough up 2000Ft). At the changing room (*öltöző*), an attendant will direct you to a cabin or locker and – in the steam baths on single-sex days – give you a *kötény* – a small loincloth for men or an apron for women – which offers a vestige of cover. Once you've changed, lock your door with your "wrist watch" and make note of your cabin number, taking with you any supplementary tickets.

In the baths The best way to enjoy the steam baths is to go from room to room, moving on whenever the heat gets too much. A popular sequence is: sauna (dry steam – often divided into three rooms, the furthest being the hottest), cool pool, steam room, cold plunge (if you can bear it), hot plunge (this makes your skin tingle wonderfully, but don't stay in for long), followed by a wallow in the larger, warmer pools that are usually at the centre of the baths. Most people then repeat the whole thing again, but the sequence you choose is entirely up to you. When you're completely finished, take a sheet from the pile to dry yourself and relax in the rest room if you feel exhausted – certainly don't plan on anything too strenuous afterwards.

THE BATHS

Császár Komjádi Uszoda II, Árpád fejedelem útja 8 ☎1 212 2750; map p.87. Hungary's national swimming stadium is a large, modern pool complex just north of Margit híd on the Buda side – the entrance faces the river. The large outdoor swimming pool (bathing caps compulsory) is covered over in winter. As it's one of the major waterpolo venues in Budapest, this means one of its pools may be given over to the players on weekdays. Daily 6am–7pm; 1800Ft.

Gellért Gyógyfürdő XI, Kelenhegyi út 4 ☎1 466 6166, ⓦgellertbath.com; map p.107. The most popular of the city's baths, and also one of the oldest – although nothing remains of the medieval buildings – the Gellért has it all: a magnificent main pool for swimming, hot pools for sitting around in both inside and outside on the terrace, fabulous Art Nouveau steam baths, and a large outdoor area, including a wave machine in the main pool (May–Aug) and shaded terraces. To enjoy the waters you must first reach the changing rooms by a labyrinth of passages. At the far end of the pool are steps leading down to the separate thermal baths, with segregated areas and ornate plunge pools for men and women – though they go

mixed at weekends. The Gellért attracts a lot of foreigners, and many of the attendants speak German or English. Daily 6am–8pm; Mon–Fri 4900ft with locker, 5300Ft with cabin; Sat & Sun 5100ft with locker, 5500Ft with cabin.

★**Hajós Alfred Sport Uszoda** XIII, southern end of Margit-sziget; map p.116. One of the nicest places for proper swimming, this is a beautiful 1930s lido renovated for the 2001 European waterpolo championships. There's a small sauna, and two large outdoor pools against a backdrop of trees; one is normally given over to waterpolo. In the winter you can swim out along a channel to the larger of the pools without walking outside. Mon–Fri 6am–3.30pm, Sat & Sun 6am–5.30pm; 1800Ft.

Király Gyógyfürdő II, Fő utca 84 ☎1 202 3688; map p.87. Fabulous Turkish baths, in the Víziváros in Buda, easy to spot thanks to the four copper cupolas. This was formerly the most popular of the steam baths with the gay community, but is now mixed sex every day. The main pool under the cupola is surrounded by smaller – hotter and cooler – pools, with doors leading off to the steam massage rooms. Daily 9am–9pm; 2400Ft.

19

★**Lukács Gyógyfürdő** II, Frankel Leó út 25–29 ☎1 326 1695; map p.87. This spa complex just north of the Margit híd in Buda has four small but delightful open-air pools, as well as mud baths and a medical treatment section – its waters are said to be good for rheumatism, arthritis and other complaints. The open-air facilities, including a thermal pool, a cooler and smaller swimming pool, and a bubbling pool with whirling currents, are in two intimate courtyards. Enter via the folly-like drinking hall (where you can take a sample) and head to the left (past plaques declaring gratitude from those who have benefited from the medicinal waters), following the signs for the *uszoda* (pool). The swimming pool and adjacent baths are mixed. Daily 6am–9pm; Mon–Fri 3000ft with locker, 3100Ft with cabin; Sat & Sun 3400ft with locker, 3500Ft with cabin with reductions before 8am and after 6pm.

Palatinus Strand XIII, Margit-sziget ☎1 236 0040; map p.116. Set among a sprawling park halfway up the island on the west side, the Palatinus is the city's most popular pool, with a large outdoor set of pools, including a wave pool and children's pools, all set in a big expanse of grass. Other facilities include football pitches and volleyball courts, as well as snack bars. The sunroof above the changing rooms is something of a gay centre. Daily May–mid Sept 9am–7pm, mid-June–mid-Aug 9am–8pm; Mon–Fri 2600ft with locker; Mon–Thurs after 4pm 1900Ft; Sat & Sun 3000Ft.

Rác Gyógyfürdő I, Hadnagy utca 8–10; map p.107. One of the oldest baths – the medieval King Mátyás is said to have used the baths on this site in the Tabán – but nothing remains from those times. It has been closed for several years, pending the completion of the new *Rácz Hotel & Spa* complex.

Rudas Gyógyfürdő I, Döbrentei tér 9 ☎1 356 1010; map p.107. One of the city's original Turkish baths, at the Buda end of the Erzsébet híd, this is at its best when the sun shines through the holes in the dome to light up the beautiful interior. The steam baths were for many years a male preserve, but women now get a day to themselves (Tues). There's an apron system in the steam section on single-sex days, but swimming costumes are compulsory on mixed days (Fri night, Sat & Sun). There is also a nineteenth-century swimming pool, open to both sexes, to the left of the main entrance – normal swimwear compulsory here. Daily 6am–8pm, plus Fri & Sat night swimming 10pm–4am; Mon–Fri 3000Ft, Sat & Sun 3300Ft, Fri & Sat night 3700Ft.

Széchenyi Fürdő XIV, Állatkerti körút 11 ☎1 363 3210; map p.69. A magnificent nineteenth-century complex in the Városliget, with its entrance opposite the entrance to the Budapest Circus. There are sixteen pools in all, including the various medicinal sections, but you'll probably use just the three outdoor ones: the hot pool where people play chess (bring your own chess set if you want to play); a pool for swimming (bathing caps compulsory); and a whirlpool. Across the far side of the hot pool from the changing rooms is a mixed sauna with a maze of hot and cold pools. Go before 8am if you want to avoid the tourist rush. Staff speak good English, guide you through the locker and cabin system and also tell you about treatments you can get, such as fish pedicures. Mon–Fri 4100Ft for locker, 4600Ft for cabin; Sat & Sun 4300Ft for locker, 4800Ft for cabin, reductions before 8am and after 5pm. Daily 6am–10pm.

★**Veli Bej Fürdő** II, Árpád fejedelem útja 7 ☎1 438 8641; map p.87. The sixteenth-century Veli Bej, the city's oldest Ottoman spa, has finally been restored in a pleasantly simple fashion. The large central cupola is surrounded by four smaller pools, with adjacent modern steam chambers, saunas and jacuzzis. The spa is run by a religious order, the Irgalmasok, and the presence of their hospital in the complex is a reminder of the very medicinal role of the thermal waters. Only eighty people are allowed into the bath at any one time. It gets full at weekends, but on weekday mornings you might have the place to yourself. Children under 14 not allowed in. Daily 6am–noon, 3–8pm; 2800Ft entry.

19

THE ZOO

Kids' Budapest

Budapest offers a healthy range of activities for kids, from adventure and roller-skating parks, to indoor play centres and state-of-the-art playgrounds. Moreover, the zoo – always a sure-fire hit with the little ones – is one of the most impressive anywhere in the region. There's plenty by way of artistic entertainment, too, and the capital retains a strong tradition of children's theatre – particularly puppetry – and dance. Don't expect anything too high-tech, however, as a lack of cash dogs many of the facilities, but many of the city's playgrounds have been refurbished in recent years, and plenty of places have activities specifically for children, from the Palace of Arts, which has events most weekends, to the Millenáris Park with its regular workshops. Concessions for under-14s are available at most attractions.

Budapest's public transport – under-6s travel free – will keep children happily entertained. **Trams** are an endless source of fun, the best ride being along the embankment in tram #2. Across the water, the **Sikló** (see p.101) is a great experience, rising up above the rooftops from the Lánchíd to the Royal Palace. A popular way for families to spend an afternoon in the Buda Hills is to go on the "railway circuit": the **Cogwheel Railway**, the **Children's Railway** and the **chairlift** (see p.119) – but note that the chairlift can be unnerving for smaller children. From April to October there's the added thrill of **boat rides** on the Danube – either short tours of the city up to Margit-sziget and back, or further afield to Szentendre and on to Esztergom – though for young children, boredom is less likely to kick in on the shorter rides. Throughout the summer there are lots of **craft activities** and children's entertainment at the Open-Air Museum in Szentendre, and a lot of the summer **festivals** also have craft stalls and activities for children, such as the August 20 festivities around the Royal Palace.

PLAYGROUNDS, PARKS AND THE ZOO

Caves Underground Buda is good fun for children as long as they aren't scared of the dark. The caves under the Várhegy (see p.94) offer some underground exploration, while the Pálvölgyi and Szemlőhegyi Caves (p.115) display dramatic geological formations. Note the Pálvölgyi doesn't admit children under 5.

Challengeland (Kalandpálya) XII, Konkoly Thege Miklós út 21 ⓦ kalandpalya.com; p.119. Up in the Buda Hills and offering some of the city's best in outdoor fun, this is a real adventure playground, where children over 100cm in height can go on ropewalks and swing from tree to tree. The shade of the trees makes this a good place to take kids on hot days. Safety is paramount with all children taught how to use harnesses. To get here, take the Children's Railway to Csillebérc Station, or catch the #21 bus from Széll Kálmán tér. Entry 3200–3600Ft depending on the height of child – this is for a 3hr 30min session. It is also worth renting gloves (200Ft). April–mid Sept daily 10am–6pm; Nov–March Sat & Sun 10am–4pm, depending on weather.

Görzenál Skatepark III, Árpád fejedelem útja ☎ 1 250 4799 ⓦ gorzenal.hu; p.113. Space to rollerblade, skateboard and cycle, with ramps and jumps, all to your heart's content. You can get here by taking the Szentendre HÉV to Tímár utca. Day ticket is 500Ft on weekdays, 900Ft at weekends. Mon–Fri 2–8pm, Sat & Sun 9.30am–8pm.

Kids' Park (Kölyökpark) II, Mammut 2 (shop 328), Lövőház utca 1–5 ☎ 1 345 8512; p.103. Indoor play area (for ages 1–11) in a city mall that comes into its own on wet days. You pay 800Ft for half an hour's use of slides, climbing walls and more – parents can leave the kids here while they go shopping. Mon–Sat 10am–9pm, Sun 9am–8pm.

Margit-sziget See p.116. The island in the Danube is a great open space where you can rent bikes, pedaloes and electric cars (from the northern end of the island, though it is worth asking on the island, as the hire points move around). The Palatinus lido (see p.197) has a wave machine

and lots of small pools for kids – there have been issues about locker security here, so don't take all your valuables. The petting zoo across on the eastern side has been vastly improved, and the varied scenery and open areas for frisbee and ball games all create a very pleasant atmosphere.

Playgrounds There are a lot of playgrounds in the squares and parks, such as the Károlyi kert, with the longest sandpit in town, near the Astoria (Belváros), Szabadság tér (Lipótváros), Szent István park (Újlipótváros), Klauzál tér (Erzsébetváros), on the Margit-sziget and at several locations in the Városliget, one of the best being near Dembinsky utca, while in Buda you can find them at the Millenáris Park near Széll Kálmán tér (see p.104), on the Gellért-hegy and at the Feneketlen tó (see map, p.107).

Tropicarium See p.125. You can get close to the sharks, feed stingrays and experience the rainforests in this huge aquarium-terrarium in southern Buda.

Városliget See p.71. The park has the largest concentration of activities and attractions for children: playgrounds, the zoo (see below), a circus and a fairground. The Széchenyi Baths (see p.197) are popular with bigger children – especially the large outdoor hot pool and the whirlpool – but it's not a great place for splashing around in as the old ladies don't want their hairdos messed up. For those who prefer to stay above water level, there's also rowing in summer and ice-skating in winter (see p.71) on the lake by Hősök tere.

Zoo (Állatkert) See p.73. With its visionary director, the zoo gets better every year. The latest development is the new Once Upon a Time Park in the grounds of the former Funfair (Vidámpark): kids can stroke the animals in the petting farm, ride ponies or go on the grand old Carousel. There's also the **Zoo Funhouse (Állatkert Játszóház**; ⓦ jatekmester.hu), for babies and children aged up to ten. In addition to a well-constructed activity centre, you get the chance to be taken by the zookeepers to see the

20

animals being fed. You can enter from the zoo (Mon–Fri 900Ft/hr, Sat–Sun 1100Ft), or from the street entrance between the zoo and the circus Állatkert Játszóház (Mon–Fri 1200Ft/hr, Sat–Sun 1500Ft). Daily 9am–8pm.

MUSEUMS

Hospital in the Rock See p.94. With gory waxworks, spooky Cold War bunkers and an excellent guided tour, this could be great fun for kids (especially boys) – but unfortunately you can't run around or touch anything and admission charges are steep.

Hungarian Open-Air Museum See p.132. Children's programmes every weekend, a playground and frequent folk-craft and folk-dancing displays in this museum outside Szentendre.

Natural History Museum See p.84. Full of colour and activity, with interactive games and lots to look at, plenty of it at child height. Well thought out, it certainly grabs children's attention, but make sure you take snacks – if the café is closed, there is not much else nearby. Across the road is the Botanical Garden (p.84).

Palace of Miracles See p.125. This great interactive playhouse has sadly moved to smaller premises at the Campona Mall but it still has plenty to keep children entertained for an hour or two. Activities such as the bed of nails and square-wheeled car serve as a back-door way of explaining scientific principles. Good explanations in English.

Railway History Park See p.124. Strong child appeal here: lots of big old engines and carriages, and in summer you can even drive an engine yourself.

Telephone Museum See p.94. A hands-on museum, which is a rarity in Budapest; children enjoy sending faxes and calling one another on vintage phones.

Transport Museum Városliget; see p.72. Vehicles, trams, ships and trains of all kinds, plus model train sets that run every hour until 5pm. On the first floor of the nearby Petőfi Csarnok is an Aviation and Space Flight display.

DANCE, THEATRE AND CREATIVE FUN

20 The fact that successful music ensembles such as the Budapest Festival Orchestra and the folk group Muzsikás hold regular events designed specifically for children says a lot about Hungarian attitudes to young people. Budapest also has a strong tradition in puppetry, and many big Hungarian writers have contributed to its children's repertoire. There are some English-language performances, but again, puppet shows are good visual entertainment even without the language. Morning and matinée performances are for kids. Tickets are also available from the ticket offices listed on p.179.

Budapest Festival Orchestra Cocoa Concerts III, Selmeci utca 14–16, Óbuda ☎1 388 6538, ⓦbfz.hu; the website has details of dates. Hour-long concerts for children aged 5–12, where the musicians introduce the music and the instruments – and give out a cup of cocoa, too. The concerts are usually every other month on either a Saturday or a Sunday at 2.30pm and 4.30pm, Sept–May; tickets cost 2500Ft.

Budapest Puppet Theatre (Budapest Bábszínház) VI, Andrássy út 69 ☎1 342 2702, ⓦbudapest-babszinhaz.hu (see p.183). One of the most established puppet theatres – it also does shows for adults.

Kolibri Theatre (Kolibri Színház) VI, Jókai tér 10 ☎1 353 4633, with two other venues nearby at VI, Andrássy út 74 and 77 ⓦkolibriszinhaz.hu. All three Kolibri venues have shows for children of all ages, but those at the Andrássy út 74 theatre are usually better for smaller children. Closed early June to Aug.

Millenáris Park See p.104. Some exhibitions and shows in the various buildings around the site, but best of all is the large indoor play centre in the Fogadó building. Millipop has activities for all ages: a big complex of tunnels and slides and climbing frames, interactive and electronic games, Rubik's cubes and puzzles and pottery painting. Good café on the mezzanine. Daily 10am–8pm.

Muzsikás Children's House TEMI Fővárosi Művelődési Háza, XI, Fehérvári út 47 ⓦmuzsikas.hu. While members of the Muzsikás folk band play, dancers take children (and their parents) through some basic steps, chanting Hungarian children's songs and rhymes – don't worry, non-Hungarian children will enjoy the dancing anyway. The venue is a couple of stops beyond Móricz Zsigmond körtér on trams #18 and #47. Most Tuesdays at 5.30pm Sept–May, 400Ft for children, 700Ft for adults. There is another children's dance organised by Aranytíz Club (see p.182).

Plaster Age VII, Gozsdu udvar, near entrance at Dob utca 16 ⓦgipszkorszak.hu. Workshops for children to paint mugs, plates and assorted shapes – part of a new trend across the city. If you are painting pottery that needs firing, check it will be ready in time for you to take with you. There's another branch in the Millipop play centre at Millenáris park (see p.164); alternatively try Made by You in V, Király Pál utca 11 (ⓦmadebyyou.hu,) where you can paint ceramics.

GAY PRIDE MARCH

Gay Budapest

Of all the cities in the former eastern bloc, Budapest perhaps has the most active gay scene, albeit still very underground compared to its Western counterparts. The city's annual Pride event is one of the most established and well attended in the region and equality is formalised by law – the age of consent is 14 for homosexuals and heterosexuals alike, while, in 2009, Parliament passed a new bill allowing registered partnerships for same-sex couples. However there has been a distinct chill since 2010, as the popular conservative government pushes the idea that the good Hungarian is straight and God-fearing – the 2012 Constitution stressed that marriage is between opposite-sex couples. So even though Budapest is a cosmopolitan city, gays must still tread warily and lesbians even more so.

21

Gay venues are mostly to be found within the **Nagykörút** – there is a collection of bars off Kossuth Lajos utca in the Belváros too. The major event in the gay calendar is **Budapest Pride**, a well-established week-long festival taking place in June and culminating in the colourful Pride March at the weekend. The threat of disruption by right-wing groups means that the march now takes place between barriers along a carefully policed route, but the participants are determined not to let this dampen their spirits. At the big Sziget festival in August (see p.179) there is a gay tent, the Magic Mirror. There are also two events in November, LIFT (Lesbian Identities Festival) and an LGBTQ film festival at the end of the month – though the present conservative climate has put the financial squeeze on any such "disapproved" events.

Budapest's gay scene is very male-dominated. Perhaps the best spots for **lesbians** are *Club 93* and *Why Not* – though there are a couple of lesbian groups that hold regular events: Labrisz (ⓦlabrisz.hu/english) and Ösztrosokk, that arrange parties at various venues, usually on the second Saturday of every month (10pm–4am; entry from 1000Ft; ⓦosztrosokk.hu).

As far as **accommodation** is concerned, the major hotels should all welcome gay guests, or you can go through the website ⓦgaystay.net, which handles flats and also books rooms in the KM Saga guest house (IX, Lonyay utca 17; ⓦkm-saga.hu).

ESSENTIALS

Information The largest gay and lesbian organization in town is Háttér, which runs a helpline (daily 6–11pm; ☎1 329 3380, ⓦhatter.hu) offering advice and information on events – although some of the operators only speak Hungarian.

Listings and websites You can find listings for places and events in English in the gay freebie monthly *Company* found at most gay venues. The Magnum Szauna website (ⓦmagnumszauna.hu) has a very useful and up-to-date section on the city's best gay restaurants, bars, clubs and so on. The website ⓦgayguide.net has the latest on gay accommodation, bars, clubs, restaurants, baths and events in the city. It is also worth looking at the website ⓦbudapestpride.hu, though it is not always up to date on events.

BARS AND RESTAURANTS

Most of the bars listed here levy an **entry fee** or set a minimum consumption level – being gay in Budapest is an expensive privilege. Some venues give you a card when you enter, on which all your drinks are written down; you pay for your drinks and the entry fee as you leave. Be warned that if you lose the card, you'll have to cough up a hefty penalty. Otherwise, be on the lookout for overcharging.

THE BELVÁROS

Action V, Magyar utca 42 ☎1 266 9148, ⓦaction.gay.hu; map p.38. The most hardcore of the gay bars, full of young men looking for one-night stands. Dark room, video room and live shows on Friday (1000Ft entry). Minimum consumption 1000Ft Fri and Sat only. The entrance is hard to find – it's 15m along from the big "A" sign on the door. Daily 9pm–4am.

Madrid V, Semmelweis utca 17 ☎0670 410 2185, ⓦmadridcafebar.com; map p.38. Large, friendly bar close to the Astoria junction, with a large dark room downstairs. Karaoke every Wed, Fri and Sun. Daily 3pm–4am.

★**Why Not?** V, Belgrád rakpart 3-4 ☎0670 557 2727 ⓦwhynotcafe.hu; map p.38. Relaxed small café bar with terrace near the Pest end of the Szabadság híd, with great views across the Gellért hegy. Its clientele is mixed in the daytime, turning more gay in the evening. Serves drinks, snacks and sandwiches, and has karaoke sessions Tues and Sun. Daily 10am–4am.

ELSEWHERE IN THE CITY

★**Club 93** V, Vas utca 2; map p.58. Simple, cheap pizzeria halfway between Astoria and Blaha Lujza tér just off Rákóczi út that's popular with gays and lesbians. The gallery and window seating make it a good place to people-watch. Daily 11am–midnight.

CoXx V, Dohány utca 38 ☎1 344 4884, ⓦcoxx.hu; map p.58. One of the popular gay bars in town, this men-only venue is a friendly place to meet. The ground floor is a gallery and internet café; downstairs holds a dancefloor, video rooms and numerous other spaces. Regular themed party nights. Free entry, minimum consumption 1000Ft. Daily 9pm–4am.

Fenyőgyöngye II, Szépvölgyi út 155 ☎1 325 9783; map p.113. This restaurant is gay-owned, not that many who go there know that. It's at the last stop of the #65 bus from Kolosy tér in Óbuda. Good Hungarian food, polite service. Daily noon–11pm.

Mystery Café V, Nagysándor József utca 3 ☎1 312

1436, ⓦmysterybar.hu; map p.48. Otherwise known as the *Le Café M*, this is a small, friendly place near the Arany János utca metro, that's more suited to chatting rather than dancing (there's no disco). It's a good place to start or end the evening. Internet café too, with wi-fi. Free entry. Daily 5pm–4am.

BATHS

The once famed gay activity in the public steam baths is far less widespread today. The Király has gone mixed (prompted in part by an undercover TV programme about gay sex there) and the Rác has become entombed in a luxury hotel that is waiting to open; there is some action at the Rudas but it is all very discreet. One reason for this decline is that gays can meet elsewhere – cruising bars, or in private saunas such as Magnum that offer dedicated facilities to gay visitors. However, the sun terrace at the Palatinus strand and the roof terrace at the Széchenyi remain popular meeting places.

Magnum Szauna VIII, Csepreghy utca 2 ☎1 267 2532, ⓦmagnumszauna.hu; near the Corvin negyed metro stop. Budapest's first private gay bath, Magnum offers a steam room and dry sauna, gym, lounge, dark rooms and cabins. Dark and Naked parties take place on Fridays at 10pm and parties on some Saturdays at 8pm, as well as other regular events. 2490Ft for under-30s, 2990Ft for over-30s, Wed 1700Ft for all. Mon–Thurs 1pm–midnight, Fri 1pm–4am, and open continuously Sat 1pm–Mon 1am.

Szauna 69 IX, Angyal utca 2 ☎1 210 1751, ⓦgaysauna .hu. Finnish sauna, jacuzzi and private rooms, as well as a bar. 1600Ft for under-25s, 2100Ft for over-25s, Happy Hours Mon 1600Ft & Wed 1700Ft for all. Mon–Thurs & Sun 1pm–1am, Fri 1pm–2am, Sat 1pm–6am.

STATUE OF MÁTYÁS CORVINUS ON THE MÁTYÁS FOUNTAIN

Contexts

History

Although Budapest has only formally existed since 1873, when the twin cities of Buda and Pest were united together, the city has loomed large in European history. Besieged and invaded by Roman legions, Turkic nomads, Nazi stormtroopers and Soviet tanks, it retains a strong identity of its own and remains "Janus faced", looking both east and west. What follows is the briefest sketch of a complex and fascinating past (for more on which see p.219).

In 35 BC the Danube Basin was conquered by the **Romans** and subsequently incorporated within their empire as the province of Pannonia, whose northern half was governed from the town of **Aquincum** on the west bank of the Danube. Ruins of a camp, villas, baths and an amphitheatre can still be seen today in Óbuda and Rómaifürdő. Roman rule lasted until 430 AD, when Pannonia was ceded to **Attila the Hun**. Attila's planned assault on Rome was averted by his death on his wedding night, and thereafter Pannonia was carved up by **Germanic tribes** until they were ousted by the Turkic-speaking **Avars**, who were in turn assailed by the Bulgars, another warlike race from the Eurasian steppes. Golden torques and other treasures from Hun, Goth and Avar burial sites – now on display in the National Museum – suggest that they were quite sophisticated rather than mere "barbarians".

The coming of the Magyars

The most significant of the invaders from the east were the **Magyars**, who stamped their language and identity on Hungary. Their origins lie in the Finno-Ugric peoples who dwelt in the snowy forests between the Volga and the Urals, where today two Siberian peoples still speak languages that are the closest linguistic relatives to Hungarian; along with Finnish, Turkish and Mongolian, these languages make up the Altaic family. Many of these Magyars migrated south, where they eventually became vassals of the Khazar empire and mingled with the Bulgars as both peoples moved westwards to escape the marauding Petchenegs.

In 895 or 896 AD, seven Magyar tribes led by Árpád entered the Carpathian Basin and spread out across the plain, in what Hungarians call the "**landtaking**" (*honfoglalás*). They settled here, though they remained raiders for the next seventy years, striking terror as far afield as France (where people thought them to be Huns), until a series of defeats persuaded them to settle for assimilating their gains. The runic-style writing the Magyar tribes used is increasingly visible today – often used by hardline nationalists to underline their Hungarianness. According to the medieval chronicler, known today simply as Anonymous, the clan of Árpád settled on Csepel-sziget, and it was Árpád's brother, Buda, who purportedly gave his name to the west bank of the new settlement.

8000BC	35BC	895	1000
Homo sapiens appeared in Budapest area	Danube Basin conquered by Romans	The seven Hungarian tribes enter the Carpathian Basin under Árpád	Pope Sylvester II sends crown for King Stephen's coronation

The Árpád dynasty

Civilization developed gradually after Árpád's great-grandson **Prince Géza** established links with Bavaria and invited Catholic missionaries to Hungary. His son **Stephen** (István) took the decisive step of applying to Pope Sylvester for recognition, and on Christmas Day in the year 1000 AD was crowned as a Christian king. With the help of the Italian Bishop Gellért, he then set about converting his pagan subjects. Stephen was subsequently credited with the **foundation of Hungary** and canonized after his death in 1038. His mummified hand and the crown of St Stephen have since been revered as both holy and national relics, and are today some of Budapest's most popular tourist attractions.

Despite succession struggles after Stephen's death, a lack of external threats during the eleventh and twelfth centuries enabled the **development of Buda and Pest** to begin in earnest, largely thanks to French, Walloon and German settlers who worked and traded here under royal protection. However, the growth in royal power caused tribal leaders to rebel in 1222, and Andrew II was forced to recognize the noble status and rights of the **nation** – landed freemen exempt from taxation – in the Golden Bull, a kind of Hungarian Magna Carta.

Andrew's son **Béla IV** tried to restore royal authority, but the **Mongol invasion** of 1241 devastated the country and left even the royal palace of Esztergom in ruins. Only the timely death of Ghengis Khan spared Hungary from further ravages. Mindful of a return visit, Béla selected the **Vár** as a more defensible seat and encouraged foreign artisans to rebuild Buda, which German colonists called "*Ofen*" after its numerous lime-kilns (the name Pest, which is of Slav origin, also means "oven").

Renaissance and decline

After the Árpád dynasty expired in 1301, foreign powers advanced their own claims to the throne and for a while there were three competing kings, all duly crowned. Eventually **Charles Robert** of the French Angevin (or Anjou) dynasty triumphed. Peacetime gave him the opportunity to develop the gold mines of Transylvania and northern Hungary – the richest in Europe – and Charles bequeathed a robust exchequer to his son **Louis the Great**, whose reign saw the population of Hungary rise to three million, and the crown territories expand to include much of what are now Croatia and Poland. The oldest extant strata of the Buda Palace on the Vár date from this time.

After Louis' demise, the throne was claimed by **Sigismund of Luxembourg**, Prince of Bohemia, whom the nobility despised as the "Czech swine". His failure to check the advance of the Turks through the Balkans was only redeemed by the Transylvanian warlord **János Hunyadi**, whose lifting of the siege of Belgrade caused rejoicing throughout Christendom. Vajdahunyad Castle in the Városliget is a romantic nineteenth-century replica of Hunyadi's ancestral seat in Transylvania.

Hunyadi's nephew, **Mátyás Corvinus**, is remembered as the **Renaissance king** who, together with his second wife Beatrice of Naples, lured humanists and artists from Italy to their court. Mátyás was an enlightened despot, renowned for his fairness, but when he died in 1490, leaving no legitimate heir, the nobles took control, choosing a pliable successor and exploiting the peasantry. However in 1514 the peasants, led by **György**

1458	1541	1556	1686
Mátyás Corvinus accedes to the throne, ushering in a golden age	Ottoman armies occupy Budapest	Rudas Baths constructed on orders of Pasha Sokoli Mustafa	Habsburg armies capture Budapest from Turks

Dózsa, rebelled against the oppression. The savage repression of this **revolt** (over seventy thousand peasants were killed and Dózsa was roasted alive) and subsequent laws imposing "perpetual serfdom" alienated the mass of the population – a situation hardly improved by the coronation of the 9-year-old **Louis II**, who was barely 16 when he had to face the full might of the Turks under Sultan Süleyman "the Magnificent".

The Turkish conquest: Hungary divided

The Battle of **Mohács** in 1526 was a shattering defeat for the Hungarians – the king and half the nobility perished, leaving Hungary leaderless. After sacking Buda, the Turks withdrew to muster forces for their real objective, Vienna. To forestall this, Ferdinand of Habsburg proclaimed himself king of Hungary and occupied the western part of the country, while in Buda the nobles put János Zápolyai on the throne. Following Zápolyai's death in 1541, Ferdinand claimed full sovereignty, but the Sultan occupied Buda and central Hungary and made Zápolyai's son ruler of Transylvania, which henceforth became a semi-autonomous principality – a tripartite division known as the **Tripartium**, formally recognized in 1568. Despite various truces, warfare became a fact of life for the next 150 years, and national independence was not to be recovered for centuries afterwards.

Turkish-occupied Hungary was ruled by a Pasha in Buda, with much of the land either deeded to the Sultan's soldiers and officials, or run directly as a state fief. The towns, however, enjoyed some rights and were encouraged to trade, and the Turks were largely indifferent to the sectarian bigotry practised in Habsburg-ruled Hungary. The Habsburg **liberation of Buda** in 1686 was actually a disaster for its inhabitants, as the victors massacred Jews, pillaged at will and reduced Buda and Pest to rubble. The city's Turkish baths and the tomb of Gül Baba were among the few surviving buildings.

Habsburg rule

Habsburg rule was a bitter pill, which the Hungarians attempted to reject in the **War of Independence** of 1703–11, led by Prince **Ferenc Rákóczi II**. Though it was unsuccessful, the Habsburgs began to soften their autocracy with paternalism as a result. The revival of towns and villages during this time owed much to settlers from all over the empire, hence the Serb and Greek churches that remain in Pest and Szentendre. Yet while the aristocracy commissioned over two hundred palaces, and Baroque town centres and orchestras flourished, the masses remained all but serfs, mired in isolated villages.

Such contradictions impelled the Reform movement led by **Count István Széchenyi**. His vision of progress was embodied in the construction of the Lánchíd (Chain Bridge) between Buda and Pest, which proved an enormous spur to the development of the two districts. The National Museum, the Academy of Sciences and many other institutions were founded at this time, while the coffee houses of Pest became a hotbed of radical politics. Széchenyi's arch-rival was **Lajos Kossuth**, small-town lawyer turned member of parliament and editor of the radical *Pesti Hirlap*, which scandalized and delighted citizens. Kossuth detested the Habsburgs, revered "universal liberty", and demanded an end to serfdom and censorship. Magyar chauvinism was his blind spot, however, and the law of 1840, his greatest pre-revolutionary achievement, inflamed

1800	1848	1849
Beethoven plays in Budapest	Crowds gather on March 15 in front of the National Museum, the start of the War of Independence	Opening of István Széchenyi's Lánchíd, the first permanent bridge between Buda and Pest

dormant nationalist feelings among Croats, Slovaks and Romanians by making Hungarian the sole official language.

When the empire was shaken by revolutions that broke out across Europe in **March 1848**, local radicals seized the moment. Kossuth dominated Parliament, while **Sándor Petőfi** mobilized crowds on the streets of Pest. A second war of independence followed, which again ended in defeat and Habsburg repression, epitomized by the execution of Prime Minister Batthyány in 1849, and the construction of the Citadella atop Gellért-hegy, built to intimidate citizens with its guns.

Budapest's Belle Époque

Gradually, brute force was replaced by a **policy of compromise**, by which Hungary was economically integrated with Austria and, as Austrian power waned, given a major shareholding in the Habsburg empire, henceforth known as the "Dual Monarchy". The compromise (*Ausgleich*) of 1867, engineered by **Ferenc Deák**, brought Hungary prosperity and status, but tied the country inextricably to the empire's fortunes. Buda and Pest underwent rapid expansion and formally merged. Pest was extensively remodelled, acquiring the Nagykörút (Great Boulevard) and Andrássy út, a grand approach to the Városliget, where Hungary's millennial anniversary celebrations were staged in 1896, marking a thousand years since the arrival of the Hungarian tribes in the Carpathian Basin. (In fact they arrived in 895 but preparations were late, so the official date was adjusted to 896.) New suburbs were created to house the burgeoning population, which was by now predominantly Magyar, though there were still large German and Jewish communities. Both elegance and squalor abounded, café society reached its apogee, and Budapest experienced a **cultural efflorescence** in the early years of the twentieth century to rival that of Vienna. Today, the most tangible reminders are the remarkable buildings by Ödön Lechner, Béla Lajta and other masters of Art Nouveau and National Romanticism – the styles that characterized the era.

The Horthy years

Dragged into **World War I** by its allegiance to Austria and Germany, Hungary was facing defeat by the autumn of 1918. The Western or Entente powers decided to dismantle the Habsburg empire in favour of the "**Successor States**" – Romania, Czechoslovakia and Yugoslavia – which would acquire much of their territory at Hungary's expense. In Budapest, the October 30 "Michaelmas Daisy Revolution" put the Social Democratic party of Count **Mihály Károlyi** in power, but his government avoided the issue of land reform, attempted unsuccessfully to negotiate peace with the Entente and finally resigned when France backed further demands by the Successor States.

On March 21, 1919, a **Republic of Councils** (*Tanácsköztársaság*) was proclaimed led by **Béla Kun**, which ruled through local Soviets. Hoping for radical change and believing that "Russia will save us", many initially supported the new regime, but enforced nationalization of land and capital and attacks on religion soon alienated the majority. After 134 days, the regime collapsed before the advancing Romanian army, which occupied Budapest.

1873	1896	1898	1905
Uniting of Buda, Pest and Óbuda to form Budapest	Underground railway inaugurated as part of Millennial celebrations in Budapest	Sisi, Empress Elizabeth, assassinated in Switzerland	St Stephen's Basilica is completed after 54 years' work

Then came the **White Terror**, as right-wing gangs moved up from the south killing "Reds" and Jews, who were made scapegoats for the earlier Communist "Red Terror" – especially in Budapest, the Bolshevik capital. **Admiral Miklós Horthy**, self-appointed regent for Karl IV, who had been exiled by the Western allies ("the Admiral without a fleet, for the king without a kingdom") entered what he called the "sinful city" on a white horse, and ordered a return to "traditional values". Meanwhile, at the Paris Conference, Hungary was obliged to sign the **Treaty of Trianon** (July 4, 1920), surrendering two-thirds of its historic territory and three-fifths of its total population (three million in all) to the Successor States. The bitterest loss was **Transylvania** – a devastating blow to national pride. Horthy's regency was characterized by gala balls and hunger marches, revanchism and growing **anti-Semitism**, enshrined in law from 1925. Yet Horthy was a moderate compared to the **Arrow Cross** Fascists waiting in the wings, whose power grew as **World War II** raged, and the Hungarian Second Army perished at Stalingrad.

Anticipating Horthy's defection from the Axis in October 1944, Nazi Germany staged a coup, installing an Arrow Cross government, which enabled them to quicken the pace of the Holocaust in Hungary and begin the massacre of the **Jews** of Budapest. It was only thanks to the valiant efforts of foreign diplomats like Wallenberg and Lutz that half of them survived, when ninety percent of Hungary's provincial Jews perished. In late December, the Red Army smashed through the defensive "Attila Line" and encircled the capital, held by German troops. During the seven-week **siege of Budapest**, citizens endured endless shelling amid a bitter winter, as street-fighting raged. In January the Germans withdrew from Pest, blew up the Danube bridges and holed up in Buda, where the Vár was reduced to rubble as the Red Army battered the Wehrmacht into submission. Aside from the Jews in the ghetto – for whom it meant salvation from the Arrow Cross – the city's **liberation** on February 13, 1945 brought little joy to Budapestis, as the Red Army embarked on an orgy of rape and looting, followed by a wave of deportations to Siberia.

The Communist takeover and the 1956 Uprising

As Budapestis struggled to rebuild their lives after the war, the Soviet-backed **Communists** took control bit by bit – stealthily reducing the power of other forces in society, and using the threat of the Red Army and the **ÁVO secret police**, who took over the former Arrow Cross torture chambers on Andrássy út. By 1948 their hold on Hungary was total, symbolized by the red stars that everywhere replaced the crown of St Stephen, and a huge statue of Stalin beside the Városliget, where citizens were obliged to parade before Hungary's "Little Stalin", **Mátyás Rákosi**.

The power struggles in the Moscow Communist Party leadership that followed the death of Stalin in 1953 were replicated in the other Eastern European capitals, and in Hungary Rákosi was replaced by **Imre Nagy**. Nagy's "New Course" allowed Hungarians an easier life before Rákosi struck back by expelling him from the Party for "deviationism". However, society had taken heart from the respite and intellectuals held increasingly outspoken public debates during the summer of 1956. The mood came to a head in October, when 200,000 people attended the funeral of László Rajk (a victim of the show trials in 1949) in Kerepesi Cemetery, and Budapest's students decided to march to the General Bem statue near the Margit híd.

1912	1919	1920	1944
The magnificent Elephant and Giraffe Houses unveiled in Budapest's Zoo	Admiral Horthy enters Budapest, marking the start of the anti-Semitic White Terror	Treaty of Trianon carves up old Hungarian kingdom	Budapest ghetto set up in Jewish quarter

On October 23, demonstrators chanting anti-Rákosi slogans crossed the Danube to mass outside Parliament. As dusk fell, students demanding access to the Radio Building were fired upon by the ÁVO, and a spontaneous **1956 Uprising** began, which rapidly took hold throughout Budapest and spread across Hungary. The newly restored Nagy found himself in a maelstrom, as popular demands were irreconcilable with realpolitik – independence and withdrawing from the Warsaw Pact were anathema to the Kremlin. It was Hungary's misfortune that the UN was preoccupied with the Suez Crisis when the Soviets reinvaded on November 10, crushing all resistance in six days. An estimated 2500 Hungarians died and some 200,000 fled abroad; back home, hundreds were executed and thousands jailed for their part in the uprising.

"Goulash socialism" and the end of Communism

After Soviet power had been bloodily restored, **János Kádár** gradually normalized conditions, embarking on cautious reforms to create a "**goulash socialism**" that made Hungary the envy of its Warsaw Pact neighbours and the West's favourite Communist state in the late 1970s. Though everyone knew the limits of the "Hungarian condition", there was enough freedom and consumer goods to keep the majority content. Decentralized management, limited private enterprise and competition made Hungary's economy healthy compared to other Socialist states, but in the 1980s it became apparent that the attempt to reconcile a command economy and one-party rule with market forces was unsustainable. Dissidents tested the limits of criticism, and even within the Party there were those who realized that changes were needed. Happily, this coincided with the advent of Gorbachev, which made it much easier for the reform Communists to shunt Kádár aside in 1988.

The **end of Communism** was heralded by two events the following summer: the ceremonial reburial of Imre Nagy, and the dismantling of the barbed wire along the border with Austria, which enabled thousands of East Germans to escape to the west while "on holiday". In October 1989, the government announced the legalization of other parties as a prelude to free elections, and the People's Republic was renamed the Republic of Hungary in a ceremony broadcast live on national television. Two weeks later this was eclipsed by the fall of the Berlin Wall, closely followed by the Velvet Revolution in Czechoslovakia and the overthrow of Ceaușescu in Romania on Christmas Day.

The post-Communist era

Hungary's first **free elections** in the spring of 1990 resulted in a humiliating rejection of the reform Communists' Hungarian Socialist Party (MSzP), and the installation of a centre-right coalition government dominated by the **Hungarian Democratic Forum (MDF)** under Premier **József Antall**. Committed to a total break with Communism, the MDF aimed to restore the traditions and hierarchies of prewar Hungary and its former position in Europe.

After Antall's premature death in 1993, his successor failed to turn the economy around and the 1994 elections saw the **Socialists** (under the **MSzP**) return to power. To allay fears of a Communist return to power, they included the **Free Democrats (SzDSz)**

1945	1949	1953	1956
Soviet troops capture Budapest from the Nazis	First trolleybus line inaugurated, #70, on Stalin's seventieth birthday	Hungary's football team demolishes England 6–3	Hungarian Uprising breaks out on October 23

in government, and reassured Hungary's foreign creditors with austerity measures that angered voters who had expected the Socialists to reverse the growing inequalities in society. It soon became obvious that they were riddled with corruption; some party members became millionaires almost overnight.

The 1998 elections were narrowly won by the **Fidesz-Hungarian Civic Party** of **Viktor Orbán**, a figure of undeniable charisma who repositioned his party to the right, stressing the need to revive national culture and using the buzz-word *polgári* (meaning "civic", but redolent of bourgeois middle-class values) to appeal to a broad constituency. The youngest prime minister in Hungarian history, the Oxford-educated Orbán promoted a conservative Christian agenda with an acute understanding of national and religious symbolism.

With an expanding economy, falling inflation and low unemployment levels – plus the achievement of steering Hungary into NATO – Orbán anticipated victory in the parliamentary elections of 2002. Instead, after a vitriolic campaign, his Fidesz–MDF coalition was ousted, the electorate preferring a return to the centre-left alliance of Socialists and Free Democrats, whose most important achievement was to preside over Hungary's accession to the **European Union** in 2004.

In August 2004, the premiership passed to the sports minister and millionaire businessman **Ferenc Gyurcsány**, who revitalized the jaded Socialists by appointing a cabinet of fellow millionaires who got rich during the privatization of state assets in the 1990s. Like previous governments, however, they faced the dilemma that Hungary was living beyond its means – its budget deficit of ten percent of GDP was the highest in the EU – while voters opposed further belt-tightening or reforms of the health system. By promising better welfare while secretly running up deficits, Gyurcsány managed to delay a reckoning long enough to win the April 2006 election – the first time a government had been re-elected since democracy was restored.

In September 2006, however, national radio broadcast a **tape-recording** of him telling his cabinet that austerity measures were inevitable "because we fucked up. Not a little, a lot… We lied in the morning, we lied in the evening." While both the context of the speech and the leaking of the tape have aroused much debate, a furore ensued, with weeks of demonstrations outside Parliament led by Fidesz and the MDF. On October 23, **rioting** erupted, protesters battling police around Kossuth tér and Nyugati station. In a throwback to 1956, they waved Hungarian flags with a hole cut out, and even managed to activate an old Soviet tank from a museum (which stalled before it reached Parliament).

Gyurcsány clung to office but the government was robbed of all authority. Even after he resigned in 2009, the Socialists were a broken force, and in the elections of 2010 Fidesz, led by a resurgent Orbán, stormed to a massive victory securing more than two-thirds of the vote. He promptly announced that a **national declaration** "May there be peace, freedom and unity" be posted in every building, an act which soon had the press cynically dubbing him the "Dear Leader".

An even clearer sign of the change in Hungarian politics was the success of the far-right **Jobbik (Movement for Better Hungary)**, which received sixteen percent of the vote, coming third. The rise of this media-savvy group under Gábor Vona was based on its appeal to younger Hungarians – anti-Semitic nationalism is no longer the preserve of old embittered Magyars. Jobbik proudly waved its flags bearing the "Árpád stripes"

1958	1978	1989	1990
Imre Nagy executed for his role in the 1956 revolt	St Stephen's crown returned to Hungary from Fort Knox	The Iron Curtain is dismantled	First free elections after the fall of Communism

of the Arrow Cross and openly flaunts its links with the banned Magyar Gárda (Hungarian Guard), the paramilitary group that parades through villages in eastern Hungary "restoring order" – ie terrorizing Gypsy villagers.

The new Hungary

Orbán's determination to shape a new Hungary, transforming its economy and its culture, has required a pugnacious, centralised and **interventionist state**. A legal avalanche – no fewer than nine hundred laws were drafted between 2010 and 2014 – has swept most opposition aside. When independent bodies voiced criticism, they were stripped of powers, as happened to the Constitutional Court; stuffed with government supporters, as at the National Bank; or simply abolished. Government money poured into the coffers of its business supporters with the declared aim of building a right-wing entrepreneurial class that could challenge the old communist elite.

At home Fidesz did all it could to bolster the **Catholic Church**, giving it control of schools and hospitals and hoping it could once again become the moral backbone of the nation; and beyond the borders it has **extended voting rights** to Hungarian minorities, drawing criticism from its neighbours and the EU that Hungary was ignoring Europe's borders. Most embarrassingly Fidesz attempted to commemorate the Holocaust and so alienated the Jewish community that local organisations decided to boycott it.

Orbán himself aroused intense opposition, both at home and abroad, for his trampling on **media freedom** (state tv news now resembles the propaganda arm of government) and his raiding of private pension funds, but he turned this round as evidence that he was the defender of Hungarian interests against the EU and foreign banks and businesses. The government's order to cap the fees charged by foreign-owned public utility companies by ten percent in 2013 was typical of his populist approach. Similarly for a nation that feels it was treated unfairly by the twentieth century the Fidesz line that seems to absolve the Hungarians of any complicity in the Nazis atrocities had a strong appeal.

Come the **2014 elections**, however, the electorate clearly was not put off by the controversies, as Fidesz's support held up well across the country. The party only polled 43 percent of the votes, but it still won a two-thirds majority in parliament. Voters had few alternatives. The remnants of left-wing opposition have been embroiled in their own corruption scandals with **Gábor Simon**, a former deputy-chariman of the Socialist Party, arrested for failing to declare €770,000 in an Austrian bank account. Meanwhile the **far-right Jobbik party** has grown its share of the vote to twenty percent, with support growing in the west of the country.

The view from Budapest

In **Budapest**, while governments came and went after 1990, **Mayor Gábor Demszky** steered the city forwards without any major upsets for twenty years, finally securing state funding for the **fourth metro line**, running from Keleti Station in Pest to Etele tér in Buda. However, he stepped down at the 2010 elections before he was engulfed by the Fidesz tide. His successor, **István Tarlós**, an engineer by trade, ran as an independent

1999	2001	2002	2004
Hungary joins NATO	*Gresham Palace* hotel restored to its 1907 glory	National stadium renamed after Ferenc Puskás, the legendary Hungarian footballer	Hungary joins EU

with Fidesz backing. He immediately stamped his mark on the city by changing several **street names**, offending both the Russians (by renaming Moszkva tér) and the Americans (by renaming Roosevelt tér), and vowed to make the city a leaner, cleaner place by tackling the corruption of the Budapest transport authority – particularly the soaring cost of the fourth metro line.

The city's intellectuals viewed Tarlós with suspicion: his attempt to ban a gay stall at the Sziget festival in 2001 when he was mayor of Óbuda did little to endear him to them. Their fears seemed confirmed when the new mayor overruled an appointment committee to put two anti-Semitic right-wingers in charge of the New Theatre, a move that provoked widespread protest.

Under Tarlós the city has certainly been spruced up. Streets and major junctions have been made more pedestrian- and cyclist-friendly, the gleaming new metro line is running smoothly and **restoration projects** have transformed public buildings from the Music Academy to the Várkert Bazár. In some ways, however, the city has been sanitised – a law in 2013 banned the homeless from the streets of the city centre and ruin bars (see p.173) are now seen as cash cows rather than counter culture. That said, there is an undeniable buzz about the place as the economy sparks to life together with a palpable political edginess as Hungarians remain deeply divided.

2006	**2007**	**2010**	**2014**
Riots after Prime Minister's admission of "lies, lies, lies"	The neo-fascist Magyar Gárda formed in Budapest	Viktor Orbán leads Fidesz to crushing electoral victory	Orbán reelected with large parliamentary majority

Music

Hungarian classical music enshrines the trinity of Liszt, Bartók and Kodály: Liszt was the founding father, Bartók one of the greatest composers of the twentieth century, and Kodály (himself no slouch at composition) created a widely imitated system of musical education. When you also take into account talented Hungarian soloists such as András Schiff and ensembles such as the Budapest Festival Orchestra, it's clear that this small nation has made an outstanding contribution to the world of classical music. After classical, the musical genres most readily associated with Hungary are folk and Gypsy, both of which have some excellent exponents, the former led by Muzsikás and the wonderful singer Márta Sebestyén, and the latter by the likes of the cimbalom player Kálmán Balogh. The increasing popularity of jazz is manifest in the growing number of clubs in Budapest and other larger cities, as well as several terrific summer jazz festivals held around the country. Meanwhile, Hungarian popular music, while not exactly cutting-edge, is becoming more adventurous as a new generation of DJs and bands soaks up the influence of Western European and American artists.

Classical music

Franz Liszt (1811–86), who described himself as a "mixture of Gypsy and Franciscan", cut a flamboyant figure in the salons of Europe as a virtuoso pianist and womanizer. His *Hungarian Rhapsodies* and other similar pieces reflected the "Gypsy" side to his character and the rising nationalism of his era, while later work like the *Transcendental Studies* (whose originality has only recently been recognized) invoked a visionary "Franciscan" mood. Despite his patriotic stance, however, Liszt's first language was German (he never fully mastered Hungarian), and his expressed wish to roam the villages of Hungary with a knapsack on his back was a Romantic fantasy.

That was left to **Béla Bartók** (1881–1945) and **Zoltán Kodály** (1882–1967), who began exploring the remoter districts of Hungary and Transylvania in 1906, collecting peasant music. Despite many hardships and local suspicion of their "monster" (a cutting stylus and phonograph cylinders), they managed to record and catalogue thousands of melodies, laying down high standards of musical ethnography, still maintained in Hungary today, while discovering a rich source of inspiration for their own compositions.

Bartók created a personal but universal musical language by reworking the raw essence of Magyar and Finno-Ugric folk music in a modern context – in particular his six String Quartets – although Hungarian public opinion was originally hostile. Feeling misunderstood and out of step with his country's increasingly pro-Nazi policies, Bartók left Hungary in 1940, dying poor and embittered in the United States. Since then, however, his reputation has soared, and the return of his body in 1988 occasioned national celebrations, shrewdly sponsored by the state.

Kodály's music is more consciously national: Bartók called it "a real profession of faith in the Hungarian soul". His *Peacock Variations* are based on a typical Old Style pentatonic tune and the *Dances of Galánta* on the popular music played by Gypsy bands. Old Style tunes also form the core of Kodály's work in musical education: the

"Kodály method" employs group singing to develop musical skill at an early age. His ideas made Hungarian music teaching among the best in the world.

The classical tradition was continued by a two of the leading avant-garde composers of the late twentieth century, **György Ligeti** and **György Kurtág**. Both were born in Transylvania, and both were strongly influenced by their time in the west in the late 1950s. Ligeti never returned, and completely embraced the experimental techniques around him, while Kurtág returned to Budapest to develop his very individual style that retains a strong Bartokian influence.

Folk music

Hungarian folk music (*Magyar népzene*) originated around the Urals and the Turkic steppes over a millennium ago, and is different again from Gypsy or Roma music. The haunting rhythms and pentatonic scale of this "Old Style" music (to use Bartók's terminology) were subsequently overlaid by "New Style" European influences – which have been discarded by more modern enthusiasts in the folk revival centred around Táncház.

The "Dance House" movement was born in the 1970s when folk musicians in Budapest began to recreate the rural dance gatherings that were still part of everyday life in Hungarian villages in Transylvania. It struck a chord with the urban middle classes, who were left cold by the official version of Hungarian folk music industry and attracted by the forbidden fruits of Hungarian culture. Official disapproval (the dance houses were tolerated but were carefully monitored by the authorities) lent them an underground thrill: their popularity spread – the musicians noted that even the police informers couldn't resist joining in. Since then, the shouting, whistling, and slapping of boots and thighs has continued unabated, and has managed to survive the official embrace that the Fidesz government has predictably flung round the folk movement – folk now has its own kitsch talent show *Fölszállt a Páva*.

The two biggest names to emerge from the Táncház movement were **Muzsikás** and **Márta Sebestyén**, who have been regular collaborators for years. A four-piece ensemble comprising bass, violin and flute, Muzsikás (pronounced *Mu-zhi-kash*) started out in the early 1970s by exploring the musical archives of village folk music, from which they derived their own distinctive repertoire, combining traditional Hungarian music with the sounds of Transylvania, across the border in Romania – while their recorded output is not that prolific, they do tour regularly, both at home and abroad.

Unquestionably Hungary's finest folk singer, and one of the best in Europe, Sebestyén's gorgeous and distinctive voice has seen her become firmly established on the world music scene in recent years, a reputation that was sealed after she featured on the soundtrack to the film *The English Patient*. Aside from her regular appearances with Muzsikás, Sebestyén has also sung with **Vujicsics**, a seven-strong ensemble from Pomáz near Szentendre who specialize in Serbian and Croatian folk melodies. As both of these bands grow older, they have spawned a second generation of bands: two of the top new ensembles are the **Buda Folk Band** and **Söndörgő**, formed respectively by the sons of Muzsikás and Vujicsics members.

Two dance house specialists that play regularly in the city are the **Ökrös** and **Tükrös** bands, while other bands upholding folk traditions are **István "Szalonna" Pál** and his band, **Róbert Lakatos and the Rév** – Lakatos's viola (*brácsa*) gives the music a wonderfully mellow sound – and three Roma ensembles from Transylvania, the **Szászcsávás** and **Magyarpalatkai Band** bands and the brilliant violinist **Kis Csípás** and his band. The **Csík** Ensemble has moved away from its folk roots towards folk-style cover versions of pop songs – though they alienated some followers by backing the Fidesz electoral campaign.

Three artists to look out for are **Miklós Bóth**, a guitarist who sounds like Jimi Hendrix jamming with Muzsikás; the American violinist **Bob Cohen**, whether with the Budapest klezmer outfit **Di Naye Kapelye** or in other configurations; and perhaps the best known of the three, **Félix Lajkó**, a Hungarian virtuoso violinist and zither player from the Vojvodina region of Serbia, whose eccentric fusion of folk, Gypsy and jazz inspires a devout following.

The new generation of female singers is a very strong one: **Bea Palya**, who spans Hungarian, Roma and Jewish music traditions, **Ági Szaloki**, who has sung with the Ökrös Band as well as performing solo, **Ági Herczku**, **Éva Korpás** and **Szilvi Bognár**, who sing with a range of bands.

Gypsy music

Played on anything from spoons and milk jugs to guitars, **Gypsy or Roma music** ranges from haunting laments to playful wedding songs. The band that pioneered this sound in the 1980s was **Kályi Jág**, whose success transformed the way Roma communities played their own music. For a primer check out Tony Gatliff's excellent film *Latcho Drom*, which explores Roma music from India to Spain. The next generation of Hungarian Roma musicians includes the groups **Romengo**, **Vojasa**, **Parno Graszt** and the **Karaván Familia** – all of whom tour extensively and are the focal point of most Roma festivals in Hungary and abroad. The Transylvanian dance house bands listed above are from a different Roma tradition, but they are also worth catching. The distinctive voice of Mónika Juhász-Miczura, or **Mitsoura**, is featured on many CDs – she has also recorded albums as a solo artist.

Three of the best known Roma artists are **Kálmán Balogh**, one of the world's foremost exponents of the cimbalom, a hammer dulcimer (stringed instrument) played with little mallets, with a repertoire ranging from Gypsy tunes to Bach; the jazz guitarist **Ferenc Snétberger**; and the wizard violinist **Roby Lakatos**, who tours extensively around the world from his base in Brussels. A seventh-generation descendant of János Bihari (aka "King of the Gypsy Violinists"), Lakatos hails from the Romungro tradition of "Gypsy music" that you will see advertised at touristy restaurants, known in Hungarian as **Magyar nóta**. Consisting of a series of mid-nineteenth-century Hungarian ballads traditionally played by Roma musicians, Magyar nóta is usually performed by one or two violinists, a bass player and a guy on the cimbalom. The more famous restaurants boast their own musical dynasties, such as the Lakatos family, who have been performing this sort of music for over a century.

In recent years a decline in demand for Gypsy restaurant bands has sent younger Romungro musicians in new directions, such as **Roma jazz** – look out for tenor saxophonist **Gábor Bolla** in particular – or the cabaret-style music of **Budapest Bár,** led by Róbert Farkas.

Popular music and jazz

Budapest has undergone a **popular music** revival in the last few years: radio stations and music magazines have taken off and the city has become part of the international tour circuit – the Sziget Festival each August (see p.179) is now one of the premier music gatherings on the continent. This has all had a knock-on effect on local music. **Heaven Street Seven** call their version of guitar pop Dunabeat, while **Quimby**'s Tibor Kiss is the Hungarian equivalent of Tom Waits. Two newer outfits on the circuit are the rapping **Anna and the Barbies** and the alternative rock band **30Y**. The one-time underground local radio station **Tilos Rádió** has done much to promote **DJs**, and there are now a host of them around the country – Palotai and Mango do a lot of wild mixing using a mass of sources and sounds. Slam poetry is big in the city – **Akkezdet Phiai** is one of the more accessible acts.

A popular crossover style blends pop with Hungarian folk or Thirties swing: **MagyarVista Social Club** (a play on the name of the famous Cuban outfit – Magyar Vista is the

Hungarian name of a village in Romania) and **Tárkány Művek** combine jazz, rock and folk. The bands backing the gloriously clear voice of **Flóra Herczeg** combine folk, pop and jazz.

Jazz has always had a devout, but small, following in the country and more and more clubs and bars offer live jazz. Names worth checking out are **Béla Szakcsi Lakatos**, a jazz pianist who frequently plays in Budapest clubs, **Mihály Dresch**, the saxophonist who draws on folk traditions, **Miklós Lukács**, a pupil of the cymbalomist Kálmán Balogh, and two fine singers, **Harcsa Veronika** and **Nikoletta Szőke**.

Discography

An excellent online source for all CDs is the Hangvető website (⒲hangveto.hu). A full discography of the works of Liszt, Bartók and Kodály, conductors like Dohnányi and Doráti, and contemporary Hungarian soloists and singers would fill a catalogue, but look out for the following names: pianists András Schiff, Zoltán Kocsis (who also conducts) and Dezső Ránki; the Liszt Ferenc Chamber Orchestra, the Budapest Festival Orchestra and the Hungarian Radio and TV Symphony; conductors Iván Fischer and Tamás Vasáry; and singers Mária Zádori, Ingrid Kertesi, Andrea Rost, Adrienne Csengery, József Gregor and Kolos Kovats.

Folk and Gypsy music can be bought at all record stores – Fonó is the biggest label. Note that a CD with a picture of a Gypsy orchestra all dressed up in red waistcoats is of the "*nóta*" variety – listen before you buy to check this is the kind of Gypsy music you want. As well as the artists listed here, there are hundreds of great recordings in the above fields. The following simply offer an introduction; particular recommendations are marked with the ★ symbol.

INDIVIDUAL ARTISTS

★**Kálmán Balogh** *Kálmán Balogh and the Gipsy Cimbalom Band* (Fonó). A terrific collection of tunes from Hungary and the wider region, including the heart-rending version of the folk song "A csitári hegyek alatt". Recorded with artistic director Romano Kokalo, *Gipsy Colours* (Fonó, Budapest) is a fabulous selection of Gypsy dance tunes from the region.

★**Félix Lajkó** *Remény*, *Félix* (both on Tilos), *Lajkó Félix and his Band* (Fonó). The best recordings so far of this Hungarian virtuoso violinist from Subotica in northern Serbia – *Remény (Hope)* features previously unreleased concert recordings alongside pieces from the soundtrack to *Othello*, while *Lajkó Félix and his Band* is a highly charged set of recordings made in the woods near his home. He also features with the Boban Markovic Orchestra, the fantastic Serbian Gypsy ensemble, on the CD *Srce Cigansko*, which combines typically rumbustious Serbian brass with Lajkó's busy violin.

★**Roby Lakatos** Earlier works include *Lakatos* (Deutsche Grammophon), which features new workouts of favourites by the likes of Brahms alongside traditional Hungarian folk

songs; *Later with Lakatos* (Deutsche Grammophon), a homecoming concert in Budapest's Thália Theatre in 1999. More recent albums (all on the Avanti label) are *Firedance*, a sizzling record exploring Gypsy themes from around the world; *Klezmer Karma*, a funky, Jewish-influenced recording featuring performances by Miriam Fuks and the Franz Liszt Chamber Orchestra; and *Roby Lakatos with Musical Friends*, an all-jazz project boasting some stellar guests such as Stephane Grappelli and Marc Fossett.

Bea Palya *Ágról ágra* (Orphea). Starting with a Hungarian folk prayer at dawn Palya moves across borders to embrace Romanian and Persian songs with the same authority she brings to her own tradition.

Márta Sebestyén *Kismet* (Hannibal). On this wide-ranging album, Hungary's leading Táncház singer draws upon various folk traditions, with Bosnian, Hindi and Irish songs, among others; otherwise, Sebestyén is best known for her recordings with the folk group Muzsikás (see p.220), while her international star has risen thanks to significant contributions to the Grammy-award-winning Deep Forest album *Boheme* and the film *The English Patient*.

GROUPS

★**Bazseva** *Első Bekezdés* (Fonó). Formed in 2013, Bazseva is a new Budapest band on the circuit. Its six members want to rid folk of the kitsch image of boots and hats and moustaches and show what a life force it can be.

Béla Lakatos and The Gypsy Youth Project

Introducing (World Music Network). Lively and refreshing debut album from this talented outfit, with songs pertaining to rural Roma life. Wonderful vocals and some fabulous instrumental improvisation.

Besh o Drom Vibrant large ensemble that produces a

feverish Balkan blend of dance music with its driving brass and whirling rhythms perhaps at its rawest on their first album, *Macsó Hímzés* (Fonó).

★**Buda Folk Band** *Magyar Világi Népzene* (Fonó). The first recording by "Sons of Muzsikas" band – which includes Sándor Csoóri and Márton Éri – develops traditional Hungarian folk, drawing on its melodies and instrumentation.

★**Budapest Bar** *Budapest Bar 1* (EMI). The first album of the Robert Farkas cabaret band is their best, with the supreme opening song "Szivemben bomba van" (There's a bomb in my heart).

Csik Ensemble *Ez a vonat, ha elindult, Hadd menjen...* (Fonó). Rooted in the folk tradition, the band works with pop musicians such as Tibor Kiss of the band Quimby, to powerful effect.

★**Di Naye Kapelye** The band's three albums to date are the eponymous *Di Naye Kapelye*, *A Mazeldiker Yid* and *Traktorist* (all Oriente Musik), all terrific, and typically exuberant, klezmer recordings, which make for immensely enjoyable listening. *Traktorist* features a wonderfully jolly Communist-era ode to the Yiddish tractor.

★**Herczeg Flóra és a Például Igen** *Mi Jöhet még!* Very enjoyable collection of songs by this young singer from Eger and her group, led by trumpeter János Hámori.

★**Muzsikás** *The Bartók Album* (Hannibal). Featuring Márta Sebestyén and the Romanian violinist Alexander Balanescu, this manages to set the music of Bartók in its original context – three of Bartók's violin duos are presented alongside original field recordings and recordings of his transcriptions by Muzsikás.

★**Morning Star** (Hannibal) is another fine Muzsikás volume – interestingly, their record company recommended slight changes and a softening of edges for this foreign edition of *Hazafelé* (Hungaroton), the original Hungarian recording. Their latest release, 2004's *Live at the Liszt Academy of Music*, which again stars Sebestyén, is a compilation of recordings taken from successive appearances at the Budapest Spring Festival.

★**Lakatos Róbert és a Rév** *BrácsaTánc* (FolkEuropa), A pleasantly low-key CD by this group from Komarom in Slovakia, led by the mellow viola of Róbert Lakatos. *Rév* means ferry, and the group moves happily between the different musics of the region – Lakatos himself is also at home in the classical tradition, playing Bartók.

Tükrös Ensemble Two of the best CDs by this established folk band present tunes from the Mezőség region of Transylvania (*A mi Mezőségünk*) and from the Szatmár region of eastern Hungary (*Szatmári népzene*, both FolkEuropa).

Vujicsics Ensemble *Serbian Music from South Hungary* (Hannibal). More complex tunes than most Magyar folk music, with a distinct Balkan influence. Two albums featuring Márta Sebestyén are *25 – Live at the Academy of Music* (R-E-Disc 005), a concert in Budapest celebrating the group's twenty-fifth anniversary, and *Podravina* (R-E-Disc 004), a selection of Croatian dance melodies.

COMPILATION ALBUMS

Magyar népzene 3 (*Hungarian folk music*; Hungaroton). A four-disc set of field recordings covering the whole range of folk music, including Old and New Style songs, instrumental and occasional music, that's probably the best overall introduction. In the West, the discs are marketed as "Folk Music of Hungary Vol.1".

★**Rendhagyó Prímástalálkozó 1** (*Prímás Parade 1*; FolkEuropa*)*. A fascinating supergroup that brings together folk musicians, a rock guitarist, a classical violinist, jazz saxophonist and more – but all rooted in Hungarian and Roma traditions of Transylvania. The result sparkles, never more so than when the electric guitar of Miklós Both plays the role of the violin *primás*. The follow-up CD struggles to match its sparkle.

Rough Guide to Hungary (World Music Network). The second Rough Guide to Hungarian music is an excellent introduction to the many wildly differing sounds of Hungarian music. It includes a bonus CD by Tarkány.

Rough Guide to the Music of Eastern Europe (World Music Network). Although most of the songs on this CD are from the Balkans, there is a healthy representation from Hungary, featuring songs by Márta Sebestyén, Vízöntő and Kálmán Balogh and the Gypsy Cimbalom Band.

Rough Guide to the Music of Hungarian Gypsies (World Music Network). All the big-hitters are here on this thoroughly comprehensive introduction to the many strands of Hungarian Gypsy music – the highlight is a ripping tune by Mitsoura performed with the brilliant Romanian band Fanfare Ciocarlia. Also worth checking are the *Rough Guide to Music of the Gypsies*, with Hungary represented by Kálmán Balogh and the Joszef Lacatos Orchestra, and the *Rough Guide to Klezmer Revival* (RGNET 1203), which features a track by Di Naye Kapelye.

Tánczházi muzsika (*Music from the Táncház*; Hungaroton). A early double album of the Sebő Ensemble playing Táncház music from various regions of Hungary. Wild and exciting rhythms by pioneers of the movement.

Táncház-Népzene (*Dance House – Folk Music*; Hagyományok Háza). An excellent series that has been going since 2003, produced by the Hungarian Heritage House.

Új élő népzene. The series the *Living Village Music* has been going for twenty years, and its twenty albums feature a great mixture of dances, ballads and instrumental pieces by local artists from all over the Carpathian Basin.

Books

There is a wide range of books on Budapest available in the city, particularly architecture titles, or translations of Hungarian literature. Books tagged with the ★ symbol are particularly recommended. See p.188 for a list of Budapest's better bookshops, most of which can take orders.

ART, ARCHITECTURE AND PHOTOGRAPHY

Our Budapest. A very informative series of pocket-size books: written in Hungarian and English by experts in their fields, and published by Budapest City Hall, they cover the city's architecture, baths and parks, and are very cheap, though unfortunately the standard of English varies.

★**Irén Ács** *Hungary at Home*. Excellent collection of photos covering all walks of life in postwar Hungary. Her other books, including *Rendezvous*, are also worth looking out for in bookshops.

★**Bruno Bourel & Lajos Parti Nagy** *Lightscapes*. One of the most interesting collections of photos available. Taken around the city by Bourel, a sharp-eyed French photographer who has lived there for many years, they are accompanied by words from a leading contemporary Hungarian writer.

Bob Dent *Budapest: A Cultural and Literary History*. A wide-ranging background to the city by an English journalist who has lived in Budapest for many years.

Györgyi Éri et al *A Golden Age: Art and Society in Hungary 1896–1914*. Hungary's Art Nouveau age captured in a beautifully illustrated coffee-table volume.

★**János Gerle** *et al Budapest: An Architectural Guide*. The best of the small new guides to the city's twentieth-century architecture, covering almost 300 buildings, with brief descriptions in Hungarian and English.

Ruth Gruber *Jewish Heritage Travel: A Guide to Central and Eastern Europe*. The most comprehensive guide to Jewish sights in Budapest and elsewhere.

Edwin Heathcote *Budapest: A Guide to Twentieth-Century Architecture*. A useful and informative pocket guide to the city, though with some curious omissions.

Tamás Hofer et al. *Hungarian Peasant Art*. An excellently produced examination of Hungarian folk art, with lots of good photos.

Imre Móra *Budapest Then and Now*. A personal and very informative set of accounts of life in the capital, past and present.

★**László Lugo Lugosi** et al. *Budapest – On the Danube; Walks In the Jewish Quarter; The Castle District; Jewish Budapest; Walks Around the Great Boulevard*. A series of small-format architectural guides – the last one is especially recommended.

Tamás Révész *Budapest: A City before the Millennium*. Excellent collection of black and white photographs of the city, though the text can be irritating.

Dora Wieberson et al. *The Architecture of Historic Hungary*. Comprehensive illustrated survey of Hungarian architecture through the ages.

HISTORY, POLITICS AND SOCIETY

Robert Bideleux & Ian Jeffries *A History of Eastern Europe: Crisis and Change*. An excellent and wide-ranging history of the region.

Judit Frigyesi *Béla Bartók and Turn-of-the-century Budapest*. Placing Bartók in his cultural milieu, this is an excellent account of the Hungarian intellectual world at the beginning of the twentieth century.

Jörg K Hoensch *A History of Modern Hungary 1867–1994*. An authoritative history of the country.

László Kontler *Millennium in Central Europe: A History of Hungary*. Another very thorough and reliable history of the country, although its archaic style lets it down somewhat.

Paul Lendvai *The Hungarians: 1000 Years of Victory in Defeat*. Refreshing and authoritative book on Hungary's complex and often tragic history, with particularly stimulating accounts of the Treaty of Trianon and the subsequent Nazi and Communist tyrannies – there are some fascinating pictures, too.

Bill Lomax *Hungary 1956*. Still probably the best – and shortest – book on the Uprising, by an acknowledged expert on modern Hungary. Lomax also edited *Eyewitness in Hungary*, an anthology of accounts by foreign Communists (most of whom were sympathetic to the Uprising) that vividly depicts the elation, confusion and tragedy of the events of October 1956.

John Lukács *Budapest 1900*. Excellent and very readable account of the politics and society of Budapest at the turn of the century, during a golden age that was shortly to come to an end.

John Man *Attila the Hun*. A beautifully written biography of the Magyars' mythical ancestor, illuminating horsemanship and warfare as practised by the Seven Tribes that later colonized the Carpathian basin.

★ **Michael Stewart** *The Time of the Gypsies*. This perceptive book on Roma culture is based on anthropological research conducted in a Roma community in northern Hungary in the 1980s.

Peter Sugar (ed) *A History of Hungary*. A useful and not too academic survey of Hungarian history from pre-Conquest times to the close of the Kádár era, with a brief epilogue on the transition to democracy.

Tony Thorne *Countess Dracula*. An intriguing biography of the sixteenth-century "Blood Countess" Erzsébet Báthory, which argues that she was framed by her uncle to safeguard the Báthory fortune.

BIOGRAPHY AND TRAVEL WRITING

Magda Dénes *Castles Burning: A Child's Life in War*. A moving biographical account of the Budapest ghetto and postwar escape to France, Cuba and the United States, seen through the eyes of a Jewish girl. The author died in 1966, shortly before the book was published.

★ **George Faludy** *My Happy Days in Hell* (Penguin Modern Classics). A remarkable autobiographical account of Faludy's horrendous experience of both Nazi and Soviet repression, including starvation and torture in a labour camp, told with ironic good cheer. His *Selected Poems 1933–80* presents fiery, lyrical poetry with themes of political defiance and the nobility of the human spirit.

Ray Keenoy *Eminent Hungarians*. Everything you always wanted to know about Hungary's most renowned historical and contemporary figures – from Lajos Kossuth and Attila József, to Harry Houdini and Ernő Rubik, creator of the Rubiks cube.

★ **Patrick Leigh Fermor** *A Time of Gifts; Between the Woods and the Water*. In 1934 the young Leigh Fermor started walking from Holland to Turkey, reaching Hungary in the closing chapter of *A Time of Gifts*. In *Between the Woods and the Water* the inhabitants of the Great Plain and Transylvania – both Gypsies and aristocrats – are wonderfully evoked. Lyrical and erudite. Artemis Cooper's biography, *Patrick Leigh Fermor: An Adventure*, also sheds interesting light on his account.

Edward Fox *The Hungarian Who Walked to Heaven*. A brief account of the life of Sándor Kőrösi Csoma, the Hungarian who went in search of the roots of the ancient Hungarians and got sidetracked into making the first Tibetan dictionary.

John Paget *Hungary and Transylvania*. Paget's massive book attempts to explain nineteenth-century Hungary to the English middle class, and, within its aristocratic limitations, succeeds. Occasionally found in secondhand bookshops.

Giorgio and Nicola Pressburger *Homage to the Eighth District*. Evocative short stories about Jewish life in Budapest, before, during and after World War II, by twin brothers who fled Hungary in 1956.

Ernő Szép *The Smell of Humans*. A first-rate but harrowing memoir of the Holocaust in Hungary.

Rogan Taylor & Klára Jamrich (eds) *Puskás on Puskás*. This splendid book not only depicts the life of one of Hungary's – and the world's – greatest footballers, but also provides an intriguing insight into postwar Communist Hungary.

★ **Nick Thorpe** *The Danube: A Journey Upriver from the Black Sea to the Black Forest* (Yale). The BBC's Central European Correspondent, Thorpe (who lives in Budapest) has both the background knowledge and the journalist's eye to put together a fascinating volume that presents the living river in its historical setting.

LITERATURE

Hungary's fabulously rich **literary heritage** has been more widely appreciated in recent years thanks to the success of authors such as Antal Szerb, Sándor Márai and the Nobel Prize-winning Imre Kertész. A useful starting point is *Hungarian Literature* (Babel Guides, 2001), an informative guide to the best Hungarian fiction, drama and poetry in translation, with selected excerpts. There are also numerous collections of short stories published in Budapest, though the quality of translations varies from the sublime to the ridiculous. Works by nineteenth-century authors such as Mór Jókai are most likely to be found in secondhand bookshops (see p.188). The list of volumes published by Bloodaxe has done much to spread the word about Hungary's poets.

ANTHOLOGIES

Loránt Czigány (ed) *The Oxford History of Hungarian Literature from the Earliest Times to the Present*. Probably the most comprehensive collection in print to date. In chronological order, with good coverage of the political and social background.

György Gömöri and George Szirtes (ed) *Colonnade of* *Teeth*. In spite of its strange title, this is a good introduction to the work of young Hungarian poets.

Michael March (ed) *Description of a Struggle*. A collection of contemporary Eastern European prose, featuring four pieces by Hungarian writers including Nádas and Esterházy.

George Szirtes (ed) *An Island of Sound: Hungarian Poetry* *and Fiction Before and Beyond the Iron Curtain*. This anthology features the cream of Hungarian prose and poetry from the end of World War II through to 1989.

POETRY

Endre Ady *Poems of Endre Ady*. Regarded by many as the finest Hungarian poet of the twentieth century, Ady's allusive verses are notoriously difficult to translate.

Attila József *The Iron-Blue Vault*. József's powerful verse, which made him enemies on both the left and right, is some of the finest poetry in Hungarian.

Miklós Radnóti *Forced March* (Enitharmon) There are several translations of Radnóti's sparse, anguished poetry. This collection of his final poems, found in his coat pocket after he had been shot on a forced march to a labour camp, translated by György Gömöri and Clive Wilmer, is an excellent place to start.

Zsuzsa Rakovszky *New Life*. Well-received volume translated by the Hungarian-born English poet George Szirtes.

FICTION

Géza Csáth *The Magician's Garden and Other Stories; Opium and Other Stories*. Disturbing short stories written in the magic realist genre. The author was tormented by insanity and opium addiction, killing his wife and then himself in 1918.

Tibor Déry *The Portuguese Princess*. Wry short stories by a once-committed Communist, who was jailed for three years after the Uprising and died in 1977.

Péter Esterházy *Celestial Harmonies*. Written by a descendant of the famous aristocratic family, this is a dense and demanding book, chronicling the rise of the Esterházys during the Austro-Hungarian empire and their downfall under Communism. His latest novel (yet to be translated), was born of his shock at discovering that his father had been an informer for the Communist secret police.

★**Tibor Fischer** *Under the Frog, A Black Comedy*. "Under a frog down a coalmine" is a Hungarian expression meaning "Things can't get worse", but this fictional account of the 1956 Uprising will have you in stitches. Fischer's parents fled to Britain in 1956.

Jenő Rejtő *The Blonde Hurricane*. Like Antal Szerb and Miklós Radnóti, Rejtő was a great Hungarian writer who was killed in the Holocaust for his Jewish descent: all three could have escaped, but they thought it would never happen in Budapest. He wrote a series of excellent romps – this translation succeeds better than Rejtő's *Quarantine in the Grand Hotel*.

★**Imre Kertész** *Fateless*. Drawing from the author's own experiences as an Auschwitz survivor, this Nobel prize-winning book tells the tale of a young boy's deportation to, and survival in, a concentration camp. A brilliant translation by Tim Wilkinson.

Dezső Kosztolányi *Skylark*. A short and tragic story of an old couple and their beloved child by one of Hungary's top writers of the twentieth century, in a masterly translation by Richard Aczél. Kosztolányi's *Esti Kornél* is a Hungarian classic, a series of whimsical short tales that offers a wonderful portrait of prewar Budapest.

Gyula Krúdy *Adventures of Sinbad*. Stories about a gourmand and womanizer by a popular Hungarian author with similar interests to his hero.

Sándor Márai *Embers*. An atmospheric and moving tale about friendship, love and betrayal by one of Hungary's most respected pre-World War II writers; a beautiful read, as is his early novel *The Rebels*, translated by George Szirtes.

Péter Nádas *A Book of Memories*. This translation of a novel about a novelist writing about a novel caused a sensation when it appeared in 1998. A Proustian account of bisexual relationships, Stalinist repression and modern-day Hungary in a brilliant translation by Iván Sanders.

★**Antal Szerb** *Journey by Moonlight*. This Hungarian classic, written in 1937, tells the story of a Hungarian businessman on honeymoon in Italy who embarks upon a mystical and dazzling journey through the country. Len Rix's translation captures the atmosphere of the original beautifully. Two more brilliant Szerb novels are *The Pendragon Legend* and *Oliver VII*, one set in Wales and the other mainly in Venice, while his *Martians' Guide to Budapest* is a delightful portrait of the city.

FOOD AND WINE

Carolyn Bánfalvi *Food, Wine, Budapest*. A very useful primer on Hungarian cuisine and drink, with information about shopping, markets and restaurants. This first edition was printed in 2007, but a new edition is on the cards.

Susan Derecskey *The Hungarian Cookbook*. A good, easy-to-follow selection of traditional and modern recipes.

Stephen Kirkland *The Wine and Vines of Hungary*.

Authoritative and accessible guide with tips on what to order. Covers the different wines of the country's regions, and their wine-makers too.

George Lang *The Cuisine of Hungary*. A well-written and beautifully illustrated work, telling you everything you need to know about Hungarian cooking, its history and how to do it yourself.

Hungarian

Hungarian is a unique, complex and subtle tongue, classified as belonging to the Finno-Ugric linguistic group, which includes Finnish and Estonian. If you happen to know those languages, however, don't expect them to be a help: there are some structural similarities, but lexically they are totally different. In fact, some scholars think the connection is completely bogus and have linked Hungarian to the Siberian Chuvash language and a whole host of other fairly obscure tongues. Essentially, the origins of Hungarian remain a mystery and, although a few words of Turkish have crept in, together with some German, English and (a few) Russian neologisms, there's not much that the beginner will recognize.

Consequently, foreigners aren't really expected to speak Hungarian, and locals are used to being addressed in **German**, the lingua franca of Hungarian tourism. However, **English** is gaining ground rapidly, and is increasingly understood. That said, a few basic Magyar phrases can make all the difference. Hungarians are intensely proud of their language and pleased when foreigners make an effort to learn a few courtesies. Note that **signage** is mostly in Hungarian only, though multilingual signs can be found on the metro, in most museums and in many restaurants.

The Rough Guides' *Hungarian for Travellers* is a useful **phrasebook** and, if you're prepared to study the language seriously, the best available book is *Colloquial Hungarian* (Routledge). As a supplement, invest in one of the handy little *Angol–Magyar/Magyar–Angol Kisszótár* dictionaries, available from bookshops in Hungary.

BASIC GRAMMAR

Although its rules are complicated, it's worth describing a few features of **Hungarian grammar**, albeit imperfectly. Hungarian is an agglutinative language – in other words, its vocabulary is built upon **root-words**, which are modified in various ways to express different ideas and nuances. Instead of prepositions "to", "from", "in" etc, Hungarian uses **suffixes**, or tags added to the ends of genderless **nouns**. The change in suffix is largely determined by the noun's context: for example the noun "book" (*könyv*) will take a final "*et*" in the accusative (*könyvet*); "in the book" = *könyvben*; "from the book" = *könyvből*. It is also affected by the rules of vowel harmony (which take a while to get used to, but don't alter meaning, so don't worry about getting them wrong!). Most of the nouns in the vocabulary section below are in the nominative or subject form, that is, without suffixes. In Hungarian, "**the**" is *a* (before a word beginning with a consonant) or *az* (preceding a vowel); the word for "**a/an**" is *egy* (which also means "one").

Plurals are indicated by adding a final "k", with a link vowel if necessary, giving -ek, -ok or -ak. Nouns preceded by a number or other indication of quantity (eg, many, several) do not appear as plural: eg *könyvek* means "books", but "two books" is *két könyv* (using the singular form of the noun). **Adjectives** precede the noun (*a piros ház* = the red house), adopting suffixes to form the comparative (*jó* = good; *jobb* = better), plus the prefix *leg* to signify superlative (*legjobb* = the best). **Negatives** are usually formed by placing the word *nem* before the verb or adjective. *Ez* (this), *ezek* (these), *az* (that) and *azok* (those) are the **demonstratives**.

PRONUNCIATION

Achieving passably good **pronunciation**, rather than grammar, is the first priority (see below for general guidelines). **Stress** almost invariably falls on the first syllable of a word and all letters are spoken, although in sentences the tendency is to slur words together. Vowel sounds are greatly affected by the bristling **accents** (that actually distinguish separate letters) which, together with the "double letters" *cs, gy, ly, ny, sz, ty,* and *zs,* give the Hungarian **alphabet** its formidable appearance.

a o as in h**o**t	**o** aw as in s**a**w, with the tongue kept high
á a as in f**a**ther	**ó** aw as in s**a**w, as above but longer
b b as in **b**est	**ö** ur as in f**u**r, with the lips tightly rounded but without
c ts as in ba**ts**	any "r" sound
cs ch as in **ch**urch	**ő** ur as in f**u**r, as above but longer
d d as in **d**ust	**p** p as in si**p**
e e as in y**e**t	**r** r pronounced with the tip of the tongue like a
é ay as in s**ay**	Scottish "r"
f f as in **f**ed	**s** sh as in **sh**op
g g as in **g**o	**sz** s as in **s**o
gy a soft dy as in **d**ue	**t** t as in si**t**
h h as in **h**at	**ty** ty as in **T**uesday
i i as in b**i**t, but slightly longer	**u** u as in p**u**ll
í ee as in s**ee**	**ú** oo as in f**oo**d
j y as in **y**es	**ü** u as in the German "**ü**ber" with the lips tightly
k k as in sic**k**	rounded
l l as in **l**eap	**ű** u as above, but longer
ly y as in **y**es	**v** v as in **v**at
m m as in **m**ud	**w** v as in "**V**alkman," "**v**hiskey" or "**W**C" (vait-say)
n n as in **n**ot	**z** z as in **z**ero
ny ny as in o**ni**on	**zs** zh as in mea**s**ure

WORDS AND PHRASES

BASICS

Do you speak ...	beszél ...
... *English*	... angolul
... *German*	... németül
... *French*	... franciául
yes	igen
OK	jó
no/not	nem
and	és
or	vagy
I (don't) understand	(nem) értem
please	kérem
excuse me (apology)	bocsánat, or elnézést
excuse me (to attract attention)	legyen szíves
two beers, please	két sört kérek
thank you (very much)	köszönöm (szépen)
you're welcome	szívesen
hello/goodbye	szia (informal)
good morning	jó reggelt
good day	jó napot
good evening	jó estét
good night	jó éjszakát
goodbye	viszontlátásra (formal)
see you later	viszlát (more informal)
how are you?	hogy vagy? (informal)
how are you?	hogy van? (formal)
could you speak more slowly?	elmondaná lassabban?
what do you call this?	ennek mi a neve? or ezt hogy hívják?

please write it down	kérem, írja le
today	ma
tomorrow	holnap
the day after tomorrow	holnapután
yesterday	tegnap
the day before yesterday	tegnapelőtt
in the morning	reggel
in the evening	este
at noon	délben
at midnight	éjfélkor

QUESTIONS AND REQUESTS

Hungarian has numerous interrogative modes whose subtleties elude foreigners, so it's best to use the simple *van?* ("is there?"), to which the reply might be *nincs* or *nincsen* ("there isn't"/"there aren't any"). In shops or restaurants you will immediately be addressed with the one-word *tessék*, meaning "Can I help you?", "What would you like?" or "Next!". To order in restaurants, shops and markets, use *kérek* ("I'd like ...") plus accusative noun; *Kérem, adjon azt* ("Please give me that"); *Egy ilyet kérek* ("I'll have one of those").

I'd like/we'd like	Szeretnék/szeretnénk
Where is/are ...?	Hol van/vannak ...?
Which way is/are ...?	Merre van/vannak ...?
Hurry up!	Siessen!
How much is it?	Mennyibe kerül?
for one night	egy éjszakára
per week	egy hétre
a single room	egyágyas szoba
a double room	kétágyas szoba

hot (cold) water	meleg (hideg) víz
a shower	egy zuhany
It's very expensive	Ez nagyon drága
Do you have anything cheaper?	Van valami olcsóbb?
Do you have a student discount?	van diák kedvezmény?
Is everything included?	Ebben minden szerepel?
I asked for …	Én … -t rendeltem
The bill please	Fizetni szeretnék
We're paying separately	Külön-külön fizetünk
what?	mi?
why?	miért?
when?	mikor?
who?	ki?

SOME SIGNS

entrance	bejárat
exit	kijárat
arrival	érkezés
departure	indulás
open	nyitva
closed	zárva
push	tolni
pull	húzni
free admission	szabad belépés
women's toilet	női mosdó (or WC – "Vait-say")
men's toilet	férfi mosdó
shop	bolt
market	piac
room for rent	szoba kiadó or Zimmer frei
hospital	kórház
pharmacy	gyógyszertár
(local) police	(kerületi) Rendőrség
caution/beware!	vigyázat!/vigyázz!
no smoking	tilos a dohányzás/ dohányozni tilos
no bathing	tilos a fürdés/fürdeni tilos

DIRECTIONS

Which way is the …?	Merre van a …?
campsite	kemping
hotel	szálloda/hotel
railway station	vasútállomás
bus station	buszállomás
bus-stand	kocsiállás
(bus or train) stop	megálló
inland	belföldi
international	külföldi
Is it near (far)?	Közel (messze) van?
Which bus goes to …?	Melyik busz megy … -ra/ re?

a one-way ticket to … please	egy jegyet kérek … -ra/ re csak oda
a return ticket to …	egy retur jegyet … -ra/re
Do I have to change trains?	Át kell szállnom?
towards	felé
on the right (left)	jobbra (balra)
straight ahead	egyenesen előre
(over) there/here	ott/itt
Where are you going?	Hova mész/megy? (informal/formal)
Is that on the way to …?	Az a … úton?
I want to get out at …	Le akarok szállni … -on/ en
please stop here	itt álljon meg
I'm lost	eltévedtem
arrivals	érkező járatok (or érkezés)
departures	induló járatok (or indulás)
to/from	hova/honnan
change	átszállás
via	át

COMPUTER/TECHNOLOGY

charger	töltő
@	kukac (literally, worm)
mobile phone	mobil (telefon)
plug	dugó
socket	konnektor
website	honlap, weboldal

DESCRIPTIONS AND REACTIONS

nothing	semmi
perhaps	talán
very	nagyon
good	jó
bad	rossz
better	jobb
big	nagy
small	kicsi
quick	gyors
slow	lassú
now	most
later	később
beautiful	szép
ugly	csúnya
Help!	Segítség!
I'm ill	beteg vagyok

NUMBERS AND MEASURES

In shops and markets, items are priced per piece (*darab*, abbreviated to *db.*) or per kilogram. Shoppers commonly request purchases in multiples of ten grams (*deka*); one hundred grams is *tíz deka*. The measure for fluids is the *deci* (decilitre, abbreviated to dl., equivalent to about 3.5 fl oz) – see "Drinks" (p.229) for how this applies in bars and restaurants.

1	egy	800	nyolcszáz
2	kettő	900	kilencszáz
3	három	1000	egyezer
4	négy	**half**	fél
5	öt	**a quarter**	negyed
6	hat	**each/piece**	darab (db.)
7	hét	**10 grams**	egy deka
8	nyolc	**100 grams**	tíz deka
9	kilenc		
10	tíz		

TIME, DAYS AND DATES

Luckily, the 24-hour clock is used for timetables, but on cinema programmes you may see notations like 1/4, 3/4, etc. These derive from the spoken expression of time which, as in German, makes reference to the hour approaching completion. For example 3.30 is expressed as *fél négy* – "half (on the way to) four"; 3.45 – *háromnegyed négy* ("three quarters on the way to four"); 6.15 – *negyed hét* ("one quarter towards seven"), etc. However, " ... o'clock" is ... *óra*, rather than referring to the hour ahead. Duration is expressed by the suffixes – *től* ("from") and *-ig* ("to"); minutes are *perc*; to ask the time, say *"Hány óra?"*

11	tizenegy		
12	tizenkettő		
13	tizenhárom		
14	tizennégy		
15	tizenöt		
16	tizenhat		
17	tizenhét		
18	tizennyolc		
19	tizenkilenc		
20	húsz	**Monday**	hétfő
21	huszonegy	**Tuesday**	kedd
30	harminc	**Wednesday**	szerda
40	negyven	**Thursday**	csütörtök
50	ötven	**Friday**	péntek
60	hatvan	**Saturday**	szombat
70	hetven	**Sunday**	vasárnap
80	nyolcvan	**on Monday**	hetfőn
90	kilencven	**on Tuesday**	kedden
100	száz	**on Wednesday**	szerdán
101	százegy	**on Thursday**	csütörtökön
150	százötven	**on Friday**	pénteken
200	kettőszáz	**on Saturday**	szombaton
300	háromszáz	**on Sunday**	vasárnap
400	négyszáz	**day**	nap
500	ötszáz	**week**	hét
600	hatszáz	**month**	hónap
700	hétszáz	**year**	év

HUNGARIAN FOOD AND DRINK TERMS

The food categories here refer to the general divisions used in menus. In cheaper places you will also find a further division of meat dishes: ready-made meals like stews (*készételek*), and freshly cooked (in theory) dishes such as those cooked in breadcrumbs or grilled (*frissensültek*). *Tészták* is a pasta-doughy category that can include savoury dishes such as *turoscsusza* (pasta served with cottage cheese and a sprinkling of bacon), as well as sweet ones like *somlói galuska* (cream and chocolate covered sponge). Two popular **snacks** which are nicer than they sound are *zsirós kenyér* (bread spread with lard and sprinkled with paprika; often sold in old-fashioned wine bars); and *lángos* (fried dough served with soured cream or a variety of other toppings, and available in markets).

BASICS		ecet	vinegar
borravaló	tip	egészségedre!	Cheers!
bors	pepper	étlap	menu
cukor	sugar	jó étvágyat!	Bon appétit!

kenyér	bread
kifli	croissant-shaped roll
méz	honey
mustár	mustard
rizs	rice
sajtos or vajas pogácsa	cheese or butter scones
só	salt
tejföl	sour cream
tejszín	cream
vaj	butter
zsemle or péksütemeny	bread rolls

COOKING TERMS

comb	leg
mell	breast
angolosan	(English-style) underdone/rare
főtt	boiled
főzelék	creamed vegetable dishes – better than it sounds
jól megsütve	well done (fried)
jól megfőzve	well done (boiled)
paprikás	in a paprika sauce
pörkölt	stewed slowly
rántott	deep-fried in breadcrumbs
roston sütve	grilled
sülve	roasted
sült/sütve	fried
töltött	stuffed

SOUPS (LEVESEK)

bakonyi betyárleves	"Outlaw soup" of chicken, beef, noodles and vegetables, richly spiced
csirke-aprólék leves	mixed vegetable and giblet soup
erőleves	meat consommé often served with noodles (tésztával or metélttel), liver dumplings (májgombóccal), or an egg placed raw into the soup (tojással)
gombaleves	mushroom soup
gulyásleves	goulash in its original Hungarian form as a soup, sometimes served in a small kettle pot (bográcsgulyás)
halászlé	a rich fish soup often served with hot paprika
húsleves	meat consommé
jókai bableves	bean soup flavoured with smoked meat
kunsági	chicken soup
pandúrleves	seasoned with nutmeg, paprika and garlic
lencseleves	lentil soup
hideg meggyleves	chilled sour cherry soup
palócleves	mutton, bean and sour cream soup
paradicsomleves	tomato soup
tarkonyos borjúraguleves	lamb soup flavoured with tarragon
ujházi tyúkleves	chicken soup with noodles, vegetables and meat
zöldségleves	vegetable soup

APPETIZERS (ELŐÉTELEK)

These comprise both hot (*meleg*) and cold (*hideg*) dishes.

füstölt csülök tormával	smoked knuckle of pork with horseradish
hortobágyi palacsinta	pancake stuffed with minced meat and served with creamy paprika sauce
körözött	a paprika-flavoured spread made with sheep's cheese and served with toast
libamáj	goose liver
rakott krumpli	layered potato casserole with sausage and eggs
rántott gomba	mushrooms fried in breadcrumbs, sometimes stuffed with sheep's cheese (juhtúróval töltött)
rántott sajt, Camembert, karfiol	Camembert or cauliflower fried in breadcrumbs
tatárbeefsteak	raw mince mixed with an egg, salt, pepper, butter, paprika and mustard, and spread on toast
tepertő	crackling (usually pork, sometimes goose)
velőcsont fokhagymás pirítóssal	bone marrow spread on toast rubbed with garlic, a special delicacy associated with the gourmet Gyula Krúdy

SALADS (SALÁTÁK)

Salads are not Hungary's strong point; they are usually simple, and are often served in a vinegary dressing, although other dressings include blue cheese (*rokfortos*), yogurt (*joghurtos*) or French (*francia*).

csalamádé	mixed pickled salad
fejes saláta	lettuce
idénysaláta	fresh salad of whatever is in season
jércesaláta	chicken salad
paradicsom saláta	tomato salad
uborka saláta	cucumber; can be gherkins (*csemege* or *kovászos*) or the fresh variety (*friss*)

FISH DISHES (HALÉTELEK)

csuka tejfölben sütve	fried pike with sour cream
fogas	a local fish of the pike-perch family
fogasszeletek Gundel modra	breaded fillet of *fogas*
harcsa	catfish
harcsa paprikás	catfish in paprika sauce
kecsege	sterlet (small sturgeon)
nyelvhal	sole
pisztráng	trout
pisztráng tejszínes mártásban	trout baked in cream
ponty	carp
ponty filé gombával	carp fillet in mushroom sauce
rántott pontyfilé	carp fillet fried in breadcrumbs
rostélyos töltött ponty	carp stuffed with bread, egg, herbs and fish liver or roe
süllő	another pike-perch relative
sült hal	fried fish
tonhal	tuna

MEAT DISHES (HÚSÉTELEK)

baromfi	poultry
bécsi szelet	Wiener schnitzel
bélszin	sirloin
bélszinjava	tenderloin
csirke	chicken
fácán	pheasant
fasírt	meatballs
hátszin	rumpsteak
kacsa	duck
kolbász	spicy sausage
liba	goose
máj	liver
marha	beef
nyúl	rabbit
őz	venison
pulyka	turkey
sertés	pork
sonka	ham
vaddisznó	wild boar
vadételek	game
virsli	frankfurter
borjúpörkölt	closer to what foreigners mean by "goulash": veal stew seasoned with garlic
cigányrostélyos	"gypsy-style" steak with brown sauce
csikós tokány	strips of beef braised in bacon, onion rings, sour cream and tomato sauce
csülök Pékné módra	knuckle of pork roasted with potatoes and onions
erdélyi rakott-káposzta	layers of cabbage, rice and ground pork baked in sour cream (a Transylvanian speciality)
hagymás rostélyos	braised steak piled high with fried onions
pacal	tripe (usually in a paprika sauce)
paprikás csirke	chicken in paprika sauce
rablóhús nyárson	kebab of pork, veal and bacon
sertésborda	pork chop
sült libacomb tört burgonyával és párolt káposztával	grilled goose leg with potatoes, onions and steamed cabbage
töltött káposzta	cabbage stuffed with meat and rice, in a tomato sauce
töltött paprika	peppers stuffed with meat and rice, in a tomato sauce
vaddisznó borókamártással	wild boar in juniper sauce
vasi pecsenye	fried pork marinated in milk and garlic

SAUCES (MÁRTÁSOK)

bormártásban	in a wine sauce
ecetes tormával	with horseradish
fokhagymás mártásban	in a garlic sauce
gombamártásban	in a mushroom sauce
kapormártásban	in a dill sauce

meggymártásban	in a morello cherry sauce
paprikás mártásban	in a paprika sauce
tárkonyos mártásban	in a tarragon sauce
tejszínes paprikás mártásban	in a cream and paprika sauce
vadasmártásban	in a brown sauce (made of mushrooms, almonds, herbs and brandy)
zöldborsós	in a green-pea sauce
zöldborsosmártásba	in a green peppercorn sauce

ACCOMPANIMENTS (KÖRETEK)

galuska	noodles (though *Somlói galuska* is different – see introduction)
gombóc	dumpling
hasábburgonya	chips, french fries
krokett	potato croquettes
petrezselymes burgonya	boiled potatoes served with parsley
rizs	rice
zöldköret	mixed vegetables

VEGETABLES (ZÖLDSÉGEK)

bab	beans
borsó	peas
burgonya/krumpli	potatoes
fokhagyma	garlic
gomba	mushrooms
hagyma	onions
(vörös) káposzta	(red) cabbage
karfiol	cauliflower
kelkáposzta	savoy cabbage
kukorica	sweetcorn
lecsó	tomato and green pepper stew that's a popular ingredient in Hungarian cooking
padlizsán	aubergine/eggplant
paprika (édes/erős)	peppers (sweet/hot)
paradicsom	tomatoes
sárgarépa	carrots
spárga	asparagus
spenót	spinach
uborka	cucumber
zöldbab	green beans
zöldborsó	peas
zukkini	courgette
rakott krumpli	layered potatoes with egg and sausage
Sólet	a superior baked beans (a Jewish speciality)

spenót főzelék	a garlicky creamed spinach (often served with a fried egg)
tök főzelék	creamed marrow with dill

FRUIT AND NUTS (GYÜMÖLCSÖK ÉS DIÓK)

alma	apple
birsalma	quince
bodza	elderflower
citrom	lemon
dió	walnut
eper	strawberry
földi mogyoró	peanut
füge	fig
(görög) dinnye	(water) melon
körte	pear
málna	raspberry
mandula	almond
meggy	morello cherry
mogyoró	hazelnut
narancs	orange
őszibarack	peach
sárgabarack	apricot
szilva	plum
szőlő	grape
tök (sütőtök)	marrow (pumpkin/ squash)

CHEESE (SAJT)

Cheeses made in Hungary are a rather limited selection, the most interesting being the soft *juhtúró*.

füstölt sajt	smoked cheese
juhtúró	sheep's cheese
kecske sajt	goat's cheese
márvány	Danish blue cheese
trappista	rubbery, Edam-type cheese
túró	a cross between cottage and curd cheese

DESSERTS (ÉDESSÉGEK)

almás pite	apple pie
aranygaluska	golden dumpling cake
diós metélt	pasta with walnuts
fánk	doughnut
gesztenye puré	chestnut purée
gundel palacsinta	pancake with walnuts in a chocolate sauce
mákos or diós beigli	poppyseed or walnut roll
mákos guba	poppy seed pudding
palacsinta	pancake
párolt alma	stewed apple
rétes	strudel

SPRITZERS

Most bars serve **spritzers** – wine mixed with soda water – on request and increasingly you can see them on menus too. Given the quality of the wine in cheaper wine bars, it is a much nicer way to drink it, and very thirst-quenching. A popular drink among the younger generation is VBK, wine mixed with cola (see below).

Hungarians give their mixes curious names:

Kifröccs – small spritzer:	1dl. soda water, 1dl. wine
Fröccs – spritzer:	1dl. soda water, 2dl. wine
Hosszúlépés – long step:	2dl. soda water, 1dl. wine
Viceházmester – deputy janitor:	3dl. soda, 2dl. wine
Haziúr – landlord:	1dl. soda, 4dl. wine

szilva gombóc	dumpling stuffed with a plum
túrógombóc	cottage cheese dumpling

DRINKS (ITALOK)

The drinks list (*itallap*) is usually divided into wine, beer, spirits and soft drinks. **Wine** is often served by the *deci* (dl.), or 100ml, and may be charged as such, so that the sum on the drinks list may be multiplied by two or three times on the bill. To avoid ambiguity over glass sizes, you can specify *egy deci, két deci* or *három deci* (respectively, 100ml, 200ml or 300ml). **Pálinka** is a popular aperitif, distilled from apricots (*barackpálinka*), plums (*szilva*), William's pears (*Vilmoskörte*) or other fruit; and **Unicum** a dark, bitter digestif that Hungarians swear is good for the stomach. Due to Hungary's abundant thermal springs there are numerous local brands of **mineral water**; it's sold with colour-coded bottle-caps for easy recognition of still (*szénsavmentes* – pink caps), mildly fizzy (*enyhe* – green) or sparkling (*szénsavas* or *buborékos* – blue).

ásányvíz	mineral water
bor	wine
borsmenta teá	peppermint tea
csapalt sör	draught beer
édes bor	sweet wine
fehér bor	white wine
félédes bor	medium-dry wine

gyümölcslé	fruit juice
kávé	coffee (espresso)
koffeinmentes kávé	decaffeinated coffee
korsó	half-litre of beer
menta teá	mint tea
narancslé	orange juice
pálinka	schnapps-like fruit brandy, in a range of flavours
pezsgő	sparkling wine
pohár	300dl. of beer, or a glass of wine
rosé	rosé wine
sima (csap) víz	ordinary (tap) water
sör	beer
száraz bor	dry wine
szódavíz	soda water
teá	tea
tejeskávé	coffee with milk
Traubiszóda	sparkling grape-flavoured soft drink
Unicum	a bitter medicinal *digestif*
üveg	bottle (of wine)
(csap) víz	(tap) water
vörös bor	red wine
vörösboros kola (VBK)	red wine mixed with cola

Glossary of Hungarian terms

ÁFA Goods tax, equivalent to VAT.

Állatkert Zoo.

Arrow Cross see Nyilas.

Áruház Department store.

ÁVO The dreaded secret police of the Rákosi era, renamed the ÁVH in 1949.

Barlang Cave.

Belváros Inner city.

Biedermeier Heavy nineteenth-century style of Viennese furniture that became very popular in Budapest homes.

Borkostoló Wine tasting.

Borozó Wine bar.

Botanikuskert Botanical garden.

Büfé Snack bar.

Cigány Gypsy/Roma (can be abusive).

Cigánytelep Gypsy settlement.

Cigányzene Gypsy music.

Csárda Inn; nowadays, a restaurant with rustic decor.

Csárdás Traditional wild dance to violin music.

Cukrászda Cake shop.

Diszterem Ceremonial hall.

Domb Hill.

Duna River Danube.

Egyetem University.

Erdély The Hungarian word for Transylvania, the region of Romania where a large Hungarian minority lives.

Erdő Forest, wood.

Étterem Restaurant.

Fasor Avenue.

Fogadó Inn.

Folyó River.

Forrás Natural spring.

Fürdő Public baths.

Gözfürdő Steam bath.

Gyógyfürdő Mineral baths fed by thermal springs with therapeutic properties.

Hajó Boat.

Hajóállomás Boat landing stage.

Halászcsárda/halászkert Fish restaurant.

Ház House.

Hegy Hill or low mountain.

HÉV Commuter trains running from Budapest.

Híd Bridge.

Hídfő Bridgehead.

Honvéd Hungarian army.

Ifjúsági szálló Youth hostel.

Iskola School.

Kápolna Chapel.

Kapu Gate.

Kert Garden, park.

Kerület (*ker*.) District.

Kiállítás Exhibition.

Kiáltó Lookout tower.

Kincstár Treasury.

Kirakodó vásár Fair, craft or flea market.

Kollégium Student hostel.

Korzó Promenade.

Körönd Circus (road junction, as in Piccadilly Circus).

Körtér Circus (as *körönd*).

Körút (*krt*.) Literally, ring road, but in Budapest refers to the main boulevards surrounding the Belváros.

Köz Alley, lane; also used to define narrow geographical regions.

Kulcs Key.

Kút Well or fountain.

Lakótelep High-rise housing estate.

Lépcső Flight of steps.

Liget Park, grove or wood.

Lovarda Riding school.

Magyar Hungarian (pronounced "*mod*-yor").

Magyarország Hungary.

MÁV Hungarian national railways.

Megálló Railway station or tram or bus stop.

Megye County; the county system was originally established by King Stephen to extend his authority over the Magyar tribes.

Mozi Cinema.

Műemlék Historic monument, protected building.

Művelődési ház/központ Arts centre.

Nádor Palatine, highest administrative office in Hungary in the Habsburg empire pre-1848.

Nyilas "Arrow Cross"; Hungarian Fascist movement.

Palota Palace; *püspök-palota*, a bishop's residence.

Pályaudvar (*pu*.) Rail terminus.

Panzió Pension.

Patak Stream.

Pénz Money.

Piac Outdoor market.

Pince Cellar.

Rakpart Embankment or quay.

Református The reformed church, which in Hungary means the Calvinist faith.

Rendőrség Police.

Repülőtér Airport.

Rév Ferry.

Rom Ruined building.

Roma The romany word for gypsy, preferred by many Roma in Hungary.

Romkocsma Bar located in a ruined building or courtyard.

Sétány "Walk" or promenade.
Skanzen Outdoor ethnographic museum.
Sor Row, as in *fasor*, row of trees, ie avenue.
Söröző Beer hall.
Strand Beach, open-air baths or any area for sunbathing or swimming.
Szabadtér Open-air.
Szálló or **szálloda** Hotel.
Szent Saint.
Sziget Island.
Szoba kiadó Room to let.
Tájház Old peasant house turned into a museum, often illustrating the folk traditions of a region or ethnic group.
Táncház Venue for Hungarian folk music and dance.
Temető Cemetery.
Templom Church.
Tér Square; *tere* in the possessive case.
Terem Hall.

Tilos Forbidden; *tilos a dohányzás* means "smoking is forbidden".
Tó Lake.
Torony Tower.
Türbe Tomb or mausoleum of a Muslim dignitary.
Udvar Courtyard.
Uszoda Swimming pool.
Út Road; in the possessive case, *útja*.
Utca (*u.*) Street.
Vár Castle.
Város Town.
Városháza Town hall.
Vásár Market.
Vásárcsarnok Market hall.
Vasútállomás Railway station.
Vendéglő Restaurant.
Verbunkos Folk dance, originally a recruiting dance.
Völgy Valley.
Zsidó Jew or Jewish.
Zsinagóga Synagogue.

Small print and index

Rough Guide credits

Editor: Andy Turner
Layout: Anita Singh
Cartography: Deshpal Dabas
Picture editor: Marta Bescos
Proofreader: Stewart Wild
Managing editor: Alice Park
Assistant editor: Prema Dutta
Production: Charlotte Cade

Cover design: Nicole Newman, Anita Singh
Photographers: Eddie Gerald, Michelle Grant
Editorial assistant: Rebecca Hallett
Senior pre-press designer: Dan May
Programme manager: Helen Blount
Publisher: Joanna Kirby
Publishing director: Georgina Dee

Publishing information

This sixth edition published January 2015 by
Rough Guides Ltd,
80 Strand, London WC2R 0RL
11, Community Centre, Panchsheel Park,
New Delhi 110017, India
Distributed by Penguin Random House
Penguin Books Ltd,
80 Strand, London WC2R 0RL
Penguin Group (USA)
345 Hudson Street, NY 10014, USA
Penguin Group (Australia)
250 Camberwell Road, Camberwell,
Victoria 3124, Australia
Penguin Group (NZ)
67 Apollo Drive, Mairangi Bay, Auckland 1310,
New Zealand
Penguin Group (South Africa)
Block D, Rosebank Office Park, 181 Jan Smuts Avenue,
Parktown North, Gauteng, South Africa 2193
Rough Guides is represented in Canada by Tourmaline
Editions Inc. 662 King Street West, Suite 304, Toronto,
Ontario M5V 1M7
Printed in Singapore by Toppan Security Printing Pte. Ltd.

MIX
Paper from
responsible sources
FSC
www.fsc.org FSC™ C018179

Help us update

We've gone to a lot of effort to ensure that the sixth
edition of **The Rough Guide to Budapest** is accurate
and up-to-date. However, things change – places get
"discovered", opening hours are notoriously fickle,
restaurants and rooms raise prices or lower standards. If
you feel we've got it wrong or left something out, we'd like
to know, and if you can remember the address, the price,
the hours, the phone number, so much the better.

Please send your comments with the subject line
"**Rough Guide Budapest Update**" to ✉ mail@uk
.roughguides.com. We'll credit all contributions and send a
copy of the next edition (or any other Rough Guide if you
prefer) for the very best emails.

Find more travel information, connect with fellow
travellers and plan your trip on Ⓦ roughguides.com.

ABOUT THE AUTHORS

Charles Hebbert fell in love with Budapest in 1982 and lived there for more than ten years. He regularly visits the city with his family when he isn't working as an editor in London, playing his accordion or updating Rough Guides in northern Italy.

Norm Longley has spent the past fifteen years writing Rough Guides to countries in Eastern Europe and the Balkans, including Hungary and Budapest. More recently he has co-authored guides to Scotland and Wales. He lives near Bath and can occasionally be seen erecting marquees on the Rec.

Acknowledgements

Charles Hebbert wants to thank Caroline (and Molly and Fergus), Fazakas Péter, and Lőrincz Anna, and all those who have answered my endless questions, including Rachel Appleby, "Rozi" Rozgonyi Zoltan, Körösényi Bori, Korentsy Endre, Kosa Judit, Weyer Balázs, Pallai Péter, Bisztray Sándor, Biber Kriszta, Michael V Griffin, Bob Cohen, Bozoki Bánfalvi Gábor, András, Hudi László, Tolnai Lea, Vágvölgyi András and Richard Robinson, and at the Hungarian Tourist Office Karin Jones and Zsebő-Ferenczi Ági in London and Sztojanovits Kristóf and Szűcs-Balás Vera in Budapest. He also thanks Andy Turner for his understanding editing and Marta Bescos for her photo work.

Norm Longley would like to thank Andy and Charles for making this such an easy book to work on; thanks too, to Timea Major, Kristof Sztojanovics and Vera Szucs-Balas in Budapest, Karin Jones in London, and most importantly, Christian, Luka, Patrick and Anna.

Readers' updates

Thanks to all the readers who have taken the time to write in with comments and suggestions (and apologies if we've inadvertently omitted or misspelt anyone's name):

George Gomori, Denyse Kozub, Phil Thomas, Ken Lee, Martin Fearns and Jonathan Barker.

Photo credits

All photos © Rough Guides except the following:
(Key: a-above; b-below/bottom; c-centre; f-far; l-left; r-right; t-top)

p.1 Neil Farrin/Robert Harding Picture Library
p.2 Paul Panayiotou/4Corners
p.4 Travel Library/SuperStock
p.7 Age fotostock Spain, S.L/Alamy Images (c); Howard Stapleton/Alamy Images (b); Ivan Vander Biesen/Dreamstime.com (t)
p.8 Ollirg/Dreamstime.com
p.10 Mauricio Abreu/AWL Images
p.11 David Kilpatrick/Alamy Images (tr); David Soulsby/Alamy Images (b); Adam Batterbee (tl); Pierre Merimee/Corbis (c)
p.12 Simon Reddy/Alamy Images (t); The Bridgeman Art Library (cl); Brody House Group (cr); REBEL Media/Getty Images (b)
p.13 Stefano Amantini/4Corners (t); Paul Williams/Alamy Images (b)
p.14 David Ball/Alamy Images (b); Tim E. White/Alamy Images (t)
p.15 Art Kowalsky/Alamy Images (tr); Nitu Mistry/Alamy Images (br)
p.16 Scanrail/Dreamstime.com
p.41 Art Kowalsky/Alamy Images (b); Rawdon Wyatt/Alamy Images (t)
p.46 Don Klumpp/Getty Images
p.56 Paul Williams/Alamy Images
p.67 Robert Harding Picture Library/Alamy Images
p.83 Peter Forsberg/Alamy Images

p.86 Hideo Kurihara/Alamy Images
p.91 Stock Connection Blue/Alamy Images (t); Paul Williams/Alamy Images (b)
p.118 David Kilpatrick/Alamy Images
p.126 Danita Delimont/Alamy Images
p.131 Ken Welsh/Alamy Images
p.156 EPA European Pressphoto Agency b.v./Alamy Images
p.161 PixMenStudio/Alamy Images (bl); Ket Szerecsen (t); Montenegrói Gurman (br)
p.171 Tim E. White/Alamy Images
p.178 Roberto Finizio/Alamy Images
p.187 imageBROKER/Alamy Images
p.191 David Poole/Alamy Images
p.198 Paul Williams/ Alamy Images
p.201 Attila Kisbenedek/Getty Images
p.204 Interfoto/Alamy Images

Front cover & spine Ceiling of Central Hall at Hungarian Parliament © Massimo Pizzotti/Robert Harding Picture Library

Back cover Parliament Building and the Danube © Doug Pearson/AWL Images (t); Gellert Spa © Doug Pearson/AWL Images (bl); Violinist busking on the Fisherman's Bastion, Buda Hill © Doug Pearson/AWL Images (br)

Index

Maps are marked in grey

Map index

Listings key

- Accommodation
- Restaurant/café/bar
- Shop

City plan

The **city plan** on the pages that follow is divided as shown:

N

```
0                    500
        metres
```

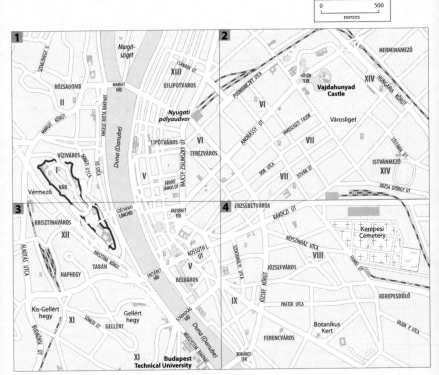

Map symbols

⎯⎯ Main road	✉ Post office	✡ Synagogue	⌒ Arch
⎯⎯ Minor road	ⓘ Tourist office	◠ Cave	🏛 Monument
▦ Motorway	✚ Hospital	⋀ Campsite	♙ Castle
▦ Pedestrianised road	🅿 Parking	▲ Peak	♱ Church (regional map)
⊞ Steps	◆ Point of interest	✈ International airport	Church (town map)
▦ Railway	@ Internet access	Ⓗ Hév station	Building
- - - - Path	⊠ Gate	Ⓜ Metro station	☐ Market
⎯⎯ Wall	⊙ Statue	★ Bus stop	⬭ Stadium
⎯ - Ferry route	⊤ Garden	Formula 1 circuit	☐ Park/forest
●-●-● Chairlift	⚓ Swimming pool	⚓ Ferry dock	⊞ Christian cemetery
⏑ Bridge	∴ Ruins	⚡ Viewpoint	☐ Jewish cemetery

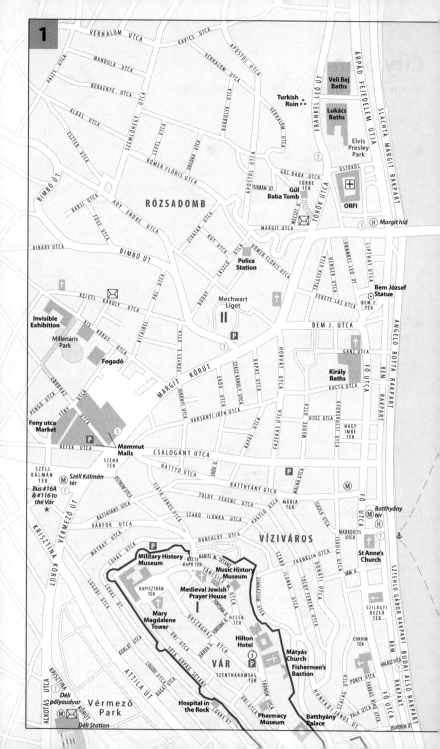

Hajós Alfréd
Swimming pool

Margit-
sziget

Centenary
Monument

GOGOL UTCA
GOGOL UT
IPOLY UTCA
VÁCI ÚT
PANNÓNIA UTCA
HEGEDŰSGYULA UTCA
VISEGRÁDI UTCA
IPOLY UTCA
Lehel Market
THURZÓ UTCA
RÖNTGEN UTCA
ALIG UTCA
KASSÁK LAJOS UTCA
Szent
István
Park
POZSONYI ÚT
HOLLÁN ERNŐ UTCA
TÁTRA UTCA
CSANÁDY UTCA
VICTOR HUGO UTCA
Lehel tér
Lehel tér
(M)
ÚJPESTI RAKPART
CARL LUTZ RAKPART
RAKPART
GERGELY G. UTCA
BALZAC UTCA
KRESZ GÉZA UTCA
CSANÁDY UTCA
LEHEL
TÉR
LEHEL UTCA
RADNÓTI MIKLÓS UTCA
XIII
FERDINÁND HÍD
FÓSONYI ÚT
TELKA UTCA
ÚJLIPÓTVÁROS
GYÖNGYHÁZ UTCA
BALZAC UTCA
MARGIT HÍD
KATONA JÓZSEF UTCA
WALLENBERG UTCA
PANNÓNIA UTCA
HEGEDŰSGYULA UTCA
VISEGRÁDI UTCA
RADNÓTI MIKLÓS UTCA
BUDAI N. U.
JÁSZAI
MARI TÉR
Budapest
Jazz Club
TÁTRA UTCA
Vigszinház
Theatre
KRESZ GÉZA UTCA
WestEnd
Center
Duna (Danube)
SZENT ISTVÁN KÖRÚT
KATONA JÓZSEF UTCA
BORBÉLY UT
KÁDÁR UTCA
Nyugati
Station
ID. ANTALL JÓZSEF RAKPART
SZÉCHENYI RAKPART
BÁLINT UTCA
BALATON UTCA
BALATON UTCA
(P)
SZÉCHENYI RAKPART
BALASSI UTCA
FALK MIKSA UTCA
HONVÉD UTCA
(M)
NYUGATI TÉR
Eiffel
Tér
Olimpia
Park
HONVÉD TÉR
STOLLÁR B. UTCA
CSENGERY UTCA
MARKÓ UTCA
NAGY IGNÁC UTCA
SZEMERE UTCA
MARKÓ UTCA
BIHARI UTCA
JÓKAI UTCA
PODMANICZKY UTCA
SZOBI UTCA
SZONDI UTCA
EÖTVÖS UTCA
Visitors'
Centre
SZALAY UTCA
TÁTKAY UTCA
SZALAY UTCA
Police
Station
WEINER LEÓ UTCA
VI
TERÉZ KÖRÚT
Museum of
Ethnography
ALKOTMÁNY UTCA
HONVÉD UTCA
LIPÓTVÁROS
LOVAG UTCA
JÓKAI UTCA
Parliament
KOSSUTH LAJOS TÉR
KOZMA UTCA
KÁLMÁN IMRE UTCA
HOLD UTCA
TERÉZVÁROS
Ministry of
Agriculture
BÁTHORY UTCA
BAJCSY-ZSILINSZKY ÚT
NAGYMEZŐ UTCA
D UTCA
MOZSER UTCA
(P)
JÓKAI TÉR
(M)
Kossuth
Lajos tér
VÉRTANÚK
TERE
Bedö
House
ARBLICH UTCA
VECSEY UTCA
FÁBRI UTCA
Glass
House
DESSEWFFY UTCA
Operetta
Theatre
(P)
GARIBALDI UTCA
NÁDOR UTCA
Market
Hall
PERCZEL M. UTCA
NAGYSÁNDOR J. UTCA
HAJÓS UTCA
Mai Manó
House
Paris
Department
Store
SZÉCHENYI RAKPART
ZOLTÁN UTCA
SZABADSÁG
TÉR
KISS E. UTCA
State
Treasury
ZICHY FERENC UTCA
State Opera
House
DALSZÍNHÁZ UTCA
PAULAY EDE UTCA
V
TV
Building
BANK UTCA
PODMANICZKY TÉR
(M)
Opera
STEINDL I. UTCA
AKADÉMIA UTCA
SZÉCHENYI UTCA
TÜKÖRY U.
(P)
ARANY JÁNOS UTCA
ARANY JÁNOS UTCA
Arany
János
utca
LÁZÁR UTCA
RÉVAY UTCA
NAGYMEZŐ UTCA
VASVÁRI P. UTCA
SZÉKELY M. UTCA
KIS DIÓFA UTCA
Hungarian Academy
of Sciences
(P)
VIGYÁZÓ F. UTCA
NÁDOR UTCA
OKTÓBER 6 UTCA
SAS UTCA
HERCEGPRIMÁS UTCA
St Stephen's
Basilica
(P)
KÁLDY GYULA U.
PAULAY EDE UTCA
ANDRÁSSY ÚT
New
Theatre
SZÉCHENYI
ISTVÁN
TÉR
CEU
ZRÍNYI UTCA
SZENT
ISTVÁN
TÉR
(P)

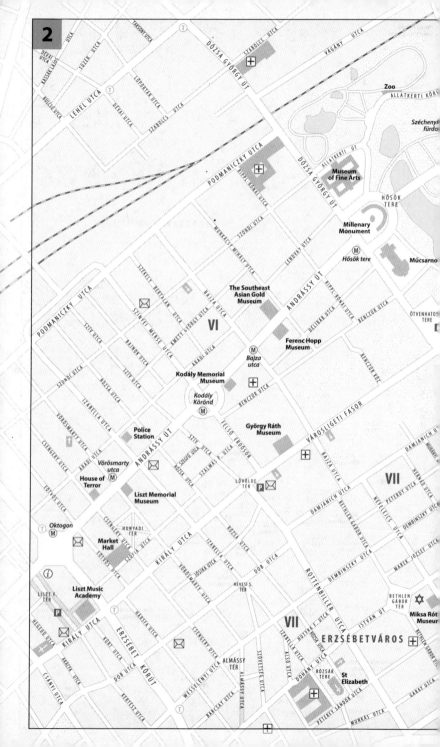

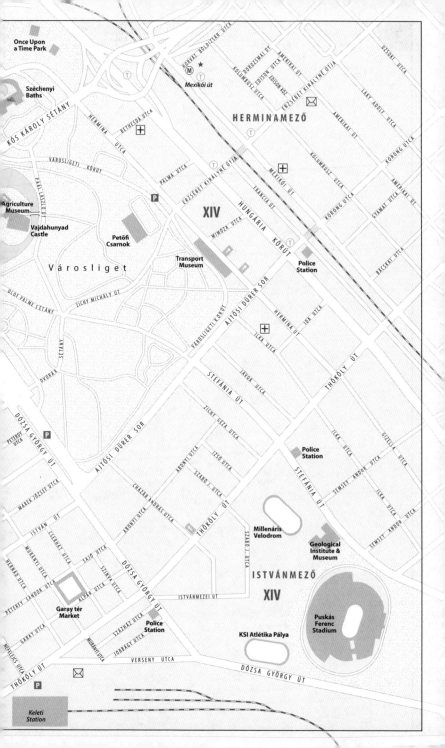

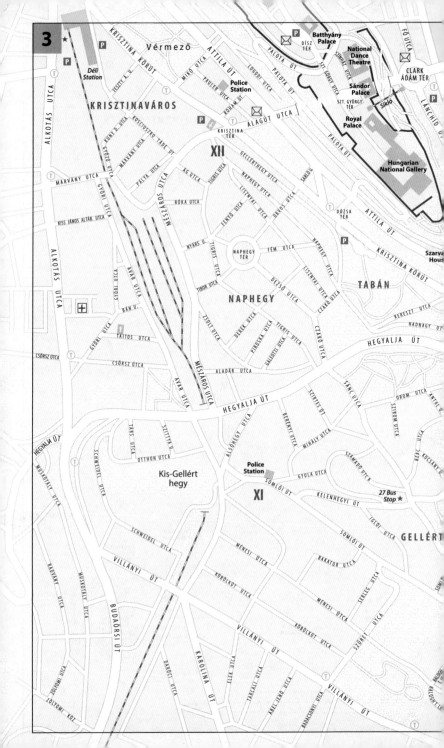

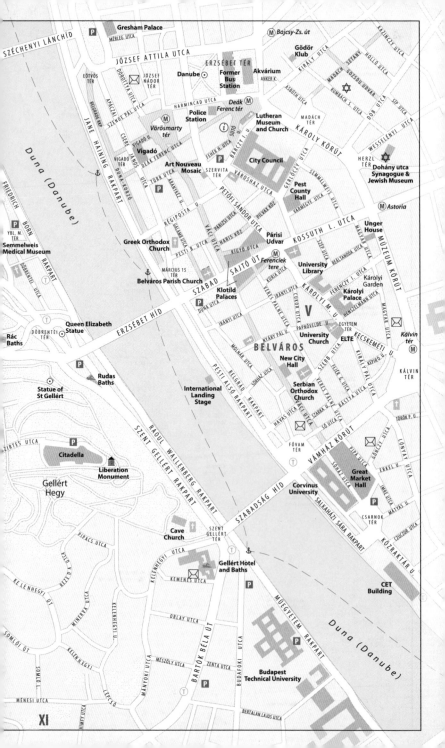

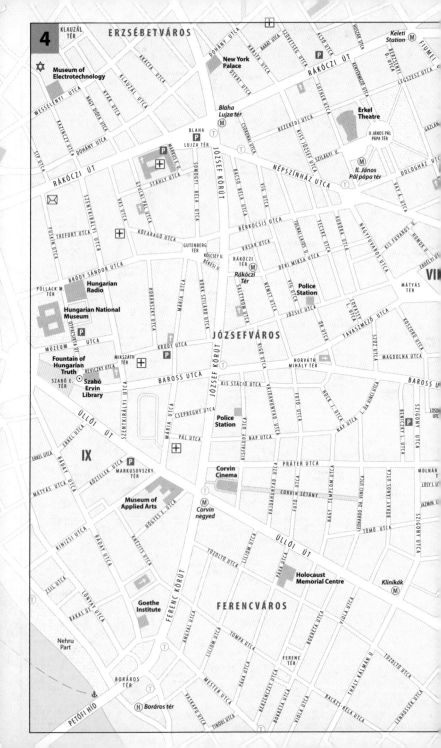

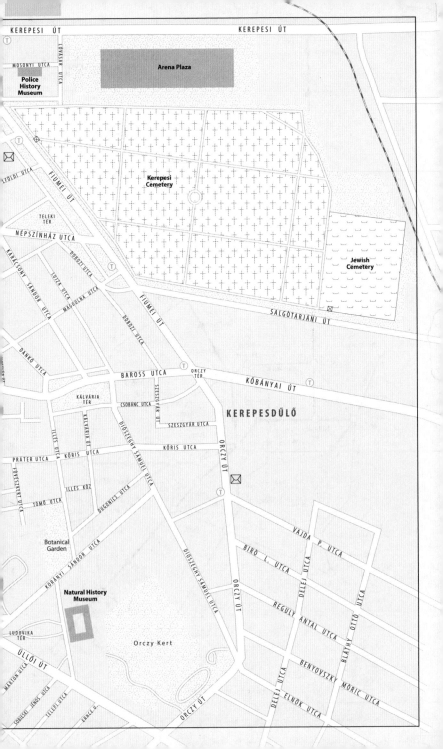

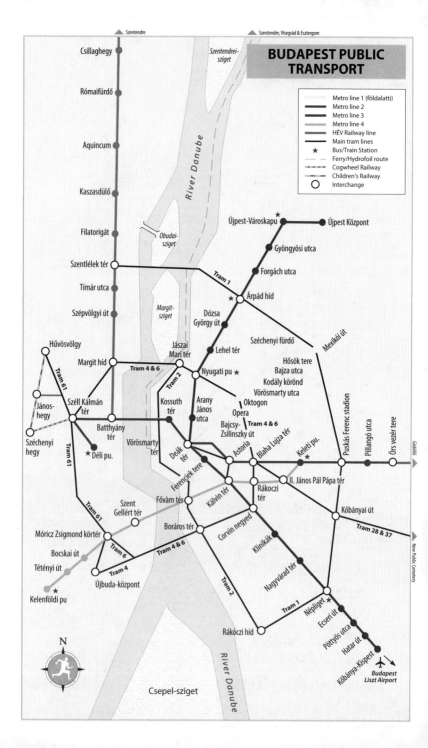

A ROUGH GUIDE TO
ROUGH GUIDES

Published in 1982, the first Rough Guide – to Greece – was a student scheme that became a publishing phenomenon. Mark Ellingham, a recent graduate in English from Bristol University, had been travelling in Greece the previous summer and couldn't find the right guidebook. With a small group of friends he wrote his own guide, combining a highly contemporary, journalistic style with a thoroughly practical approach to travellers' needs.

The immediate success of the book spawned a series that rapidly covered dozens of destinations. And, in addition to impecunious backpackers, Rough Guides soon acquired a much broader and older readership that relished the guides' wit and inquisitiveness as much as their enthusiastic, critical approach and value-for-money ethos.

These days, Rough Guides feature recommendations from shoestring to luxury and cover more than 120 destinations around the globe. Our ever-growing team of authors and photographers is spread all over the world, particularly in Europe, the US and Australia.

Rough Guides now number around 200 titles, including Pocket city guides, inspirational coffee-table books and comprehensive country and regional titles, plus technology guides from iPods to Android. As well as print books, we publish groundbreaking ebooks for every major digital device.

Visit ⓦ roughguides.com to see our latest publications.

Rough Guide travel images are available for commercial licensing at ⓦ roughguidespictures.com.